WMU Studies in Maritime Affairs

Volume 5

More information about this series at http://www.springer.com/series/11556

Lisa Loloma Froholdt
Editor

Corporate Social Responsibility in the Maritime Industry

Springer

Editor
Lisa Loloma Froholdt
Maritime Education and Training
World Maritime University
Malmö, Sweden

ISSN 2196-8772 ISSN 2196-8780 (electronic)
WMU Studies in Maritime Affairs
ISBN 978-3-030-09873-5 ISBN 978-3-319-69143-5 (eBook)
https://doi.org/10.1007/978-3-319-69143-5

Softcover re-print of the Hardcover 1st edition 2018

Printed on acid-free paper

This Springer imprint is published by the registered company Springer International Publishing AG part of Springer Nature.
The registered company address is: Gewerbestrasse 11, 6330 Cham, Switzerland

President's Message

The focus of this volume on 'corporate social responsibility' (CSR) is most relevant at a time when governments, businesses, NGOs and all other stakeholders have committed to and are expected to make their contribution to the United Nations Sustainable Development Goals (UNSDGs) in the context of the United Nations 2030 Agenda for Sustainable Development. The 17 UNSDGs provide a renewed momentum for business, including the maritime industry in its broadest sense of the term, to refocus and step up their efforts to contribute to the achievement of these goals while continuing to contribute to the facilitation of international trade. The maritime industry is expected, in line with the UNSDGs, to align their corporate strategies, of which CSR is an important pillar, to better respond to the social, environmental and economic issues facing the world today. The UNSDG goals encourage action on the part of all stakeholders to contribute to a more sustainable world. CSR sets the focus on delivering economic, social, environmental benefits for all stakeholders, particularly with respect to the poorest and most vulnerable.

The maritime industry has a unique opportunity to make its contribution to help achieve some of the UNSDG goals by promoting responsible behaviour and taking proactive measures. This includes action with respect to the following five goals: combat climate change through energy efficiency measures (Goal 13) through mitigation and adaptation; protect the ocean by contributing to the reduction of CO2 and life below the water by collecting plastics (Goal 14); promote gender equality (Goal 5); promote sustained, inclusive and sustainable economic growth, full employment and decent work for all (Goal 8); and build resilient infrastructure (Goal 9).[1] The maritime industry is already taking steps to reduce emissions by 50% by 2050 through the use of new fuels, and the International Maritime Organization has addressed greenhouse gas emissions through its emissions regulation scheme requiring ships to log and report to their respective flag states their fuel oil

[1] See the 2030 Agenda for Sustainable Development, 67th Session, Technical Cooperation Committee, July 2017 (TC 67/5(d)).

consumption beginning in 2018. With respect to Goal 8, the International Labour Organization's Maritime Labour Convention, 2006, has made and will continue to make an important contribution, and compliance with this social pillar by the industry will make a significant contribution to promoting decent work at sea. The shipping industry is playing an important role to ensure that the MLC, 2006, is fully complied with on-board ships.

This academic contribution to the CSR literature on maritime issues is the first of its kind. I am sure that the UNSDGs will provide a stimulus for more academic research in this field. The contributors to this book provide historic and contemporary perspectives on CSR in the maritime industry, an industry that has come to this field much later than others. Actions have been taken and are ongoing as the contributors to this book demonstrate, with a focus on the social, environmental and economic dimensions of the CSR.

United Nations' initiatives on CSR include the United Nations Global Compact (United Nations, 2010), which was the first and the largest voluntary CSR initiative promoted directly by the UN, focusing on the impact of business on people, planet and profit. The outcome document of the United Nations Conference on Sustainable Development (Rio+20) (June 2012) entitled 'The Future We Want' renewed the political commitment to sustainable development. It recognized that the active participation of the private sector is critical to achieving sustainable development and invited the private sector to contribute to this commitment with due regard to business practices, such as those endorsed by the United Nations Global Compact.

In 2011, the United Nations Guiding Principles (UNGP) on Business and Human Rights was unanimously agreed upon. It is the most authoritative reference point for business and human rights. The guidelines point to the role of business as specialized organs of society, performing special functions, required to comply with all applicable laws and to enhance standards and practices with due regard to human rights. The aim of the UNGP is to assist business to achieve tangible results for affected individuals and communities in order to ensure socially sustainable globalization.

A former secretary general and WMU chancellor, Mr. Efthimios Mitropoulos set out the general initiatives on CSR by the International Maritime Organization (IMO) in 2007. He affirmed that a

> proactive safety and security orientated culture, coupled with environmental consciousness, must be established among all those involved with the operation and running of ships. The part played in this by shipowners and operators at senior management level cannot be overestimated; a strong message from them that a culture of corporate social responsibility is a major contributing factor to their company's overall productivity, vitality and profitability will be all the more readily assimilated by all their staff.[2]

Another IMO secretary general and WMU chancellor, Mr. Koji Sekimizu, in his address to the Northern European Maritime industry CSR conference in Helsingor, Denmark, in November 2013, entitled 'CSR, A business case for the maritime

[2]Lekakou et al. (2015). Mr. Efthimios Mitropoulos was presented with a CSR leadership award at Capital Link's Shipping & Offshore CSR Forum in London on 4 November 2014.

industry', referred to efforts to support CSR with IMO promoting the proactive application of new regulations, the welfare of seafarers, and the important role that WMU plays in educating maritime policy makers.[3] At the United Nations Conference on Sustainable Development, Rio+20, in 2012, the IMO issued a report entitled 'A concept for a sustainable transportation system',[4] which sought to bring IMO on par with the efforts within the UN system. The report consisted of ten goals and actions and provided a platform for governmental international, regional and industry collaboration. The report called for global partnerships and awareness of the need for SD-coordinated maritime policies and governance. Action was required not only by intergovernmental organizations but also non-governmental organizations, multinational corporations, the global capital market and citizens.

In November 2016, speaking at the World Maritime Day Parallel Event in Turkey, the current secretary general of IMO, Mr. Kitack Lim, acknowledged the sophistication and technological advancement of ships and hoped that economic and regulatory incentives would encourage the shipping industry to invest in green technologies, which are not only beneficial for the environment but can also mean cost savings in the longer term.

CSR is very important to us at the World Maritime University (WMU), and a course is delivered on this topic, across our specializations. Our students are offered both practical and theoretical insights on how CSR can be implemented, acknowledging our mission and commitment to capacity building. Our deepest thanks go to the Danish Maritime Authority and Danish Shipping, supported by the Danish Maritime Fund, who provided funding for the development of this course. At WMU, we address the issues of CSR in our educational offerings covering all three dimensions of CSR—the economic, social and environmental dimensions—with respect to the maritime industry. We have expanded our programmes to include ocean governance and energy efficiency while leading the charge to expand our intake of female students to our MSc programme. We also offer a course on business integrity, which is the result of industry collaboration. These are but a few of the areas included in the UNSDGs to which we are committed.

Thirteen external and fifteen internal authors have contributed to this volume of the WMU book series, a true accomplishment. I would like to express my sincere thanks to the authors and the editor for their invaluable contribution to this important subject. These contributions highlight the action that the maritime industry is and must continue to take under the umbrella of CSR and in line with the UNSDGs.

Finally, I am grateful to the academic and technical staff at WMU for their continued effort in pursuing these commitments through education, scholarship, capacity building and research. While there is still much work to be done in both

[3]The Nippon Foundation supported the Northern European Maritime industry CSR conference, which was a unique collaboration between WMU, Danish Shipping and the Baltic and International Maritime Council (BIMCO).

[4]See http://www.imo.org/en/About/Events/WorldMaritimeDay/WMD2013/Documents/CONCEPT%20OF%20%20SUSTAINABLE%20MARITIME%20TRANSPORT%20SYSTEM.pdf.

the academia and the wider maritime industry, it is my deep hope that this anthology will make an important contribution to academic literature on the subject. I am sure that some of the important outcomes achieved to date, and which have been highlighted in the anthology, can inspire further action and set us on course for a truly sustainable future for the maritime industry underpinned by corporate social responsibility.

World Maritime University, Malmö, Sweden
Cleopatra Doumbia-Henry

Reference

Lekakou, M., Stefanidaki, E., & Theotokas I. (2015). *Corporate social responsibility in shipping: A theoretical approach.* The 5th International Symposium on Ship Operations, Management & Economics (SOME), 28 and 29 May 2015, Athens, Greece.

Foreword

This book captures the intersection of two major waves of changes; why is catching this intersection important and why now? To quote the editor, 'We need industry, the regulators, education and research—the whole triple helix!' to get together to 'make our planet great again', to quote President Macron. That this work, which stands at the intersection of these two significant waves of change, is published in a book by the World Maritime University (WMU) is a fitting example of synergy and the importance of these two waves of change. My hope is that this publication will spur and support another wave of change in the shipping and logistic sector showing that CSR is not just about regulations but also about voluntary actions—it also offers concrete proof that small-scale voluntary action is decidedly a positive step to making 'our planet great again'.

The two waves of change are the following: one wave is related to the change in perception and understanding of the term 'maritime'—originating as a term to refer to the carrying of cargo by ships going back to early settlements and now used to encompass the complete logistic chain from manufacturer to consumer where ships are a vital part of a complex logistic chain. The focus on ships and logistics tends to hide the other facet of the term 'maritime', namely, the biodiversity, ecosystem services and resources in our oceans and the use/misuse of those resources. The second wave of change is that of corporate social responsibility (CSR)/sustainability. CSR has shifted from a focus on social justice and philanthropy to the concept of planet, people and profit well illustrated by the publication of the first-ever international consensus standard on (C)SR 'Guidance on social responsibility' ISO 26000:2010 where the term (C)SR encompasses planet, people and profit. The two terms CSR and sustainability are used interchangeably. And for good reason, sustainability can be tracked back to the first UN conference in Stockholm in 1972 and the subsequent publication of *Our Common Future* in 1986, which led to many twists and turns to the agreement of the UN Sustainable Development Goals (SDG) in 2015.

The growth in the relevance of CSR/sustainability can be briefly illustrated by the rise in inclusion of CSR elements into national regulations relating to financial reports, the increase in voluntary CSR reports by about 400% from 2000 to 2010 based on GRI data, and SSI (Sustainable Shipping Initiative) being set up in 2010 and its 'Call to Action' in 2011. The growth in the broader use of the term 'maritime' can simply be illustrated with two examples outside the regulatory environment (UNCLOS and IMO): the publication by IMO of its concept 'The Sustainable Maritime Transport System' in 2013, which encompasses shipping and its associated logistic chain, and the setting up of WOC (World Ocean Council) in 2008, which involves the biodiversity, ecosystem services and resources in our oceans as well as shipping and its logistic chain.

The word 'holistic' springs to mind when describing how the volume has been put together, the topics it covers, the authors and the cooperation and communal learning it illustrates. The editor has collated an eclectic, interesting and diverse set of essays to illustrate the two waves of change and their intersection covering national/regional issues and influences, as well as the relevant organizational issues. It covers many different facets of CSR, but for me perhaps the most interesting, because they rarely get covered together with the issues facing our planet, are those that reflect the people and profit side of CSR as well as governance and voluntary action.

The inclusion of essays on financial risk management and how that can be used to support CSR, as well as the important topic of the economic opportunities for green ports, green navigation and circular economy, provide an answer to that ever-occurring question 'what is the financial argument for making this investment?' CSR is not just about money or environment, and the volume also deals with matters of social inclusion and getting the benefit of contributions from all people. Another reoccurring concern in the shipping industry is the lack of real examples of the benefit of voluntary adoption specifically in small shipping companies, remembering that much of the world fleet is owned by small ship owners who have less than ten ships each in their fleet. The book deals with this challenge by presenting a case study of 16 ship owners and their voluntary adoption of CSR. The importance of governance in relation to CSR is illustrated with essays that cover international, regional and national requirements, whether as regulations or not, that exist in the sphere of the term 'maritime' covering as it does shipping and its logistics chain as well as the biodiversity, ecosystem services and resources in our oceans.

The volume also presents us with the new realization that the lines between informal and formal rules and between public and private are merging and becoming less defined, with regulation beginning to enhance responsibility and sustainability in both developing and developed countries. The essays on what is and where did the CSR concept arise provide a new perspective, tracking it back to Indian thinking via the Italian Renaissance political theorist Machiavelli to the CSR concept of today.

This book allows WMU and other university scholars' knowledge to be shared with a broader audience and ably supports WMU work with UNEP on UNSDG. It is not WMU's first involvement in CSR; their postgraduate programmes include a maritime governance (MG) and corporate social responsibility (CSR) module whose development was funded by the Danish Maritime Fund through the Danish Shipowners' Association and the Danish Maritime Authority.

Anne Marie Warris

Ecoreflect Ltd., Guildford, UK
CCell Project Board, London, UK
Environmental Management System Committee (ISO TC 207/SCI), London, UK
UK Expert Supporting Revision of ISO 14064 and ISO 14065 (GHG MRV Standards), London, UK

Contents

Introduction

Lisa Loloma Froholdt

This publication is very timely and very relevant.

It is timely due to the fact that the maritime industry is always called a laggard when it comes to Corporate Social Responsibility (CSR), and it is necessary to flag that there are a lot of possibilities and good initiatives taking place around the world, which merit some credit, and these examples need to be disseminated in order to try and change this attitude.

It is relevant that this book is published as it shows how academia and the industry can work together and promote the CSR agenda. We need to pull together in the industry, across organisations and disciplines to lift this task in a sustainable manner and to cover the whole range of CSR pillars; the social, environmental and economic pillar. We need industry, the regulators, education and research—the whole triple helix!

Another explanation for the relevance of this publication is that the book will serve well as course reading in the CSR course offered to our post-graduate students here at World Maritime University (WMU). The development of this course was funded by the industry, by Danish Shipping and the Danish Maritime Authority through the Danish Maritime Fund. A lot of effort has been invested in promoting CSR here at WMU and in the broader industry, to push knowledge barriers and enhance awareness about CSR. This must also be seen in the context of educating our students from developing countries, by giving them theoretical handles and practical tools to enhance implementation and actions, and to address the Sustainable Development Goals (SDGs). It is our responsibility as faculty at WMU to capacity-build in this respect.

Some of the chapters (Chapters 'The Perception of Corporate Social Responsibility in the Maritime Industry', 'The Growth of CSR and Its Acceptance in the

L. L. Froholdt (✉)
World Maritime University, Malmö, Sweden
e-mail: lf@wmu.se

L. L. Froholdt (ed.), *Corporate Social Responsibility in the Maritime Industry*, WMU Studies in Maritime Affairs 5, https://doi.org/10.1007/978-3-319-69143-5_1

Maritime Industry’, ‘Maritime and Ocean Governance’ and ‘Effective and Efficient Maritime Administration and Corporate Social Responsibility’) in this anthology discuss the aspect of voluntary in the concept of CSR, and how the lines between informal and formal rules are merging and becoming rather fuzzy, and discussing that we are seeing how regulation is enhancing responsibility and sustainability in the maritime industry. This is the case in both developing and developed countries, and it is both timely and relevant to convey this.

Following the President’s message by the President of the WMU, Dr. Cleopatra Doumbia-Henry and the Foreword by Dr. Anne Marie Warris, here follows an introduction to each of the 15 chapters that this book contains.

The second chapter discusses the perception of CSR. The chapter begins with a discussion of definitions of CSR and how these definitions are both similar and different. The chapter moves into a discussion of how CSR is understood in the maritime industry, using perception surveys and other studies conducted in the maritime sector. The chapter recognizes that the perception of CSR is ever changing, and the divisions between public and private become somewhat blurred.

Chapter ‘The Growth of CSR and Its Acceptance in the Maritime Industry’ presents an overview of how the concept of CSR has developed including Machiavelli, Plato and earlier Indian literature and the global role of corporations’ social responsibility. This chapter also reflects on the fact that not all societies in the world have the same histories, values and traditions. What may be considered suitable in one part of the world may not be effective in another, and CSR can take different shapes in different countries.

Chapter ‘Maritime and Ocean Governance’ presents the legal, policy and institutional aspects of maritime governance agreements and institutions established under the United Nations Convention on the Law of the Sea (UNCLOS). The author argues that the rules of UNCLOS cannot be seen in isolation, as sectoral rules and standards are taken into account in considering the fulfilment of the obligations under UNCLOS on a number of issues. Policy instruments developed within intergovernmental organizations, such as the United Nations General Assembly, also provide guidance to the governance of maritime activities. Voluntary CSR initiatives would be complementary to regulatory initiatives and have a potential to fill existing regulatory gaps.

Chapter ‘Methods to Promote Improved Governance in Maritime Administrations of Developing Nations’ discusses the concept of “governance” and defines it on the basis of various notions, such as rule of the law, public participation, transparency, accountability, control of corruption and government effectiveness, which are considered to be elements of “good governance”. In order to understand how a good governance system can be promoted in developing nations, the chapter discusses the importance to understand how relevant international regulations on safety and security mirror good maritime governance. The chapter explores how selected incentive schemes can promote CSR in maritime administrations shipping companies.

Chapter ‘Arctic Governance and Gender: Climate Change or Social Change?’ reviews how companies and industries as well as governmental bodies can be seen as being responsible for including wider social issues on the organizational as well as the public agenda. Based in such extended and external perspectives of CSR, the authors argue how industry as well as government actors have a responsibility for the social inclusion of women in their dealings on all levels. As an illustration, gender issues in the Arctic region on a broad level are examined. The CSR concept allows industrial actors to engage in activities and responsibilities that traditionally lie outside of their organizational boundaries.

Chapter 'Effective and Efficient Maritime Administration and Corporate Social Responsibility' presents discusses how CSR is connected to a maritime administration through the concepts of effectiveness and efficiency. Using several examples, the authors discuss the need for maritime administrations to be effective and efficient. Once this is achieved, administrations can proceed to ensure that shipping companies align their business with society's expectations by putting social responsibility alongside their business goals.

Chapter 'Energy Management in the Maritime Industry' discusses the importance of how energy management and how it can serve and contribute to the targets set by a CSR policy of a shipping company or a port authority. The authors put forward a new definition of maritime energy management. The chapter discusses the increasing awareness among industries, innovators and decision-makers to move towards a more sustainable circular model of consumption in which raw materials are retained in the value chain and where growth is sustained in a world with rising populations. However, as the authors argue, moving from a linear economy to a circular economy requires a concerted effort both politically and on a business level.

Chapter 'Sulphur Directive, Short Sea Shipping and Corporate Social Responsibility in a EU Context' discusses how the Sulphur directive is important to analyse European Union legislation on SO_2 emission against the backdrop of CSR and examines how the voluntary aspect of CSR functions under emission reduction strategies that are "strict compliance" in nature. The authors examine how the environmental dimension of CSR has become an issue of compliance, rather than choice for shipping operators.

Chapter 'Green Ports and Economic Opportunities' discusses the usefulness of implementing policy instruments in the port sector with a conceptual model that is based upon the system dynamics (SD) technique. As the authors argue, it has been known that there is a good business case for making a port greener. Greening ports could therefore be used as a development tool to generate new business in a port region.

Chapter 'Energy-Efficient Ship Operation - The Concept of Green Manoeuvring' investigates how green manoeuvering can be utilised as a CSR activity in order to address air pollution which is one of the identified negative effects of shipping. The authors discuss the findings in several research studies and show how there is an opportunity to maneuver ships in a more environmentally friendly manner. However, education is an important part of enabling successful efforts by shipping companies to minimize potential negative effects of operating their fleets.

Drawing on theoretical and empirical work that has been conducted in the field, Chapter 'A Financial Business Case for Corporate Social Responsibility' presents a financial risk management case for CSR. The authors argue that there is ample room for shipping owners to undertake considerations in their priorities through a more holistic approach. The thesis of the chapter is that CSR can lead to the generation of sustainable comparative advantages and via this avenue to improved operating/ financial performance and reduced exposures to various risks.

Chapter 'Impacts of CSR on Women in the Maritime Sector' offers a comprehensive view of the development of women's integration in the maritime sector, and examines the impact of CSR initiatives by shipping companies on gender equality and equity in shipping. While encouraging the industry's voluntary initiatives on gender equality and equity, legal instruments developed by the International Labour Organization (ILO) as well as global initiatives created by the International Maritime Organization (IMO), however, cooperation between public and private sectors is necessary to create the synergy effect needed to promote maritime women from international to national levels.

Chapter 'Safety and Risk Management Considerations for CSR' discusses issues and principles of safety and risk management that relate to CSR. The chapter traces the generic evolution of the concept of CSR and presents different perspectives/ approaches. It then discusses how principles of safety and risk management may apply to CSR as elucidated by previous research and the literature, and what organizations should consider integrating strategic safety and risk management into CSR policies and practices.

Finally, Chapter 'Response to Institutional Processes - A Study of Corporate Social Responsibility in Danish Shipping Companies' presents a study undertaken of how 16 Danish shipowners integrated a CSR policy. Combined with a text analysis of annual reports, CSR reports, environmental reports, and transcribed interviews with key employees, the author determines the strategy that the companies apply. The study demonstrates that the coercive isomorphic process is the dominating factor when the shipping companies introduce CSR policies, and the findings support the argument that national legislation can awaken and introduce social responsibility to the shipping industry.

The Perception of Corporate Social Responsibility in the Maritime Industry

Lisa Loloma Froholdt

1 Introduction

There has been a debate surrounding the increasing interest in the concept Corporate Social Responsibility (CSR) (Carroll and Shabana 2010). The debate has sometimes arisen as a response to social, environmental or economic issues, involving discussions such as whether a business can or should profit from CSR activities. But the debate has largely been driven by an increasing social awareness of how commercial activities have an impact on the environment and how in turn the impact affects the public (Froholdt et al. 2015). CSR is developing out of the increased public awareness in ethical issues, such as improper treatment of workers, and faulty production that endangers workers and or customers. CSR is also gaining more ground as governments cannot control the global reach of companies today. However, much of the discussion about the conceptualization of CSR has involved Milton Friedman's (1962) argument that there is only one responsibility of business, namely to use its resources and engage in activities that increase its profits. It was his view that CSR imposes inappropriate costs for stakeholder funds due to investments in CSR activities, and these expenses are unrelated to the organisations core competencies (Friedman 1970). Friedman has since received criticism for his views, some arguing that social responsibility can be a win-win situation, and that ethical awareness and profitability are not necessarily opposites.

Many developments of the concept of CSR have come into existence during the debate, such as governance, corporate sustainability and corporate responsibility that have contributed to the discussion of how to define CSR, as no uniform definition exists. This chapter sets out to present and discuss how CSR is perceived in general

L. L. Froholdt (✉)
World Maritime University, Malmö, Sweden
e-mail: lf@wmu.se

L. L. Froholdt (ed.), *Corporate Social Responsibility in the Maritime Industry*, WMU Studies in Maritime Affairs 5, https://doi.org/10.1007/978-3-319-69143-5_2

and how it is perceived in the maritime industry in particular. This includes a brief historical overview of CSR and a discussion of maritime research.

2 Defining CSR

Dahlsrud (2008) has coined 37 different definitions of CSR, which is complicated by the fact that the terms such as public policy, society and business are interpreted differently across the range of theories that are being used in connection with CSR. Dahlsrud (2008) found that despite the many different ways of defining CSR, definitions are largely congruent with five emerging categories of CSR across the many definitions: The dimensions of stakeholders, social, economic, voluntariness and environment. These five categories are an integrated part of the widely used in the first CSR definition by the European Commission (EC) (2001) to be presented:

> A concept whereby companies integrate social and environmental concerns in their business operations and in their interaction with their stakeholder on a voluntary basis.

This definition has since been revised (2011) and is more elaborate. However the aspect of "a voluntary basis" which is inserted in the definition by the EC above has been debated and is relevant to bring to the foreground when defining CSR. This is in part due to the fact that if a company acts on a voluntary basis, the company goes beyond mere compliance of regulation (McWilliams and Siegel 2001). However, some researchers have argued that compliance is a part of a CSR agenda, and that in fact to 'obey the law' is part of how a company learns how to be responsible (Carroll 1991). This argument is also visible in the way that some companies present their CSR activities and when they disclose how they planned their CSR strategy, stating that compliance is their first step in committing to a CSR agenda. In fact, Brammer (2012) argue that CSR lies between a liberal notion of voluntary engagement as a core CSR trait on the one hand, and the contrary implication of socially binding responsibilities on the other. The theme of voluntary behavior of companies is a recurring issue in the CSR debate, and business leaders purport that CSR is voluntary and must be free of state regulation (Brammer 2012). Looking to other definitions of CSR, the following have been selected for the purpose of this chapter.

1. "UNDP views CSR as a spectrum of business activities ranging from philanthropy on one end via strategic social investments to how business processes can become more sustainable and contribute more effectively to equitable development."

   *United Nations Development Program (UNDP) (*2007*)*
2. "Corporate Social Responsibility (CSR) is the commitment of business to contribute to sustainable development, working with employees, their families, local communities, and society at large to improve their quality of life, that are both good for business and good for development".

   *The World Bank (*2005*)*

3. "Corporate Social Responsibility is the continuing commitment by business to contribute to economic development while improving the quality of life of the workforce and their families as well as of the community and society at large."
   World Business Council on Sustainable Development (WMCSD; 1998)
4. "Corporate responsibility involves the search for an effective "fit" between businesses and the societies in which they operate. The notion of "fit" recognises the mutual dependence of business and society – a business sector cannot prosper if the society in which it operates is failing and a failing business sector inevitably detracts from general well-being. "Corporate responsibility" refers to the actions taken by businesses to nurture and enhance this symbiotic relationship".
   *The Organisation for Economic Co-operation and Development (OECD) (*2001*)*
5. "CSR is a way in which enterprises give consideration to the impact of their operations on society and affirm their principles and values both in their own internal methods and processes and in their interaction with other actors. A voluntary enterprise-driven initiative and refers to activities that are considered to exceed compliance with the law".
   *The International Labour Organisation (ILO) (*2006*)*

All of these definitions claim or imply that CSR is a voluntary action that goes beyond what the law requires, in line with the definition by the EC presented earlier. The definitions describe CSR as the environmental, social and economical responsibility of a company to society, with activities ranging from more philanthropic activities to more strategic actions. Sustainability is part of the first two definitions and it is important to understand that sustainability is not the same as responsibility. The concept of sustainability first arose in what is often referred to as the Brundtland report (1987), or the report entitled "Our common future: A global agenda for change", produced by the World Commission on Environment and Development (WCED). Here it was defined as: *"sustainable development (SD) is development that meets the needs of the present without compromising the ability of the future generations to meet their own needs"*. It contains two key concepts:

- The concept of 'needs', in particular the essential needs of the worlds' poor, to which overriding priority should be given
- The idea of limitations imposed by the state of technology and social organisation on the environments ability to meet present and future needs (The Brundtland report 1987, p. 41).

The report purported that all nations should define and plan their economic and social development based on sustainable development. It further argued that there must be a strategic framework and appropriate policies in place, for SD to be realised. This report was not only renowned for the formal introduction of the definition of SD, but also due to the fact that the report was endorsed by the United Nations (UN). Put into a maritime context, the most important aspects of SD are ensuring the safety of people, the environment security, pollution prevention and resource conservation, while at the same, focusing on providing efficient and reliable services (IMO 2013). The concept has developed over time, and it is argued that there are even fraudulent and abusive uses of the concept that are predominantly based on defensive actions to protect the more dominant economic system (Bemejo 2014). It can be noted that this chapter draws on this definition of SD which is also used in the UN 2030 Agenda for Sustainable Development. Here it is defined; "*development that meets the needs of the present without compromising the ability of future generations to meet their own needs*" (A/RES/70/1).

The interest in the concept of sustainability has also had an impact on the development of CSR. In fact, sustainability has become one of the most prominent issues of the global economy (Isaksson and Steimle 2009). John Elkington (1994) attempted to measure sustainability during the mid-1990s by presenting a new framework to measure corporate performance. This accounting framework, called the triple bottom line (TBL), went beyond what is traditionally measured in terms of profits, return on investment, and shareholder value to also include environmental and social dimensions. By focusing on comprehensive investment results respecting the areas of the social, economic and environment, triple bottom line reporting can be an important tool to support sustainability goals. There is a substantial awareness about sustainable development, and for many good reasons. One of the reasons was the financial turmoil that began late 2007 (ASR 2010). Due to financial shortcomings, many companies decreased the amount of CSR activities (Karaibrahimoglu 2010). However, by focusing on sustainability of the company and reporting their performance, companies have realised that there are benefits to be gained (Waworuntu 2014).

If we return to the aspect of 'voluntary' in the definition of CSR, this has also developed over the years as previously mentioned. Some companies and public entities are seeing this aspect as an opportunity and they are proactively engaging in what could be called, the place where CSR drifts into regulation. This is the case in the example of what has taken place in India. In 2013 the Companies Act (CA) was amended to include a new provision (Clause 135), which came into effect 1 April, 2014 (Froholdt 2016). The Act defines CSR as activities that promote poverty reduction, education, health, environmental sustainability, gender equality, and vocational skills development. Companies can choose which area to invest in, or contribute the amount to central or state government funds earmarked for socio-economic development. The provision was designed to improve the lives of the community through sustainable interventions in the fields of education, environment, health, water and environment (Kumar Thakur et al. 2015). This provision applies to Indian companies and to branch and project offices of a foreign company, operating in India with (a) net worth of Rupees (Rs) 5 billion or more (83 million USD), (b) a turnover of Rs. 10 billion or more (160 million USD), or (c) a net profit of Rs. 50 million or more (830.000 USD) during any of the previous three financial years. The provision requires companies to spend at least 2% and max 5% of their average net profit on CSR related activities. This means that approximately 8.000 companies will be spending up to Rs. 150 billion (2 billion USD) on CSR activities. It is required that a committee be constituted comprising one-third independent directors and at least one woman. The committee is required to formulate a CSR policy to indicate the activities to be undertaken, and preference is given to activities in local areas in which the company operates. The company must disclose the contents of the policy and provide transparent monitoring. If a company fails to comply with this legislation, it must state the reasons.

Another example of this can be seen in the case of the legislation by the Danish government, and its efforts to facilitate CSR (Danish Companies and Commerce Agency 2010). As of 2009, large Danish companies had to report on their CSR policy. If the company does not have a CSR policy, the company has to state this fact. So, CSR is still voluntary in Denmark. Yet, if the company did have a CSR policy, the company had to include the policy, an explanation of how it was implemented and an assessment of what had been achieved and what would be the future goals. Although CSR is still voluntary, the Danish government installs this regulation in order to facilitate the responsibility of companies. It can also be noted here, that the Danish shipping company Maersk only first began its CSR reporting in 2009, precisely the time of this regulation (Froholdt 2016). Finally, in 2015, Stena Line began to convert the engines from its fleet to methanol gas driven engines on Stena Germanica (Froholdt 2016). The emissions of sulphur (SOx) are going to be reduced by 99%, nitrogen NOx) by 60%, particles (PM) by 95% and carbon dioxide (CO2) by 25% when compared to other fuels available at the time. Stena Line has recently ordered four more gas driven ro-pax ships to be delivered in 2019, which will be run on either methanol or LNG. Although it could be argued that the conversion is a result of the SOx regulation in Northern Europe from 1st January, 2015, it can be noted that the solution chosen by Stena Line, does go beyond the SOx issue in relation to the other emissions mentioned.

Another development that is changing the way we can perceive CSR is the concept of circular economy. This was internationally presented during the establishment of the Ellen MacArthur Foundation in 2010. Here circular economy is characterised as an economy that is restorative and regenerative by design and aims to keep products, components, and materials at their highest utility value at all times, distinguishing between technical and biological cycles (Ellen MacArthur Foundation 2013). Circular economy does away with the more traditional linear economy, where natural resources are mined, produced, consumed and thrown away as garbage. Many valuable resources are lost. Larger organisations such as UN and EU have understood that this necessity of this understanding as a more holistic approach. It was already included in EU's strategy in 2014 and defined; "Circular economy systems keep the added value in products for as long as possible and eliminate waste. They keep resources within the economy when a product has reached the end of its life, so that they can be productively used again and again and hence create further value" (EU 2014). The Danish container shipping company, Maersk, has also began to work with this concept and has begun to investigate how this concept can be used to build ships that can be recycled, using the 'cradle to cradle' design philosophy by McDonough and Braungart (2003). The Korean shipyard DSME (Daewoo Shipping & Marine Engineering) and Maersk have started to address recycling through a 'Cradle-to-Cradle Passport' which will be implemented on the new Triple-E ships. The passports will document approximately

95% (by weight) of the materials used to build the ships, thereby enabling better recycling of parts and materials used in the construction of the vessels. More about circular economy can be read in chapter 8, entitled 'Maritime Energy Efficiency' Ballini and Olcer (2017).

The developments of these concepts obviously influence how CSR can be perceived. Institution theory provides a lens that can be used to understand how the aspect of voluntary can be viewed, not as the central premise of CSR but only one side of the coin. Institution theory can be defined as how the forms, outcomes, and dynamics of economic organisation (firms, networks, markets) are influenced and shaped by other social institutions and with what consequences for economic growth, innovation, employment, and inequality. Institutions are usually defined as formal or informal rules, regulations, norms, and understandings that constrain and enable behaviour (Morgan et al. 2010, p. 3). With this lens we should then not be too concerned with the aspect of voluntary. CSR is both constrained and enabled through such a formal rule as the Indian Companies Act, and companies will thus be shaped by each other and by the social institution that has installed the Act. From this perspective, CSR can then be understood not only as a voluntary set of practices, but as one of the many corporate activities that can and does take place at the interface of business and society (Brammer 2012). CSR then becomes more dynamic and is not merely a decision to be made by a manager as to whether he or she chooses to be responsible and incorporate CSR into the company.

Of the definitions presented earlier, this chapter adopts definition 5: "CSR is a way in which enterprises give consideration to the impact of their operations on society and affirm their principles and values both in their own internal methods and processes and in their interaction with others. A voluntary enterprise-driven initiative and refers to activities that are considered to exceed compliance with the law" (ILO 2006). Moreover, using the lens of Institutional Theory, CSR is viewed as one activity that can take place at the interface of business and society.

The next section will present a brief historical view of how the concept of CSR has come into existence.

3 Historical Overview of CSR

Carroll (2008) argues that the Industrial Revolution from the mid-to-late 1800s shows social initiatives and practices that can be viewed as the beginning of CSR. Here the impacts of businesses on society arose as a dimension in society. Businesses also became concerned with how they could make their employees more productive, and issues arose relating to the employment of women and children in factories both United Kingdom and United States. These issues included labour unrest, social problems and child labour, and the industry's response to these issues, was a blend of humanitarianism, philanthropy and business acumen (Wren 2005). In fact, Murphy (1978) classifies the period up to the 1950s as the 'philanthropic era', in which businesses predominantly contributed to charities. However, the good practice example of the Cadbury Chocolate business that prospered in the 1870s, provides an example of being ahead of its time. Moving the company to a site called Bourneville Village, the company established a housing plan, and a plan for a green environment, where one-tenth of the village would be laid out as parks, recreation grounds and open spaces (Bailey and Bryson 2006). George Cadbury introduced an employee and community education programme, set up work councils—one for men and one for women, with equal numbers of workers and management as member, who were selected by secret ballot. Finally, work committees were also set up, consisting of employees, to discuss all matters affecting employees.

Up throughout the 1920s there were societal discussions about the social responsibility of businesses, and although Peter Drucker argued that businesses have a social dimension as well as an economic, in his second book in 1942 entitled, "The future of industrial man", it is Howard R. Bowen (1953) that has been noted to mark the beginnings of modern CSR. In his book entitled, "Social Responsibility of the businessman", he questioned what kind of responsibility to society a businessman can reasonably be expected to undertake. As Carroll (2008) interestingly notes, this question is still being asked today. Bowen (1953, p. 6) addressed the doctrine of social responsibility, defining it as; *"the obligations of businessmen to pursue those policies, to make those decisions or to follow those lines of action which are desirable in terms of the objectives and values of our society."* It is not difficult to see how this definition has spurred the discussions that followed and the discussions that still prevail today. Carroll purports that Bowen in fact, is the contemporary father of CSR (Carroll 2008).

In the 1960s, social activist groups worked vigorously for a broader notion of corporate responsibility through their activities and interventions. Up through the 1960s and the 1970s, the creation of a range of national and international conventions and agreements drove the discussion about the responsibility of businesses further, such as The International Bill of Human Rights, consisting of the Universal Declaration of Human Rights (adopted in 1948), the International Covenant on Civil and Political Rights (1966) with its two Optional Protocols and the International Covenant on Economic, Social and Cultural Rights (1966), the Environmental Protection Agency (EPA), the Equal Employment Opportunity Commission (EEOC), the Occupational Safety and Health Administration (OSHA) and the Consumer Product Safety Commission (CPSC). Towards the end of the 1970s, Carroll (1979) presented his three dimensional CSR conceptual model, which consisted of corporate responsibilities, social issues of business and corporate actions. Today, the UN Global Compact is the largest voluntary CSR initiative promoted directly by the UN, focusing on businesses impact on People, Planet and Profit, the so-called three Ps. It was formed in July, 2000, and is a framework for businesses to adopt sustainable and socially responsible policies. It states ten principles in the area of human rights, labour, the environment and anti-corruption. The UN Conference on Sustainable Development Rio + 20 was held in Rio de Janeiro, Brazil in June 2012, and its outcome document entitled "The future we want" was adopted in which the political commitment to sustainable development was renewed. It is recognised that the active participation of the private sector is critical to achieving sustainable development and the private sector is invited to explore this with due reference to business practices, such as those endorsed by the UN Global Compact. Further guidance is provided by ISO 26000 "Guidance on Corporate Social Responsibility" which states "the aim of social responsibility is to contribute to sustainable development". Following the above outcome, The International Maritime Organisation (IMO) selected "Sustainable Development: IMOs contribution beyond Rio+20" as the World Maritime Day theme for 2013. Alongside these developments, there have been many authors who have contributed to the CSR literature, some of which have offered definitions and criticisms of CSR (Eels 1956; Selekman 1959; Davis 1960; Frederick 1960; Heald 1979; Johnson 1971; Carroll 1991, 2010).

In June 2011, the UN Guiding Principles on Business and Human Rights (UNGPs) were unanimously endorsed by the UN Human Rights Council, authored by Professor John Ruggie, the former Special Representative of the UN Secretary-General for Business and Human Rights (Froholdt 2016). A critical contribution of the UNGPs has been to set out clearly the duties of States and the responsibilities of companies to ensure that businesses operate in full compliance with human rights principles (Froholdt 2016). The UNGPs are reflected in frameworks such as the International Labour Organisation (ILO) Tripartite Declaration of Principles concerning Multinational Enterprises and Social Policy (revised, 2006), the Organisation for Economic Co-operation and Development (OECD) Guidelines for Multinational Enterprises, the International Organisation for Standardization ISO 26000 standard on social responsibility, the International Finance Cooperation (IFC) Performance Standards, the UN Global Compact's Ten Principles and a growing number of commitments by various industry and multi-stakeholder initiatives. These frameworks institutionalise CSR at a global level, by creating norms, rules and standardised procedures for CSR (Brammer 2012). In that trans-national entities do not have the legal power of national enforcement, they offer standardised rules through frameworks that afford companies to engage in self-regulation.

Today CSR is a specific kind of self-regulation that penetrates the sphere of the public administrative domain. Some companies are addressing issues that are usually addressed by the public sector, and at the same time, the public sector is increasingly promoting CSR in its own policies. The lines of the private and the public domain therefore merge into new forms of governance (Froholdt 2016). These influences contribute to the shift in governance from mere command-and-control to a form of participatory governance and to new forms of institutionalism, all of which can be supported by Institution Theory. The command-and-control kind of governance is also often criticised on the grounds that it does not solve the actual problem, but provides a more last resort solution (Gritsenko 2014). The suggestions are to promote more private voluntary actions in shipping, such as green practices (Gritsenko 2014; Lai et al. 2010), although this cannot be entirely relied upon either. Unfortunately, neither regulation nor innovation has proved to be a catalyst for good governance in shipping (Haralambides 1998; Shinohara 2005).

There is an opportunity for countries to utilize the increasing interest in CSR to mandate, facilitate, partner and endorse the CSR agenda alongside key public policy goals, in order to enhance results in both respects. Tax and royalty revenues are often used for example in the case of upstream extractive industries, which can provide economic opportunities, however, they can result in poor governance. Sometimes governments are forced to ease regulation in order to keep investment and production, as the threat of capital disinvestment is a concern. Some private actors realise that it is better to control the regulatory process themselves than to be forced to succumb to a regulation they would have little control over. Visser (2006) argues that CSR is perceived differently in developing countries contra developed countries, and CSR is also perceived differently when United Kingdom (UK) and United States (US) are compared. This argument is also supported by Matten and Moon (2008), who state that this is due to a variety of longstanding, historically entrenched institutions. For example, the US institutional framework has resisted public health insurance, which leaves room to include this in a company's CSR policy. The absence of a range of employment related issues in European CSR policies are often due to the fact that corporations and other taxpayers contribute to this through the taxation system. European companies also seem less inclined to philanthropy than in the US. In some countries, the failure of legal institutions and government results in the inability to guarantee, define and administer the market and act on behalf of societal values and preferences, which in turn, creates a different context for CSR activities.

The concept of corporate social responsibility (CSR) is a relatively new phenomenon in academia, and whether CSR is equivalent with a financial benefit is still debated amongst researchers. There are studies that show a positive connection between CSR and some values in corporate performance. For example, the study by Pava and Krausz (1996) shows a positive connection between CSR and financial performance. Stanwick and Stanwick (1998) show a connection between CSR and good stakeholder relationships, and Ruf et al. (2001) show a relationship between CSR and growth in sales and return on sales. Yet Lee et al. (2009) claim that there is a negative relation between profit rate and the amount of information about CSR activities posted. Studies conducted specifically within a maritime context are limited, however, Drobetz et al. (2013) claim that corporate governance has an influence on financial performance when considering the unique conditions that exist in the shipping industry. These few studies show how the findings are rather varied.

From a historical perspective, CSR is not a new phenomenon. It is the latest manifestation of earlier debates on the role of business in society. Examples of this have been presented earlier in this chapter. However, what is new, according to Fabig and Boele (1999), is that *"today's debates are conducted at the intersection of development, environment and human rights, and are more global in outlook than earlier in this [the twentieth] century or even in the 1960s"*.

4 The Perception of CSR in the Maritime Industry

In the shipping industry, the number of companies engaging in CSR activities has increased. This is in part due to support from larger companies, but also in part due to the support from the ILO (Froholdt et al. 2015; Froholdt 2016). However, the maritime industry has been called a laggard when it comes to CSR (Skovgaard 2008). The level of CSR maturity in the maritime industry has been said to be rather low, and maritime companies are slow to incorporate CSR policies or engage in CSR activities compared to other industries (Skouloudis et al. 2011). Skovgaard discusses some of the reasons behind this reluctance to engage, in his chapter (Skovgaard, chapter 'Response to Institutional Processes: A Study of Corporate Social Responsibility in Danish Shipping Companies') in this book. One reason for this has been due the absence of a direct contact between shipping companies and the end consumers (Kunnaala 2013).

However, CSR activities in the maritime industry are evolving and transforming market conditions. There are now new demands from companies, regulators, customers, investors and NGOs in regards to energy efficiency, climate change, pollution, waste, hazards, spills and sustainable supply chain management. These new demands are in turn transforming market conditions by creating new challenges for shipping companies. Despite a predominant focus on environmental issues, the industry has taken other important initiatives (Kunnaala 2013). Some companies are not only exporting their products and services, but also their codes of conduct, hereby demanding that their suppliers abide by the same code of conduct or are required to submit their own sustainability report (Froholdt 2016). Other companies implement CSR activities predominantly when there are cost-savings or other financial benefits to be made (Mansouri et al. 2015).

A study of short sea shipping companies in Greece, Fafaliou (2006), found three approaches towards CSR. Firstly there was the 'adverse' approach where companies who operated at the lowest cost often avoided complying with international legislation (Froholdt et al. 2015). The second approach was 'typical', where companies complied by the law whilst focusing on financial benefits. Lastly, there was the 'supportive' approach, where companies went beyond compliance, either by complying with soft-law initiatives or self-regulation. The study concluded that size of company does matter in relation to which of the three approaches will be relevant. In the study by Sampson (2015) it is argued that the maritime industry has a CSR approach, but this approach is not value-driven, and is more proned to focus on the environment, than on issues that involve health and the welfare of sea-based employees.

A perception study undertaken by Froholdt et al. (2013) of the perception of CSR amongst 96 maritime professionals in developing countries showed that the maritime professionals find human and social issues to be the most significant challenge in the industry, secondly the environment and lastly bribery. It is not surprising that human and social issues are rated the highest for maritime professionals, as developing countries are where the social and environmental crises are usually most acutely felt

(WRI 2005). The fact that there are differences in how the CSR agenda is viewed in developing countries is not a new phenomenon, as Visser (2006) has also explained when he compared Carroll's CSR Pyramid to an African context (South Africa and Kenya). The differences between cultural understandings of CSR have also been evident in other studies (Edmondson and Carroll 1999; Burton 2000).

If we return to the aspect of bribery and corruptive behaviour that was brought up in the study by Froholdt et al. (2013), it can be noted that former Secretary General of IMO Mr. Mitropoulis (2014) has called for action from maritime companies on this issue. At a Capital Link Forum event he argued, "In the 21st century it is no longer sufficient for your business to be efficient. Now businesses have to operate within ethical boundaries. The challenge now is to understand them and then set about implementing them meaningfully" (Mitropoulis 2014). Ethical behavior has been increasingly addressed in the maritime industry via the CSR debate and through the introduction of the UN Global Compact (UNGC) with a section on anti-bribery and corruption as a CSR tool. CSR and the UNGC tool have enabled the topic of ethical behavior and corruption to be more openly addressed by shipping companies, which can be seen for example with the establishment of the Maritime Anti-Corruption Network their anti-corruption principles—"Seven principles" that apply to members essentially.

A number of international institutions have addressed the issue of corruption, such as the UN Convention against Corruption adopted in 2003 and the OECD Anti-Corruption Convention of 2009. Practical tools and standards have also been made available. The OECD released in April 2016 an anti-corruption toolkit[1] that can be used by governments around the world. The toolkit provides guidance to examine channels of corrupt payments. Finally, the Baltic and International Maritime Council (BIMCO) have recently provided an Anti-corruption Clause for Charter parties. At the national level, in 2010 United Kingdom (UK) introduced the Bribery Act to update and enhance UK law on bribery including foreign bribery in order to address better the requirements of the 1997 OECD anti-bribery Convention. It is now among the strictest legislation internationally on bribery. It introduces a new strict liability offence for companies and partnerships of failing to prevent bribery, and strict penalties for active and passive bribery by individuals as well as companies. MACN was created after the update of the UK Bribery Act due to the risk of fines and imprisonment for shipowners if they do not have procedures to mitigate corruption (Rytter Sørensen 2013).

While a shipping company must comply with international law, it can also decide to commit to CSR 'soft law', through a CSR tool. However, this commitment is not without challenges (Froholdt 2016). A recent report from Seafarers International Research Centre (SIRC) (Sampson 2015) showed how unethical behaviour takes place between seafarers and an array of port officials such as health inspectors, quarantine, customs and immigration officers, agents, pilots and terminal staff. These gifts made life easier for the crew on board, due to the risk of delays, if the

[1]www.oecd.org.

gifts were not provided, and they were often mediated by vessel agents. In some ports, early approval of documents was given upon the receipt of a facilitation gift. It is also expressed that there is a need for attitudinal change in regards to corruption, which is viewed as a large problem in the industry (Froholdt et al. 2013). A number of the responses describe how circumstance and location can determine whether you must participate in bribery or corruptive actions, despite the fact that it is against your own personal ethics. In some areas of the industry, even amongst large players, corruption is the norm. Some respondents 'play by the rules' and report violations, but there is still a need for more enforcement.

The data in the Froholdt et al. study (2013) showed that respondents from all regions and sectors suggest 'stronger enforcement' as a preferred approach to encourage anti-corruption awareness and knowledge about CSR, which is scored higher by respondents than 'better national laws' and 'better international laws'. This is in line with research on government capacity which concludes that a lack of enforcement remains a limitation and reduces the effectiveness of legislation as a driver for CSR (Visser 2006). In specific relation to Africa, governance reform is needed in order to provide what Fox (2004) has coined "*the enabling environment for responsible business*". Using the Institutional theory approach, the data shows that there is a possibility that companies can influence social institutions by demanding better governance in order to facilitate the development of CSR. Ultimately, the data shows the importance of the regional context in regard to determining which CSR agenda is appropriate for a specific context.

The data in the Froholdt et al. (2013) study indicated that CSR is present in the maritime industry, but it still needs maturing. Some organisations have no policy but they are aware that they are conducting activities that fall under the CSR umbrella. Some respondents express a wish to have a CSR agenda, or a policy but need help to accomplish this. Several express a need for some central point where they could find help, tools or knowledge about how to learn about CSR and what to do when creating and implementing a CSR agenda. This shows that maritime professionals are interested in learning more about CSR. However, as the study only yielded 96 responses, the study can only indicative at best.

Another perception study of CSR that was undertaken by Froholdt et al. (2015) showed how 82 maritime professionals in the Philippines perceived CSR. The respondents indicated that the concept of CSR is known and implemented by some shipping companies and maritime educational institutions. Respondents believed that there was a good CSR awareness in the Philippines, and that "*CSR is big in Asia*". Some of the respondents took part in a range of CSR activities that were available in their company, such as environment relief, soup kitchens, family services, entrepreneur courses and other programs offered to the respondents and their families. Respondents also expressed that companies should engage more in CSR activities, and some believed that this could be accomplished if companies would take part in and discuss CSR issues in more open forums, forums for companies and forums for individual companies and their employees. Although CSR is big in the Philippines, the CSR activities that exist, are predominantly of philanthropic character (Carroll 1991, 1999). As this study yielded 82 responses and is therefore small in scope, it is only indicative at best.

CSR was not known or implemented at all by the manning agencies in the Philippine study (Froholdt et al. 2015). The manning agencies all responded that it was the responsibility of the company that they performed the recruiting services for, to undertake any training or activities in relation to CSR. The manning agencies expressed that they did not see the necessity in being socially responsible. The indication that manning agencies do not find it necessary to engage in CSR is problematic. This issue of the role and responsibility of third party manning agencies also arose in a study by Taudal Poulsen and Johnson (2015), who investigated incentives in maritime companies for energy efficiency monitoring. Taudal Poulsen and Johnson (2015) found that it is difficult to influence the necessity for energy efficiency monitoring training for crews employed through third parties. Ultimately the question is who is responsible for this training, the principal company engaging the services of the manning agency or the manning agency. This is a matter that needs to be resolved, not just at a local level, but at a global level too.

An interesting category of comments in the study by Froholdt et al. (2015) were related to monitoring or regulating CSR as the way to ensure that shipping companies will implement CSR. This is in line with the recent development that has been taken by the Panama Maritime Authority (AMP). AMP has adopted a resolution requiring maritime concessionaires to pay a fee that will support social projects (Froholdt 2016). As of January, 1, 2016, AMP implemented a special three (3) year discount for ships already registered or for ships that register under the Panama Flag. To apply for this discount the applicant must present evidence of the implementation of CSR programs that are focused on the reduction of air and sea pollution from shipping. This initiative will seemingly push the environmental and social pegs of the CSR agenda, however the social projects do have a philanthropic flavour to them. In line with Institutional theory, this regulation will influence corporations, and the outcome still remains to be seen.

A concept that arose as a matter of interest for shipping companies when discussing CSR in the study by Froholdt et al. (2013) was the concept of shared value. Skovgaards (2017, chapter 'Response to Institutional Processes: A Study of Corporate Social Responsibility in Danish Shipping Companies' in this book) study also shows that perception of CSR amongst some of the Danish shipping companies is that it is important that there is a business case for CSR, and where CSR activities have been undertaken by the larger companies, it more than often takes the form of shared value. Shared value does not have the same meaning as CSR, and is a concept that has been put forward by Porter and Kramer, who define the concept as a focus on connections between societal and economic progress (Porter and Kramer 2006).

The central premise behind shared value is that there is the generation of economic value by a company in a way that also produces value for society, by addressing some of its challenges (Froholdt 2016). This provides for new opportunities for economic development that enables a community to achieve social development to which a given company investment contributes—a joint company and community value creation. The European Commission (EC) has also discussed the development of the concept of creating shared value (European Commission 2011). According to the EC, the concept refers to the way in which enterprises seek to generate a return on investment for their owners and shareholders by means of creating value for other stakeholders and society at large. This links CSR strongly to innovation, especially in terms of developing new products and services that are commercially successful and help to address societal challenges. The Danish shipping company Maersk has engaged in shared value by facilitating growth markets in Ghana, Somalia and East Africa, which is also documented in the company's Sustainability report 2016. Companies in other industries such as WalMart, Unilever and Nestle have also engaged in shared value initiatives. Shared value is however not necessarily connected to sustainability, as it is exclusively about generating economic and societal benefits relative to cost. Where CSR includes both responsibility and sustainability, shared value is more about creating commercial value and is integral to cost optimization. Although voluntary, some of these activities are more related to occasional profit maximization, rather than related to CSR (Kurucz et al. 2008).

The studies and examples mentioned above show that the perception of CSR is continuously changing, where the aspect of voluntary evolves into self-regulation and the lines between hard law and soft law become somewhat blurred (Froholdt 2016). Through the lens of Institutional theory, we can understand CSR as a dynamic force that is not so demarcated or rigid, and is used by both public and private actors. These actors in turn influence and are influenced by the way that CSR can be perceived. This process is however also influenced by the inertia that is argued by Sampson (2015). While there is still a need for attitudinal change in the maritime industry in regards to understanding the scope of CSR and the necessity to address not only the environmental leg, but also the social and the economic legs as well, CSR in the maritime industry is moving forward.

5 Concluding Remarks

This chapter has sought to present and discuss perceptions of CSR, and has done so by presenting the definition by ILO and using Institutional theory, and discussing how CSR can be understood. A brief historical overview of how CSR came into existence was also presented. This chapter then presented the findings of different studies and examples that shed some light on the way CSR is perceived.

The data from the studies presented showed that the respondents although respondents did not recognise the term CSR, they took part in actual company CSR activities. Although the study by Froholdt et al. (2013) of the perception of CSR amongst maritime professionals across the maritime industry indicated that CSR was seemingly well known in Asia, it was predominantly philanthropic in character. This is in line with other studies. Noteworthy was the response from manning agencies, and their lack of responsibility for engaging or providing training in CSR as their own CSR activity. This was left for the company hiring their services to accommodate. This can account for the respondents responding that they did not understand what CSR is. They were simply not subjected to it through their main contact, the manning agencies. However, this is an issue that needs to be addressed at both a local and a global level.

The perception study by Froholdt et al. (2015) that was undertaken in the Philippines showed that it was predominantly maritime professionals in public institutions that had heard of CSR, although maritime professionals in private organisations displayed an interest to learn more about CSR. It also showed that there are differences in the way that the CSR agenda is perceived by maritime professionals, and contextual and cultural differences across the regions have an important influence on how CSR is understood. These differences not only shed light on knowledge gaps, but they also indicate large differences in business ethics that need to be addressed. African region respondents from the Froholdt et al. (2013) study viewed the environmental and the social to be of equal importance, followed by bribery at second place. Asian region respondents viewed social issues to be of primary importance, then environmental issues, and bribery rated as third most important. For the Latin American region respondents, the social and bribery issues were rated most important, and the environment as second. The differences in these responses show that different contexts for CSR activity, as discussed earlier in this chapter and argued by Brammer (2012). Public maritime professionals were more aware of CSR than maritime professionals in private companies, and stronger enforcement was valued as a response to encourage CSR awareness by all respondents. This is interesting in relation to the Institution theory approach, and could indicate that public professionals across the regions see the value of facilitating or regulating the CSR agenda. Actions that could nurture this interest could be to offer business services or awareness programs. Other studies (Skovgaard 2008; Sampson 2015) also indicate differences in the way that CSR is perceived in the maritime industry, although the environmental leg of CSR is still prominent. There are seemingly CSR activities and an increasing awareness of CSR in the maritime industry, whether these activities are responses to regulation or actions that go beyond, and these developments are contributing to the maturation of CSR in the industry and the perception of CSR on a global perspective. Here education has a responsibility and an important role to play. If we are to change the way in which business processes take place in the maritime industry, this task begins by changing the curriculum in maritime education and training institutions and universities, by including CSR.

Institution theory provides a lens through which we can see CSR in a broader perspective. It is not merely a question of voluntary versus regulation, nor is it narrowed down to the scenario where a manager must decide whether or not to engage in CSR activities. Institution theory provides a place where CSR and governance can meet, where we can discuss how informal and formal rules provide both constraints and contingencies for maritime professionals in both public and private organisations. This theory can explain that maritime administrations can both facilitate and regulate CSR, and maritime companies can both self-regulate and dictate CSR. The studies presented indicate that this theory can be practically realised and recent development within and outside the maritime industry reflect this.

Further research could focus on investigating the influence of CSR policies in larger shipping on business activities in the maritime industry, and to monitor the impact of the initiatives that follow, on both public and private organisations.

References

Asian Sustainability Rating. (2010). *Sustainability in Asia: ESG reporting uncovered*, September, 2010.

Bailey, A. R., & Bryson, T. R. (2006). A Quaker experiement in town planning: George Cadbury and the construction of Bournville model village. *Quaker Studies, 11*(1), Article 6.

Bemejo, R. (2014). Sustainable development in the Brundtland report and its distortion. In *Handbook for a sustainable economy* (pp. 69–82). Springer.

Bowen, H. (1953). *Social responsibilities of the businessman*. New York: Harper and Row.

Brammer, S. J. (2012). Corporate social responsibility and institutional theory: New perspectives on private governance. *Socio-Economic Review, 10*, 3–28.

Brundtland Report. (1987). *'Our common future'. A global agenda for change*. United Nations Commission on Environment and Development, August 4, 1987.

Burton, F. A. (2000). A cross-cultural comparison of corporate social responsibility orientation: Hong Kong vs United States students. *Teaching Business Ethics, 4*(2), 151–167.

Carroll, A. B. (1979, October). A three-dimensional conceptual model of corporate performance. *The Academy of Management Review, 4*(4), 497–505.

Carroll, A. (1991). The pyramid of corporate social responsibility: Toward the moral management of organizational stakeholders. *Business Horizons, 34*(4), 39–48.

Carroll, A. B. (1999). Corporate social responsibility evolution of a definitional construct. *Business and Society, 38*(3), 268–295.

Carroll, A. B. (2008). A history of corporate social responsibility: Concepts and practices. In *The Oxford handbook of corporate social responsibility* (pp. 19–46). University Press.

Carroll, A. B. (2010). The business case for corporate scoial responsibility: A review of concepts, research and practice. *International Journal of Management Reviews*, 85–105.

Carroll, A. B., & Shabana, M. K. (2010). The business case for corporate social responsibility: A review of concepts, research and practice. In *International journal of management reviews* (pp. 85–105). Blackwell Publishing Ltd and British Academy of Management.

Dahlsrud, A. (2008). How corporate social responsibility is defined: An analysis of 37 defintions. *Corporate Social Responsibility and Environmental Management*, 1–13.

Davis, K. (1960). Can business afford to ignore social responsibilities? *California Management Review, 2*, 70–76.

Drobetz, W., Gounopoulos, D., Merikas, A., & Schröder, H. (2013). Capital structure decisions of globally-listed shipping companies. *Transportation Research Part E: Logistics and Transportation Review, 52*, 49–76.

Drucker, P. F. (1942). *The future of industrial man*. Routledge.

Edmondson, V. C., & Carroll, A. B. (1999). Giving back: An examination of the philanthropic motivations, orientations and activities of large black-owned businesses. *Journal of Business Ethics, 19*(20), 171–179.

Eels, R. (1956). *Corporate giving in a free society*. New York: Harper.

Elkington, J. (1994). Towards the sustainable cooporation: Win-win-win business strategies for sustainable development. *California Management Review, 36*(2), 90–100.

Ellen MacArthur Foundation. (2013). *Towards a circular economy: Business rationale for an accelerated transition*.

European Commission. (2001). *Promoting a European framework for corporate social responsibility*. Brussels, COM (2001) 366.
European Commission. (2011). Communication from the Commission to the European Parliament, the Council, the European Economic and Social Committee and the Committee of the Regions. A renewed EU strategy 2011–2014 for corporate social responsibility. COM(2011)681.
European Commission. (2014). *Towards a circular economy: A zero waste programme for Europe*. Brussels: European Commission.
Fabig, H., & Boele, R. (1999). The changing nature of NGO activity in a globalizing world: Pushing the corporate responsibility agenda. *IDS Bulletin, 30*(3), 63.
Fafaliou, I. L. (2006). Is the Euopean shipping industry aware of corporate social responsibility? The case of the greek-owned short sea shipping companies. *Marine Policy, 20*(4), 412–419.
Fox, T. (2004). Corporate social responsibility and development: In quest of an agenda. *Development, 47*(3), 29–36.
Frederick, W. C. (1960). The growing concern over business responsibility. *California Management Review, 2*, 54–61.
Friedman, M. (1962). *Capitalism & freedom*. University of Chicago Press.
Friedman, M. (1970). The social responsibility of business is to increase its profit. In *The New York Times Magazine*, September 13, 1970.
Froholdt, L. (2016). *Maritime governance and corporate social responsibility: a context for a responsible maritime industry*. World Maritime University, Malmo. Unpublished.
Froholdt, L. L., Baldauf, M., Progoulaki, M., & Pawlik, T. (2015). *IAMU capacity building report. corporate social responsibility (CSR) in shipping; A CSR awareness program to enhance capacity building in good governance of multicultural employees and safe operations – Good Governance of Multi-cultural Safety (PGMS)*. Tokyo, Japan: International Association of Maritime Universities.
Froholdt, L. L., Johansen, T., & Williams, E. (2013). *CSR report project deliverable CSR maritime; Maritime governance and corporate social responsibility*. Project funded by The Danish Maritime Authority and The Danish shipowners through The Danish Maritime Fund.
Gritsenko, D. (2014). Governing external cost of shipping in emission control areas: An instrumentation approach. *Journal of Maritime Research, XI*(II), 89–95.
Haralambides, H. (1998). *Quality shipping: Market mechanism for safer shipping and cleaner oceans*. Rotterdam: Erasmus Publishing.
Heald, M. (1979). *The social responsibility of business: Company and community, 1900–1960*. Cleveland: The Press of Case Western Reserve University.
International Labour Organisation (ILO). (2006). *InFocus initiative on corporate social responsibility (CSR)*. GB.295/MNE/2/1, Governing Body 295th session, Geneva, 2006.
International Maritime Organisation (IMO). (2013). *A concept of a sustainable Maritime Transportation System*.
Isaksson, R., & Steimle, U. (2009). What does GRI-reporting tell us about corporate sustainability? *The TQM Journal, 21*(2), 168–181. https://doi.org/10.1108/17542730910938155.
Johnson, H. (1971). *Business in contemporary society: Framework and issues*. Belmont, CA: Wadsworth Publishing Co. Inc..
Karaıbrahımoglu, Y. (2010). Corporate social responsibility in times of financial crisis. *African Journal of Business Management, 4*(4), 382–389.
Kumar Thakur, A., Narula, S. A., & Zutshi, A. (2015). Integrating and implementing CSR. A case of CONCOR (container corporation of India) in India. In *Developmet-oriented corporate social responsibility Vol. 2, Locally led initiatives in developing economies* (pp. 143–158).
Kunnaala, V. H. (2013). Corporate social responsibility in the Baltic Sea maritime sector. In *IMISS2013-Proceedings of the international scientific meeting for corporate social responsibility (CSR) in shipping, 2nd international maritime incident and near miss reporting conference*, 11–12 June (pp. 60–76). Turku: Publications of the Centre for Maritime Studies, University of Turku.

Kurucz, E., Colbert, B., & Wheeler, D. (2008). The business case for corporate social responsibility. In A. Crane, A. McWilliams, D. Matten, J. Moon, & D. Siegel (Eds.), *The Oxford handbook of corporate social responsibility* (pp. 83–112). Oxford: Oxford University Press.

Lai, C. S., Chiu, C. J., Yang, C. F., & Pai, D. C. (2010). The effects of corporate social responsibility on brand performance: The mediating effect of industrial brand equity and corporate reputation. *Journal of Business Ethics, 95*, 457–469.

Lee, D. D., Faff, R. W., & Langfield-Smith, K. (2009). Revisiting the vexing question: Does superior corporate social performance lead to improved financial performance? *Australian Journal of Management, 34*(1), 21–49.

Maersk Sustainability Report: www.maersk.com/ files/2016.

Mansouri, S., Lee, A., & Aluko, O. (2015). Multi-objective decision support to enhance environmental sustainability in maritime shipping: A review and future decisions. *Transportation Research Part E, 78*, 3–18.

Matten, D., & Moon, J. (2008). Implicit and explicit CSR. A conceptual framework for a comparative understanding of corporate social responsibility. *The Academy of Management Review, 33* (2).

McDonough, W., & Braungart, M. (2003). Toward sustaining architecture for the 21st century: The promise of Cradle to cradle design. *Industry and Environment.*

McWilliams, A., & Siegel, D. (2001). Corporate social responsibility: A theory of the firm perspective. *Academy of Management Review, 26*, 117–127.

Mitropoulis, E. E. (2014). *Raising the profile of corporate social responsibility.* Presentation at Capital links 4th Annual shipping and offshore CSR Forum.

Morgan, G., Campbell, J. L., Crouch, C., Pedersen, O. K., & Whitley, R. (2010). *The Oxford handbook of comparative institutional analysis*. Oxford University Press.

Murphy, E. A., Jr. (1978). An evolution. Corporate social responsiveness. *University of Michigan Business Review*, (November), 20–22.

Organisation for Economic Co-operation and Development (OECD). (2001). *Corporate responsibility. Private initiatives and public Goals*. OECD.

Pava, M. L., & Krausz, J. (1996). The association between corporate social responsibility and financial performance:the paradox of social cost. *Journal of Business Ethics, 15*(2), 321–357.

Porter, M. E., & Kramer, M. R. (2006, December). Strategy and society: The link between competitive advantage and corporate social responsibility. *Harvard Business Review, 84*(12), 78–92.

Ruf, B. M., Muralidhar, K., & Brown, R. M. (2001). An empirical investigation of the relationship between change in corporate social performance and financial performance: A stakeholder theory perspective. *Journal of Business Ethics, 32*(2), 143–156.

Rytter Sørensen, E. (2013). *On a course for a better world.* Unpublished paper for the "On Course for a Better World" project that was initiated by the Danish Business Authority and the Danish Shipowners' Association. The project is financed by the Danish Maritime Fund, Lauritzen Foundation, D/S NORDEN // D/S Orients Fond and the TORM Foundation.

Sampson, H. (2015). Seabirds matter more than us! Understanding the complex exercise of CSR in the global shipping industry. *Journal of Sustainable Mobility, 3*(2), 101–119.

Selekman, B. (1959). *A moral philosophy for business*. New York: McGraw-Hill.

Shinohara, M. (2005). Quality shipping and incentive schemes: From the perspective of the institutional economics. *Maritime Economics and Logistics, 7.*

Skovgaard, J. (2008). *Sustainable knowledge platform for the european maritime and logigtics industry: CSR-policy, the case of shipping: A global frontrunner whilst a CSR laggard.* Seventh Framework Programme, SKEMA Coordination Action.

Skouloudis, A., Evangelinos, K., & Nikolaou, I. (2011). An overview of corporate social responsibility in Greece. Perceptions, developments and barriers to overcome. *Business Ethics: European Review, 20*(2), 205–226.

Stanwick, P. A., & Stanwick, S. D. (1998). The relationship between corporate social performance and organizational size, financial performance and environmental performance: An empirical examination. *Journal of Business Ethics, 17*(2), 195–204.
Taudal Poulsen, R., & Johnson, H. (2015). The logic of business vs. the logic of energy management practice: Understanding the choices and effects of energy consumption monitoring systems in shipping companies. *Journal of Cleaner Production, 112*(5), 3785–3797.
The Danish Commerce and Companies Agency. (2010). *Redegørelse for samfundsansvar (Statement of CSR).* [online] http://www.retsinformation.dk/Forms/R0710.aspx?id=126096. Accessed 04 January 2012.
United Nations Development Programme (UNDP). (2007). UNDP/Private Sector strategy; Promoting Inclusive Market Development. September, 2007.
United Nations Global Compact: http:unglobalcompact.org.
Visser, W. (2006). Revisiting Carrol's CSR pyramid: An African perspective. In E. R. Pedersen & M. Huniche (Eds.), *Corporate citizenship in developing countries* (pp. 29–56).
Waworuntu, R. W. (2014). CSR and financial performance analysis: Evidence from top ASEAN listed countries. *Procedia - Social and Behavioral Sciences, 164*, 493–500.
World Bank. (2005). *Opportunities and options for governments to promote corporate social responsibility in Europe and Central Asia.* Working Paper. DevComm The World Bank, 2005.
World Resources Institute (WRI). (2005). *The wealth of the poor. Managing ecosystems to fight poverty.* World Resource Report.
Wren, D. A. (2005). *The history of management thought* (5th ed.). Wiley.

The Growth of CSR and Its Acceptance in the Maritime Industry

Devinder Grewal

1 Introduction

Corporate Social Responsibility (CSR) has become an increasingly expected role of business. It has become a regular subject of study in most business schools, libraries are adding books on this topic to their collections, the UN is promoting CSR through its Global Compact, national and regional governments increasingly require public companies to report on their social and environmental programs. Leading companies proudly promote their CSR practices in their marketing efforts.

The role of business engaging in CSR has not been universally accepted. There have been prominent opponents who believe that business should focus on its main objective, which is making a profit, and not worry about its social responsibility since that is already included in the economic outcomes to society (Friedman 1970). An insightful negation to Friedman was provided by Denning, writing in Forbes (2013). Friedman's view has been loyally supported by The Economist newspaper which has long held the view that companies support society by paying tax and adding jobs through investment (e.g., *Just Good Business (2008), Global Business Barometer (*2008b*), Social Saints, Fiscal Fiends (*2016*)*). The view of The Economist is that CSR is often misguided but cannot be ignored by businesses. The main reasons for this, according to The Economist, include (1) protection of their reputation in a time where trust in big business is being questioned by a very networked society which does not hesitate to share images, (2) the role of ranking and ratings of companies in social media, and (3) demand from employees who want to work with companies that share their values. Forbes, through a post by Steve Denning, offers a comment of the Economist's position, asserting that the role of business is bigger than just creating shareholder value—it must create a customer.

D. Grewal (✉)
World Maritime University, Malmö, Sweden
e-mail: dg@wmu.se

L. L. Froholdt (ed.), *Corporate Social Responsibility in the Maritime Industry*, WMU Studies in Maritime Affairs 5, https://doi.org/10.1007/978-3-319-69143-5_3

In *Just Good Business*, The Economist (2008a) lists three layers of corporate CSR engagement:

1. Philanthropy using pre-tax profits
2. Reputational risk management following spectacular accidents *inter alia* the oil spill from the *Exxon Valdez*, the Union Carbide Bhopal disaster of 1984, the refusal of big pharmaceutical companies to make retroviral drugs available cheaply to HIV AIDS sufferers in developing countries, the Bangladesh clothing factory fire in 2012, obesity connected with the fast food industry
3. Create value, as proposed by Porter and Kramer (2006).

These can be compared with the four reasons for CSR put forward by Porter and Kramer (2006),

- Moral obligation
- Sustainability
- Licence to operate
- Reputation

while they promote the development of shared value between society and business for long term outcomes. The example of Pfizer can be offered as an example of a large pharmaceutical company that makes a commitment to make its products available to the world's less well off. This is promoted as its socially responsible behaviour but critics point to its tax inversion as it plans to shift its base from the USA to Ireland to avail of a favourable regime. Davis et al. (2016) reporting on a study on the relationship between tax payment and CSR, find that CSR in companies is positively related to tax avoidance lobbying expenditures, effectively making CSR and tax payment substitutes.

The Friedman school of thought would support this finding with a view that firms exist to support the goals of their owners (shareholders) and CSR should only be practiced to support that goal.

It is of interest to compare the above with the model of social responsibilities suggested by Carroll (1998), comprising economic (profit making), legal (stay within the law), ethical (just and fair as judged by the host society) and discretionary (which can be seen as oxymoronic with being a responsibility but may include philanthropic activities and may well be considered the umbrella of ethical responsibilities). This bears striking resemblance to the earlier practices of CSR discussed in the following section.

The issue at the heart of this dialogue is the nature of the firm. By itself, the firm is inanimate, unable to take a decision or undertake any action. It is run by its managers who make decisions on its behalf, based on their own values and needs.

2 Early Practice of CSR

Early reflections on socially responsible behaviour are found in the literature of many countries of the old world. Machiavelli (1513) in *The Prince* writes about the need for princes to appear virtuous so that their subjects are not antagonised. Machiavelli goes on to say that the prince should not let virtue stop him from what he needs to do to protect his own interests. This is Homeric thinking that the virtues to be pursued are riches, power, status and prestige and personal attributes must support their achievement. Managers of modern firms can also be seen to be guided by similar thinking.

Plato, on the other hand, took the view that the decisions taken by individuals lead to good or bad outcomes. His view in *The Republic* is that the first care of rulers is education, developing a realm of knowledge in which 'kings are philosophers and philosophers are kings; and there is another and higher education . . . of science as well as of art, and not of youth only but of the whole of life'.

The early Indian literature that addresses holistic social responsibility tends to draw upon the Bhagawad Gita, said to be composed sometime between 2000 and 5000 BC. Several Indian and other authors (e.g., Aurobindo 1928/1997; Chatterjee 2009; Chakraborty 1999; Krishnan 2003, etc.) identify 'pillars of wisdom' from this work in the organisational and social context. These pillars may be identified as:

- Right action without desires
- Purity of intent
- Identification of the dynamics between goodness, ignorance and passion
- Holistic development
- Enlightened collective welfare
- Integrated vision for the individual, organisation and society.

The Indian approach places emphasis on the 'cause and effect' nature of decision making and the responsibility of the manager with the right ingredients of decision making defining its quality with the effects accruing to society and not necessarily only to the organisation.

3 CSR and the Corporation

Corporate regulations, environmental and labour laws remain inadequate in controlling every aspect of a firm's decisions. Developing regulation to cover every aspect of a firm's behaviour, and expecting that each of such laws will be followed, is unreasonable and its implementation will be inefficient, even in centrally controlled economies. A closer examination of Friedman's essays on business and social responsibility shows that he advocated that businesses remain within the accepted norms of corporate behaviour and ethical custom.

If we consider CSR as a component of a social contract between the community and the firm, we must consider another dimension that we have touched upon earlier—self-regulation to gain trust, particularly in the context of unexpected future developments that may have a negative impact on the firm's reputation and community relations. The element of ethics must be recognised to exist, even if it sits just below the surface of the dialogue.

The first element of the discussion in this context is the nature of self-regulation of CSR, which precludes enforcement (not merely auditing) by an external authority. The nature of a self-imposed discipline, which is shared in its objectives with the community, is that it removes any motivation to move away from the declared performance under mutually expected beliefs. This self-discipline, over time, generates a trust that leads further to reputational capital for the firm, built upon responsible relationships with its stakeholders. In turn, this reputation induces trust and cooperation and lowers the costs of control or negotiation. In this situation, if the firm were to abuse its trust, it will lose all its reputational capital with the stakeholders. Once this social contract is broken, there are often no agreed processes between the firm and the community (or stakeholders) to regain trust and reputation.

The response to this fragile situation is the existence of specific and appropriately structured standards that can be adopted by a firm for its practice and reporting of CSR. The practice of CSR can still remain voluntary but can be made compliant to an announced and known standard, such as the Global Reporting Initiative (GRI) Standards 101, 102 and 103. These standards specify to both the firm and the stakeholders what can be expected in the relationship so that such a relationship can be initiated.

Grewal and Darlow (2007) referred to a move from "trust me" to "show me" in a firm's relationship with its community. The adoption of a known standard allows the transition from a firm seeking acceptance to one that undertakes to conform to a rule of conduct with an ethical principle of CSR management standards.

There is, therefore, a gap which must be covered by means other than formal regulation. This gives rise to the concept of a hypothetical "social contract" that a firm may elect to enter into and define its own methods of compliance with it. These are most often behavioural approaches to a given strategy and the firm's decision-making guided by enlightened self-interest that is based on maintaining the trust of all its stakeholders. This extends the firm's fundamental principle of self interest in making a profit to include maintaining the trust of its stakeholders through a regime of declared self-discipline. In turn, this extension induces a reciprocal reputation of trust among its stakeholders, which the firm sees as the benefit of discretionary self-regulation. In doing this, a firm puts forward some essential elements of understanding to convince its stakeholders that it deserves their trust:

1. That it is honest and seeks to develop trust in its activities.
2. The firm seeks no singular benefits to itself from this trust—it is in mutuality with its stakeholders.
3. The operations and the results are in an observable state through reports and other disclosures to its stakeholders.

The conflict with this position is that stakeholders cannot be present to observe all the firm's transactions which may be undertaken under the discretion of the management authority structures such as collusion or risk taking. The structure of the trust mechanism is therefore asymmetrical, in favour of the firm.

In response to this imbalance, the practice of CSR has established standardised norms. A firm, in voluntarily declaring its practice of CSR, explicitly declares that it will follow norms whose structure and content are shared with the stakeholders through a declared standard. These norms allow the stakeholders to develop expectations of the conduct that the firm will follow in expected and unforeseen situations, putting in place a mechanism that supports the development of reputation as well as effecting of any punishment if the standard is not followed.

The practice of CSR then becomes a factor against which a firm's reputation may be measured. The decision that the firm has to make is *to what extent must it comply with the standard to maintain the relationship of trust with its stakeholders.* This can be a business decision which can involve costs and trade-offs and can range from the minimum compliance necessary to maintain the trust to going all the way, regardless of cost implications, because that is the brand expectation of the business in its market.

The reasons for firms to accept the contract of CSR has been mainly voluntary so far. The motives for doing so can be either reputational or long-term sustainability, or a combination of both. The level of compliance may range from minimalist, to opportunistic non-compliance to full compliance. In a competitive market environment, the level of compliance can be expected to be high when the trust standard to which compliance is expected is uniform and accepted by the other participants in the market. In times of low returns when the cost of compliance can be high, firms may resort to opportunistic non-compliance to save costs, as evidenced in a few recent instances (ABC News 2015; Maritime Executive 2015).

4 Recognition of the Social Role of Business

Over the last 50 years, a spectrum of models to illustrate the social role of business has emerged. These go by various names, including, *inter alia*, enlightened self-interest, corporate citizenship and CSR. Some companies, such as Scott Bader (http://www.scottbader.com) took an early lead in socially responsible and enlightened management and governance to include the internal and the external communities with which the company interacts. Others take a more philanthropic approach, contributing to charities, social, disadvantaged or sports groups. Many support the unemployed or homeless people or similar community initiatives.

Against the backdrop of large corporate scandals in recent years, businesses are concerned about their reputation and the support of the community. Similarly, almost as an extension of the public-private paradigm, governments are driving government owned companies towards having a formal CSR program in their management.

The relationship between business and government is fundamentally shaped by the history of development of that country. In the New World (North America and Australia are examples), business relationships were defined by European settlement and its accompanying needs to take ownership of the land and conduct commerce to the support of settlers and very often to the cost of indigenous populations. It is acknowledged that not all the developments were to support the government of the day because relationships between settlers and governments were not always mutually supportive. In the USA, freedom of business from government interference is still strongly embedded in the liberal tradition. Large business houses often have a history of supporting social causes through charitable foundations. The Bill and Melinda Gates Foundation, Ford Foundation, Getty Trust, Wellcome Trust are examples of a very large number that exist in nearly every country in the world. This separation of government and private or non-governmental development initiative includes developing educational institutions.

This social effort also contributed strongly to the reputation of the business and its economic welfare.

In Europe, the welfare state started to emerge in the mid-1800s but got progressively strengthened after the two world wars as social structures and capabilities were drained of energy after the war effort. Business owners played a small role in supporting social welfare.

Australia has traditionally followed the European, more specifically the British, model of social welfare and the state took the main role of social support.

With the progress of time, the welfare needs have grown to occupy a large percentage of the national budget. The government has taken the added position of defining a liveable minimum wage for workers while having measures that will protect the interest of business in the economy. An environment of mutual support is thus seen to emerge in the welfare countries. As demand from the wider social welfare sectors of health, education, social security continue to demand greater attention in competition with infrastructure and economic growth, governments have turned to reviewing the existing models and developing new ones.

The 1970s and 80s were a lean time for business in the developed world, with oil price hikes and their far-reaching effects on production. Governments responded by developing a more market driven approach, particularly during the Thatcher and Major years in the UK. An example is the "Business in the Community (BITC)" initiative in the UK, which came out of the Anglo-American corporate-community conference in 1980 to explore the concept of CSR. BITC formed in 1982 with 30 corporations as its members and the Prince of Wales as its President, growing to 108 members in the next 3 years. Over the next 30 years, BITC has gone through the phases of *corporate community involvement*, to *corporate community investment* and then to *responsible business*.

In Australia, similar transitions have happened through various initiatives, including the *Working Nation* in the mid-1990s of the Keating government, the community-business partnership of the late 1990s, the *Social Coalition* in the mid-2000s of the Howard government.

Together, these initiatives have raised the profile of corporate involvement in community issues, without any transfer of responsibilities from either government or the community to business. At the same time, it allows communities and individuals to engage more in their life environment. This includes communities and individuals both external and internal to the business, who have found a way of making a direct connection with their communities and understanding the sentiment about their products and operations before they impact on customer engagement.

Regardless of the widespread understanding of community involvement, each business takes its own unique approach based on the values of its management. Management literature has seen the growth of the concept of "employer of choice" which aims at attracting employees whose values will be matched by the business (Pfeffer 1998), creating a cycle of high expectations between them. At the same time, the inter-connected worlds of work and leisure assure both employers and employees that internal and external sentiment will soon flow across any boundaries. Managing corporate information, which may not only be commercially confidential, is an issue of concern to managers and owners of businesses, particularly in the transport sector.

5 Society and the Corporation

The role of business in a community can be seen through various lenses that are designed by mutual and separate expectations. They include:

The role of business to make a profit: This paradigm, endorsed by Friedman, takes the view that a business has a primary role to work in the interest of its owners, including shareholders. In providing a profit, it fulfils its primary fiduciary function to them as well as providing employment to its workers and contractors. In addition, the salaries and wages it pays to its workforce permeate through the community. The re-investment it makes in its functions provides continued employment and related benefits to everybody. A business and its managers are skilled only in the job they are trained for and cannot address social needs with any competence. However, at the discretion of its shareholders, a business may make some philanthropic contributions to society.

The role of business to follow socially responsible principles in its own self-interest: In addition to its commercial role, businesses recognise the need to keep in mind the interest of other stakeholders. This approach is driven by management perception of what is good for them and the goodwill they need to maintain with their community. Businesses provide some sponsorship to local activities and expect to gain a measure of support in return. This can be termed an insurance or a contingency approach such that a business invests in developing goodwill that it may need to call upon sometime in the future.

The role of business in engaging its stakeholders and community: The business takes a proactive role in engaging with all its stakeholders—internal and external—seeing them as partners in its continued successful operations. In this process, the business portrays that its corporate values are aligned with the values of the society within which it operates. This engagement delivers a message of mutual dependency, implying and expecting mutual support.

The role of business as a corporate citizen: The business involves its community through the involvement of its employees. This approach restructures the internal and external priorities of the business by aligning the values of the individuals within the company with those of the community outside. This alignment provides a larger stakeholder network to the business whose interests appear to be more mutually congruent.

Over the last 20 years, there has been an increasing interest by businesses as well as academics in the areas of community involvement and CSR. The outcomes have most often been to further promote the business-community involvement. One early example of this work is *Building Corporate Community Economic Development Team* by the Conference Board of Canada (1998). The volume of literature continued to grow and in 2002 the United Nations Research Institute for Social Development (UNRISD) and the UN Non-governmental Liaison Service (NGLS) published a bibliography and websites resource guide on this topic. These publications have provided businesses a basis for defining and measuring performance against external benchmarks.

Philanthropy has had a progressively growing profile in corporate community involvement. It is most developed in the US, where *inter alia* premier educational institutions like Harvard have large endowment funds in place to support their functions, but it has been in existence, perhaps in less overt forms, throughout most of the world for a long time. Organisations of all sizes have increasing social demands for their contributions, both in money and in other forms of engagement. As resources have become more constrained and targeted on corporate goals, businesses have taken a more strategic and value-creating approach to this interaction that encompasses the fundamental wealth creating role of business through its value chains and the voluntary contributions it makes. The broad trends (Conference Board) have been to

- seek alignment with business goals
- get a measurable return from investment in the community
- image enhancement for the business which, embedded increasingly into employee involvement, results in increased employee loyalty
- connect community investment with customer concerns.

These trends manifest themselves through

Charitable support, which may be intermittent, for a range of community needs, usually with the business receiving some visibility

Strategic investment in long term projects that enhance the reputation of the business

Partnerships with charities structured to enhance the corporate image of the business.

Community involvement for a business is one of the most complex issues to rationalise and understand. Most large businesses have a community involvement commitment. The reasons for doing this can be various, depending really on the outcomes the business desires.

Since businesses effectively invest in the community through their involvement, they seek to know the worth of their investment. For this, they use a wide range of strategies, including surveys of different stakeholders, measuring competence gain (skills gained through employees volunteering), or comprehensive social or sustainability audits. Large companies may have their own measurement frameworks. Other strategies for measurement include the Balanced Scorecard, the European Foundation for Quality Management (EFQM), BITC's Ten Principles of Corporate Community Investment and Standards of Excellence in Community Relations developed by Boston College Centre for Corporate Citizenship.

The elements of measurement relate to defining and commitment to the company's social vision, business-like management of community relations, internal and external corporate communication and developing community involvement programs that reflect both company and community objectives.

While all the other methods of discovering the benefits of community engagement may be defined as qualitative, a more difficult quantitative approach can be taken by conducting a cost benefit analysis (CBA) or a return on investment (ROI) analysis.

In defining the cost of the community involvement, the planning and design aspects of the engagement are considered. The detail may include any resources committed, including money and personnel, communications, staff training and opportunity costs of the initiative.

In defining benefits, items that may be considered include tax rebates attracted, free advertising gained, legal costs saved, future savings in image management in the event of a crisis, employee attraction and retention, and customer attraction and retention, any sales generated directly or indirectly from the initiative, market exposure of new goods or services generated by the business, mitigate negative impacts such as noise and dust generation of operations and provide opportunities for innovation, with a consequential benefit seen in the share price.

Allocation of the benefits to community involvement may not be free of internal disagreement. Community involvement can be seen as an intangible function with managers often questioning their tangible benefits. For instance, marketing may want to claim some responsibility for increased sales, just as HR may wish to claim ownership of employee attraction and retention. A suggested way may be to weigh the prospect of these benefits accruing in the absence of a community involvement program.

6 Choosing the Area of Community Involvement

Businesses identify areas of community involvement and activity that are easy for their core competencies to engage with. The involvement is likely to provide opportunities for leveraging benefits from existing corporate strengths, including through infrastructure, management capability, or business networks. Several examples can be found: mining companies associated with environmental and local community projects; insurance companies with crime prevention and health and safety initiatives; financial groups with support for disadvantaged sectors of society; IT companies with cause related marketing; shipping industry with trade related issues awareness.

As businesses get more strategic in their effort, they will focus more on where their returns are likely to come from. The community involvement may have long term returns such as developing skills in and maintaining strong communities from which future employees and customers of the business will come. In the process, businesses can seed development in the community through their involvement which progressively provides development, freeing up the business to develop new initiatives.

At the same time, businesses can support community projects in completely different areas. Examples are the Tattersall Foundation in Australia, which is a gaming and lottery business. Out of its profits, it is a major supporter of charities and philanthropic activity. Similarly, the Nippon Foundation derives its income from motorboat racing in Japan but shares a proportion of it with the global community through a wide variety of community development programs at all levels that include individual scholarships for studying to intergovernmental work.

The support that mining companies provide local communities is particularly interesting to study. Mining is known to be a severely damaging industry to the environment and the local communities. Mining companies are also the biggest givers to and investors in the local communities. This is seen as a strategic move to assuage the harm and buy goodwill from the locals for the business to retain its "social licence to operate".

While this can be the perspective from the business, the picture can only be complete when the expectations of the community also align with this view. Communities do expect a commercial entity to contribute financially as well as through its expertise but more importantly, they expect the involvement to be long term, make the difference that the business states it sets out to do, and be honest and transparent in its activities and intentions.

The key message that emerges from these initiatives is that regardless of extent or stated purpose of working to shared common values of society, engagement in CSR is essentially an exercise in developing competitive advantage. The shape of the initiative is driven by organisational values, relationship with stakeholders, the ideologies of senior management who shape policy and the power enjoyed by shareholders.

The benefits of community involvement are a direct result of a business investing its resources to enhance its reputation and image in the eyes of both the internal and external stakeholders. That is not to say that a business must not pursue profits. For its sustainability, its stakeholders will expect it to do that *a priori* but will also want it to be cognizant of the social values of the community within which it operates. CSR practices are the bridge that connects profitability and commercial success with the values of the community.

From the time of Friedman's position about the role of business in 1970, there has been a major shift in the way business is expected to work, not only by the wider stakeholders but even by its own shareholders, driven mainly by real experience of events that required lessons to be learnt. Businesses have long defined themselves as distinct bodies of society, with clear corporate goals. They have their own mission statements, objectives, structures and management philosophies. While keeping all these, they have had to mature into less self-focused ways of working and include the expectations of the external communities in which they work in their principles. The banking scandals of the last few years (Channel 4 2015) have made governments and the community at large more aware of the operations and misconduct that can happen in this sector of society which is entrusted with the care of its monetary wealth. As the global economic function has slowed down, shareholders have been questioning of the salaries paid to senior bank officials, as the ABC (2016) reports about the Commonwealth Bank of Australia. Banks are expected to be an integral part of the community working on the basis of keeping its confidence in their commitment to providing a competitive and sustainable service to their corporate and individual customers.

7 CSR's Role in the Global Market

Before examining CSR's role in the market, it is worth reflecting on how markets are traditionally controlled.

The basic method of controlling a market is through permits, allocations, taxes on goods/services sold and purchased, or a complete prohibition on some trades that may be seen as contrary to desired social values of that society (guns in some countries, licences to operate businesses, drugs of certain types, pharmaceuticals that require a prescription, and human trade are examples). This is prescriptive market control. Businesses operate within certain socio-legal parameters that protect the wider interests of the people, including, for example, specifically protecting union activity and having regulatory control over safety aspects of operations. In controlled market economies, which are society oriented, such traits are commonly evidenced and businesses tend to be aligned with stakeholder interests.

In liberal market economies, businesses tend to be shareholder oriented and take the profit-making approach that Friedman sponsored.

Regardless of the type of control exercised on the market, there is accepted to exist a rule of law under a functioning state that enshrines public governance and allows markets a certain operational freedom for the conduct of commerce while maintaining institutional accountability.

This perspective implies the existence of a regulatory regime that is enforced through suitable governance structures. These governance structures may include the enforceable control mechanisms, such as those mentioned above, through regulation, or policy statements that guide social behaviour.

Not all rules or policies need to come from government. Industry or societal groups can establish rules that define their operational behaviour. Examples of this can be supply chain enablers (transport and logistics groups) that can define their behaviour with their contracted partners and the wider community. These rules may be made legally binding through contracts or are simply expectations of performance norms. In this respect, they become self-regulating or jointly regulating.

In a wider understanding of the term, regulation can therefore be considered to include any method used to achieve a certain outcome, whether that is behavioural or monitoring of conduct or enforcement.

The working of regulation (and regulators) must also be considered in the current environment of privatisation, deregulation and delegation of powers (for example in shipping, to classification societies by flag state control). It is seen that even more than governments, non-state actors can become increasingly influential in defining corporate or individual behaviour. This is the space in which CSR can be seen to operate through its self-regulating or private governance modalities.

As reported by Froholdt (2016), CSR can take various forms in different contexts. Its function changes in different parts of the world and can include taking a role in poverty alleviation, spreading literacy, addressing human rights abuses, providing clean drinking water and light, addressing effects of climate change, etc. Large corporations are particularly expected to play a major role in this regard and Froholdt offers the example of India where a CSR tax is paid by corporations with a certain threshold revenue. Not without justification, multinational corporations (MNCs) are seen with some suspicion as shareholder-interest driven, avoiding tax, taking wealth out of the country, adding to corruption by influencing government decisions and destroying local competition. At the same time, the same businesses are seen to be developing jobs and introducing new technologies.

Against the backdrop of such diverse views of large business, national market governance measures have widely accommodated CSR into public policy. This is seen in statements and policy promulgated by

The UN:

> As companies, markets, and economies become more global and interdependent, businesses and investors are becoming increasingly aware of the overlap between public and private interests. They realize that their ability to prosper and grow depends on the existence of a prosperous and sustainable society. Conversely, they see that social and income inequality, as well as environmental damage, are already having negative material impacts on supply chains, capital flows, and employee productivity. (Global Compact International Year Book 2015).

The EU:

> … the new Post 2015 Framework, and the Sustainable Development Goals, will be more ambitious, far-reaching and universal. We want to see a new set of [Strategic Development Goals] SDGs that are underpinned by human rights and designed to end poverty, transform lives, and protect the planet. (EU 2015a)

The International Labour Organisation (ILO 2016):

> Corporate Social Responsibility (CSR) is a way in which enterprises give consideration to the impact of their operations on society and affirm their principles and values both in their own internal methods and processes and in their interaction with other actors. CSR is a voluntary, enterprise-driven initiative and refers to activities that are considered to exceed compliance with the law.

This quote is from the ILO's work on CSR and captured in the Tripartite Declaration of Principles concerning Multinational Enterprises and Social Policy (MNE Declaration), agreed by governments, employers' and workers' organisations. The document is from 2006 and is being overtaken by later initiatives by other supranational bodies.

The EU, in its CSR Strategy, discusses CSR as "… a multi-dimensional issue relevant to a variety of European policies including: enterprise and industrial policy; social affairs and employment; corporate governance and company law; environment; consumer affairs; trade; development; external relations; human rights; justice and home affairs; research; and education and training" (EU 2015b).

The primary issue that emerges from this overview is that attempts are being made to globalise CSR in a world which is not uniformly governed both in terms of economic development and in terms of the philosophy of governance. Different countries have different histories, cultures and ideologies. Taking a western developed-economy market-based approach may not be suitable in all contexts. This is reflected by Froholdt (2016). The obvious reality is that never in mankind's history have national characteristics disappeared in the face of an external, even globalising, influence. Taking the globalised CSR approach at the supra-governmental level is likely to have a similar response, with national businesses incorporating it into their distinctive nature of operations. The approach of governments is also likely to be similar.

Further, during a time of financial downturn when every national government in the world is seeing increasing demands on its budgets from social needs (infrastructure, services and security), CSR can provide a welcome alternative source of funds from the private sector which can be channelled into some sectors of society as well as corporate governance. At the same time, some practices that were not wholesome but were accepted by multinational companies (such as child labour, lack of environmental control on production, lack of employee benefits and/or terms of their employment, conditions of work, etc.) (Global Issues 2006) have become difficult to ignore at home and are driving awareness and change in those host countries. However, cultural and institutional changes in work practices are likely to take a long time to permeate through layers of distant societies and their hierarchies of control. At the same time, it must be acknowledged that CSR does provide an inclusive and ethical perspective on business operations in society through its administrative, legal, social and public policy aspects. Its key output currently remains in the management of business externalities as they blend with these aspects.

Responding to the growth of CSR internationally, the International Organisation for Standardisation (ISO) in 2010 developed IS0 26000, which includes as its "seven pillars" the main themes of CSR:

- Organizational governance
- Community involvement and development
- Human rights
- Labour practices
- The environment
- Fair operating practices
- Consumer issues

The reservations with the applicability of a common standard to all businesses in all countries, whether private of state owned, have been touched upon in the discussion above. The concept of CSR matures with the continuing implementation, study and reporting that it has attracted over the last few decades, just as Total Quality Management (TQM) and Quality Assurance (QA) and ISO 9000 did earlier.

8 CSR in the Maritime Industry

Like any other sector of the economy, the maritime industry has gradually taken up CSR, sometimes under persuasion from shippers or other stakeholders or in pursuit of a sustainable and differentiating strategy in a competitive market. Shipping companies traditionally compete on the basis of price and service characteristics. CSR provides a new factor that can be connected to various aspects of its functions and used to stand out from the competition.

Intense competition in shipping has led to the cyclic nature of the industry, with mergers and acquisitions, outsourcing and cost-cutting becoming an accepted way of how it operates. Driving costs down to kill off competition has been a long established way of doing business, followed by short periods of good profits before more competition enters the market. Profits from customers and cost cutting have remained the main focus of the shipping business. At the same time, for those customers who value only price of service, CSR may have little value or attraction in making a decision to use a particular shipping service.

CSR has put a new stakeholder oriented approach in place to develop customer allegiance and support that goes beyond only making profit. In an industry that has traditionally cut cost through reducing crews and related expenditure, employee welfare and the other elements identified as the "seven pillars" in CSR have become part of the context.

While a majority of shipping companies remained focused on providing a cheap mode of transport at the least possible cost, the better operators have differentiated themselves by taking on added responsibilities such as for being environmentally and socially responsible. That it remains a strategic marketing tool is illustrated by the examples of leading shipping lines professing a public commitment to CSR but sometimes operating with purely commercial outcomes in mind. Shipping companies that are competing purely on the basis of price in the market and minimising cost of operations are unlikely to have the incentive to engage in CSR. However, those companies that participate in the market on the basis of differentiating their services from the competitors (e.g., Exxon Mobil) and have a larger cost absorptive capacity are likely to engage in initiatives like CSR which will be valued by their stakeholders and the wider community.

The amount of resources and level of complexity in developing new activity is often determined by similarity to earlier activities and is supported by the existing knowledge, available assets and capabilities of the business. Within the parameters of CSR, the main focus in shipping has remained on the environment. This is driven to a great extent by the cost of environmental accidents and the negative publicity that they generate for the business. In addition to the well-known large oil pollution incidents, there are several small instances that do not make it to the popular media but result in large fines for the shipping companies.

The focus on the environment has expanded to include ship scrapping. Ships can have large amounts of toxic material on them, both as part of their structure as well as that accumulated over time through their operations. The Basel Convention of the UN restricts trade in toxic materials. These are hazardous to the labour used to dismantle the ships as well as the environment where the work is done. Non-governmental organisations, like Greenpeace and Basel Action Network (BAN), have been instrumental in bringing this to public attention. The response has been both regulatory (the Hong Kong Convention of the IMO) and voluntary with shipping companies declaring that they will only scrap their ships responsibly. Very often, national navies elect to sink their ships at sea, ostensibly to convert them to diving sites or to artificial reefs when in fact these ships may contain quite toxic materials. Similarly, a large number of oil rigs are now approaching the end of their operating lives but are prevented from being scrapped because of their toxic contents and high costs associated with scrapping (IHS Fairplay 2016).

The other side of the operational maritime industry is ports, which are the confluence of the land and water side operations. All the modes of land and sea transport can come together in one place at a port, with intense and large scale operations often being carried out in one place. Ports also have a strong focus on the environment but they are also usually located close to population centres. Their functions can not only interfere with the lives of the surrounding community but can also have an impact on their health and amenity through traffic, noise, dust, odour and light emissions. Most ports are today controlled by their regulatory operating licence conditions. Operating close to the community, ports, like trucking, bus and rail companies, also have a "social licence" which is support or permission given to them by the local community to operate in it. The understanding is that both sides benefit from the operations. If one side causes harm to the other, this support may be withdrawn and the port can come against several types of restrictions imposed on it, as in the case of Esperance port in Western Australia (The Stringer 2016).

The cost of sustaining a CSR program can be proportionately higher on small businesses when compared to large ones. This is because large businesses have larger budgets and revenues. Small businesses can often be working to very tight margins and may need to maintain a CSR program as a contractual condition of a bigger company with whom they may be trading. In both shipping and ports, CSR is seen as alternative advertising and is driven largely by shippers and other participants in the industry. The financial support to the initiative is often found in tax rebates which are available to businesses for engaging in socially beneficial initiatives.

Perhaps the largest role in being socially responsible by any business is to pay taxes that will contribute to the wider community budget that is available to the government. On this, shipping has a long established expertise and history in tax avoidance through an international network of corporate and ship registration and company structures. Even the best known shipping companies may spend large amounts of money to obtain the services of the best tax lawyers and accountants and pay little tax while they espouse the cause of community wellbeing. Many shipping companies may well have a number of charitable foundations and activities that they support in the community. These ship owners may be seen as economic conservatives who oppose tax and government interference in their business but will go to great lengths to support specific causes locally and internationally.

9 Summarising

The concept of CSR has existed for a long time, taking shape over the centuries to its current form. Even so, it is not clearly defined in itself—its outcomes are expressed, as shown by the quotes from supranational bodies, provided in this chapter. Large sections of literature on CSR tend to focus on the ethical and social aspects of CSR. These tend to concern themselves with businesses sharing benefits with society. Commercial purists resist this approach and seek to keep business unburdened of a responsibility for which it may have no capability. Progressives take the view that businesses can integrate better with society if they go beyond profit seeking and engage at multiple levels with society.

This chapter also reflects on the fact that not all societies in the world have the same histories, values and traditions. What may be considered suitable in one part of the world may not be effective in another. CSR can take different shapes in different countries. A forced globalised view of this concept may not be accepted everywhere.

From a business perspective, CSR must be considered to be an investment of time and resources which must provide tangible benefits. This approach is being increasingly adopted as "strategic CSR". Businesses engage in it not for purely altruistic reasons but because they see benefits for themselves. The maritime industry can be seen to adopt this approach in its acceptance of, and engagement in, CSR.

References

ABC News. (2016). *Commonwealth Bank of Australia Remuneration Report*. http://www.abc.net.au/news/2016-11-10/cba-remuneration-report-voted-down/8012454. Accessed 10 Nov 2016.

ABC News - Greek Shipping Companies Fined $1.5 Million. http://abcnews.go.com/US/wireStory/greek-shipping-companies-fined-15m-pollution-cover-42974349. Accessed 23 Oct 2016.

Alperson, M. (1998). *Building the corporate community economic development team* (p. 57). The Conference Board, Inc., July 7, 1998.

Aurobindo, S. (1928, reprinted 1997). *Essays on the Gita* (p. 607). Pondicherry: Sri Aurobindo Ashram Publication Department.

Basel Action Network (BAN). http://www.ban.org/green-ship-recycling/. Accessed 28 Nov 2016.

Business in the Community (BITC). http://www.bitc.org.uk/.

Carroll, A. (1998). The four faces of corporate citizenship. *Business and Society Review*, September, 1–7.

Chakraborty, S. (1999). *Wisdom leadership: Dialogues and reflections*. New Delhi: Wheeler Publishing.

Channel 4. (2015). *Five other banking scandals since 2008*. https://www.channel4.com/news/five-other-banking-scandals-since-2008. Accessed 10 Nov 2016.

Chatterjee, S. (2009). Managerial ethos of the Indian tradition: Relevance of a wisdom model. *Journal of Indian Business Research, 1*(2/3), 136–162.

Davis, A., Guenther, D., Krull, L., & Williams, B. (2016). Do socially responsible firms pay more taxes? *The Accounting Review, 91*(1), 47–68.

EU. (2015a). *From MDGs to SDGs: An unprecedented year for international development*. Neven Mimica, EU Development Commissioner. https://ec.europa.eu/commission/2014-2019/mimica/blog/mdgs-sdgs-unprecedented-year-international-development_en. Accessed 17 Nov 2016.

EU. (2015b). *Policy coherence for development 2015 EU report*. http://ec.europa.eu/europeaid/sites/devco/files/policy-coherence-for-development-2015-eu-report_en.pdf. Accessed 18 Nov 2016.

Exxon Mobil. http://corporate.exxonmobil.com/en/company/multimedia/energy-lives-here. Accessed 29 Nov 2016.

Forbes. (2013). *The origin of 'the World's Dumbest Idea': Milton Friedman*. http://www.forbes.com/sites/stevedenning/2013/06/26/the-origin-of-the-worlds-dumbest-idea-milton-friedman/#35d3609f214c. Accessed 24 Oct 2016.

Friedman, M. (1970). *The social responsibility of business is to increase profits*. The New York Times Magazine, 13 September 1970.

Froholdt, L. (2016). *Maritime governance and corporate social responsibility: A context for a responsible maritime industry*. World Maritime University, Malmo. Unpublished.

Global Compact International Year Book. (2015). https://globalgoals-yearbook.org/editions/#toggle-id-3. Accessed on 22 Nov 2016

Global Issues. (2006). *Corporations and worker's rights*. http://www.globalissues.org/article/57/corporations-and-workers-rights. Accessed 28 Nov 2016.

Global Reporting Initiative. https://www.globalreporting.org/standards/gri-standards-download-center/. Accessed 16 Nov 2016.

Grewal, D., & Darlow, N. J. (2007). The business paradigm for corporate social reporting in the context of Australian seaports. *Maritime Economics & Logistics, 9*, 172–192.

http://www.forbes.com/sites/stevedenning/2016/04/03/the-economist-defends-the-worlds-dumbest-idea/#5a3806b570bb. Accessed 24 Oct 2016.

IHS Fairplay. (2016). http://fairplay.ihs.com/commerce/article/4265261/cold-stacking-a-better-option-than-scrapping-jack-up-rig-owners-told. Accessed 28 Nov 2016.

ILO. (2016). *InFocus Initiative on Corporate Social Responsibility (CSR), Governing Body, 295th Session, Geneva, 2006*. http://libguides.ilo.org/corporate-social-responsibility-en. Accessed 18 Nov 2016.

Krishnan, V. (2003). Modernisation without demolishing cultural roots: The role of transformational leadership. In J. Gifford & G. Zezulka-Mailoux (Eds.), *Culture and the state, Volume IV (alternative interventions)* (pp. 164–173). Edmonton: University of Alberta.

Machiavelli, N. (1513). *The Prince*. Translated by Daniel Tanno, Bantam Classics 2003.

Maritime Executive – Maersk Shipbreaking Practices. http://www.maritime-executive.com/article/maersk-pushes-back-on-shipbreaking-practices. Accessed 23 Oct 2016.

Pfeffer, J. (1998). *The human equation: Building profits by putting people first*. Boston: Harvard Business School Press.

Plato Plotinus (c. 380 BC) The Republic. http://www.idph.net/conteudos/ebooks/republic.pdf. Accessed 24 Oct 2016.

Porter, M., & Kramer, M. (2006). Strategy and society: The link between competitive advantage and corporate social responsibility. *Harvard Business Review*, December, 78–93.

The Economist. (2008a). *Just good business*. http://www.economist.com/node/10491077. Accessed 23 Oct 2016.

The Economist. (2008b). *Global business barometer*. http://www.economist.com/media/pdf/20080116CSRResults.pdf. Accessed 23 Oct 2016.

The Economist. (2016). http://www.economist.com/news/business-and-finance/21684770-social-saints-fiscal-fiends-opinions-vary-whether-firms-can-be-socially-responsible. Accessed 23 Oct 2016.

The Stringer. (2016). http://thestringer.com.au/esperance-wa-sacrifice-zone-for-the-profits-of-the-uranium-industry-10583#.WDyKzfkwiUk. Accessed 28 Nov 2016.

UNRISD. (2002). *Corporate social and environmental responsibility: Selected sources of information*. http://www.unrisd.org/80256B3C005BCCF9%2F(httpAuxPages)%2F44B23434F64FF980C1256CE600599CDD%2F$file%2Falvangls.pdf. Accessed 7 Nov 2016.

Governance of Maritime Activities: Legal, Policy and Institutional Aspects

Yoshinobu Takei

1 Introduction

The concept "governance" has increasingly been invoked in the context of maritime activities. The term "maritime" is sometimes used in relation to particular activities, such as "navigation, shipping or commerce" (Juda 2007, pp. 270–271) or focusing "on issues such as ports and harbours, shipping, transportation and other sectorally oriented activities, including naval interests" (Haward and Vince 2008, p. 72). In fact, when commentators consider the concept "maritime governance", they often pay considerable attention to shipping (Roe 2013; Mukherjee and Brownrigg 2013, pp. 173–197). However, the term "maritime" could also be used in an integrated and holistic manner.[1] Used in this way, the concept "maritime governance" is not limited to the governance of shipping-related activities.

While no agreed definition of the concept "maritime governance" exists (Rothwell and VanderZwaag 2006),[2] the pillars of maritime governance include,

The views expressed in this chapter are those of the author and do not necessarily reflect those of the United Nations.

[1]For example, the Integrated Maritime Policy of the European Union refers to a vision "for an integrated maritime policy that covers all aspects of our relationship with the oceans and seas" (European Commission (2007) Communication from the Commission to the European Parliament, the Council, the European Economic and Social Committee and the Committee of the Regions, An Integrated Maritime Policy for the European Union, COM(2007) 575 final, p. 4).

[2]The concept "governance" is used by commentators in different ways. Rhodes (1996, p. 653) suggests that there are at least six different ways in which governance can be used. The concept "good governance", which is increasingly used in discussion on "governance", includes the rule of law, public participation, transparency, accountability, control of corruption and government

Y. Takei (✉)
Division for Ocean Affairs and the Law of the Sea, Office of Legal Affairs, United Nations, New York, NY, USA
e-mail: takei@un.org

L. L. Froholdt (ed.), *Corporate Social Responsibility in the Maritime Industry*, WMU Studies in Maritime Affairs 5, https://doi.org/10.1007/978-3-319-69143-5_4

inter alia, legal and institutional aspects (Juda 1996, p. 2; Treves 2010, pp. 7–8; de Souza Patu 2011, p. 31; Rothwell and Stephens 2010, p. 462; de Marffy 2004, pp. 162–163). Principles and approaches often advocated in governance discussions in the maritime/ocean context include: the precautionary approach, ecosystem-based management, integrated management, transparency, science-based decision-making, accountability, compliance, enforcement and sanctions (de Souza Patu 2011, p. 36; Freestone 2008, p. 391; Haward and Vince 2008, pp. 18–25; Oude Elferink 2012; Rothwell and Stephens 2010, pp. 462–470; Tanaka 2008).

The concept "maritime governance" is linked to the other central theme of this book, namely, "corporate social responsibility" (CSR), despite different focuses in these concepts (i.e., interactions by a broader set of stakeholders in governance discussions, notably States and intergovernmental organizations, *versus* corporate/industry in CSR discussions). Although there is no universally-agreed definition of CSR,[3] for example, Coady et al. (2013) conclude that "[v]oluntary CSR collaborations and initiatives are helping to facilitate the implementation of international shipping regulations and drive beyond-compliance improvements in sustainability performance—fundamentally, reinforcing, supplementing and filling gaps in the international regulatory regime. The relevance of CSR to the international legal framework for the oceans has also been pointed out by legal scholars (Bonfanti and Romanin Jacur 2014).

This chapter considers legal, institutional and policy aspects concerning maritime activities. Following the Introduction, the chapter considers the legal and institutional framework established by the United Nations Convention on the Law of the Sea (UNCLOS).[4] Then, it discusses the activities of the United Nations relating to maritime activities, in particular the work of the General Assembly, which is at the centre of policy-making relating to any activities in the oceans and seas, and the outcome of summits and conferences on sustainable development. This is followed by the discussion of other legal instruments and institutions related to the governance of maritime activities, as well as cooperation and coordination between relevant institutions. The chapter concludes with brief concluding remarks.

---

effectiveness (Brown Weiss and Sornarajah 2009). See also International Law Association (2002). Resolution 3/2002, New Delhi Declaration of Principles of International Law Relating to Sustainable Development of 6 April 2002, available at http://www.ila-hq.org/en/committees/index.cfm/cid/25 and Kaufmann et al. (1999).

[3]On the concept of CSR, see chapter "The Perception of Corporate Social Responsibility in the Maritime Industry" of this book.

[4]United Nations Treaty Series (UNTS), vol. 1833, No. 31363.

2 The International Legal Framework Under the United Nations Convention on the Law of the Sea (UNCLOS)

This section discusses the legal framework established under UNCLOS, by first looking at the provisions of UNCLOS, as well as institutions established by UNCLOS, and then considering its Implementing Agreements. The section also examines the provisions relating to rules of reference under UNCLOS and their implications for the legal regime for maritime activities.

2.1 UNCLOS

UNCLOS sets out the legal framework within which all activities in the oceans and seas must be carried out.[5] Often considered a "Constitution for the Oceans",[6] UNCLOS was adopted in 1982 as a result of the extensive negotiations during the Third United Nations Conference on the Law of the Sea, held from 1973 to 1982,[7] as well as discussions during the preceding meetings under the United Nations, such as the Committee on the Peaceful Uses of the Sea-Bed and the Ocean Floor beyond the Limits of National Jurisdiction.[8] These developments, indeed, were preceded by codification efforts throughout the twentieth century, notably under the League of Nations as well as the First and Second United Nations Conferences on the Law of the Sea in 1958 and 1960, respectively, based on the work of the United Nations International Law Commission.

UNCLOS serves numerous important functions in the governance of maritime activities. Among such functions, it sets out delineation of various maritime zones and rights and obligations of States therein.

In terms of maritime zones, UNCLOS determines the breadth of the existing maritime zones (e.g., the territorial sea, contiguous zone and continental shelf), while it establishes the concept of several new maritime zones (e.g., archipelagic waters, exclusive economic zone (EEZ) and the "Area").[9] It ended decades-long conflicts regarding the breadth of the territorial sea by fixing the outer limit of the territorial sea at 12 nautical miles from the baselines.[10] Beyond the territorial sea, it newly

[5]UN Doc. A/RES/71/257, preamble.

[6]"A Constitution for the Oceans", Remarks by Tommy T.B. Koh, of Singapore, President of the Third United Nations Conference on the Law of the Sea, available at: http://www.un.org/depts/los/convention_agreements/texts/koh_english.pdf.

[7]See Final Act of the Third United Nations Conference on the Law of the Sea, available at: http://www.un.org/depts/los/convention_agreements/texts/final_act_eng.pdf.

[8]See http://www.un.org/depts/los/convention_agreements/convention_historical_perspective.htm.

[9]Under UNCLOS, the "Area" means the seabed and ocean floor and subsoil thereof, beyond the limits of national jurisdiction. UNLOS, article 1(1)(1).

[10]Ibid., article 3.

introduced the concept of EEZ, up to 200 nautical miles from the baselines.[11] For the continental shelf, where coastal States have sovereign rights and jurisdiction for certain purposes,[12] UNCLOS provides its new definition and stipulates complex criteria for the delineation of the outer limit of the continental shelf beyond 200 nautical miles.[13] In addition, while the regime of the high seas applies to all parts of the sea beyond the EEZ,[14] UNCLOS established the Area and its resources as the Common Heritage of Mankind.[15]

Provisions of UNCLOS explicitly concern a number of maritime activities, including: navigation, overflight, laying of submarine cables and pipelines, fishing, exploitation of non-living resources, the establishment of artificial islands, installations and other structures, generation of renewable energy, hydrographic surveys, marine scientific research and transfer of marine technology. These provisions define rights and obligations of States with regard to particular activities in specific maritime zones. For example, UNCLOS provides for navigational rights of all States in different zones. In internal waters, foreign ships do not have navigational rights, except for force majeure and distress.[16] In archipelagic waters, foreign ships enjoy the right of archipelagic sea lanes passage.[17] In the territorial sea, foreign ships enjoy the right of innocent passage.[18] In straits used for international navigation, States have the right of transit passage.[19] In the EEZ and the high seas, all States enjoy the freedom of navigation.[20] On the high seas, ships are subject to the exclusive jurisdiction of their flag States, unless otherwise expressly provided,[21] while coastal States also have extensive jurisdiction over ships in areas under their national jurisdiction.

UNCLOS also has detailed provisions concerning the protection and preservation of the marine environment, including in particular in Part XII, which is dedicated to this issue. In Part XII, UNCLOS provides for general obligations concerning the protection and preservation of the marine environment,[22] as well as detailed provisions for each of the six sources of marine pollution (i.e., land-based pollution,

---

[11] Ibid., article 57.

[12] Ibid., article 77.

[13] Ibid., article 76.

[14] Ibid., article 86.

[15] Ibid., article 136. For the purposes of Part XI of UNCLOS, "resources" means all solid, liquid or gaseous mineral resources *in situ* in the Area at or beneath the seabed, including polymetallic nodules. Ibid., article 133(a).

[16] See ibid., article 8.

[17] Ibid., article 53.

[18] Ibid., articles 17–21.

[19] Ibid., articles 37–42.

[20] Ibid., articles 58 and 87.

[21] Ibid., article 92.

[22] For example, ibid., articles 192–193.

vessel-source pollution, pollution by dumping, pollution from seabed activities, pollution from activities in the Area, and pollution from or through the atmosphere).[23] The rights and obligations of States relating to navigation described above need to be considered in the light of such provisions. For example, while ships enjoy freedom of navigation in the EEZ, navigation of ships therein is subject to the rules and regulations concerning the prevention, reduction and control of marine pollution from ships in the EEZ.[24]

Another important feature of UNCLOS is its comprehensive system of dispute settlement. In addition to the duty to settle disputes peacefully, UNCLOS provides for several means of dispute settlement, including: negotiations, conciliation, arbitration and judicial means.[25] Of particular note here are the provisions on compulsory dispute settlement entailing binding decisions, with limitations under article 297, as well as optional exceptions under article 298, for specific categories of disputes. For disputes which allow unilateral recourse to compulsory dispute settlement provisions entailing binding decisions, four types of means of dispute settlement entailing binding decisions exist: arbitration under Annex VII of UNCLOS, special arbitration under Annex VIII, the International Tribunal for the Law of the Sea (ITLOS) and the International Court of Justice (ICJ), with Annex VII arbitration in place as the default mechanism for a number of disputes unless otherwise agreed.[26] There are preconditions for resorting to these procedures (e.g. exchange of views under article 283) and circumstances which may preclude the use of these procedures (e.g. articles 281 and 282).

2.2 *Institutions Established Under UNCLOS*

UNCLOS has established three bodies, namely, the International Seabed Authority (ISA), ITLOS and the Commission on the Limits of the Continental Shelf (CLCS). The ISA is the organization through which States Parties to the Convention shall organize and control activities in the Area, particularly with a view to administering the resources of the Area.[27] The ISA has been developing the Mining Code, including regulations concerning prospecting and exploration of three types of mineral resources and recommendations for the guidance of contractors.[28] It has

---

[23]Ibid., Sections 5–6 of Part XII.

[24]Ibid., articles 211(5)–(6) and 220(3)–(8).

[25]Ibid., Sections 1–2 of Part XV.

[26]Ibid., article 287.

[27]Ibid., article 153(1) provides: Activities in the Area shall be organized, carried out and controlled by the Authority on behalf of mankind as a whole in accordance with this article as well as other relevant provisions of this Part and the relevant Annexes, and the rules, regulations and procedures of the Authority.

[28]ISA, "The Mining Code", available at: https://www.isa.org.jm/mining-code. Currently, a regulatory framework for mineral resource exploitation is being considered at the ISA.

also adopted the Environmental Management Plan for the Clarion-Clipperton Zone.[29] In accordance with UNCLOS and the Mining Code, 15-year contracts for exploration for polymetallic nodules, polymetallic sulphides and cobalt-rich ferromanganese crusts have been entered into with 26 contractors.[30]

ITLOS is a judicial body established by UNCLOS to adjudicate disputes arising out of the interpretation and application of the Convention, having jurisdiction over all disputes and all applications submitted to it in accordance with UNCLOS and over all matters specifically provided for in any other agreement which confers jurisdiction on it.[31] It not only has jurisdiction for cases where both parties to the dispute give consent to its jurisdiction but also exercises jurisdiction with regard to prompt release cases and requests for provisional measures as a default mechanism, unless parties otherwise agree.[32]

Established in accordance with article 76 and Annex II of UNCLOS, CLCS is a body composed of 21 members who are experts in the field of geology, geophysics or hydrography, serving in their personal capacities.[33] The CLCS plays two roles: make recommendations for the delineation of the outer limit of the continental shelf beyond 200 nautical miles from the baselines in accordance with article 76 and advise coastal States in making submissions of information in respect of the continental shelf beyond 200 nautical miles from the baselines.[34] So far, 77 submissions (exclusive of revised submissions) have been received by the CLCS. To date, it has adopted 29 recommendations.[35]

In addition, in accordance with article 319(2)(e) of UNCLOS, the Secretary-General of the United Nations has convened the meeting of States parties to UNCLOS since its entry into force.[36] The meeting of States parties annually considers, inter alia, administrative and budgetary issues whereas there have been discussions on whether the meeting of States parties can discuss substantive matters.[37]

---

[29]ISA, "Environmental management plan for the Clarion-Clipperton Zone", available at: https://www.isa.org.jm/environmental-management-plan-clarion-clipperton-zone.

[30]ISA, "Overview", available at: https://www.isa.org.jm/deep-seabed-minerals-contractors/overview.

[31]ITLOS was established under Annex VI of UNCLOS.

[32]Ibid., articles 290 and 292.

[33]Ibid., Annex II, article 2(1).

[34]Ibid., Annex II, article 3(1).

[35]See CLCS website, available at: http://www.un.org/depts/los/clcs_new/commission_submissions.htm.

[36]See http://www.un.org/depts/los/meeting_states_parties/meeting_states_parties.htm.

[37]See, e.g., Report of the twenty-fifth Meeting of States Parties, New York, 8-12 June 2015, SPLOS/287, available at: http://www.un.org/ga/search/view_doc.asp?symbol=SPLOS/287, para. 81: "Divergent views were expressed concerning the mandate of the Meeting of States Parties to discuss matters of a substantive nature relating to the implementation of the Convention. Some delegations indicated that the Meeting had the mandate to consider all issues pertaining to the application and implementation of the Convention. Other delegations were of the view that the

The institutions established under UNCLOS are not the only bodies where the implementation of UNCLOS and other legal and policy issues relating to oceans and seas have been considered. Indeed, a number of processes have been established in this regard (see below) and their works are inter-related to those of institutions under UNCLOS.

2.3 *Implementing Agreements*

UNCLOS has been supplemented by two Implementing Agreements: the Agreement relating to the implementation of Part XI of the United Nations Convention on the Law of the Sea of 10 December 1982 (the "Part XI Agreement" or the "1994 Implementing Agreement")[38]; and the Agreement for the Implementation of the Provisions of the United Nations Convention on the Law of the Sea of 10 December 1982 relating to the Conservation and Management of Straddling Fish Stocks and Highly Migratory Fish Stocks (the "United Nations Fish Stocks Agreement").[39]

Provisions of Part XI of UNCLOS relating to deep seabed mining, which significantly reflected the move towards the establishment of a New International Economic Order, did not gain wide support by many industrialized countries—indeed, many of them did not become parties to UNCLOS in the 1980s. Without the participation of these countries, implementation of UNCLOS, including institutions established by it, was deemed to undergo considerable difficulties. Under the initiative of the Secretary-General of the United Nations, States held consultations to address this problem. These consultations resulted in the adoption of the 1994 Implementing Agreement.[40] According to article 2 of the 1994 Implementing Agreement, which deals with the relationship between the Agreement and Part XI of UNCLOS, the two instruments shall be interpreted and applied together as a single instrument. In the event of an inconsistency between the Agreement and Part XI, however, the provisions of the Agreement shall prevail. After the adoption of the 1994 Agreement, States were only able to become party to both UNCLOS and the 1994 Agreement.[41] Therefore, the 1994 Implementing Agreement in effect amended

---

Meeting should limit itself to the consideration of financial and administrative matters relating to the bodies established by the Convention, namely, [ITLOS, ISA and CLCS], as prescribed under the Convention. In that connection, some delegations emphasized that the Meeting should not be regarded as a forum for discussion and resolution of bilateral disputes concerning the application and interpretation of the Convention." Some parties have also expressed similar views at the twenty-sixth Meeting of States parties in 2016. Report of the twenty-sixth Meeting of States Parties, 20–24 June 2016, SPLOS/303, available at: http://www.un.org/ga/search/view_doc.asp?symbol=SPLOS/303, para. 92.

[38]UNTS, vol. 1836, No. 31364.

[39]Ibid., vol. 2167, No. 37924.

[40]See http://www.un.org/depts/los/convention_agreements/convention_overview_part_xi.htm.

[41]Part XI Agreement, article 4.

the relevant provisions of UNCLOS. The Agreement provisionally entered into force in 1994 and definitively in 1996.[42] The Agreement deals with issues that prevented industrialized States from becoming parties, such as costs to States parties, institutional arrangements, decision-making mechanisms for the ISA, the Review Conference, transfer of technology, production policy and economic assistance.

The 1995 United Nations Fish Stocks Agreement, the other Implementing Agreement, was negotiated and adopted in a different context. The problem of managing fish stocks bordering the outer limit of the 200-mile EEZ was already known at the Third United Nations Conference on the Law of the Sea, but attempts to extend coastal State jurisdiction over these stocks were not accepted at that time. Instead, UNCLOS has general provisions for these stocks in the part dealing with the EEZ (Part V)[43] and provisions concerning conservation and management of marine living resources in the high seas (Part VII).[44] In response to the call by the United Nations Conference on Environment and Development in 1992, the General Assembly requested convening the United Nations Conference on Straddling Fish Stocks and Highly Migratory Fish Stocks, which was held from 1993 to 1995.[45] The Conference adopted the United Nations Fish Stocks Agreement in 1995. The Agreement entered into force in 2001.

The Agreement provides for the international legal regime for the conservation and sustainable use of these fish stocks, incorporating modern approaches to fisheries management, such as the precautionary approach, and ecosystem considerations into fisheries management.[46] It assigns an important role to regional fisheries management organizations (RFMOs) and arrangements,[47] sets out compatibility requirements between measures for areas under national jurisdiction and those for the high seas,[48] provides for detailed provisions on flag State responsibilities and implementation, including boarding and inspection,[49] provides for the requirements of developing States,[50] and contains provisions concerning dispute settlement, including both compulsory dispute settlement applying the relevant UNCLOS provisions mutatis mutandis, and mechanisms for the settlement of disputes of a technical nature.[51]

---

[42]For the status of treaties deposited with the Secretary-General of the United Nations, see the website of the Treaty Section of the Office of Legal Affairs, at https://treaties.un.org/Pages/ParticipationStatus.aspx?clang=_en.

[43]UNCLOS, articles 63(2) and 64.

[44]Ibid., articles 116–119.

[45]Final Act of the United Nations Conference on Straddling Fish Stocks and Highly Migratory Fish Stocks, A/CONF.164/38, available at: https://documents-dds-ny.un.org/doc/UNDOC/GEN/N95/272/03/PDF/N9527203.pdf?OpenElement.

[46]See, e.g., United Nations Fish Stocks Agreement, articles 5–6 and Annex II.

[47]E.g., ibid., article 8.

[48]Ibid., article 7.

[49]Ibid., articles 18–23.

[50]Ibid., articles 24–26.

[51]Ibid., articles 27–32.

After the entry into force of the Agreement, the Secretary-General of the United Nations has convened the Informal Consultations of States Parties to the Agreement since 2002.[52] The meetings, with the participation both by States parties and by States non-parties to the Agreement, considered, inter alia, preparations for the Review Conference, implementation of the Agreement at the global, regional and national levels, and the establishment of the Assistance Fund under Part VII.

While the United Nations Fish Stocks Agreement does not anticipate annual meetings of parties, it provides for a Review Conference four years after the entry into force of the Agreement. Pursuant to article 36 of the Agreement, the Review Conference on the Agreement was held in 2006 and suspended to keep the Agreement under review. Subsequently, the Conference was resumed (and again suspended) in 2010 and 2016. The Conference agreed on a number of important recommendations, addressing the following issues: conservation and management of stocks; mechanisms for international cooperation and non-members; monitoring, control and surveillance and compliance and enforcement; developing States and non-parties.[53] Although it is not a standing conference of parties as in the case of many multilateral environmental agreements in the formal sense, the Review Conference has become a de facto body to conduct regular reviews, with a view to strengthening the legal regime established by the Agreement.

2.4 Development of an International Legally Binding Instrument Under UNCLOS on the Conservation and Sustainable Use of Marine Biological Diversity of Areas Beyond National Jurisdiction

On the basis of the work of the Ad Hoc Open-ended Informal Working Group to study issues relating to the conservation and sustainable use of marine biological diversity beyond areas of national jurisdiction (BBNJ Working Group) from 2006 to 2015 (see below),[54] the General Assembly decided to develop an international legally binding instrument under UNCLOS on the conservation and sustainable use of marine biological diversity of areas beyond national jurisdiction.[55] In this context, pursuant to General Assembly resolution 69/292, prior to holding an intergovernmental conference under the auspices of the United Nations, a Preparatory Committee was established to make substantive recommendations on the

[52]See http://www.un.org/depts/los/convention_agreements/fish_stocks_agreement_states_parties.htm.

[53]For information on the Conference and its recommendations, see http://www.un.org/Depts/los/convention_agreements/review_conf_fish_stocks.htm.

[54]Information on the Working Group is available at: http://www.un.org/depts/los/biodiversityworkinggroup/biodiversityworkinggroup.htm.

[55]UN Doc. A/RES/69/292, para. 1.

elements of a draft text of an international legally binding instrument under UNCLOS on the conservation and sustainable use of marine biological diversity of areas beyond national jurisdiction.[56]

Pursuant to General Assembly resolutions 69/292 and 71/257, the Preparatory Committee held four sessions in 2016 and 2017. It addressed the issues identified in the package agreed in 2011, namely, the conservation and sustainable use of marine biological diversity of areas beyond national jurisdiction, in particular and together, marine genetic resources, including the questions on the sharing of benefits, measures such as area-based management tools, including marine protected areas, and environmental impact assessments, capacity-building and transfer of marine technology.[57]

At the end of the fourth session in July 2017, the Preparatory Committee adopted, by consensus, its recommendations to the General Assembly, which contain non-exclusive elements of a draft text of an international legally binding instrument under UNCLOS that generated convergence among most delegations (Section A) and some of the main issues on which there is divergence of views (Section B).[58] Furthermore, the Preparatory Committee recommended to the General Assembly to take a decision, as soon as possible, on the convening of an intergovernmental conference, under the auspices of the United Nations, to consider the recommendations of the Preparatory Committee on the elements and to elaborate the text of an international legally binding instrument under UNCLOS (para. 2).[59]

2.5 *Rules of Reference*

UNCLOS does not purport to provide detailed rules and regulations for all activities. Instead, it is aimed to accommodate existing and newly developed rules and regulations as part of its legal regime. For a number of fields, UNCLOS anticipates that detailed rules and regulations will be developed by competent/relevant

[56]Ibid., para. 1(a).

[57]Ibid., para. 2.

[58]Sections A and B do not reflect consensus (para. 1). For the recommendations, see para. 38 of the Report of the Preparatory Committee established by General Assembly resolution 69/292: Development of an international legally binding instrument under the United Nations Convention on the Law of the Sea on the conservation and sustainable use of marine biological diversity of areas beyond national jurisdiction. The Advance, unedited version of the report is currently available at: http://www.un.org/Depts/los/biodiversity/prepcom_files/Procedural_report_of_BBNJ_PrepCom.pdf.

[59]General Assembly resolution 69/292, in para. 1(k), reads: "Decides that, before the end of its seventy-second session, and taking into account the aforementioned report of the preparatory committee, it will decide on the convening and on the starting date of an intergovernmental conference, under the auspices of the United Nations, to consider the recommendations of the preparatory committee on the elements and to elaborate the text of an international legally binding instrument under the Convention."

international organizations at the global and regional levels, as well as individual States. The competent/relevant international organizations that may be involved in this work would include: specialized agencies of the United Nations (e.g., the International Maritime Organization (IMO), the International Labour Organization (ILO), the Food and Agriculture Organization of the United Nations (FAO), the Intergovernmental Oceanographic Commission (IOC) of the United Nations Educational, Scientific and Cultural Organization (UNESCO) and the International Civil Aviation Organization (ICAO)); funds and programmes (e.g., the United Nations Environment Programme (UNEP) and the United Nations Development Programme (UNDP); institutions established under, inter alia, UNCLOS, the Convention on Biological Diversity (CBD)[60] and the Convention on International Trade in Endangered Species of Wild Fauna and Flora (CITES)).[61] Such organizations are not limited to global bodies; in several areas, regional bodies may also play an important role in this regard[62]

In the case of shipping, the IMO, which was formerly called Inter-Governmental Maritime Consultative Organization, has been developing detailed rules and regulations. Already at the time of the adoption of UNCLOS, the body of rules and regulations developed by the IMO existed and, since then, the IMO continued to provide for the regulation of shipping, within the framework of the International Convention for the Safety of Life at Sea (SOLAS),[63] the International Convention for the Prevention of Pollution from Ships (MARPOL), 1973, as modified by the Protocol of 1978 relating thereto[64] and by the Protocol of 1997, and the International Convention on Standards of Training, Certification and Watchkeeping for Seafarers (STCW),[65] as well as other IMO conventions.[66] For maritime labour standards, the ILO has also provided detailed rules concerning seafarers and fishers.

UNCLOS extensively uses a technique, often called "rules of reference", whereby detailed generally accepted international rules and standards developed outside UNCLOS are incorporated into the legal framework of UNCLOS, and State parties to UNCLOS are required to use them. In other words, to implement UNCLOS, States are also required to follow the rules and standards contained in instruments other than UNCLOS, regardless of the legal status of these instruments

[60]UNTS, vol. 1760, no. 30619.

[61]Ibid., vol. 993, no. 14537.

[62]For a list of competent/relevant international organizations in relation to UNCLOS, see ""Competent or relevant international organizations" under the United Nations Convention on the Law of the Sea", *Law of the Sea Bulletin*, No. 31 (1996), pp. 79–95. However, it should be noted that, after the preparation of this list, a number of new bodies have been established.

[63]UNTS, vol. 1184, No. 18961.

[64]Ibid., vol. 1340, No. 22484.

[65]Ibid., vol. 1361, No. 23001.

[66]See, e.g., Implications of the United Nations Convention on the Law of the Sea for the International Maritime Organization: Study by the Secretariat of the International Maritime Organization (IMO), LEG/MISC.8, available at: http://www.imo.org/en/OurWork/Legal/Documents/LEG%20MISC%208.pdf.

vis-à-vis these States (Division for Ocean Affairs and the Law of the Sea 2004). The formulation of the relevant provisions of UNCLOS varies (e.g., "conforming to and giving effect to",[67] "taking into account",[68] "shall at least have the same effect as",[69] and "shall be no less effective than"),[70] and therefore the stringency with which States need to follow these rules and standards varies, depending on the provisions concerned.

For example, generally accepted international rules and standards developed at "the competent international organization"[71] are minimum standards to be required for flag States. For coastal States, on the other hand, their laws and regulations regarding navigation by foreign ships in their EEZ need to be formulated to give effect to such international rules and regulations.

3 The Work of the United Nations Relevant to the Governance of Maritime Activities

3.1 The General Assembly and Other Organs of the United Nations

At the global level, the United Nations General Assembly plays an overall policy guidance role. It adopts annual resolutions on oceans and the law of the sea and on sustainable fisheries, and covers all aspects of ocean affairs. Annual General Assembly resolutions provide an overall review of major developments related to the oceans. Policy guidance provided by the General Assembly has bearings on developments at various competent/relevant international organizations and entities in their specific sectors.

To achieve its objectives, the General Assembly has established several bodies/processes dedicated to specific tasks, in particular:

- United Nations Open-ended Informal Consultative Process on Oceans and the Law of the Sea (ICP);
- Regular Process for Global Reporting and Assessment of the State of the Marine Environment, including Socioeconomic Aspects;
- Ad Hoc Open-ended Informal Working Group to study issues relating to the conservation and sustainable use of marine biological diversity beyond areas of national jurisdiction; and

---

[67] UNCLOS, article 211(5).

[68] Ibid., articles 207(1) and 212(1).

[69] Ibid., article 211(2).

[70] Ibid., articles 208(3) and 209(2).

[71] The singular term "the competent international organization" in this context is widely recognized to mean the IMO. See, e.g., LEG/MISC.8, p. 7.

- Preparatory Committee established by General Assembly resolution 69/292: Development of an international legally binding instrument under the United Nations Convention on the Law of the Sea on the conservation and sustainable use of marine biological diversity of areas beyond national jurisdiction.[72]

The Secretary-General of the United Nations is entrusted with numerous mandates related to oceans and the law of the sea. The Division for Ocean Affairs and the Law of the Sea (DOALOS) of the Office of Legal Affairs provides various secretariat services to assist the Secretary-General in discharging his mandates under UNCLOS and related Agreements. DOALOS also provides substantive secretariat services to the General Assembly and its subsidiary bodies in this regard.[73] The Secretary-General annually prepares reports on oceans and the law of the sea to be submitted to the General Assembly for its consideration as well as to the meeting of States parties to UNCLOS, which are comprehensive reports on developments and issues relating to ocean affairs and the law of the sea, including the implementation of relevant General Assembly resolutions.

Other organs of the United Nations also play important roles. The Security Council has occasionally dealt with matters related to oceans, in particular piracy off the coast of Somalia[74] and migration by sea.[75] Its decisions under Chapter VII of the Charter of the United Nations[76] are legally binding upon States (see article 25). The Economic and Social Council (ECOSOC) covers issues related to oceans, in particular in the context of sustainable development. The International Court of Justice has contributed to the development of the international law of the sea through its judgments and advisory opinions for several decades. In addition, the High-level Political Forum on Sustainable Development (HLPF), established following the United Nations Conference on Sustainable Development (UNCSD), now plays a primary role in follow-up and review for the implementation of "Transforming our world: the 2030 Agenda for Sustainable Development" (2030 Agenda),[77] including its Sustainable Development Goals (SDGs).

---

[72]On the work of these bodies, see http://www.un.org/depts/los/. In addition, while UN-Oceans (see below) was not established by the General Assembly, its revised Terms of Reference have been approved by the General Assembly in its resolution 68/70. Furthermore, it should be noted that the General Assembly has been addressing the impacts of bottom fisheries on vulnerable marine ecosystems and the long-term sustainability of deep-sea fish stocks since 2004, through recurring reviews of actions taken by States and regional fisheries management organizations and arrangements (RFMO/As).

[73]For the core functions of DOALOS, see Secretary-General's bulletin, Organization of the Office of Legal Affairs, ST/SGB/2008/13, available at: http://legal.un.org/ola/media/st-sgb-2008-13.pdf.

[74]See S/RES/1816 (2008) and subsequent resolutions.

[75]See S/RES/2240 (2015).

[76]https://treaties.un.org/Pages/ViewDetails.aspx?src=IND&mtdsg_no=I-1&chapter=1&lang=en.

[77]UN Doc. A/RES/70/1.

3.2 Summits and Conferences on Sustainable Development

The successive conferences and summits on sustainable development have adopted various declarations and action plans, which have had important implications for the oceans. In particular, chapter 17 of Agenda 21,[78] adopted at the United Nations Conference on Environment and Development held in Rio de Janeiro in 1992, has set essential and detailed programmes of action for governance in this field. The Johannesburg Plan of Implementation,[79] adopted in 2002, developed the agenda set by Agenda 21 and added several important elements.

"The future we want", the outcome document of the UNCSD held in 2012,[80] set out another important policy guidance in relation to the oceans. Furthermore, "The future we want" strengthened institutional frameworks for sustainable development by establishing, inter alia, the HLPF and decided to develop sustainable development goals which would be integrated into the post-2015 development agenda.

On the basis of the work of the Open Working Group on Sustainable Development Goals,[81] as well as other contributions to the process, the intergovernmental negotiations on the post-2015 development agenda finalized the post-2015 development agenda over the course of 2015.[82]

The 2030 Agenda, the outcome document of the United Nations summit to adopt the post-2015 development agenda, held from 25 to 27 September 2015, is critically important in the context of the governance of maritime activities. Whereas it is an instrument that sets an international development agenda for the next 15 years, the SDGs contained in the 2030 Agenda explicitly integrate sustainable development into the development agenda. SDGs contain various Goals and targets relating to the oceans. While all Goals and numerous targets relate to the oceans and their resources, most importantly, Goal 14, entitled "Conserve and sustainably use the oceans, seas and marine resources for sustainable development", contains ten important targets for the oceans.

After the adoption of the 2030 Agenda, the global indicator framework for SDGs has been developed in accordance with the mandate under the Agenda, with a view to measuring progress in the implementation of the Goals and targets contained in the 2030 Agenda. The General Assembly and the Economic and Social Council adopted the global indicator framework for the Sustainable Development Goals and targets of the 2030 Agenda for Sustainable Development, developed by the

---

[78]https://sustainabledevelopment.un.org/content/documents/Agenda21.pdf.

[79]http://www.un.org/esa/sustdev/documents/WSSD_POI_PD/English/WSSD_PlanImpl.pdf (in particular, paras. 30–36).

[80]UN Doc. A/RES/66/288, Annex.

[81]For the Report of the Open Working Group of the General Assembly on Sustainable Development Goals, see A/68/970.

[82]On the intergovernmental negotiations, see https://sustainabledevelopment.un.org/post2015/negotiations.

Inter-Agency and Expert Group on Sustainable Development Goal Indicators, as agreed upon by the Statistical Commission, in 2017.[83]

In connection with Goal 14, pursuant to General Assembly resolutions 70/226 and 70/303, the high-level United Nations Conference to support the implementation of Goal 14: Conserve and sustainably use the oceans, seas and marine resources for sustainable development was held in June 2017.[84] The Conference adopted an intergovernmentally-agreed declaration, entitled "Our ocean, our future: call for action", which was endorsed by the General Assembly in its resolution 71/312. It calls, inter alia, on all stakeholders to conserve and sustainably use the oceans, seas and marine resources for sustainable development by taking a number of actions on an urgent basis, including by building on existing institutions and partnerships.[85] The report of the Conference also contains the Co-Chairs' summaries of the seven Partnership Dialogues and the list of voluntary commitments made in the context of the Conference.[86]

With regard to the follow-up and review of the implementation of the 2030 Agenda, including the SDGs, the 2030 Agenda makes it clear that the HLPF will have the central role in overseeing follow-up and review at the global level.[87] The General Assembly decided that the HLPF in 2017 would review Goal 14, together with Goals 1, 2, 3, 5, 9, as well as 17, in depth, under the theme "Eradicating poverty and promoting prosperity in a changing world".[88] In the Ministerial Declaration adopted at the HLPF in 2017, the Ministers and high representatives, inter alia, called on all stakeholders to urgently undertake, inter alia, the actions highlighted in the call for action adopted during that Conference and by implementing the respective voluntary commitments pledged by individual Member States and other stakeholders during the Conference.[89]

4 Other Legal Instruments and Institutions Relevant to Maritime Activities

In addition to the global legal framework under UNCLOS, sectoral rules have been developed by numerous international organizations and institutions at the global and regional levels. For example, as noted above, the IMO, a specialized agency of the United Nations, has been developing rules and standards for shipping under

[83] A/RES/71/313; E/RES/2017/7.

[84] A/RES/70/226.

[85] Para. 13.

[86] See A/CONF.230/14 (advance unedited version is available at: https://oceanconference.un.org/).

[87] A/RES/70/1, paras. 47 and 82.

[88] A/RES/70/299, para. 5. Means of implementation, including with respect to Goal 17, are reviewed annually. Para. 4.

[89] Currently available as E/2017/L.29–E/HLPF/2017/L.2.

numerous IMO Conventions. In particular, an array of international instruments, such as codes and guidelines, have been developed under IMO conventions, and regularly revised. Through the Sub-Committee on Implementation of IMO Instruments (formerly, Sub-committee on Flag State Implementation) and other organs, it has also been engaged in the monitoring and facilitation of the implementation of IMO instruments. The ILO, another specialized agency of the United Nations, has contributed to international standard-setting in the field of labour standards, including maritime labour standards. In particular, in 2006, it adopted the Maritime Labour Convention, which entered into force in 2013, updating and consolidating over 60 conventions and recommendations relating to maritime labour. Through regular and ad hoc supervisory mechanisms, the ILO has been monitoring the implementation of the instruments adopted under its auspices.

While the bulk of the above-mentioned instruments regulate activities at sea, some of them also deal with other activities. For example, port is an interface between ships and land, and indeed an essential part for maritime activities. Many IMO and ILO instruments concern regulatory requirements relating to ports, e.g., port State control and the implementation of the International Ship and Port Facility Security (ISPS) Code. Regulation concerning maritime affairs even goes further landward (e.g. ship recycling).

In some cases, region-specific provisions are found in the global instruments dealing with maritime activities, e.g., designation of areas to be avoided under SOLAS, Special Areas under MARPOL, and Particularly Sensitive Sea Areas.[90] Implementation of these global rules and standards are undertaken not only at the national level, but also through regional cooperative mechanisms, such as regional port State control memoranda of understanding (MOUs) and regional seas conventions and action plans.

Related to the body of sectoral rules dedicated to the governance of maritime activities, there are other multilateral treaty regimes developed separately from the international law of the sea yet applicable or relevant to maritime activities, such as the General Agreement on Tariffs and Trade (GATT)/World Trade Organization (WTO).[91]

5 Cooperation and Coordination

In view of the co-existence of various international organizations and entities with competence in ocean and coastal issues, inter-agency cooperation and coordination to maintain consistency among the relevant organizations and entities is a major

[90]Region-specific instruments also exist, e.g., the Polar Code, which was made mandatory under SOLAS and MARPOL.

[91]See Marrakesh Agreement establishing the World Trade Organization, UNTS, Vol. 1867, No. 31874.

challenge. At the global level, there are several mechanisms that are intended to further cooperation and coordination. For example, UN-Oceans serves as the cooperation and coordination mechanism of the United Nations System agencies and the ISA on ocean and coastal issues.[92] The biennial work programme of UN-Oceans for 2016–2017 was agreed on and presented in June 2016, which contains several items related to the implementation of ocean-related SDGs, including SDG 14. The ICP is another platform for cooperation and coordination among agencies. Annually, under the agenda item "Inter-agency cooperation and coordination", the meetings of the ICP offer opportunities for the Member States of the United Nations to give feedback to inter-agency cooperation and coordination, including to the activities of UN-Oceans. In addition, with regard to scientific aspects, the Joint Group of Experts on the Scientific Aspects of Marine Environmental Protection (GESAMP), which is an advisory body, established in 1969, that advises the United Nations system on the scientific aspects of marine environmental protection, also assists in the cooperation and coordination of participating agencies.[93]

At the regional level, there are mechanisms for cooperation and coordination among bodies working in the same sector (e.g., cooperation between RFMO/As),[94] as well as cross-sectoral cooperation and coordination (e.g., cooperation between RFMO/As and regional marine environmental protection organizations).[95]

Similarly, some attempts of cooperation and coordination involving global and regional bodies have been undertaken. An example of this type of cooperation concerns the proposed cooperation among the OSPAR Commission, NEAFC, the IMO and the ISA for the North-east Atlantic. The OSPAR Commission sought to conclude a collective arrangement between competent authorities on the management of selected areas in areas beyond national jurisdiction in the North-East Atlantic, in this regard. While the proposal for the quadruple arrangement did not yield immediate result, the OSPAR Commission enhanced its cooperation with NEAFC and also concluded a MOU with the ISA.[96] Another example for this type of cooperation relates to the activities by UNEP and regional seas conventions and action plans. In addition to the relationship between UNEP and its regional seas

[92]See http://www.unoceans.org. The United Nations Legal Counsel/DOALOS functions as the focal point of UN-Oceans. The revised terms of reference for the work of UN-Oceans were approved by the General Assembly in its resolution 68/70 in 2013. These terms of reference are scheduled to be reviewed by the General Assembly at its seventy second session in 2017. See A/RES/71/257, para. 346.

[93]See http://www.gesamp.org.

[94]Examples include the Regional Fishery Body Secretariats Network (RSN) (see http://www.fao.org/fishery/rsn/en) and joint meetings of tuna RFMOs (see http://www.tuna-org.org/).

[95]See, e.g., cooperation between the North-East Atlantic Fisheries Commission (NEAFC) and the OSPAR Commission (for example, the MOU, available at: http://www.neafc.org/system/files/opsar_mou.pdf). In addition, it is noted that the Sustainable Ocean Initiative (SOI) Global Dialogue with Regional Seas Organizations and Regional Fisheries Bodies on Accelerating Progress Towards the Aichi Biodiversity Targets was convened by the CBD Executive Secretary in September 2016. See https://www.cbd.int/doc/?meeting=SOIOM-2016-01.

[96]See http://www.ospar.org/site/assets/files/1357/mou_isa.pdf.

programmes, cooperation took place also involving non-UNEP mechanisms, such as the OSPAR Commission, as exemplified by the holding of successive Global Meetings of the Regional Seas Conventions and Action Plans.[97]

In addition, it is interesting to recall that, in the context of the review of actions addressing the impacts of bottom fisheries, the overall policy guidance provided by the United Nations General Assembly has been responded to not only by States but also by RFMO/As and FAO.[98] Interactions between global and regional bodies have proved to be an essential element in addressing such impacts in a continuous manner.

6 Conclusion

In this chapter, we have considered the important pillars of the governance of maritime activities, namely, a complex web of legal and policy instruments and institutional arrangements governing maritime activities. The legal framework governing maritime activities consists of the international law of the sea, as reflected in UNCLOS. UNCLOS and its Implementing Agreements are complemented by a number of rules and standards developed in sectoral bodies at the global and regional levels. The rules of UNCLOS cannot be seen in isolation, as sectoral rules and standards are taken into account in considering the fulfilment of the obligations under UNCLOS on a number of issues. Policy instruments developed within intergovernmental organizations, such as the United Nations General Assembly, also provide guidance to the governance of maritime activities. Many of the institutions involved in the governance of maritime activities exist in parallel. Where necessary, cooperation among these bodies, as well as coordination of their activities, to achieve better governance remains a major challenge.

As noted at the beginning of the chapter, the concept "maritime governance" is linked to CSR, the other central theme of this book. Indeed, voluntary CSR initiatives would be complementary to regulatory initiatives and have a potential to fill existing regulatory gaps. CSR initiatives would be able to contribute to addressing social and environmental concerns, and thereby help to achieve better maritime governance.

[97]See http://www.unep.org/regionalseas/globalmeetings/default_ns.asp.

[98]See A/71/351 and preceding reports of the Secretary-General on this issue.

References

Bonfanti, A., & Romanin Jacur, F. (2014). Energy from the sea and the protection of the marine environment: Treaty-based regimes and ocean corporate social responsibility. *International Journal of Marine and Coastal Law, 29*, 622–644.

Brown Weiss, E., & Sornarajah, A. (May 2009). Good Governance. In: *Max Planck Encyclopedia of Public International Law*. http://opil.ouplaw.com/home/EPIL.

Coady, L., Lister, J., Strandberg, C., & Ota, Y. (2013). The role of corporate social responsibility (CSR) in the international shipping sector: A phase 2 research paper, prepared for The Northern European Symposium on CSR in Shipping, Copenhagen, Denmark. Retrieved November 12, 2013, from http://corostrandberg.com/wp-content/uploads/2013/11/ubc-csr-in-shipping-denmark.pdf

de Marffy, A. (2004). Ocean governance: A process in the right direction for the effective management of the oceans. *Ocean Yearbook, 18*, 162–192.

de Souza Patu, G. N. (2011). *Scope and evolution of ocean governance: Improving cross-sectoral management by the adoption of principles of international law*. Thesis, University of Wollongong. http://ro.uow.edu.au/theses/3545

Division for Ocean Affairs and the Law of the Sea. (2004). *Obligations of states parties under the United Nations convention on the law of the sea and complementary instruments*. New York: United Nations. http://www.un.org/depts/los/doalos_publications/publicationstexts/E.04.V.5.pdf

Freestone, D. (2008). Principles applicable to modern oceans governance. *International Journal of Marine and Coastal Law, 23*, 385–391.

Haward, M., & Vince, J. (2008). *Oceans governance in the twenty-first century: Managing the Blue Planet*. Cheltenham: Edward Elgar.

Juda, L. (1996). *International law and ocean use management: The evolution of ocean governance*. London: Routledge.

Juda, L. (2007). The European Union and ocean use management: The marine strategy and the maritime policy. *Ocean Development and International Law, 38*, 259–282.

Kaufmann, D., Kraay, A., & Zoido-Lobatón, P. (October 1999). Governance Matters. Policy Research Working Papers. http://elibrary.worldbank.org/doi/pdf/10.1596/1813-9450-2196.

Mukherjee, P. K., & Brownrigg, M. (2013). *Farthing on international shipping* (4th ed.). Heidelberg: Springer.

Oude Elferink, A. G. (2012). Governance principles for areas beyond National jurisdiction. *International Journal of Marine and Coastal Law, 27*, 205–259.

Rhodes, R. A. W. (1996). The new governance: Governing without government. *Political Studies, 44*, 652–667.

Roe, M. (2013). *Maritime governance and policy-making*. London: Springer.

Rothwell, D. R., & Stephens, T. (2010). *The international law of the sea*. Oxford: Hart Publishing.

Rothwell, D. R., & VanderZwaag, D. L. (2006). The sea change towards principled oceans governance. In D. R. Rothwell & D. L. VanderZwaag (Eds.), *Towards principled oceans governance: Australian and Canadian approaches and challenges* (pp. 3–15). London: Routledge.

Tanaka, Y. (2008). *A dual approach to ocean governance: The cases of zonal and integrated management in international law of the sea*. Farnham: Ashgate.

Treves, T. (2010). Principles and objectives of the legal regime governing areas beyond national jurisdiction. In E. J. Molenaar & A. G. Oude Elferink (Eds.), *The international legal regime of areas beyond national jurisdiction: Current and future developments* (pp. 7–25). Leiden: Martinus Nijhoff Publishers.

Methods to Promote Improved Governance in Maritime Administrations of Developing Nations

Patrick Donner, George Theocharidis, and Tafsir Johansson

1 Introduction

Shipping has for a long time been acknowledged as one of the strong catalysts of socio-economic development. The facilitation of international trade is one of the central aims of the shipping industry and has become an increasingly important part of a global economy. The concept "governance" has become the topic of much debate within the context of international trade and was also recently highlighted due to the fact that shipping is trans-boundary and that the shipping industry has an impact on the environment. At the same time, it has rightly been observed[1] that there is no uniform definition of the concept "governance", and definitions that do exist, only point to an uncertainty of the concept (Roe 2012). It is noteworthy that the term "governance" is used extensively in a number of academic disciplines, e.g. business administration, political science, management, economics and law (Yliskylä-Peuralahti and Gritsenko 2014). As such, the term "governance" is mainly defined on the basis of the focus of each individual discipline. For example, in the field of economics, governance is said to comprise of the processes that support economic actions and transactions by protecting property rights, enforcing contracts and taking collective action to provide appropriate physical and organisational infrastructure (Dixit 2008). In economic governance, the aforementioned processes are carried out within institutions, both formal and informal (Dixit 2008). The definition of governance as observed in the

[1]Takei Y., "Regulatory review in the maritime sector". Paper drawn up under the auspices of a research project on Maritime Governance and Corporate Social Responsibility at World Maritime University under the Reference Research group called; CSR Maritime. The project is funded by The Danish Maritime Fund through the Danish Shipowners Association and the Danish Maritime Authority.

P. Donner (✉) • G. Theocharidis • T. Johansson
World Maritime University, Malmö, Sweden
e-mail: pd@wmu.se; gt@wmu.se; tj@wmu.se

L. L. Froholdt (ed.), *Corporate Social Responsibility in the Maritime Industry*, WMU Studies in Maritime Affairs 5, https://doi.org/10.1007/978-3-319-69143-5_5

economic-discipline can be contrasted from the way it is understood in the field of law. Governance, in the law discipline, is concerned *inter* alia, with the functions of the government organs, i.e. the executive branch, the legislative branch and the judiciary branch. To ensure good governance, it is acknowledged that each of these three organs should be separate and be given independent powers so that powers, and roles and responsibilities are not in conflict with each other (Vile 1967). Again, in the field of business administration, the definition of the term "governance" is mainly company or corporation oriented whereby the fundamental principle is similar to that of the economic discipline. Fidrmuc et al. (2006) have offered an insightful definition of corporate governance that refers to a "combination of mechanisms which ensure that the management (the agent) runs the firm for the benefit of one or several stakeholders (principals)" (Fidrmuc et al. 2006). In short, governance in the corporate field revolves mainly around the conflict of interests and the prevention or mitigation of those conflicts between the providers of finance and the managers; the shareholders and the stakeholders; and the different types of shareholders (Goergen et al. 2012).

While the current trend demonstrates that the definition and concept of governance does not apply in a uniform manner in all disciplines, international organisations, which are a part of the global development network, also demonstrate dissimilarities in the way they have understood, conceptualized and defined the term governance (United Nations Economic and Social Council 2006). For example, in 1992, the World Bank published its first report titled "Governance and Development" in which it explored the meaning of governance and its connection with development (World Bank 1992). In that report, the World Bank defined governance as "the manner in which power is exercised in the management of a country's economic and social resources for development" (World Bank 1992). Five years later, in 1997, the United Nations Development Programme (UNDP) defined governance as "the exercise of economic, political and administrative authority to manage a country's affairs at all levels. It comprises the mechanisms, processes and institutions through which citizens and groups articulate their interests, exercise their legal rights, meet their obligations and mediate their differences" (UNDP 1997). From a joint perspective, the United Nations (UN) System Task Team[2] published a paper in 2012 titled "Governance and Development" that highlights significant trends and changes in governance since the Millennium Summit in 2000 (UN System Task Team 2012). In the 2012 paper, the UN System Task Team referred to governance as "the exercise of political and administrative authority at all levels to manage a country's affairs" (UN System Task Team 2012). Parallel to this reference, the Task Team highlighted the definition of governance that was first endorsed by UNDP in 1997, and subsequently recognized by the UN Committee of Experts on Public Administration in 2006 (UN System Task Team 2012). In doing

[2]The Task Team was led by the Department of Economic and Social Affairs and the United Nations Development Programme and brought together senior experts from over 50 UN entities and international organisations to provide system-wide support to the post-2015 consultation process, including analytical input, expertise and outreach.

so, the Task Team argues that the institutional and human capacities for governance help determine the way in which the effectiveness of public policies and strategies is attained (UN System Task Team 2012).

At the same time, the concept "good governance" is increasingly being included in discussions at all levels. Basic notions, such as rule of the law, public participation, transparency, accountability, control of corruption and government effectiveness, are considered as elements of "good governance" (Brown Weiss and Sornarajah 2009). At the United Nations Conference on Sustainable Development 2012 (Rio+20 Conference) the concept of "good governance" was highlighted by Kofi Annan,[3] the former Secretary General of the United Nations (UN), as being very important in achieving the goals set out. Of particular relevance is the 2030 Agenda for the Sustainable Development, which will be the new reference point for all activities in the coming 15 years. It is also noteworthy that recent discussions about the framework and definition of good governance, whether in academia or elsewhere, is centred on what makes institutions, both public and private, more effective and efficient. Governance in the corporate field, otherwise known as corporate governance, is "something much broader to include a fair, efficient and transparent administration to meet certain well-defined objectives" (Fernando 2009). When compared to Corporate Social Responsibility (CSR), i.e. treating the stakeholders of a firm ethically or in a socially responsible manner, it is generally understood that corporate governance has a much wider scope (Department of Parliamentary Services 2006). The Australian Parliamentary Joint Committee on Corporations and Financial Services considers CSR as an integral part of corporate governance in so far as "corporate responsibility is only one aspect of an organisation's governance and risk management processes" (Department of Parliamentary Services 2006, p. 7).

Since the beginning of the twentieth century, a number of researches have been carried out with the objective to link "good governance" with CSR through the idea of responsible business behaviour (Bigg and Ward 2004; Bharej 2014). Again, a number of international actors have addressed different aspects of the relationship between CSR, good governance and corporate accountability (Bigg and Ward 2004). These initiatives are exemplified through the development of the OECD Guidelines for Multinational Enterprises, the UNDP Private Sector Strategy, and the UN Global Compact/UNDP 'growing sustainable business in least developed countries' initiative (The OECD Guidelines for Multinational Enterprises 1976; UNDP 2012; UN Global Compact 2002). The interrelation between: (a) CSR and corporate governance; and (b) CSR and good governance—is obvious, albeit not absolutely clear.

In the shipping sector, Maritime Governance (MG) replaces the term corporate governance and continues to maintain a form of connection with CSR. Similar to corporate governance, MG can be considered as an area with a broad scope whereby CSR is considered as an integral element of the governance framework. It is,

[3] "Good governance" at the local, national and international levels is perhaps the single most important factor in promoting development and advancing the cause of peace.

therefore, safe to assert that good MG is an indicator of how well a shipping company is performing as a corporate and socially responsible entity with regard to environment, safety, labour issues, customer relations and increased transparency of operations (Roe 2012; Bloor et al. 2006, 2013). In this context, MG mainly touches upon core elements that are identified as law, policy and institutions relating to the regulation of maritime activities (Takei 2014). Such activities include navigation, shipping and commerce, which relate to ports, harbours, shipping *stricto senso*, transportation etc. The present regulatory scheme in the shipping industry relies on the implementation and enforcement by individual states (acting either as port, flag or coastal state). The International Maritime Organization (IMO) has no power of enforcement to ensure that nations adhere to the regulations, as the task is left to the governments of IMO Member States. Again, implementation of IMO conventions depends on whether the member state follows the dualist or monist system. On the other hand, almost invariably it is the maritime administration, which is the national agency responsible for and dedicated to ensuring the safety of ships, the protection of life and property at sea and the marine environment.

In order to understand how a good governance system can be promoted in developing nations, it is first and foremost important to gain an understanding of how relevant international regulations on safety and security mirror good MG. Because the techniques to implement good MG have already been incorporated in a number of IMO legal instruments, the methods to promote improved governance or good MG in developing nations would certainly include those IMO governance instruments, which in the event of ratification by the state are subsequently implemented and enforced by their maritime administrations. The rationale behind enforcement and adherence is self-explanatory: to make shipping companies accountable to the stakeholders as well as the international community. In other words, they recommend companies to conduct business in a corporate and socially responsible manner. While the techniques are mainly those that are derived from various international conventions that require national consideration and effective implementation by governmental departments of maritime administration, there seems to be a notion of shared-responsibility in the good MG enforcement procedure. The responsibility is shared by shipping companies that are the principal actors central to the subject matter of good MG. But "responsibility" is a word that companies with a business mind-set quite often consider as overrated. Because in fact, the objective of incorporating a company is guided by the principle of making profit, and shipping companies are no exception to this principle. This is where incentive schemes could play an invaluable role. Reward schemes, such as reduction in port fees or harbour dues, can be viewed as helping companies to increase profit by cutting down costs. Whether this profit through incentive schemes could be used to promote improved governance, parallel to the existing mechanisms adopted by maritime administrations, merits further scrutiny. With this in mind, the present chapter aims to examine some of the best practices and perceptions of improved governance, as well as incentive schemes for public and private actors, which may improve and promote social, economic and environmental responsibility among shipping companies in developing nations.

2 Governance in Maritime Administrations of Developing Nations: Facts and Proposals

It is understood that there is no specific reference to maritime or ocean governance in key international instruments. However, in trying to ascertain the means that could be used to promote good governance in maritime administrations in developing nations, due consideration can be given to certain provisions of the United Nations Convention on the Law of the Sea, 1982 (UNCLOS). Article 94 of UNCLOS clearly states that flag states have a duty to take such measures for ships flying their flag as are necessary to ensure safety at sea. This duty is more specifically defined in various international regulations. Moreover, considering the fact that there should be a common approach to shipping standards, IMO has adopted Resolution A.1054 (27) (Code for the Implementation of Mandatory IMO Instruments), which incorporates specific strategies and best practices that could be developed by member States in order to achieve the Code's objective, one of which is enhancing global maritime safety and protection of the marine environment. Administrations of Contracting States, in this context, are under an obligation to enforce the provisions of IMO Conventions as far as their shipping business is concerned and may proceed to impose penalties for infringements of national law.

At the same time, it may be observed that the policy of every maritime nation on maritime administration is charted by the government, almost invariably by a national agency responsible for and dedicated to ensuring safety of ships, protection of life and property at sea and the marine environment, and compliance with applicable international and national laws and regulations. Powers of the maritime administration spring from the national maritime legislation and the competent Minister. Accordingly, maritime administrations of states administer their own national shipping infrastructure. That being the case, in many nations there is a lack of a common notion of MG among various governmental departments.

A key question, related to the topic under examination, is whether maritime administrations of developing nations have devised and implemented methods and techniques, in order to promote governance of their maritime policies, and if not, what they could do in the coming future. Maritime administrations are run by departments, which differ in terms of structure and operation and are governed by their own state legislation. They are responsible for the enforcement of all national maritime-related activities. However, the legislation that governs parts of the maritime sector of some developing nations may, in some cases, be best described as not updated. For example, the Merchant Shipping Ordinance of 1983 is the law that governs shipping activities in Bangladesh. This needs to be replaced by a law that reflects essential elements of IMO conventions and protocols. In some cases, law reform can be marked by a slow progress. For example, the 151st Law Commission Report on Admiralty Law in India recommended that British Statutes (i.e. the Admiralty Jurisdiction (India) Act 1860 and the Colonial Courts of Admiralty Act 1890, and three other related British statutes) should be repealed. This was the situation that prevailed for a considerable period of time and it was only at the beginning of 2016 that the Indian government accepted the recommendation.

On the opposite side stands the example of Brazil, which was heavily influenced by international sources, especially the conventions created by IMO and by the uses and customs of international trade, through the *Lex Mercatoria* (Agripino de Castro Junior 2009). As it becomes apparent, in terms of maritime safety and security, marine environment, labour issues and other matters, which touch upon MG, the 'not-updated' law stands in conflict with the laws of other developing nations. This creates a complete imbalance in the way maritime administrations are governing their maritime-related activities. This has brought the following result. Early adopters of good governance started to report their environmental and safety performance (Yliskylä-Peuralahti and Gritsenko 2014). This happened when cargo owners asked for information that related to the specific performance of shipping. Today, cargo owners are asking for the same information and the focus is on the maritime transport providers of developing nations. On other matters such as environment, safety, labour issues, customer relations and transparency of operations, there is no obligatory feedback. In order to bring an overall improvement, it thus becomes important to promote improved governance in maritime administrations in developing nations.

Another important area is the enforcement of standards. Survey and certification by maritime administrations are the basic methods of such enforcement. In some cases, nations, which lack necessary expertise and experience, have found a form of convenience in delegating the aforementioned functions to non-public entities (Villanueva 2004). Expertise, experience and internationality comprise the Classification Societies' cornerstone in the effective pursuit of their safety goals, which are central to the notions of good governance. Obviously, this is in sharp contrast with the lack of capacity and competence of several flag state administrations, which has led to Classification Societies being designated as Recognized Organizations (Villanueva 2004). At the same time, it is notable that maritime administrations of developed nations have delegated part of the above functions to Recognized Organizations in order to effectively expand their capabilities on a worldwide basis (Villanueva 2004). Thus, Classification Societies exercise considerable influence in the general policy against sub-standard ships. That is so by preventing the latter from conducting business and bringing forth the rule that only ships classed in accordance with proper rules and in conformity with the applicable national and international regulations are allowed to sail (Villanueva 2004). The Danish Class Agreement of 2003 can be cited as an example, whereby Recognized Organizations, authorized by the Danish Maritime Authority, should comply with the requirements of IMO Resolutions A. 739(18) and A. 789(19) as well as the Council Directive 94/57/EU. In compliance with IMO and European Union Guidelines, DMA exercises its supervisory powers over the Recognized Organization through a system of audits, random inspections, planned inspections or expanded special surveys. The Agreement also provides for a proper reporting and communications procedure.

2.1 Governance and the Ship Port Interface

A similar area extends in the field of best practice options recommended in IMO Resolution A.1054 (27) on the continuous review and verification of the effectiveness of Contracting States in respect of meeting their international obligations. One way of continuous review can be accomplished by evaluating Port State Control (PSC) reports. PSC reports are usually published annually and contain statistics on the performance of Flag States and Recognized Organizations. In order to carry out the effective implementation of PSC provisions, many nations have already signed and accepted a Memorandum of Understanding (MoU) for regional cooperation in PSC and have established a centralized computer database system and a harmonized approach (ClassNK 2014). However, a major hindrance for effective PSC is the need for technical and financial assistance to enforce regulations by the maritime administrations of developing nations (Villanueva 2004). Even though developing nations tend to be parties to the different regional MoUs, they tend to lack sufficient resources to enforce PSC (Villanueva 2004). This is particularly apparent within the newly established regional PSC agreements. Equally, active participation of maritime administrations of all parties is crucial to the successful implementation of PSC MoUs. For the Indian Ocean region, the Indian Ocean MoU carried out a Concentrated Inspection Campaign (CIC) on Propulsion and Auxiliary Machinery from 1 September to 30 November 2013 in line with the CIC carried out by the Tokyo MoU and the Paris MoU. According to the 2013 Annual Report of the Indian Ocean MOU, a total of 5320 inspections were carried out and 376 vessels were detained in 2013. The given number does not reflect the best practice that is incorporated in the Paris MoU where the 3879 inspections during the equivalent CIC resulted in only 68 detentions or 1.8% (Paris MOU 2014). A noteworthy example that can act as guidance for developing nations is the work of the European Maritime Safety Agency (EMSA), which has assumed the technical responsibility for monitoring PSC at European Union (EU) level. A similar agency could be developed through special MoUs that can promote, develop and implement a harmonised community scheme for the training and assessment of competences of PSC inspectors by member states.

Resolution A.1054 (27) also incorporates the notion that states should implement a strategy that covers the achievement, maintenance and improvement of overall organisational performance and capability. A strategic human resource development system developed by maritime administrations of developing nations will influence organisational performance. A good quality system can assure achievement and maintenance of organisational performance. Administrations can apply the ISO 9001 management system standards or other equivalent management quality systems. Furthermore, improvement can be achieved via the new public management principle, which reflects preservation and improvement of certain aspects of Resolution A.1054 (27). This represents a major shift from the traditional public administration with far greater attention being paid to the achievement of results and the personal liability of the managers (Hughes 1998). In the new public management system, there is an expressed intention to move away from classic bureaucracy, so as to make organisations, personnel and employment terms and conditions more flexible (Hughes 1998; Pfiffner 2004; Rhodes 2000). It also provides for the identification of organisational and personal objectives, which are to be set out clearly, so as to enable measurement of their achievement through performance indicators (Hughes 1998, 2003; Rhodes 2012). Although it is not possible to implement all strategies embedded in the new public management, maritime administrations of developing nations, could opt to implement certain forms of new public management, so as to promote good governance.

Parallel to that, there should be a well-implemented crew Performance Management System (PMS), which provides valuable information for corporate management, where the purpose is to align the performance of every employee with the corporate strategy and objectives (PwC Survey 2010) of the maritime administration. A proper PMS can facilitate decisions for human resource issues, such as rewards (fixed or variable pay), training and development, career planning and promotion (PwC Survey 2010). The key areas, as defined by the crew PMS, should include performance goals, skills and competencies required to successfully perform duties and responsibilities; and finally corporate values and behaviours, which are expected to be demonstrated, so as to fit within the corporate culture (PwC Survey 2010).

If we continue from the above proposition, we will observe that the development of good governance, in conjunction with a sound PMS, can encourage maritime administrations of developing nations to define more comprehensive priorities for maritime affairs. A sound management system is the first step in ensuring a better environment for the maritime workforce, which eventually assists in protection and preservation of the marine environment. Maritime administrations are under an obligation to promote marine environmental protection awareness among seafarers of both the public and private sectors. More importantly, the maritime workforce, especially newly recruited seafarers in the public sector, must be made aware of "state responsibility" for intentional wrongful acts, which violate international obligations. This can be personal blameworthy behaviour arising out of non-respect of due diligence standards and strict liability of the State due to occurrence of damage to the victim. Finally, maritime administrations in developing nations, could strive to properly disseminate the rationale of international conventions among seafarers and crewmembers of both the public and private sector.

2.2 *Maritime Security and Governance*

Maritime security measures, as an element of good maritime governance, ensure a certain degree of protection against possible threats to the shipping business and the maritime labourers, who comprise the maritime manpower and workforce segment. Hawkes (1989) offers a very useful definition of "maritime security measures" and states that these measures are employed by maritime administrators, owners and operators of vessels, port facilities, offshore installations, and other maritime organisations or establishments to protect against seizure, sabotage, piracy, pilferage, annoyance or surprise. Moreover, all measures taken to prevent hostile interference with lawful operations may be embraced. Although the definition provided by Hawkes (1989) seems to be all-embracing, it should be noted that most of the international instruments that introduced maritime security initiatives before 9/11 were trying to insert the act of terrorism by sea within the scope of piracy (Jesus 2003). Although at first glance, terrorism by sea and piracy seem to embody the same features, researchers have argued that the two acts are rather unique and dissimilar in nature, and cannot be used interchangeably (Shie 2004; Mat Salleh 2006). While terrorism can be considered as politically driven, piracy on the other hand, can be deemed as private gain driven (Shie 2004). Post 9/11 initiatives by the United States of America (US) demonstrate the viewpoint of the government on terrorism and the various alternatives through which maritime security measures have been strengthened. To address cargo related risks, the US has incorporated three new initiatives, i.e. C-TPAT, the CSI and the 24-hour rule. Through these initiatives, the concerned authorities of the US try to ensure that all overseas partners and counterparts are genuine and operate in accordance with safe and secure procedures and practices (Mat Salleh 2006). While the US initiatives can be termed as precautionary acts to strengthen maritime security to deal with terrorism against shipping, these initiatives primarily rest with the governments of individual states, whether developing or developed. Based on what is required and what is absent, the governments may design, develop and implement security measures to protect against any form of harm to the public and private sectors, because the effects and ramifications of failing to preserve an acceptable degree of safety and security in the maritime sector are extensive and damaging in the highly sensitive maritime industry (Villanueva 2004). Therefore, maritime administrations of developing nations must ensure that the two active ingredients of maritime security, i.e. adequate warning and timely action, are properly preserved by means of proper security indoctrination and training of personnel (Hawkes 1989). This can be seen as part of the best practice system that can improve the governance system of the maritime administrations of developing nations.

Directly linked to the implementation of maritime security measures are IMO's provisions for the promotion of maritime security by virtue of the International Ship and Port Facility Security Code (ISPS Code 2002). This is achieved by appointment of competent personnel in port facilities, on board ships and in the shipping companies that will comply with the security requirements, as provided for by the Code. It also includes the preparation and implementation of port facility security plans and ship security plans, which are subject to approval by the Contracting State. In 2002, IMO initiated an ambitious programme under the heading Integrated Technical Co-operation Programme (ITCP) for the purpose of providing assistance to developing nations, in the global effort to protect shipping from terrorist attacks. Considerable sums of money were reserved for the running of the ITCP, however no follow-up on the implementation of the ISPS Code was attained—a factor which undermined the whole project. Nevertheless, this IMO initiative can be identified and recognized as an effective method of promoting good governance by maritime administrations of developing nations.

2.3 STCW as a Governance Mechanism

In the area of Maritime Education and Training (MET), the current trend is slowly shifting from knowledge-based to competency-based training. The need for constant professional updating and re-certification has brought maritime training institutions out from the grasp of the maritime administration and shipping industry (Ziarati 2006). The "Train-the-Trainer" programme developed by IMO included the objective of assisting Governments of developing nations to strengthen regulatory implementation by enlarging the pool of trained instructors capable of delivering high quality maritime security training at the national and regional level, using IMO's updated training package and its three model courses for security officers. At the same time, maritime administrations of developing nations need to be vigilant in ensuring that Maritime Education and Training Planners meet the requirements of the International Convention on Standards of Training, Certification and Watchkeeping for Seafarers (STCW 1978), as amended. Again, the current trend is slowly shifting from knowledge-based to competency-based training. While STCW 1978 focused on what seafarers are required to know in order to be competent, post STCW 1995 focuses on what seafarers need to be able to do (Lewarn 2002). That being said, maritime administrations should update themselves on the current trends and modify the training 'wants and needs' of the seafarers. An effective method to achieve this would entail that several maritime administrations gather MET experts from various developing nations, so as to establish a form of conglomeration, which would promote cooperation and coordination links, in order to benefit one from the other. This could in turn eliminate potential mistakes and misunderstandings among developing nations in terms of maritime training. Eventually a common strategy would be modelled, having as primary target the compliance with the correct international standards. A typical example would be the change of the posture of the merchant fleet due to the introduction of sophisticated ship design technologies on board commercial ships. This improvement has resulted in the need for additional education and training requirements to support highly specialized maritime operations. Also, the development of advanced navigational technologies, professional transportation technologies, pollution prevention technologies and regulations were considered important for their inclusion into the seafarers' competency standards. This outcome led to the amendment of the STCW 78 at the Manila Conference in 2010 and this is precisely what needs to be highlighted by maritime administrations of developing nations.

The STCW is central to MET, while the International Convention for the Safety of Life at Sea, 1974 (SOLAS 1974), the International Convention for the Prevention of Pollution from Ships, 1973, as modified by the Protocol of 1978 (MARPOL 73/78) and the Maritime Labour Convention, 2006 (MLC 2006) of the International Labour Organization (ILO) regulations are the key elements, which regulate most of the changes to seafarers' qualification requirements. SOLAS 1974 and MARPOL 73/78 regulations tend to change more rapidly and frequently than the STCW. Inclusion of these requirements into the STCW takes time and this situation causes delay in reflecting current requirements into qualification standards (Ziarati et al. 2011). This is considered a hindrance for maritime administrations of developing nations and in order to overcome this delay it is important to establish a link between the STCW, SOLAS 1974, MARPOL 73/78 and the ILO working-groups (Ziarati et al. 2011). As far as the joint working-groups are concerned, not only the contribution of IMO, but of other significant organisations, such as EMSA, should also be taken into account (Ziarati et al. 2011). Maritime administrations of developing nations could form a type of partnership among training institutions and the industry partners with a view to establishing Maritime Certificates of Excellence", which are equal to European maritime postgraduate courses. This may well go further than the STCW requirements. Such cooperation would create good collaboration among the developing nations' maritime sectors as well as function as a cost-saving method. More importantly it would simultaneously create a good governance environment for shipping companies, so that they would extract good practices from each other.

3 Incentives for Shipping Companies and Promotion of Corporate Social Responsibility

Over the past 50 years, there has been a debate surrounding the growing interest in the CSR concept (Carroll and Shabana 2010). In the early 1990's, CSR was labeled as an umbrella term for a concept of operations that public and private companies use, to act in a responsible manner (Carroll 1991; Jones 1995). It is understood that through this term, companies are held accountable to the people and other entities that may be affected in the operation of their business. In retrospect, efforts to gather one single uniform definition is observed in relevant literatures, some of which indicate that CSR has a myriad of definitions. In a number of literatures, the many available definitions of CSR are stated as having five principal dimensions (Dahlsrud 2006). These five dimensions are the environmental dimension; the social dimension; the economic dimension; the stakeholder dimension; and the voluntariness dimension (Dahlsrud 2006). In the context of social responsibility, it is observed that the stakeholder dimension seems to establish a firm connection between a company's business operation and the society. Studies also indicate that the term stakeholder has an all-embracing meaning in so far as it covers the societal aspects more transparently than any of the aforementioned dimensions (Bantekas 2004; Coady and Strandberg 2012; Krakoff 2012). It is, therefore, safe to assert that the stakeholder dimension and social responsibility are connected at the grass-roots level. This connection is also supported by Freeman's traditional definition of stakeholder, i.e. "any group or individual who can affect or is affected by the achievement of the organization's objectives, which is centred on managing the stakeholders' interests, needs and viewpoints" (Freeman 1984). Although the definition is mainly organization-based, 20 years later, this definition is still considered to be more balanced and much broader than any other definitions (Friedman and Miles 2006). The words "can affect or is affected by", as incorporated in Freeman's definition, is deemed flexible and can be taken to include individuals outside the firm and to that extent, groups may consider themselves to be stakeholders of an organisation, without the firm considering them to be such. Today, through the stakeholder dimension, CSR has evolved and expanded. From business that is solely focused on land-based activities, to companies that are engaged in sea or ocean based activities, CSR is a topic that is discussed and debated in both public and private fora.

3.1 Shipping Companies and Organisational Behaviour

It was mentioned earlier that in shipping, good governance is linked to CSR. At the same time, it should be stressed that the element of CSR within the shipping activity does not have an abstract content. Shipping companies in the exercise of their rights and duties as active bodies of MG, touch upon CSR. In other words, shipping companies, as active bodies of the maritime governance framework, have a duty to observe and understand how business operations can impact stakeholders. These impacts are numerous and may occur due to a number of reasons. One such reason could be substandard shipping where the ship is substantially below the standards required by relevant conventions. Substandard shipping can also refer to a ship, whose crew is not in conformance with the international provisions of safe manning. Again, shipping companies should act diligently so as to prevent environmental damage through collision or discharge, and this duty to act diligently may also extend to end-of-life management considerations where a shipping company should ensure that vessels are recycled in an environmental friendly manner. This may also include proper inspection and removal of hazardous and high-risk materials before the vessel is on its end-of-life journey to the recycling facility, whether domestic or foreign. It is important to mention that these governance aspects are, to a great degree, covered by international law. International maritime law prescribes rules that need to be adhered to by companies and based on compliance factors, Brammal (2012) has divided shipping companies into three main categories:

A. Companies, which are merely compliant with international maritime legislation;
B. Companies, which exhibit compliance with legislation by reacting positively to initiatives in the marketplace to improve the environment; and
C. Companies, which independent of international maritime law through their own initiative act as leaders in setting standards for their environmental performance and so go beyond mere ordinary compliance (Brammal 2012).

Brammal (2012) also observes that the current position regarding CSR is lack-lustre due to the fact that only a few shipping companies are marginally compliant and on closer inspection, in fact, may not be compliant at all (Brammal 2012). However, what is important to recognize, is the existence of a doctrine that is 'strict compliance' in nature, which prescribes that socially responsible actions need to be taken into consideration by shipping companies. Although the term strict compliance is incongruous with the fundamental concept of CSR that is characterized by its voluntary feature, there are noteworthy efforts where voluntary CSR actions have been transposed into domestic law that is also considered as a strict compliance regulatory regime. India, for example, has enacted the Companies Act in 2013 (The Companies Act 2013). Schedule VII of the said act outlines a number of CSR activities that include *inter alia*, environmental sustainability and social business projects. Through this Act, there appears to be a substantial blurring of the voluntary element of CSR. Apparently, for domestic companies or subsidiaries of a foreign company established in India, CSR activities have become obligatory. But for other countries that do not have a domestic strict compliance scheme, it is up to the companies to develop a management framework that can balance business with social responsibility that is quite often reflected in the company's code of conduct. Since CSR is still acknowledged as a voluntary act, shipping companies are, therefore, not obliged to think beyond the business mind-set. A possible alternative to alter this mind-set could be to replace the term obligation with motivation, and look into methods to steer shipping companies towards CSR. For example, benefit schemes could be an incentive that can motivate and inspire shipping companies to be more CSR oriented. These benefit schemes or incentive schemes have a high probability of encouraging shipping companies to go beyond standard compliance of environmental behaviour and set an example for other companies engaged in the same business to re-think and revisit their operational approaches. It is therefore, submitted that incentive schemes can act as a motivation for shipping companies in striving for best performance, whether in the environmental domain or societal domain.

A research project was conducted to examine the relationship between CSR and organisational performance in the container shipping industry (Lu et al. 2009). The researchers selected three critical CSR attributes and examined the above-mentioned relationship in container shipping in Taiwan through a factor analysis methodology. It comprised of community involvement and environment, disclosure and employee and consumer interest. According to the researchers, the methodology was consistent with principles outlined in ISO 26000, which is said to "provide guidance rather than requirements, so it cannot be certified to, unlike some other well-known ISO standards" (Discovering ISO 26000 2014). In the end, it would assist in clarifying the notion of CSR and subsequently help businesses and organisations in translating principles into effective actions and sharing best practices relating to social responsibility, globally (Discovering ISO 26000 2014). It should be noted that all types of organisations regardless of activity, size or location could apply ISO 26000.

3.2 *Incentives as Catalysts*

In the shipping industry, companies are usually motivated by an urge to comply with both existing regulations and anticipated future regulations (Kunnaala et al. 2013). For shipping companies, it is not only about adhering to international standards; it is also about enhancing the company's brand image (Dahalan et al. 2012). After all, shipping companies are no different from any other business entity. In the business world, clients are drawn towards companies that have a strong reputation (Caruana and Chircop 2000; Leuthesser and Kohli 1997). As such, ensuring that the company has always maintained international regulations and standards on construction standards, navigational rules and standards of crew competence, is integral to a company's reputation. For example, a client is more likely to enter into a contract of sale with a company that does not have a history of practicing substandard shipping and has not contravened any of the provisions encapsulated in chapter 3 of IMO Resolution A. 1052 (27) on Port State Control. If the company can demonstrate stakeholder involvement in its code of conduct, it projects a more positive image to clients. Being committed to addressing social and environmental concerns by adhering to the principles outlined in ISO 26000 will undoubtedly strengthen the company's portfolio. This can be seen as a competitive advantage for shipping companies whereby this additional attribute will allow a certain company to outperform its competitors and attract more clientele. In general, CSR is acknowledged as providing real business benefits by attracting both customers and high-quality employees (Kunnaala et al. 2013). The basic advantage reaped by shipping companies via applying CSR guidelines can be surmised as being guided by the intention to make profit. However, in order to motivate shipping companies to be more active and engaged in CSR matters, finding the appropriate guidance on CSR or disseminating the knowledge of CSR is not the be all and end all. Since CSR is based on voluntariness, there needs to be a catalyst that can boost a company's self-initiative on the subject matter. It is, therefore, submitted that reward schemes or incentive schemes may be an appropriate tool that can motivate a shipping company in the desired direction.

One of the issues dealt with by the project Competitive Advantage by Safety (CAFE) is whether there are incentives, which make shipping companies implement programmes deliberately intended to induce or encourage specific actions compliant with CSR (Kunnaala et al. 2013). The project revealed an emphasis on the impact of gaining a better reputation, which is one of the key elements to engage in CSR activities in the first place. But of course, CSR should be taken into account in terms of striking a balance between financial, social and environmental factors. Being socially and environmentally responsible to the stakeholders can have positive economic effects for a company through improvement of its reputation and brand. CSR makes a company attractive as an employer and strengthens the loyalty of the employees (Kunnaala et al. 2013). In this respect, maritime sector operators are similar to brand owners in any other industry sectors. They have a need to protect their brand image by demonstrating to multiple stakeholders that their ships and services are safe and environmentally sound (Kunnaala et al. 2013). Even though shipping companies do not necessarily face this kind of immediate publicity and consumer pressure issues, their customers, however, quite possibly do and in that case these customers may seek to manage the risks to their own reputation by selecting carriers, which are verifiably engaged in CSR (Neef 2012).

A typical example, according to the above rationale, may be extracted from the tanker industry. A shipping company, which has formulated and implemented a strategy paying special attention to CSR practices, leads to a number of benefits, which function, equally, as incentives (Pike et al. 2011). Being a pioneer by self-complying to rules and practices not incorporated yet in legal instruments of the international community, causes the market to react in the following manner. Oil producers are eager to ensure, not only the safe carriage of the toxic cargo, but also environmental protection, even by paying a higher freight. Oil majors are keen to protect an impeccable safety record, especially when the carriage routes pass through environmentally protected areas, something which is achieved by engaging reputable shipping companies, widely recognized for their environmental awareness. Naturally, the promotion of strong relationships with those reputable shipping companies would be achieved at the expense of a higher freight, demanded by the latter. Furthermore, having a zero accident record in oil carriage triggers insurance premium decrease, an incontrovertible benefit for the shipping company. More importantly, the socially and environmentally responsible shipping companies have a preferential treatment by the governmental authorities in the ports of call, which is totally justifiable on the basis that it is a positive reaction to the carriers that pay special attention to the quality of the environment of the visiting state. Finally, the consumers enjoy the benefit of a lower price in the fuel, since the avoidance of an accident does not disturb the market balance relating to the price formation.

Moreover, shipping companies, which promote the notion of sustainability in a free market, are clearly aware of the fact that documented and monitored social, environmental and economic impacts of their operations provide more concrete and predictable corporate results for their stakeholders (Fafaliou et al. 2006). The advantages of engaging in CSR can extend to two areas, the former is monetary and the latter is non-monetary. Companies engage in CSR activities, in order to avoid exposure to unethical business practices, poor performance or potential negative impacts on local communities etc. (Kunnaala et al. 2013). Companies may also seek to achieve competitive advantage by going beyond regulations, implementing management systems, working proactively or strengthening employee pride and loyalty, which import a sense of cohesion and symmetry in the functions of the organisational framework (Poulovassilis and Meidanis 2013). For some sectors, the pressure of external stakeholders, such as Non Governmental Organizations (NGOs), or the potential of new regulatory measures, may work as incentives to engage in CSR. Whether positive incentive or negative incentive, it depends on the end-result and the way it is perceived by the shipping company in context. This leads to the significant question of the type and nature of incentive schemes that may be implemented by shipping companies, so as to externalize that they are acting in socially/environmentally responsible manner.

3.3 Examination of Selected Globally Operating Incentives

Proactive measures based on incentive schemes have recently been introduced to promote a higher level of governance in ship management and operation. The original and the new institutional economics supplement an interesting aspect of the governance structure and the institutional environment surrounding these phenomena of shipping transactions (Williamson 2000; Shinohara 2005). The abstractions of bounded rationality and opportunism in institutional economics are also applicable to the shipping activity (Shinohara 2005). Incentive schemes, in this context, can be seen as agents of change. It is correct to state that incentive schemes are new propelling measures, which takes the term Quality Shipping to a higher plateau (Haralambides 1998). They can be classified as proactive measures, in contrast with rules and penalties that, in most cases, are implemented after a serious maritime incident has happened (Shinohara 2005). Incentive schemes may be founded on rewarding systems available to ship owners, where reduction of taxes, port dues and other charges are given to ships that have met the standard criteria for the quality of their hardware and/or software; that is, the ship and/or the work of its crew and the ship manager ashore. It is a general perception that the level of the standard criteria set by the incentive schemes, are higher than the standards set by respective legislation, hence, the implementation of the rewarding system and the basis of its appeal. From a general assessment, there are four categories of incentive schemes operating worldwide:

(1) Multinational incentives based on a quality certificate;
(2) Mitigation of the burden of Port State Control (PSC) for quality ships;
(3) Reduction of port dues for ships that have passed the hardware criteria and the Bonus/Malus system; and
(4) The Green Passport of the IMO based on EMSA 2005 (Shinohara 2005).

The first incentive scheme originated in Rotterdam in 1992, when the Ministry of Transport and Water Management of the Netherlands and the Port of Rotterdam started discussions on measures to prevent water quality deterioration, as well as accidents caused at and around the world's largest port (Shinohara 2005; "Sustainable Initiatives in the Port of Rotterdam" Incentive Scheme 2014). This is known as the Green Award incentive scheme, the idea of which was to implement a scheme to encourage shipping companies rather than restricting them with excessive pressure. This idea was finally materialized by incorporating the Green Award Foundation, which is a neutral, independent foundation, established in 1994 in the initiative of the Rotterdam Municipal Port Management and the Dutch Ministry of Transport (Green Award Foundation 1994; Stanbrook 2013). The Green Award Foundation represents the first of the four different types of incentive schemes, i.e. multinational incentives based on a quality certificate. The Green Award Foundation is said to ensure the provision of incentive premiums at various ports in the world as regards to the ships that have passed. This is initiated by the owner's voluntary application with preconditions of certain criteria of management quality on board and ashore (Shinohara

2005). In addition, the Green Award incentive scheme may be seen as a separate regime from flag-state or port-state inspection, which controls the compliance of ships in terms of existing regulations. The Green Award proceeds with an objective of creating a market preference for quality tonnage resulting in fewer incidents and accidents, which can jeopardize the marine environment (Green Award Foundation 1994). The Green Award Foundation that became independent in 2000, i.e. a non-governmental and a non-profit organisation, issues a certificate to the ships and their owners that have passed an inspection and an audit, respectively. The ports and private service providers at ports, which are in support of the Green Award scheme, provide an incentive benefit to the ship owner that has obtained that certificate when the ship calls at one of the enlisted ports (Shinohara 2005). Currently, there are 30 Green Award Ports and 21 Other Green Award Incentive Providers that provide numerous rewards (Green Award Foundation 1994). The majority of these Green Award Incentive Providers are from EU countries whereby Netherlands is marked as the country that provides the highest number of awards. The criteria are multifarious and depend on individual ports. It is important to note that India, as a developing nation, has taken a leading role as an Other Green Award Incentive Provider whereby Karishma Marine Solutions Pvt. Ltd. (KARCO) has taken a crucial step in ensuring its co-operation with its international counterparts. This is a best practice that demonstrates good governance. The benefit provided by KARCO is an entitlement to an additional 6% discount on KARCO safety videos. However, the Kitakyushu Seaport and Airport Bureau of Japan is the only Green Award Port, which provides the benefit of a 10% reduction on port dues to LNG Carriers (Green Award Foundation 1994).

The second incentive, i.e. mitigation of the burden of PSC for quality ships, is manifest in the United States of America as Quality Shipping for the 21st Century (Qualship21) that is provided by the US Coast Guard (USCG). The USCG efforts to eliminate substandard shipping are focused on improving methods to identify poor-quality vessels. According to the USCG Marine Safety Manual, a vessel is regarded as substandard if the hull, machinery or equipment, such as lifesaving, fire-fighting and pollution prevention equipment, are substantially below the standards required by the laws of the US or relevant Conventions. Some incentives are, therefore, provided for the benefit of vessels, which are in compliance with the existing national and international requirements. For example, the submission to Qualship 21 in the case of the US PSC permits *inter alia*, name recognition and reduction of PSC examination frequency (Christodoulou-Varotsi 2009; Qualship 21 – Frequently Asked Questions). As much benefit as Qualship 21 is said to provide, it simultaneously incorporates rules for revocation of Qualship 21 title, if the vessel in question is guilty of a marine violation, if it has "more than one paid Notice of Violation case (tickets), or a reportable marine casualty that meets the definition of a serious marine incident or major marine casualty in US waters (Qualship21). Similar to the eligibility criteria are the criteria of crewmember or passenger injuries, which are not related to any other serious marine incident or major marine casualty, and will not cause the vessel's eligibility to be revoked, thus operating as an exception to the criteria for revocation (USCG). In this context, a marine violation is any violation of law, regulation or order, which is enforced by the USCG and results in a final assessed monetary civil penalty by a hearing officer or a judgement by the US attorney in criminal proceedings (USCG). Moreover, an important ground for revocation also entails that the vessel in question is found with serious deficiencies (i.e. such that they may warrant the detention of the vessel), which is not being monitored by the vessel's flag administration or a Recognized Organization acting on behalf of the flag administration, or the vessel fails to report a hazardous condition prior to arrival (USCG). An exception has also been laid down against this condition, if the vessel is within the time limits imposed by the flag administration or Recognized Organization to correct deficiencies, the vessel will not lose eligibility for incentives (USCG). It should be noted that the "Qualship 21 program ended in 2015 with an enrolment of 1,433 vessels", and these enrolled vessels "will remain enrolled until their Qualship 21 certificates expire" (Department of Homeland Security 2015).

The third incentive scheme relates to reduction of port dues for ships that have passed the hardware criteria and was basically given to tankers with segregated ballast tanks or a double-hull structure (Shinohara 2005). National governments or port managers incorporated a form of incentive provision by reducing port dues on the condition that a ship had a specific type of structure in order to reduce the risk of maritime environmental pollution (Shinohara 2005). At the EU level, there exists a generic incentive, which differs in content and conditions. Sweden applies a Bonus/Malus system, under which harbour and fairway dues are reduced based on the ship-generated emissions of NOx and SOx (EMSA 2005). The Bonus/Malus certificate is renewed every 3 years (EMSA 2005). However, the philosophy of differentiated dues does not have universal acceptance (EMSA 2005). The Australian Marine Environmental Protection Association (AUSMEPA), for example, stated that "Australian ports have consistently rejected the concept of reduced port fees for quality and environmentally conscious ships . . . their view being that if port fees are discounted for some ships other ships will need to pay higher fees than the service provided is worth" (EMSA 2005). Another incentive that is collateral to the NOx and SOx emissions is the Blue Angel. The Blue Angel label refers to the certification and verification aspects of the International Safety Management Code and Guidelines on Implementation of the Code 2014 (ISM Code) (EMSA 2005). The proof of quality management is exemplified via retaining the ISM Certificate. According to EMSA 2005, for a Blue Angel ship, the previous SOx emissions must have been reduced by at least 50% and the NOx emissions by 20% (obligatory) or SOx emissions have been reduced by 85% and NOx emissions by more than 50% (optional). Despite being uncomplicated and transparent, this system was observed to have a very low acceptance in the shipping industry and, at the time of the report, there was only one shipping line that had vessels certified under the Blue Angel scheme (EMSA 2005).

Finally, the Green Passport scheme was accepted by IMO to ensure that the ship recycling is carried out in an environmentally friendly manner. The IMO adopted Guidelines on Ship Recycling in 2003, which introduced the Green Passport (Guide for the Class Notation: Green Passport 2011). The Green Passport, according to EMSA 2005, "is a document that contains guidelines and details of all potentially hazardous and high-risk materials on board a vessel". Central to the implementation scheme of the Hong Kong International Convention for the Safe and Environmentally Sound Recycling of Ships 2009 (Ship Recycling Convention), is the development and maintenance of a document referred to as the Inventory of Hazardous Materials (IHM), which was previously known as the Green Passport in IMO Resolution A. 962(23) (Guide for the Class Notation: Green Passport 2011). The Inventory is ship-specific and comprises the whole life of the ship, from construction throughout the ship's operating life to preparation for scrapping at the end of the ship's useful life. It should be noted that the IHM and Green Passport mainly differ in that IHM requires a more detailed and reasonably accurate account of the listed hazardous substances in the inventory booklet and sampling has to be carried out for existing ships (Guide for the Class Notation: Green Passport 2011). The Green Passport does not provide any monetary benefits like the other incentive schemes and its objective is to promote the Ship Recycling Convention. The objective is rational in so far as it assists prevention, reduction, minimization and, to the extent practicable, elimination of accidents, injuries and other adverse effects on human health and the environment caused by ship recycling, and enhancement of ship safety, protection of human health and the environment throughout a ship's operating life. More specifically, the Green Passport scheme stipulates that the document shall accompany the ship throughout its entire operating life. Every owner of the vessel is obliged to maintain the Green Passport and to accurately update it to reflect any relevant design and equipment changes. At the end of the vessel's life, the final owner would be expected to present it to the recycling facility (EMSA 2005).

3.4 *Criteria of Achieving Incentives and Corporate Social Responsibility: The Implied Connection*

Having examined the content of the four globally operating incentive schemes, it is now important to answer the question: how do incentive schemes externalize that those companies have acted in an environmentally and socially responsible manner? To answer this question, one must commence by distinguishing the formal (governmental) and informal or private (non-governmental) categories of the given schemes (Shinohara 2005). Qualship 21 of the USCG and the schemes of Norway, Hamburg and other ports are publicly operated and thus fall within the formal category. The incentives of the formal category can be extracted from the traditional existing regulations, yet they aim at higher standards of quality in exchange for benefits rather than imposition of penalties. The mitigation of PSC examination, as embedded in the Qualship 21 scheme, and the reduction of port dues by various port authorities are formal and regulatory and can be further categorized under the heading of Institutional Environment (Shinohara 2005). In this context, Institutional Environment is termed as a regulator of governance whereby the factors are made up of the measures taken by international organisations and national governments, changes in laws and standards, societal responses to maritime accidents, effects of cooperative campaigns, mass media and their influence, etc. (Shinohara 2005). In contrast, the Green Award, which is administered by the Green Award Foundation, is founded on a private basis by voluntary registration of ships by their respective owners. It is noteworthy that the Green Award scheme is also based on voluntary agreements with ports and maritime service providers as incentive providers. The informal incentives are clearly operated entirely by private organisations. They set out their own international standards regarding ship structure, conditions and quality of ship management. This informal category invites ports and maritime service providers to support the scheme by providing incentives to the owners of ships that have met certain criteria (Shinohara 2005). While the formal category tends to have a hard law flavour, the informal category, based on voluntary registration, can be seen to embody the soft law character. Then again, whatever the traits may be, governments, national or local, can improvise their own incentive scheme in any form and within their own capacity (Shinohara 2005). They need to ensure that the benefits under the formal category are parallel to the standards or pre-conditions of the respective incentive. In retrospect, the analysis of the Green Award incentive scheme consists a vast number of benefits furnished by Ports and Other Incentive Providers (Green Award Foundation 1994). However, this category is still informal and lacks the power of enforcement.

So, whether it is a formal or informal arrangement, or whether it is a reduction in port fees or a reduction in the number of PSC examination, if one focuses on the conditions that have been met by the ship owners, rather than the reward that has been obtained by them, it will be easy to assess how incentive schemes are an indicator that shipping companies are performing in a responsible manner. For example, the advantages sought by the incentive providers of the Green Award, i.e. "increase of quality ships; reduced risk (safety and environment); tool to address air quality issues, tool to address CSR policy; improvement of environmental awareness of administrators and port authorities; increase of efficiency in ship/shore interface; shorter visiting period of ship to port; and enhancement of positive image"—mostly yield positive outcomes for stakeholders that may be affected in the operational procedure of shipping business (Green Award Foundation 1994). These are the advantages that are explicit in the official homepage of the Green Award. It is therefore clear that the advantages that the incentive providers of the Green Award receive are not 'personal gain' in nature and can be deduced as generous acts to promote extra clean and extra safe shipping practices. Again, by opening the award scheme to dry bulk carriers, oil tankers, chemical tankers, LNG, LPG, container carriers and inland navigational vessels—the incentive providers of the Green Award ensure that the certified shipping companies have acted in a responsible manner towards the society and environment. The procedure carried out by the Bureau Green Award prior to certification broadly focuses on crew, operational, environmental and managerial elements—criteria, which can be portrayed as a test of good governance. In short, the Green Award, including the aforementioned incentive schemes, are helping shipping companies calibrate good governance strategies and deepening their engagement in CSR activities. For shipping companies, the achievement is more than just the incentive 'monetary or non-monetary' reward. Advertising these incentive-awards on the company's homepage may serve as a good marketing strategy so that they can secure more clients, build a strong network with other companies and expand their business. In return, the formal or informal organisations confirm through audits and certificate-grants that companies have achieved the required objectives. Whether it is elimination of substandard shipping in accordance with Qualship 21 or environmental awareness of administrators or port authorities pursuant to the Green Award, the objectives of the discussed incentive schemes are a positive approach to reduce the detrimental effects of shipping on stakeholders. These objectives fit well within the ambit of the five principal dimensions as classified by Dahlsrud (2006). Again, from a narrow perspective, the goals of the aforementioned incentive schemes are a way to address the interests, needs and viewpoints of others who can be or are affected by the company's business operation. That is how Freeman (1984) has defined "stakeholder", and as indicated by Dahlsrud (2006), "stakeholder" is one of the five dimensions of CSR. Therefore, it is submitted that under the guise of incentive schemes both formal and informal organisations are assisting shipping companies to be more socially and environmentally responsible, which is in the core of the discussion of CSR. CSR is promoted through the grant of incentive-certificates and rewards and is apparently implied in the underlying objective of these individual incentive schemes.

4 Concluding Remarks

The consolidated definition of governance as provided by the UN System Task Team in 2012 focuses on the powers exercised by the political and administrative authorities to administer and regulate a country's overall affairs. At the same time, researchers and representatives of the UN have marked good governance as an indicator that helps comprehend whether the exercise of political and administrative authority has helped achieve important goals. In other words, good governance can be hypothesized as being a tool to measure the operational effectiveness and efficiency of both public and private institutions. In the corporate field, good governance is a well-established theory whereby CSR is considered to be a significant aspect of an organisation's governance and risk management process.

MG is a generic term that could be used to refer to corporate governance in the maritime sector. In this context, the word "maritime" in the term MG is used to compartmentalize shipping companies into a single and strict business-category while keeping the features of the traditional concept of corporate governance intact. Corporate governance inevitably applies to shipping companies and arguments in favour of this form of application can be forwarded based on the fact that shipping companies, similar to other commercial entities, are also corporate bodies with a corporate agenda. In the maritime field, these corporate bodies with a corporate agenda that are engaged in shipping-business are responsible for registering their vessels with a certain jurisdiction whose flag they are entitled to fly in all sea-going commercial activities. From a general perspective, the flag marks the legal jurisdiction, which the vessel is subject to, and maritime administrations exercise political and administrative authority over flag administrations to ensure that they meet domestic and international standards concerning safety and security. In other words, maritime administrations of all nations, whether developed or developing, strive to be good stewards of governance and help ensure that flag administrations are conducting business in a responsible manner. A practical way of ensuring that shipping companies reflect accountability in their business is Flag State Control—a mechanism through which maritime administrations ensure a company's compliance with international regulations and standards concerning shipping. This control exercised by maritime administrations can be seen as a reflection of how well MG functions in a particular nation.

Karim (2014) has observed significant shortcomings of MG in developing states and has gone as far as to state that, "one of the main challenges for developing countries is the implementation of IMO conventions … Many States consider it contrary to their sovereignty to apply an international convention directly in the domestic sphere" (Karim 2014). The author also highlights that the "north-south" divide continues to be a dominating factor in the IMO discourse and identifies this divide as a important factor in the international law-making process (Karim 2014). In addition, the author also notes that the 48 nations that comprise the Least Developed countries do not work together in IMO negotiations pertaining to international shipping and climate change (Karim 2014). Although many of the shortcomings identified in the work of Karim (2014) are based on work-experience and research papers, e.g. Beckman (2006) and Alam (2006), there is no concrete evidence that IMO conventions are in any way biased broadly owing to the fact that governments of developing nations are at liberty to structure and implement domestic policies in any manner they deem fit. It is more to do with the political will of the elected government and the intention to govern their maritime sector to promote good governance and ensure that companies are conducting their business in a responsible corporate and social manner. As discussed in s. 2.1 of this chapter on "Governance and ship port interface", developing nations are also a part of PSC MoUs that demonstrate the intention of the government to help shipping companies meet international obligations. However, developing nations, according to Villanueva (2004), require more technical and financial resources. To address this drawback, IMO has an extensive technical co-operation program, which concentrates on improving the ability of developing countries. Assistance is, therefore, readily available as opposed to capacity, which is an area that requires self-development. As such, implementation of control mechanisms to improve good MG rests on individual developing nations.

While maritime administrations are required to follow the local laws and applicable conventions, it seems that some developing countries do not always comply with regulations. For example, in 2008, "Emery Transnational, a former subsidiary of Con-way Inc. based in the Philippines, allegedly made $244,000 in improper payments to officials at the Philippines Bureau of Customs and the Philippines Economic Zone area. This payment total allegedly consisted of hundreds of small cash payments designed to induce officials to violate customs regulations, settle customs disputes, and reduce or not enforce legitimate fines" (Sherman and Sterling 2008). However, on a more positive note, the Philippines has been considered eligible for entry into the Qualship21 Program in 2016, which can be marked as a significant improvement.

IMO observes that developing nations often face difficulties in strengthening regulations related to Flag State Implementation (FSI) (IMO 2008). Strengthening regulations on FSI has been a target of IMO, since it could help maritime administrations of developing nations to promote and maintain an improved governance system. IMO is also of the opinion that international treaties, which embody rules and standards on proactive safety, should be developed "*...in order to prevent accidents at sea, and not in response to them*" (IMO 2008). While these policies ensure that "*...flag and port States, shipowners, managers, shipbuilders, equipment manufacturers, training institutes and other stakeholders develop their capacities and exert their responsibility to the fullest*" (IMO 2008), it is observed that the MG system can be improved in developing nations through the four incentive schemes discussed earlier. Because parallel to the enforcement mechanisms adopted by maritime administrations, shipping companies also need to be made aware of the fact that good MG is a shared responsibility. Furthermore, shared responsibility has already been integrated in the notable incentive schemes established by developed countries. While the main business benefits associated with the implementation of CSR can be derived from several theoretical and empirical studies (Hopkins 2004; Grewal and Darlow 2007), one of the main targets is to improve stakeholder communication and enhance the company's image and reputation. Incentive schemes can be considered as a unique opportunity to: (1) reap more benefits in different ports around the world; and (2) improve the company's brand image and attract more clients.

In this context, maritime administrations of developing nations can also make an effort to develop incentive schemes for shipping companies registered under their flag and foreign flags. The Swedish Bonus/Malus system can be taken as a positive development that promotes good MG. The "Environmental Differentiated Fairway dues" is mainly based on an agreement between the Swedish Shipowner's Association, the Swedish Port and Stevedore Association and the Swedish Maritime Administration. The involvement of the Swedish Maritime Administration in this incentive scheme exemplifies a form of good practice that can act as a road map. Incentive schemes, as such, can be used as a tool for ensuring that shipping companies operate in a socially-environmentally responsible manner by making sure that the conditions of the incentives are well maintained. At the same time the shipping companies can obtain extra advantages from being well maintained and retaining their social license to operate. The advantages of incentive schemes are, to that extent, multifarious—thus the basis of their appeal.

References

"Sustainable Initiatives in the Port of Rotterdam" Incentive Scheme. (2014). http://www.deltalinqs.nl/uploadfiles/file/20140501_ENG_Stimuleringsregeling%20Duurzame%20initiatieven%20in%20de%20Rotterdamse%20haven%20-%20versie%20april%202014.pdf. Accessed 5.11.2016.

Agripino de Castro Junior, O. (2009). Brazilian maritime law: a general overview. *3 degree Quadrimestre, 14*(3), 255–279.

Alam, Z. (2006). *IMO conventions and their implementation*. Paper presented at the East Asian Seas Congress, Haikou City, Hainan Province, PR China (12–16 December 2006).

Bantekas, I. (2004). Corporate social responsibility in international law. *Boston University International Law Journal, 22*, 309–311.

Beckman, R. (2006). *Ratification and implementation of IMO conventions in the East Asian Seas region*. Paper presented at the East Asian Seas Congress, Haikou City, Hainan Province, PR China (12–16 December 2006).

Bharej, K. (2014). Corporate social responsibility and good governance. *International Journal of Research, 1*(5).

Bigg, T., & Ward, H. (2004). *Linking corporate social responsibility, good governance and corporate accountability through dialogue*. Discussion Paper, International Institute for Environment and Development, London.

Bloor, M., Datta, R., Gilinskiy, Y., & Horlick-Jones, T. (2006). Unicorn among the cedars: on the possibility of effective "Smart Regulation" of the globalized shipping industry. *Social & Legal Studies, 15*, 534–551.

Bloor, M., Sampson, H., Baker, S., Walters, D., Dahlgren, K., Wadsworth, E., et al. (2013). Room for manoeuvre? Regulatory compliance in the global shipping industry. *Social & Legal Studies, 22*, 171–189.

Brammal, R. (2012). *How green are shipping companies?* Research and Enterprise Working Paper Series. Working Paper Number XII. Southampton Solent University, Faculty of Business, Sport and Enterprise.

Brown Weiss, E., & Sornarajah, A. (2009, May). *Good governance*. Max Planck Encyclopedia of Public International Law. http://opil.ouplaw.com/home/EPIL. Accessed 01.05.2016.

Carroll, A. B. (1991). The pyramid of corporate social responsibility: Toward the moral management of organizational stakeholders. *Business Horizons, 34*(4), 39–48.

Carroll, A. B., & Shabana, M. K. (2010). The business case for corporate social responsibility: a review of concepts, research and practice. *International Journal of Management Reviews* (pp. 85–105). Blackwell Publishing Ltd and British Academy of Management.

Caruana, A., & Chircop, S. (2000). Measuring corporate reputation: A case example. *Corporate Reputation Review, 3*(1), 43–57.

Christodoulou-Varotsi, I. (2009). *Maritime safety law and policies of the European Union and the United States of America: Antagonism or synergy?* Berlin, Heidelberg: Springer-Verlag.

ClassNK. (2014). *Port State Control Annual Report*. http://www.classnk.or.jp/hp/pdf/publications/Publications_image/PSC13E.pdf. Accessed 15.02.2015.

Coady, L., & Strandberg, C. (2012). *Corporate social responsibility and the shipping industry: a global perspective* (p. 1). A paper prepared for the Nippon Foundation, April. http://corostrandberg.com/wp-content/uploads/2012/10/DRAFT_Key-CSR-Components-Shipping-Industry_Apr2012.pdf. Accessed 22.11.2016.

Dahalan, W. S. A. W., Zainol, Z. A., Yaa'kub, N. I., & Kassim, N. M. (2012). Corporate social responsibility (CSR) from shipping companies in the straits of Malacca and Singapore. *International Journal of Business and Society, 13*(2), 197–208.

Dahlsrud, A. (2006). How corporate social responsibility is defined: an analysis of 37 definitions. *Corporate Social Responsibility and Environmental Management, 15*(1), 1–13.

Department of Homeland Security. (2015). *Port State Control in the United States. 2015 Annual Report*. https://www.uscg.mil/hq/cgcvc/cvc2/psc/annual_report/annualrpt15.pdf. Accessed 23.11.2016.

Department of Parliamentary Services. (2006). *Corporate responsibility: managing risk and creating value*. Parliamentary Joint Committee on Corporations and Financial Services, Senate Printing Unit, Australia.

Discovering ISO 26000. (2014). *Guidance on social responsibility*. Retrieved from the World Wide Web, http://www.iso.org/iso/discovering_iso_26000.pdf. Accessed 22.03.2015.

Dixit, A. K. (2008). Economic governance. In S. N. Durlauf & L. E. Blume (Eds.), *The new Palgrave dictionary of economics* (2nd ed.). New York: Palgrave MacMillan.

European Maritime Safety Agency (EMSA). (2005). *Study on ships producing reduced quantities of ships generated waste – Present situation and future opportunities to encourage the development of cleaner ships*. EMSA/OP/05/05. file:///Users/tafsir/Downloads/prf-emsa-final-report_rev10-07%20(1).pdf. Accessed 22.03.2015.

Fafaliou, I., Lekakou, M., & Theotokas, I. (2006). Is the European shipping industry aware of corporate social responsibility? The case of the Greek-owned short sea shipping companies. *Marine Policy, 30*, 412–419.

Fernando, A. C. (2009). *Corporate governance: Principles, policies and practices*. India: Dorling Kindersley.

Fidrmuc, J., Goergen, M., & Renneboog, L. (2006). Insider trading, news releases and ownership concentration. *Journal of Finance, 61*(6), 2931–2973.

Freeman, R. E. (1984). *Strategic management: a stakeholder approach*. Boston, MA: Pitman.

Friedman, A. L., & Miles, S. (2006). *Stakeholders: theory and practice*. Oxford: Oxford University Press.

Goergen, M., Brewster, C., & Wood, G. (2012). Varieties of capitalism and investments in human capital. *Wilkinson Industrial Relations: A Journal of Economy and Society, 51*(1), 501–527.

Green Award Foundation. (1994). http://www.greenaward.org/26-foundation.html. Accessed 22.03.2015.

Grewal, D., & Darlow, N. J. (2007). The business paradigm for corporate social reporting in the context of Australian seaports. *Maritime Economics & Logistics, 9*, 172–192.

Guide for the Class Notation Green Passport. (2011). *Consolidated Version 2014*, American Bureau of Shipping. https://www.eagle.org/eagleExternalPortalWEB/ShowProperty/BEA%20Repository/Rules&Guides/Current/158_GreenPassport/GreenPassportGuide. Accessed 23.11.2016.

Haralambides, H. (Ed.). (1998). *Quality shipping: Market mechanism for safer shipping and cleaner oceans*. Rotterdam: Erasmus Publishing.

Hawkes, K. (1989). *Maritime security*. Maryland: Cornell Maritime Press.

Hopkins, M. (2004). *Corporate social responsibility: an issues paper*. Policy Integration Department, World Commission on the Social Dimension of Globalization. International Labour Office. Working Paper No. 27. International Labour Organization, Geneva.

Hughes, O. E. (1998). *Public management and administration* (2nd ed.). New York: Palgrave Macmillan.

Hughes, O. E. (2003). *Public administration and administration*. New York: Palgrave Macmillan.

International Convention on Standards of Training, Certification and Watchkeeping for Seafarers 1978, International Maritime Organization. Adoption 7 July 1978, Entry into force: 28 April 1984; Major revisions in 1995 and 2010.

International Maritime Organization. (2008). *Functions and current activities of IMO and its achievements covering technical fields of shipping engaged in international trade*. Contribution of the International Maritime Organization (IMO) to the Secretary-General's Report on Oceans and the Law of the Sea, 2008: Maritime Safety and Security.

International Ship and Port Facility Security Code and SOLAS Amendments 2002. http://www.ubak.gov.tr/BLSM_WIYS/DISGM/tr/HTML/20130304_142647_66968_1_67502.pdf. Accessed 16.02.2015.

Jesus, J. L. (2003). Protection of foreign ships against piracy and terrorism at sea: legal aspects. *International Journal of Marine and Coastal Law, 18*(3), 387.

Jones, T. M. (1995). Instrumental stakeholder theory: a synthesis of ethics. *The Academy of Management Review, 20*(2).

Karim, Md. S. (2014). *Prevention of pollution of the marine environment from vessels* (pp. 14–136). Springer.
Krakoff, S. (2012). Planetarian identity formation and the relocalization of environmental law. *Florida Law Review, 64*(1).
Kunnaala, V., Rasi, M., & Storgård, J. (2013). *Corporate social responsibility in shipping: views of Baltic Sea shipping companies on benefits of responsibility*. Project Competitive Advantage by Safety - CAFE, A70, Publications of the Centre for Maritime Studies, University of Turku.
Leuthesser, L., & Kohli, C. (1997). Corporate identity: the role of mission statements. *Business Horizons, 40*, 59–66.
Lewarn, B. (2002). Maritime education and training – The future is now! *IAMU Journal, 2*(1), 19–24.
Lu, C.-S., Lin, C.-C., & Tu, C.-J. (2009). Corporate social responsibility and organisational performance in container shipping. *International Journal of Logistics Research and Applications, 12*(2), 119–132.
Mat Salleh, N. (2006). *Post 9/11 maritime security measures: global maritime security versus facilitation of global maritime trade*. World Maritime University Dissertations. Paper 98.
Neef, D. (2012). *Corporate social responsibility comes to maritime shipping*. Safety4Sea. http://www.safety4sea.com/corporate-social-responsibility-comes-to-maritime-shipping/analysis-6-25. Accessed 22.03.2015.
OECD Guidelines for Multinational Enterprises. (1976). *Policy Brief*. http://www.oecd.org/investment/mne/1903291.pdf. Accessed 20.11.2016.
Paris MOU. (2014). *Annual Report 2013*. https://www.parismou.org/sites/default/files/Paris%20MoU%20Annual%20Report%202013%20revised_1.pdf. Accessed 31.03.2015.
Pfiffner, J. P. (2004). Traditional public administration versus the new public management: accountability versus efficiency. In A. Benz, H. Siedentopf, & K. P. Sommermann (Eds.), *Institutionenbildung in Regierung und Verwaltung: Festschrift fur Klaus Konig* (pp. 443–454). Berlin, Germany: Duncker & Humbolt.
Pike, K., Butt, N., Johnson, D., & Walmsley, S. (2011). *Global sustainable shipping: audit and overview* (pp. 6–7). A Report for WWF.
Poulovassilis, A., & Meidanis, S. (2013). *Sustainability of shipping – Addressing corporate social responsibility through management systems*. http://www.commonlawgic.org/media/files/imo-over-mbm/folders/Sustainability-of-Shipping.pdf. Accessed 22.03.2015.
PwC Survey 2010. *Shipping crew performance management systems*. www.pwc.gr. Accessed 28.02.2015.
Qualship 21 – Frequently Asked Questions. http://www.ecmeurope.net/wp-content/uploads/2014/08/QUALSHIP-21-FAQ-07.31.14.pdf. Accessed 23.11.2016.
Rhodes, R. A. W. (2000). Governance and public administration. In J. Pierre (Ed.), *Debating governance* (pp. 54–90). Oxford: Oxford University Press.
Rhodes, R. A. W. (2012). Waves of governance. In D. Levi-Faur (Ed.), *Oxford handbook of governance*. Oxford: Oxford University Press.
Roe, M. (2012). *Shipping governance and policy-making*. London: Springer.
Sherman & Sterling. (2008). *SEC v. Con-way Inc.* http://fcpa.shearman.com/?s=matter&mode=form&id=167. Accessed 25.11.2016.
Shie, T. R. (2004). *Port in a storm? The nexus between counterterrorism, counterproliferation and maritime security in Southeast Asia* (Vol. 4, No. 4, p. 14). Honolulu: Pacific Forum CSIS. https://csis-prod.s3.amazonaws.com/s3fs-public/legacy_files/files/media/csis/pubs/issuesinsights_v04n04.pdf. Accessed 21.11.2016.
Shinohara, M. (2005). Quality shipping and incentive schemes: from the perspective of the institutional economics. *Maritime Economics and Logistics, 7*.
Stanbrook, C. R. (2013). *The Port of Gibraltar joins the green award scheme*. Gibraltar Port Authority. http://www.gibraltarport.com/sites/default/files/news/Green%20Award%20Press%20Release.pdf. Accessed 23.11.2016.

Takei, Y. (2014). *Regulatory review in the maritime sector*. Working paper. Research project "Maritime Governance and Corporate Social Responsibility". World Maritime University.

The Companies Act, 2013, No. 18 of 2013, Ministry of Law and Justice, India. http://www.mca.gov.in/Ministry/pdf/CompaniesAct2013.pdf. Accessed 22.11.2016.

UN Global Compact. (2002). *Growing sustainable business for poverty reduction*. http://www.un.org/esa/coordination/Alliance/documents/GSB_overview.pdf. Accessed 20.11.2016.

UN System Task Team on the Post-2015 UN Development Agenda. (2012). *Governance and development*. Thematic think piece, UNDESA, UNDP and UNESCO. http://www.un.org/millenniumgoals/pdf/Think%20Pieces/7_governance.pdf. Accessed 20.11.2016.

United Nations Convention on the Law of the Sea. (1982). http://www.un.org/depts/los/convention_agreements/texts/unclos/unclos_e.pdf. Accessed 20.02.2015.

United Nations Development Programme. (1997). *Governance for sustainable human development*. New York: UNDP Policy Document.

United Nations Development Programme. (2012). *Strategy for working with the private sector*. http://www.undp.org/content/dam/undp/library/corporate/Partnerships/Private%20Sector/UNDP-Private-Sector-Strategy-final-draft-2012.pdf. Accessed 20.11.2016.

United Nations Economic and Social Council. (2006). *Definition of basic concepts and terminologies in governance and public administration*. Committee of Experts on Public Administration, E/C.16/2006/4. http://unpan1.un.org/intradoc/groups/public/documents/un/unpan022332.pdf. Accessed 20.11.2016.

USCG. Foreign and Offshore Compliance Division (CG-CVC-2): Qualship 21 Initiative. https://www.uscg.mil/hq/cgcvc/cvc2/psc/safety/qualship.asp. Accessed 23.11.2016.

Vile, M. J. C. (1967). *Constitutionalism and the separation of powers* (2nd ed.p. 1). Indianapolis: Liberty Fund.

Villanueva, R. E. Jr. (2004). *The emerging role of the classification society as an extension of the flag state administration*. Unpublished Master's Thesis, World Maritime University, Malmö, Sweden.

Williamson, O. (2000). The new institutional economics: taking stock, looking ahead. *Journal of Economic Literature, 38*.

World Bank. (1992). *Governance and development*. Washington, DC: The World Bank. http://documents.worldbank.org/curated/en/1992/04/440582/governance-development. Accessed 20.11.2016.

Yliskylä-Peuralahti, J., & Gritsenko, D. (2014). Binding rules or voluntary actions? A conceptual framework for CSR in shipping. *World Maritime University Journal of Maritime Affairs, 13*, 251–268.

Ziarati, R. (2006). Safety at sea-applying Pareto analysis. Commercial shipping. In *Proceedings of World Maritime Technology Conference 2006*.

Ziarati, R., Demirel, E., & Lahiry, H. (2011). International cooperation for maritime education and training. In *International Conference IMLA 19 Opatija*.

Arctic Governance and Gender: Climate Change or Social Change?

Momoko Kitada and Lise Synnøve Neeraas Langåker

1 Introduction

In the last couple of decades, especially after the Kyoto Protocol was adopted in 1992 to globally mitigate climate change, more and more attention has been paid to environmental concerns in global politics and business. Political debates on climate change have helped educating citizens and corporations around the world about the importance of behaving in an environmentally friendly manner. Parallel to the emergence of environmental issues on the agenda, the notion of corporate social responsibility (CSR) has become a major theme of business development and business ethics.

Business ethics and social auditing have been recognized by placing guidelines and standards, such as the Organization for Economic Cooperation and Development's Guidelines for Multinational Enterprises, the Social Accountability 8000 standards, and the Global Reporting Initiative; However, such guidelines and standards requires a mechanism to effectively implement in corporate practices (Kuhn and Deetz 2008). To establish principles regarding to CSR, the so-called *triple bottom line* (TBL) (Economist 2009) framework has been widely established as a useful tool with which to analyse organisations' positions regarding CSR. Through a TBL analysis, a company's economic, environmental and social performance can be simultaneously studied in order to suggest whether or not the company is grounded—or is potentially steering towards—organisational sustainability on many accounts.

M. Kitada (✉)
World Maritime University, Malmö, Sweden
e-mail: mk@wmu.se

L. S. N. Langåker
Western Norway University of Applied Sciences, Haugesund, Norway
e-mail: lise.langaker@hvl.no

L. L. Froholdt (ed.), *Corporate Social Responsibility in the Maritime Industry*, WMU Studies in Maritime Affairs 5, https://doi.org/10.1007/978-3-319-69143-5_6

There is nothing new about being occupied with organisational sustainability in *economic* terms. What is more novel, though, is the emphasis which lately is placed upon organisations' *environmental* performance and hence a wider environmental responsibility. According to the Third International Maritime Organization (IMO) Greenhouse Gas (GHG) Emission Study (2014), the international shipping accounts for 2.2% of the global CO2 emissions. Even though the industry is known as the most environmentally friendly mode of transportation, it encounters demands for responsible environmental performance when it comes to CO2 and other emissions, and not at least concerning damaging spills (for example, oil spills and ballast water spills). It is reasonable to assume that the industry's focus to prevent damaging spills might be influenced by the rather heavy fines attached to such incidents in many countries around the world (Sampson 2016).

The *social* performance factor of the TBL framework can potentially incorporate a very wide area of organisational performance. Traditionally, an organisation's social performance has been evaluated in terms of general workforce welfare with a significant emphasis upon occupational health and safety issues during the last decades. However, an organisation's social responsibility is often also seen as extending beyond the organisational boundaries, both by the organisation itself and its surroundings. For example, companies may be seen as holding a certain amount of responsibility for its local community by way of providing stable employment, by way of contributing financially and otherwise to local institutions and cultural organisations and by way of becoming a political actor when vital local issues are felt to be at stake.

But companies and industries as well as governmental bodies can also be seen as being responsible for including wider social issues on the organisational as well as the public agenda. This is an area of organisational commitment that is not much discussed in the literature up till now. Based in such extended and external perspectives of CSR, we will in this chapter argue how industry as well as government actors in our opinion have a responsibility for the social inclusion of women in their dealings on all levels. As an illustration, we have chosen to examine gender issues in the Arctic region on a broad level.

The Arctic region refers to the Arctic Council membership countries: Canada, Denmark (including Greenland and the Faroe Islands), Iceland, Finland, Norway, the Russian Federation, Sweden, the United States. The reason why the Arctic is chosen as an illustration is that the region is of particular significance to the maritime industry due to the increasing interest of shipping companies to expand business opportunities here (e.g., new shipping routes, new tourism opportunities, etc.). Also, the Arctic region is highly environmentally sensitive. Lastly, the Arctic region includes countries that like to look upon themselves as "gender equal". Thus, our example will illuminate economic as well as environmental and social aspects within a CSR mode of thought, although our emphasis will be on the extended social responsibility concerning gender issues.

2 Limited Emphasis on Gender Perspectives

The current discussions on Arctic governance include various interests and scopes. Some emphasise the economic development of the region in terms of natural resources which are becoming more accessible due to climate change. In addition to resource management in Arctic, shipping and marine activities are of interest for those who seek new business opportunities. For example, Arctic navigation and routes have been already proved to be available for use, and the legal framework such as the Polar Code needed to catch up with such a rapid business development. Marine activities include fisheries and tourism as marine resources are attractive for new business opportunities in the region.

In the twentieth century, human beings have hopefully learned that nothing will last forever and human activities must be monitored and regulated in order to sustain our earth for all living species. Arctic governance is therefore highly motivated by the idea of sustainable development, emphasising environmental protection and biodiversity. It also extends to political and military stability in the region. Both economic and political debates in conjunction with environmental concerns occupy the majority of discourses on future Arctic governance. Stelzenmüller et al. (2013) identify the challenges in implementation of the ecosystem management, for example, the lack of operational objectives, data access, and stakeholders' involvement. These elements are also considered as a key for ocean governance in the context of Arctic ecosystem management (Lawrence 1999).

Nevertheless, the maritime industry seems to be struggling with finding a balanced approach amongst economic, environmental, and social aspects of CSR. In the last two decades, *environmental* performance of maritime organisations has been emphasised. According to the Third IMO GHG Emission Study (2014), international shipping accounts for 2.2% of the global CO2 emissions. It is predicted that ships' CO2 emissions will possibly increase between 50% and 250% by 2050; however, if operational measures and implementing existing technologies are appropriately applied, there is a potential of reducing CO2 emissions by up to 75% (IMO 2009). The industry is known as the most environmentally friendly mode of transportation in terms of CO2 per ton nautical mile; yet there are still high demands for responsible environmental performance in the maritime industry. Such responsibilities include the control of CO2 and other emissions, and damaging spills (for example oil spills and ballast water spills) from ships. These negative environmental impacts of ships become even more sensitive if the maritime industry expands their business in the Arctic region. It is reasonable to assume that a wider environmental responsibility of the maritime industry to prevent damaging spills might be influenced by the rather heavy fines attached to such incidents in many countries around the world, and thus it immediately affects their reputations and business returns (Sampson 2016).

Our concern here is to see a reasonable explanation from the maritime industry about why social aspects, especially people, are not of much focus in Arctic. If the maritime industry invests in Arctic and pays their concern into environmental issues, why don't they talk about people, for example, women and men, at all?

The question of gender equality in Arctic was raised in full at the conference organised by the Arctic Council in August 2002, "Taking Wing". This initiative was followed by the 2003–2004 Arctic Council Sustainable Development Working Group (SDWG) project, "Women's participation in decision-making processes in Arctic fisheries resource management" by the Northern Feminist University and the Norwegian Ministry of Foreign Affairs. This assignment included the project called the "Women and Natural Resource Management in the Rural North", providing accounts of women's relationship with resource-based industries and industrial developments in the Arctic region, based on several fieldwork reports from Canada, Greenland, Iceland, Norway, Sweden and Finland (Sloan 2006).

Despite such efforts in early 2000s, gender equality in Arctic has not been high on the agenda until recently. In October 2014, the conference on "Gender Equality in the Arctic" was held in Akureyri, Iceland, hosted by the Ministry of Foreign Affairs, Iceland, in cooperation with the Icelandic Arctic Cooperation Network and the Centre For Gender Equality. This conference provided an overview of current state of affairs and future challenges in the Arctic from feminist perspectives (Oddsdottir et al. 2015). The conference also highlighted the absence of discourse on Arctic governance and gender, which will be further focused in this chapter.

3 Climate Change and Gender

The existing literature discusses the relevance of climate change to gender from various perspectives. The United Nations (UN) reports that women in particularly rural areas tend to be poor and affected by climate change because of their dependence on natural resources for living as well as the vulnerability of women to disasters (UN WomenWatch 2009). On a similar note, rural women in many developing countries collect fuel woods for cooking as well as part of their income-generating activities (ESMAP 2013). Such activities partly contribute to emission problems. Therefore, within the discourse of climate change, the element of gender would help the understanding of different needs and involvements between men and women. In many countries, women are under-represented in current political institutions. Important decisions relating to climate change may thus be made without women's representation. A greater focus on gender perspectives will thus ensure the effective development in improving the global issue of climate change (UNDP 2012).

Although all of the cited accounts are related to climate change, it would bring different impacts on different people in different regions at different levels. For example, economic and social status affect people's capacity to make their own choices. Poor people cannot afford modern ways of living and women may be socially restricted or excluded from decision-making. Various stakeholder groups address multiple societal issues and concerns (Wartick and Cochran 1985). Indeed, it is criticised that negotiations on climate change, including the discussions of the Kyoto Protocol, reflect Northern priorities and interests (Denton 2002). Why does a more inclusive approach become important here? The report on Arctic development for the European Union (EU) concludes that a global economy and climate change are key drivers of developments in the European Arctic (Stępień et al. 2014). In other words, the European Arctic cannot be totally independent from a global economy and climate change. An openness to various stakeholder groups will therefore help the governance structure of Arctic. As discussed earlier, if climate change is recognised as a global agenda, discussions for strategies to mitigate climate change should reflect everyone, including women. Gender issues must be high on the agenda in this context. This understanding also reflects the TBL model of CSR which supports the aspects of economic, environmental, and social responsibilities as main drivers for sustainable development of the Arctic region.

4 Political Empowerment in the Arctic

A majority of the countries in the Arctic region are regarded as highly gender-equal, compared to the rest of the world. Does this mean that the Arctic has a high political participation of women? Eva-Maria Svensson, a professor of the Arctic University of Norway UiT and University of Gothenburg, noted that the Committee on the Elimination of Discrimination against Women (CEDAW) made the observation that gender inequality exists throughout all Arctic states to a lesser or greater extent (Oddsdottir et al. 2015, p. 26). For example, while the Arctic Council has successfully enabled both women and indigenous groups to participate in discussing the development of the Arctic region, the representation of these groups and their agencies to influence the decision-making are still limited. Sinevaara-Niskanen (2015) claims that the current inclusion of gender and indigeneity is only partially done and these categories are not recognised in the representative structure of Arctic politics. The Arctic Council is based on working groups with a variety of chairpersons, participants, agendas, tasks, and meeting locations. This complex work practice makes it challenging for marginalised groups such as women and indigenous people to take part in the meetings (Sinevaara-Niskanen 2015).

This claim is supported by the statistics in the Global Gender Gap Report (World Economic Forum 2016). Among eight member states in the Arctic Council, four countries (i.e. Iceland, Finland, Norway, and Sweden) occupied the top four in the overall ranking. However, the scores for their political empowerment index were still far from 1.0 (equal) and even Iceland as the best country in the world remained its score as 0.719 only. Further, the general gender gaps between those Nordic countries and others (i.e. Canada, United States, and Russia) become wider in the political empowerment index. While the Nordic countries show 0.539 in the average score of political empowerment, the mean score of three countries (Canada, United States, and Russia) is 0.150 (see Table 1). It suggests that female leaders and politicians are still under-represented and this area of gender equality needs to be prioritised in the future.

Table 1 Political empowerment index of 6 member countries in the Arctic Council

Country	Overall rank	Political empowerment (rank)	Political empowerment (score)	
Iceland	1	1	0.719	0.539 (The mean score in Nordic countries)
Finland	2	2	0.607	
Norway	3	3	0.576	
Sweden	4	6	0.486	
Denmark	19	29	0.309	
Canada	35	49	0.222	0.150 (The mean score of 3 countries: Canada, United States, and Russia)
United States	45	73	0.162	
Russia	75	129	0.066	

Source: Adapted from World Economic Forum (2016)

In addition, gender equality is multi-dimensional and requires careful attention when it comes to cultural aspects. For example, Njåstad et al. (2009) argue that the word "gender" is not regarded to be relevant to certain indigenous cultures and communities in Arctic. Hence, gender equality may not be successfully addressed in indigenous contexts. This suggests that feminist theorists need to be flexible and find a different approach to bring gender onto the agenda. In 2008, the working group of the Vulnerability and Adaption to Climate Change in the Arctic (VACCA) suggested that gender should continue to be a topic within the discussions of vulnerability and adaptability (Njåstad et al. 2009). This exemplifies the importance of adapting to cultures and populations concerned as well as being realistic and making sense in a given context.

5 Governance and Equality

The term "governance" is broadly used for all instruments and mechanisms through which different stakeholders manage their interests and make decisions for the wider good of society. Caluser and Salagean (2007) describe the characteristics of good governance as equal participation; the rule of law; transparency of information; accountability and responsibility of the institution. These characteristics are equally important to Arctic governance.

Notwithstanding, the legitimacy for public governance tends to be weaker in regions away from the centre than in more central parts of nation states. While good governance can be applied to all citizens of a country, these regions' weaker ties to national governments could systematically work as a barrier to include *all peoples*. Unless a regional body consciously gives attention to marginalised groups, including women, good governance in the region would be difficult to become realised.

Today, the emergence of globalisation as well as European integration challenge the notion of "good governance" which was primarily applied to nation states but is now attempted to cover a wider demography. Agné (2006, p. 434) questions the principle in democratic theory that "the people be affected only by such decisions as they have participated in making and, therefore, that all decisions made externally to the people must be avoided". The notion of democratic political autonomy is challenged here, and it has to be carefully considered what degree of participation is wanted when it comes to influencing decisions.

"Equal participation" has been an ultimate goal in feminist movements, but the term "equal" may become abstract without analysing what degree of participation others have. In other words, "equal participation" does not necessarily promise "equal impact". Structural boundaries may prevent women from making as much influence as men. Such issues need to be rigorously examined instead of merely looking at numbers when it comes to gender representation.

This view is also stressed by Ostrom (1990) in the scope of the governance and management of common-pool resources (CPRs). In her work of the governance of natural resources, such as air, water, and fish, used by different individuals and institutions, the conditions of successful governance and management in "the commons" are questioned. Her study concludes that the successful implementation of inclusive policies lies in how local communities discuss relevant issues and how these discussions shall be allowed to influence the management of these communities (Ostrom 1990). In the context of the Arctic region where the environmental sensitivity is high, the Arctic "commons" are increasingly attracting the maritime industry to invest in new business opportunities. As Ostrom (1990) highlights, it is crucial whether local communities, including women, are able to raise their concerns about Arctic resources and their voice is heard by management. Considering the generally high rates of gender equality indicators among the Arctic countries (World Economic Forum 2016), it is expected that women would have been participating in discussions on Arctic governance; however, reality seems to be different.

6 Gender Mainstreaming in Arctic Governance

Social aspects of Arctic governance have been emphasised at many occasions. Attention has been given to groups of people, culture and heritage, and health and wellbeing. Nonetheless, social aspects are not limited to these topics. A wider scope of diversity issues in the Arctic should be addressed, including "indigenous and non-indigenous peoples, elders and youth, men and women, and representatives of various livelihoods, including both fishing and mining, where each other's needs and interests are respected", according to Gunn-Britt Retter, Chair of the local Saami association (Oddsdottir et al. 2015, p. 21). It is notable that gender perspectives are rarely discussed as an important agenda in Arctic governance. The absence of women in the process of Arctic development will not create a comprehensive view, and as a result, it may limit methodologies to analyse and understand Arctic development issues. Gender mainstreaming—a strategy for making the concerns and experiences of women as well as of men an integral part in all political, economic and societal spheres (UN 2002)—is an important tool in order to include women's perspectives into the Arctic developmental discourses.

Gender mainstreaming concerns not only women's but also men's experience in their Arctic lives. Williamson et al. (2004) discuss how Arctic men and women experience life differently and reveal that men in some Arctic regions (i.e. Alaska, United States, Canada, Nunavut, Western Northwest Territories) tend to be unemployed at a higher rate than women. In addition, gender specific suicide rates between 0 and 24 years old in different Arctic regions show that men have significantly higher suicide rates than women. The research also reveals that some Arctic men have lost their masculine roles and duties both inside and outside the home because of the introduction of modern living in apartments, compared to owning a family house (Williamson et al. 2004). Furthermore, Arctic men tend to stay in their villages while Arctic women seem to have a higher mobility rate than men. Arctic women are more likely to move to urban cities as job-seekers or students in higher education. Some Arctic women marry non-Arctic men who have stayed for a fixed-term mission of security or research in Arctic (Williamson et al. 2004). Because such temporary security officers and researchers are typically males, gendered interventions into Arctic territories can result in creating opportunities of coupling non-Arctic men to Arctic women. After their terms end, non-Arctic men typically move out of the Arctic with their Arctic women partners and therefore, some Arctic women become more "mobile" than men.

Without gender analysis, there may be no means to understand male problems. Gender equality includes attention to men, and men's challenges are equally important as women's. Feminist approaches can help identifying such hidden social issues in the process of Arctic development and facilitate open discussions and dialogues between women and men who may suffer from dilemmas concerning their identities and roles in society.

7 Gender Analysis for Social Change

The organising of Arctic region, similar to that of other international alliances, has many actors with different degrees of participation and access to resources. This may make the political autonomy of Arctic complex. In order to achieve gender equality in Arctic, one of the necessary processes would be to monitor the degree of women's participation in Arctic social and political dialogue.

The importance of obtaining accurate and relevant data on the status of women, men and gender relations and the constant monitoring of such data has been discussed elsewhere: "The need for sex-disaggregated data has been stressed in numerous international conventions and declarations, including the 1995 Platform for Action of the Fourth UN World Conference on Women in Beijing and the 1995 Commonwealth Plan of Action on Gender and Development" (Beck 1999).

Sex-disaggregated data will help us to see where gender biases are hidden and how to target and prioritise in policy making.

Gender analysis is useful to identify the gaps between policy and its implementation. Various methods are available, for example, gender-sensitive frameworks which are employed in the impact assessment at three different levels: the macro or societal level, the meso or organisational level, and the micro or individual level (Elson et al. 1997; Gutierrez 2003).

Gender-Sensitive Indicators (GSI) is another tool to develop a database and it is found to be particularly useful at a national level (Beck 1999). GSI includes both quantitative and qualitative indicators (Canadian International Development Agency 1997; UNESCO 2003). Quantitative GSIs are usually used as goal setting during the process of policy or project planning, for example, "women represent at least 40% of the Arctic business development committee by the end of 2020". Increasing women's participation in the process of Arctic development is important, however the quality of their experiences and participation is equally important. Qualitative indicators therefore require research on how women perceive the quality of their participation and experiences. GSI can be effectively used for three types of indicators, namely input, process and outcome. While input indicators (generally quantitative) measure "what was invested in the project", process indicators (generally qualitative) measure "how the project progressed" and outcome indicators measure "what came out of the project" (UNESCO 2003).

Canada has applied gender-based analysis (GBA) to all legislation, policies, and programmes since 1995 when the UN Beijing Platform for Action was adopted. The method was eventually evolved into GBA+, and this new format includes other demographic factors, such as age, education, language, geography, culture and income (Oddsdottir et al. 2015, p. 18). GBA or GBA+ can be developed and utilised in wider areas, such as economy, security, environment, policies, health, education and culture, and it will bring about a better picture of Arctic governance, if applied.

These analytical data and information are, needless to say, important in advocating gender equality in the process of Arctic development. The claims backed up by statistics and situational analysis would be convincing, and policy makers would have to listen to the voices of both women and men in the Arctic. It helps to draft action plans based on gender gap analysis and to step forward from the rhetoric to the practicing of gender equality in the region. Research will support the process of knowledge creation by women in particular, and magnify the effect of advocacy in public. Such efforts will meet the gender sensitive implementation of the post-2015 development framework (UNCTAD 2015).

8 Conclusion

The well-established concept of corporate social responsibility—CSR—has served to legitimatise public demands towards industries and corporations. Businesses all over the world and within all industries are thus expected to take into consideration environmental and social as well as economic issues in their business endeavours. In this chapter we have used Arctic development as an illustration of how the maritime industry—and society at large—would benefit if the industry became a promoter of social development and inclusion of women at all levels in the region.

Climate change has brought a range of new possibilities to the industrial development of the Arctic region, including Arctic navigation, natural resources, tourism, fisheries and so forth. The term "Arctic governance" is frequently used to address the responsibility of human beings for the sustainable development in the region and it is increasingly important to monitor and evaluate the impact of human activities in Arctic.

This paper highlights the under-representation of women in Arctic discourses, in particular in decision-making processes. The participation of all members in local communities, including women, is a key for the successful implementation of inclusive policies to make an impact on the community management. In line with this thought, it is discussed that the participation of women should be encouraged through monitoring and assessment in order to ensure that women on an equal basis can influence Arctic development. Gender mainstreaming is suggested as an effective tool for identifying possible structural as well as cultural challenges prohibiting women's participation in Arctic decision-making processes. Such efforts can be combined with gender analysis, including GBA+ and GSI, to analyse gender gaps and identify targets for improvement. This approach to Arctic governance will promote economic diversity and gender equality, and thus it will enable women actively to innovate and become entrepreneurs in the region. The region and the relevant regional industries will benefit greatly from such a development.

Within an CSR scope of thought, we argue that our Arctic example illustrates how powerful industries such as the maritime industry has a role to play when it comes to broader societal responsibilities. A *triple bottom analysis* based on the industry's economic, environmental and social performance has shown that there are benefits for the maritime industry as well as for the broader Arctic society if gender issues earn a more prominent place on the industrial and political agenda.

An important discussion in this respect is how far "out" CSR reaches when it comes to societal challenges such as the gender issue. It can easily be argued that industries should stick to "mere" business and leave broader societal development to other institutions. Our argument for integrating CSR into a broader public sphere, however, is that recent years' development of the CSR concept allows for positive expectations towards industries in the role of societal actors outside of their organisational boundaries, which is a limited version of the industry's responsibility for its local community. Based on this perspective, it seems appropriate to suggest that the maritime industry with its powerful industrial base and old traditions for political involvement has a great potential for the integration of a broad CSR concept in corporate business strategies. Though still a few, some good practices were reported in maritime CSR: The A.P. Moller–Maersk, for example, recognises gender as an important way of expanding the talent pool and has established a diversity and inclusion strategy. The strategy has generated various actions to increase the representation of women in management, and to implement a new maternity policy to support women's career cycles in the maritime industry.[1]

In our Arctic example, we have shown the potentially beneficial implications for the industry as well as for society by doing so. The inclusion of gender issues in maritime CSR strategies will hopefully be visible in corporate plans in the near future.

References

Agné, H. (2006). A dogma of democratic theory and globalization: Why politics need not include everyone it affects. *European Journal of International Relations, 12*, 433–458.

Beck, T. (1999). *A quick guide to using gender-sensitive indicators*. London: Commonwealth Secretariat.

Caluser, M., & Salagean, M. (Eds.). (2007). *Good governance in multiethnic communities: Conditions, instruments, best practices, ways to achieve and measure good governance at the local level*. The Ethnocultural Diversity Resource Center and the King Baudouin Foundation.

Canadian International Development Agency (CIDA). (1997). *Guide to gender sensitive indicators*. Minister of Public Works and Government Services Canada.

Denton, F. (2002). Climate change vulnerability, impacts, and adaptation: Why does gender matter? *Gender and Development, 10*(2), 10–20.

Economist. (2009). *Triple bottom line*. http://www.economist.com/node/14301663. Accessed 9 April 2017.

Elson, D., Evers, B., & Gideon, J. (1997). *Gender aware country economic reports: Concepts and sources*. GENECON Unit Working Paper 1. University of Manchester.

Energy Sector Management Assistance Program (ESMAP). (2013). *Integrating gender considerations into energy operations*. Knowledge Series 014/13. Washington, DC: World Bank.

Gutierrez, M. (2003). *Macro-economics: Making gender matter: Concepts, policies and institutional change in developing countries*. Zed Books.

IMO. (2009). *Second IMO Greenhouse Gas Study 2009*. London: IMO.

IMO. (2014). *Third IMO Greenhouse Gas Study 2014*. London: IMO.

Kuhn, T., & Deetz, S. (2008). Critical theory and corporate social responsibility: Can/should we get beyond cynical reasoning? In A. Crane, A. McWilliams, D. Matten, J. Moon, & D. S. Siegel (Eds.), *The Oxford handbook of corporate social responsibility*. Oxford: Oxford University Press.

Lawrence, J. (1999). Considerations in developing a functional approach to the governance of large marine ecosystems. *Ocean Development and International Law, 30*, 90–125.

Njåstad, B., Kelman, I., & Rosenberg, S. (Eds.). (2009). *Vulnerability and adaptation to climate change in the Arctic. Arctic Council Sustainable Development Working Group (SDWG)*. Tromsø: Norwegian Polar Institute.

Oddsdottir, E. E., Sigurosson, A. M., Svandal, S., & Arnadottir, A. K. (2015). *Gender equality in the Arctic: Current realities, future challenges*. Conference Report. Ministry of Foreign Affairs, Iceland in cooperation with Icelandic Arctic Cooperation Network and the Centre for Gender Equality.

Ostrom, E. (1990). *Governing the commons: The evolution of institutions for collective action*. Cambridge: Cambridge University Press.

[1]See the press release form the A.P. Moller–Maersk, 'Maersk Group introduces improved maternity benefits worldwide' dated 14 January 2016.

Sampson, H. (2016). "Seabirds Matter More Than Us!": Understanding the complex exercise of CSR in the Global Shipping Industry. *The Journal of Sustainable Mobility, 3*(2), 101–119. https://doi.org/10.9774/GLEAF.2350.2016.de.00007.

Sinevaara-Niskanen, H. (2015). *Setting the stage for arctic development: Politics of knowledge and the power of presence*. PhD thesis. ISBN 978-952-484-831-2.

Sloan, L. (Ed.). (2006). *Women and natural resource management in the rural north. Arctic Council Sustainable Development Working Group 2004–2006*. Nordfold: Forlaget Nora.

Stelzenmüller, V., Breen, P., Stamford, T., Thomsen, F., Badalamenti, F., Borja, Á., et al. (2013). Monitoring and evaluation of spatially managed areas: A generic framework for implementation of ecosystem based marine management and its application. *Marine Policy, 37*, 149–164.

Stępień, A., Koivurova, T., & Kankaanpää, P. (Eds.). (2014). *Strategic assessment of development of the arctic: Assessment conducted for the European Union*. Arctic Centre, University of Lapland.

UN. (2002). *Gender mainstreaming: An overview*. New York: United Nations.

UN WomenWatch. (2009). *Fact sheet: Women, gender equality and climate change*. http://www.un.org/womenwatch/feature/climate_change/ Accessed 06 August 2015.

UNCTAD. (2015). *Ensuring gender-sensitive implementation of the post-2015 development framework*. UNCTAD/PRESS/PB/2015/10. Geneva: UNCTAD.

UNDP. (2012). *Gender and energy*. New York: United Nations Development Programme.

UNESCO. (2003). *Gender sensitive quantitative and qualitative indicators*. http://www.unesco.org/new/fileadmin/MULTIMEDIA/HQ/BSP/GENDER/PDF/3.%20UNESCO%20Gender%20Lens%20for%20measuring%20performance%20guide%20for%20developing%20gender%20sensitive%20indicators.pdf. Accessed 24 August 2015.

Wartick, S. L., & Cochran, P. L. (1985). The evolution of the corporate social performance model. *Academy of Management Review, 10*(4), 758–769.

Williamson, K. J., Hoogensen, G., Lotherington, A. T., Hamilton, L. H., Savage, S., Koukarenko, N., et al. (2004). Chapter 11: Gender issues. In N. Einarsson, J. N. Larsen, A. Nilsson, & O. R. Young (Eds.), *Arctic human development report*. Akureyri: Stefansson Arctic Institute.

World Economic Forum. (2016). *The Global Gender Gap Report 2016*. Geneva: World Economic Forum.

Effective and Efficient Maritime Administration and Corporate Social Responsibility

Neil Bellefontaine and Tafsir Johannson

1 Introduction

Shipping commonly refers to maritime transportation conducted by a ship, and irrespective of size or flag, a ship does not operate in isolation and its main purpose is to transport goods and cargos from one part of the world to another (Farthing and Brownrigg 1997). In this context, maritime transport is deemed as an indispensable part of international logistics and accounts for 80% of the volume of global trade (United Nations Conference on Trade and Development 2013, p. 5). What can be gathered from the 2013 United Nations Conference on Trade and Development report is that the shipping industry has played a key role in transforming the global economy in the last few decades (United Nations Conference on Trade and Development 2013, p. 5). Transportation being the catalyst of maritime explorations, shipping, to that extent, has not only made cross-border trade possible, it has also brought innumerable opportunities since it's inception. From export-import of raw materials, consumer products, natural resources, oil and gas and chemicals to job opportunities on board ships, in the port or even in the government office—shipping in short, can be considered as a strong pillar of a nation's economy. As a forerunner of globalization, shipping has changed the way one views trade and development. While shipping can be praised by a number of positive adjectives, mostly with regard to the way it contributes to the advancement of a nations economic growth, the advantages, nevertheless, come with a number of negative externalities. Quite often, these negative externalities begin to surface in the aftermath of a maritime incident and may pose a detrimental effect on the marine environment, the coastal community, the marine biodiversity, the seafarers working on board the ships etc.

N. Bellefontaine (✉) · T. Johannson
World Maritime University, Malmö, Sweden
e-mail: nab@wmu.se; tj@wmu.se

L. L. Froholdt (ed.), *Corporate Social Responsibility in the Maritime Industry*, WMU Studies in Maritime Affairs 5, https://doi.org/10.1007/978-3-319-69143-5_7

When investigations are conducted in the aftermath of a maritime incident, the general approach is to look beyond the terms "ship" and "shipping" whereby the initial focus is on the people working on-board and subsequently, the drivers or the key people working from behind the scene. The main purpose of an investigation is to identify the causes and contributing factors through the gathering and analysis of relevant information and make necessary recommendations in order to prevent related casualties in the future. When it comes to the maritime property i.e. the ship, attention is drawn on the maritime personnel or people working on board that particular ship. Based on the type of contract or the type of shipping, this may include the ship-owner, master, operator or the seafarer who are in the forefront of a maritime operation. For the latter i.e. shipping, the focus shifts to the industry, usually a conglomeration of companies and often tends to be identified as a combination of different markets e.g. tramp market (bulk carriers), the liner market (container vessels, roll-on/roll-off ships), special or industrial shipping market and the passenger shipping market (Chrzanowski 1985). It is the shipping companies collectively operating within the shipping industry, which govern all operations with reference to the ship and is responsible for all regulatory mismanagement and business conducted via substandard-shipping. Stopford (2009, p. 53), citing the Rochdale Report (Committee of Inquiry into Shipping), offers a succinct definition of shipping:

> Shipping is a complex industry and the conditions which govern its operations in one sector does not necessarily apply to another; it might even, for the purposes, be better regarded as a group of related industries. Its main assets, the ship themselves, vary widely in size and type; they provide the whole range of services for a variety of goods, whether over short or longer distance. Although one can, for analytical purposes, usefully isolate sectors of the industry providing types of service, there is usually some interchange at the margin which cannot be ignored.

In the event of a maritime incident, whether it is a danger or imminent threat to the people and personnel on board or whether it has an impact on the marine environment, it is the respective company[1] that is held responsible and questioned by concerned stakeholders. In order to demonstrate accountability, shipping companies are asked to "...integrate social and environmental concerns in their business operations and in their interactions with their stakeholders on a voluntary basis" (COM(20001) 366 Final at p. 5). This integration of social, environmental and economical concerns, aptly termed as Corporate Social Responsibility (CSR) is to be "treated as an investment, not a cost, much like quality management" (COM (20001) 366 Final). In the maritime sector, the duty of CSR translates into "safety at sea", recognized by international actors and authorities and integrates the same concerns i.e. social and environmental (Arat 2011). This is mainly due to the fact that it is no longer publically acceptable for corporations to experience economic prosperity in isolation from those stakeholders that are likely to be affected by its

[1]That regulates all operations of the ship.

actions in the course of conducting business operations (D'Amato et al. 2009). The maritime sector is no exception to this point of view.

One of the significant aspects highlighted by the EU Commission is "identifying, preventing and mitigating..." all possible adverse impacts (COM(20001) 366 Final) and ISO 26000 Guidance Standards on Social Responsibility further substantiates the duties of an organization with respect to the adverse impacts (Official homepage of DNV GL). There have been a number of fundamental researches on "transparency and ethical behaviour" of shipping organizations where focus has been on the work of individual companies in relation to business, profit and CSR. To that extent, there exists a plethora of scholarly works on qualitative and quantitative examination with regard to the concepts of CSR in shipping and its derivatives, CSR reporting, CSR and multi-cultural human environment, CSR and the human element, CSR and maritime governance etc. (Arat 2011). The works on shipping and CSR, still continues. However, in all of these examinations of CSR, there is one topic that needs to be separated and discussed at-length. The topic that needs further assessment relates to maritime administration and the impetus it gives to shipping companies in order to be corporate and socially responsible.

Maritime administration, in order to adhere to the generic and collateral concepts of CSR, needs to achieve a certain level of organizational effectiveness and the impending question is—how can one measure organizational effectiveness in a maritime administration? From a general viewpoint, maritime administrations are comprised of integrated units in their structure and these units collectively play an important role in enforcing governmental policies that govern the maritime sector. In order to implement governmental policies successfully, maritime administrations need to be goal-oriented and organizationally effective. Broadly speaking, the concept of organizational effectiveness focuses on the goals of an organization and since maritime administrations are governmental organizations with unique characteristics, it is important to examine the role they play in making sure that the shipping companies adhere to the implemented policies and demonstrate a certain level of accountability. However, the question remains: how can maritime administrations be advocates of CSR in the shipping industry and assist the government in carrying out its state obligations as a member of the international community? To answer this question, this chapter makes an effort to examine organizational effectiveness and efficiency from a maritime administration perspective.

2 "Efficient and Effective" Maritime Administration

Maritime Administration is the centralized institution of a state that governs the essential matters of the maritime sector and seeks to enforce the respective national rules and regulations. This mandate is linked to the supra-national maritime administration being IMO, which has the United Nations (UN) mandate to implement maritime Conventions, Codes, Guidelines and practices to address global issues respecting maritime safety, security and marine environmental protection of the oceans, among other matters (Roe 2015; IMO 2013). As such, a maritime administration is generally administered and overseen by a designated Minister appointed by the government of the state. It could also be a division within a Ministry, a department of a Ministry, statutory authority or an executive agency. National Maritime Administrations can, and do, vary widely in mandate structure and operations depending on the development state of a particular country (Roe 2015). As a part of the public administration, the centralized maritime institution has features common to other public sectors and from a general point of view, the fundamental responsibility of the institution is to provide the government with the necessary tools, which would enable it to satisfactorily and "efficiently" undertake those functions which are embodied and promulgated within the country's Merchant Shipping Legislation (Vanchiswar 1996). In short, a maritime administration can be termed as an administrative unit and an executive arm of the government that assists the government to ensure implementation obligations of the country through maritime policies and laws in order to govern all maritime affairs and shipping related matters.

To ensure that the maritime administration can perform its operations as a competent executive arm, the government, at the same time, needs to ensure that the national legislation mirrors the modern approaches and keeps pace with the international strategies. From a fundamental viewpoint, it is the government that is under an international obligation to exercise due diligence when formulating, incorporating or amending the domestic rules and regulations, which are then in turn devised and implemented by the maritime administrations. This is due to the fact that maritime activities are cross-border operations are marked by their international nature and in order to fulfil the responsibility as a flag state and a port state, the government should have the most significant and effective regulations in place. By virtue of these regulations, the various departments of the maritime administration can move towards enforcement and maintain a high level of maritime quality management and thus, fulfil their functions in the administrative, legal, and operational delivery areas.

A central objective of a maritime administration is to improve the functional efficiency of the government in fulfilling its international obligations in the field of maritime affairs and international shipping in accordance with relevant international instruments (*See* 1.4.16 in Hubbard and Hoppe 2001). It can be suggested that in order to improve the government's functional efficiency and successfully carry out its international obligations, the various departments of a maritime administration need to be first and foremost, efficient in their own designated operations and secondly, they need to demonstrate organizational effectiveness. This is where the study of effectiveness and efficiency in the public sector becomes relevant. There have been a considerable number of studies related to public sector effectiveness and efficiency (Borcherding et al. 1982; Mueller 1989) and the general understanding is that effectiveness and efficiency is still a matter of dispute (Jan-Erik Lane 2000). The authors who support this viewpoint also confirm that effectiveness and efficiency apply to both administration and public service (Jan-Erik Lane 2000). Thus, the immediate question is, how can effectiveness and efficiency link maritime organizations to the notion of CSR and is it possible to create a concrete connection between effectiveness and efficiency and good governance?

The United Nations Educational, Scientific and Cultural Organization (UNESCO) acknowledges that effectiveness and efficiency are two of the eight major characteristics of good governance (Good Governance 2005) and based on this recognition, it is hypothesized that the two terms can be considered as a viable link between maritime administration and good governance (*See* Fig. 1). The international framework reflects a substance over form approach and fathoms that good governance should apply to a whole system within government (CIPFA and IFAC 2013). Moreover, good governance in the public sector is aimed to encourage better service delivery and improved accountability (CIPFA and IFAC 2013), and these two aspects relate to the all-embracing concept of organizational goodness as examined in the survey conducted by Shenhav et al. and relatively translates into effectiveness and efficiency when viewed from a maritime administration-objective angle. Finally, a number of initiatives (including the OECD Guidelines for Multinational Enterprises, the UNDP High Level Commission on the Private Sector and Development, and the UN Global Compact/UNDP 'growing sustainable business in least developed countries' initiative) are said to have addressed different aspects of the relationship between good governance, CSR and corporate accountability (Shenhav et al. 1994; Bigg and Ward 2007). These initiatives rationalize and further the nexus between maritime administration and CSR via good (maritime) governance, whether it be a government agency or a shipping company.

Although a maritime administration is a part of the public administration, it is safe to assert that administrations have a form of social responsibility towards specific and categorized stakeholders and this "responsibility" is analogous to the responsibility undertaken by private corporations. Despite the fact that CSR is a term commonly used by companies that wish to be guided by those informal regulations (Buhmann 2006) the notion can still be applied to maritime administrations when trying to define and determine the social responsibility spectrum that they have to satisfy as a part of the work-objective. For maritime administrations, the maritime

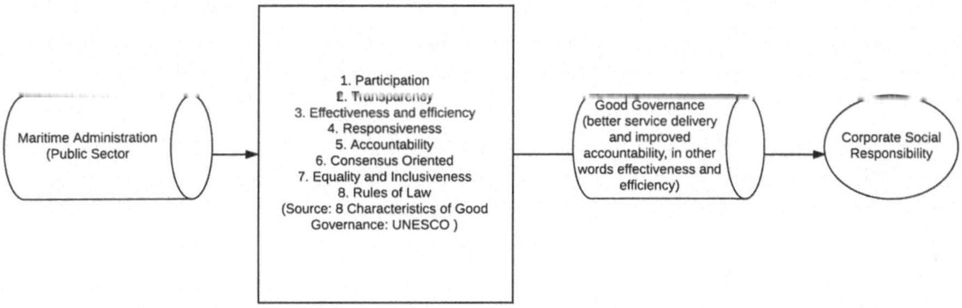

Fig. 1 Hypothesis-link between Maritime Administration and CSR. Source: Hypothesis extracted from Good Governance 2005, Official Homepage of UNESCO, Retrieved from the World Wide Web; http://portal.unesco.org/ci/en/ev.php-URL_ID=5205&URL_DO=DO_TOPIC&URL_SECTION=201.html

governance concept, will focus on institutional, legal and social policy development frameworks for good governance that addresses legal, cultural, social and environmental obstacles to good governance. Thus, for example, a maritime administration can be socially responsible by the way they control substandard shipping through inspection and survey. Whether it is port State control or flag State control, the operative word is control and the way maritime administrations exercise authority over ships, ship-owners and shipping companies. It is not only about being socially responsible as a maritime administration, it is about administering the shipping companies in a manner so that they are addressing the identified deficiencies to become more corporate and socially responsible as a whole. Intra-organizational effectiveness within the administration strengthens the roots of CSR and it is then through flag State control and port State control that success of CSR is realized. It is, therefore, submitted that an efficient and effective maritime organization with a stark organizational structure is the commencing point of CSR in the maritime sector. In light of the given conditions, hypotheses and nexus the two keywords efficiency and effectiveness merits further scrutiny with regard to the objectives and functions of a state's maritime administration.

3 Defining "Efficient and Effective"

The first keyword efficiency, is a term referential to cost estimates and is most commonly used in the field of economics that implies the relationship between input and output (Fare and Lovell 1978; Kopp 1981). A programme is said to be efficient if the target is achieved with the least possible use of resources (Hawker 1983) and for the public sector, it is often hard to measure efficiency "due to: the lack of resources to conduct evaluations; the lack of pre-reform measures of performance; the complexities in measuring efficiency in the public sector; and the problem of isolating the effects of specific institutional reforms on efficiency from other external influences" (Curristine et al. 2007 at 2). It is, therefore, understood that there is no standard procedure to calculate or measure efficiency or effectiveness and as a result both developed and developing countries have taken diverse approaches to increase efficiency in the maritime sector by reforming key institutional arrangements.

While the first condition (that relates to the concept of "efficiency") can be deemed as complex and emphasizes on managerial reform and the introduction of new working practices (Li 2000), the second condition (that relates to the concept of effectiveness) does not have a concrete definition in maritime law and its understanding demands an observation of how effectiveness has been interpreted in other disciplines. It is noteworthy that the term effectiveness is crucial to comprehend how well an organization is functioning and has been a source of motivation for the researchers of business administration who seek to understand organizational effectiveness (Henri 2004). When it comes to defining organizational effectiveness, scholars of business administration have used the term effectiveness and performance interchangeably due to the fact that their definition, measurement and explanation are virtually identical (March and Sutton 1997; Henri 2004).

In an effort to explain organizational effectiveness, a survey was conducted by Shenhav et al. in 1994 and an examination was conducted of 349 articles published by four leading management journals. According to the survey, the usage of the term "performance" has been cited as being dominant since 1978 (Shenhav et al. 1994; Henri 2004) and the authors also indicate that whether it is effectiveness or performance that is used, the term organizational effectiveness reveals the extent to which the organizational objectives have been met (*See* also Etizioni 1960). Again, similar to evaluating efficiency in the public sector, which is almost universally designated as being ineffective (Mihaiu et al. 2010 at 133), it is quite hard to evaluate organizational effectiveness in the public sector, especially maritime administrations, due to the fact that its functions are limited by statute. Despite this limitation, maritime administrations have an obligation to make sure that all relevant international requirements are met by the ship owner and the operator of the ship. These international requirements are embodied in various international laws, e.g., the International Convention for the Safety of Life at Sea of 1974, International Convention for the Prevention of Pollution from Ships 1973, as modified by the Protocol of 1978, International Convention on Load Line of 1966 (as modified by its 1988 Protocol), International Convention on Tonnage Measurement of Ships of 1969. Whether it is a flag state or a port state, the implementation of the International Maritime Organization (IMO) needs to be consistent. In this context, the IMO Member State Audit Scheme (IMSAS)[2] plays an important role by providing an audited member scheme with an objective assessment of how effectively and efficiently the state it administers and implements the relevant instruments covered by the scheme (IMO Member State Audit Scheme; IMO Resolution A.946 (23)). IMSAS has traits similar to the International Civil Aviation Organization's Safety Oversight Audit Program where safety aspects during operation are given high priority, and in the given scenario, the auditors of IMSAS are most au fait with this context setting. In retrospect, the introduction and implementation of conventions, codes and amendments seems to be relatively easy; but ensuring that these are effectively enforced is something that needs to be closely observed. So the idea to set up an audit scheme for maritime administrations may well be considered as a profound approach by the IMO to ensure that member states are up-to-date with implementation and enforcement of relevant regulations.

From a control perspective, traits of efficiency and organizational effectiveness of a maritime administration can be gathered from the way they perform flag State control and port State control. While flag State control is conducted by the officers of the maritime administration of the flag State to ensure that their fleet follows national and international regulations, port State control, on the other hand, is the inspection of foreign ships in other national ports by port state officers of respective maritime

[2]The initial framework for IMSAS was developed by a Joint Member State Working Group, largely based on a Quality Systems Approach similar to ISO 9001.

administrations. Although port State control is the next control layer after flag State control, both of these state controls can be narrowed down by the terms investigation, monitoring and in certain cases, detention. These action-terms, in short, help define the controlling-functions of a maritime administration over ships and their owners. If the maritime administration or the responsible recognized organization[3] is able to perform these duties and help maintain the high safety standards and ensure that owners and operators have the essential items of equipment in the correct condition as per international regulation, then the working practice of that administration can be deemed as efficient, and the control that is exercised can be termed as effective. It is therefore suggested that in order to understand efficiency and effectiveness of maritime administrations, the terms flag State control and port State control merits further scrutiny.

4 Flag State Control

To understand "performance" in the public sector, Kalb (2010) has relied on two essential components i.e. efficiency and effectiveness (See Worthington and Dollery 2000). According to Kalb (2010), efficiency refers to how well a decision-making unit (e.g. local government) employs resources in producing (public) goods and services, and efficiency construes the degree to which a decision making unit achieves its programme and policy objectives (Kalb 2010). When this concept is applied to maritime administrations, it can be hypothesized that an effective and efficient maritime administration has performed and continues to perform its international obligations in good faith. With regard to the maritime sector, flag state control and port state control are the two main areas of responsibility of a State government and the duties of control pursuant to standards set out by the international maritime law must be performed by the government administrations in good faith.

Article 26 of the Vienna Convention on the Law of Treaties, 1969 (hereby referred to as Vienna Convention) stipulates that, "every treaty in force is binding upon the parties to it and must be performed by them in good faith"(Vienna Convention on the Law of Treaties, 1969, "observation of treaties"). While "good faith" is a topic that belongs to the domain of contract law, it has nevertheless, been dealt with and written about at inordinate length. Good faith is a state obligation and Article 29 of the Vienna Convention further incorporates that, "unless a different intention appears from the treaty or is otherwise established, a treaty is binding upon each party in respect of its entire territory" "(Vienna Convention on the Law of

[3]In practicing their statutory functions, many maritime administrations are assisted by technical organizations that are willing to act on behalf of administrations on mutual basis. They are termed as recognized organizations. Some maritime administrations mainly focus on the commercial side and leave their statutory obligations of safety and environmental matters in the hands of recognized organizations, either fully or partially.

Treaties, 1969, "territorial scope of treaties"). In short, a state is obliged to perform its duties in good faith and in order to "effectively and efficiently" perform the duties as stated in the binding treaty, states must establish a viable and competent authority that can perform or undertake to perform the duties. The authority or the administration performs or undertakes to perform those duties on behalf of the state and the notion of "good faith" ensures the effectiveness and efficiency of such performance.

Flag State control implies that a State must exercise control over ships entitled to fly its flag and the topic related to the ability to perform its duties under relevant international Conventions has always been a sensitive issue for Flag States. Scholars in the field of maritime law support a common concept—a ship is the subject matter of flag state control and under national maritime law it is aptly recognized as a property and a business asset (Mukherjee 1993). The same concept furthers that a ship "on the international scene assumes a profile akin to a person, requiring nationality" (Mykoo 2003; Mukherjee 1993). To that extent, the question of nationality is to be determined by the respective maritime state to ensure that the ship can be subject to a regulatory scheme (Özcaryir 2001) and so that the state can continue to perform its international obligations in good faith beyond national borders. To that extent, Article 91 of the United Nations Convention on the Law of the Sea, 1981 (hereby referred to as UNCLOS) prescribes the process through which a state can confer nationality on a ship:

1. Every State shall fix the conditions for the grant of its nationality to ships, for the registration of ships in its territory, and for the right to fly its flag. Ships have the nationality of the State whose flag they are entitled to fly. There must exist a genuine link between the State and the ship.
2. Every State shall issue to ships to which it has granted the right to fly its flag documents to that effect. (UNCLOS, Article 91)

By conferring nationality on a ship, a Flag State also solves the question of jurisdiction, which is predicated on the fundamental principle and corollary of a state's sovereignty (Mykoo 2003). Through conferment of nationality, a state can exercise jurisdiction over a "ship" and from an international law perspective, jurisdiction has been defined as the power of a state to exercise its authority via legislative, executive or judicial action over persons and properties (Özcaryir 2001). Since maritime activities concern business across borders—these business activities enliven a state's intention to assert their laws extraterritorially. To assert these laws, a state needs to consider the general accepted international regulations, procedures and practices pursuant to Article 217 of UNCLOS:

> States shall ensure compliance by vessels flying their flag or of their registry with applicable international rules and standards, established through the competent international organization or general diplomatic conference, and with their laws and regulations adopted in accordance with this Convention for the prevention, reduction and control of pollution of the marine environment from vessels and shall accordingly adopt laws and regulations and take other measures necessary for their implementation. Flag States shall provide for the effective enforcement of such rules, standards, laws and regulations, irrespective of where a violation occurs (UNCLOS, Article 217(1))

An important aspect of Article 217(1) is the effective enforcement of international rules and standards and the enforcement aspects are delegated to the respective maritime administration, which must be structured to perform the duties as outlined in Article 94 of UNCLOS. It is noteworthy that the United Nations Convention on the Conditions for Registration of Ships (UNCCROS 1986) was envisaged by the United Nations Conference on Trade and Development (UNCTAD) to become a Convention, which would outline the international conditions for the registration of ships and define the exact meaning of genuine link between a vessel and the state of registry (Pamborides 1999). Although this appeared to be the climate in which UNCRROS 1986 opened in the year 1984, collateral to this objective the Convention provides that the flag state must establish a National Maritime Administration (hereby referred to as NMA), which "...shall be subject to its jurisdiction and control" (UNCCROS 1986, Article 5). Article 5(2) of UNCCROS 1986 further states that the general obligation of a flag State is to implement applicable international standards on issues related to safety and pollution prevention (UNCCROS 1986, Article 5(2)). In this context, the duty of the NMA is provided in paragraph 3 of Article 5, which sets out in detail, but not exhaustively, the tasks that need to be performed by the NMA:

> Article 5(3): The maritime administration of the flag State shall ensure:
>
> (a) That ships flying the flag of such State comply with its laws and regulations concerning registration of ships and with applicable international rules and standards concerning, in particular, the safety of ships and persons on board and the prevention of pollution of the marine environment,
> (b) That ships flying the flag of such State are periodically surveyed by its authorized surveyors in order to ensure compliance with applicable international rules and standards,
> (c) That ships flying the flag of such State carry on-board documents, in particular those evidencing the right to fly its flag and other valid relevant documents, including those required by international conventions to which the State of registration is a Party,
> (d) That the owners of ships flying the flag of such State comply with the principles of registration of ships in accordance with the laws and regulations of such State and the provisions of this Convention. (UNCCROS 1986, Article 5(3).

UNCCROS 1986 has concretely defined the route upon which NMAs should operate their registries and to elaborate this aspect, Mukherjee (1993) explains that the public law function of registration is concerned with administrative matters pertaining to the national interest comprising, *inter alia* conferment of nationality and the right to fly the national flag; extraterritorial jurisdiction over matters related to maritime safety, pollution control, manning and labour conditions, and shipboard discipline; the right to diplomatic protection including consular services; the right of the ship to naval protection; and the right to engage in cabotage activities (Mukherjee 1993, p. 32). Furthermore, a NMA can confirm compliance through a system of periodic surveys and physical inspection of the ship and if satisfied with the survey and inspection, the NMA may issue a certificate that is a proof of compliance. Due to limited technical resources, NMAs may delegate these functions to Recognized

Organizations (hereby referred to as ROs) and the delegation aspect has been developed by the IMO in Resolution A. 739(18) (See Resolution A. 739(18)). In all cases, the NMA shall fully guarantee the completeness and efficiency of the survey and the inspection and shall undertake to ensure that necessary arrangements are made to satisfy this obligation (Abe 2000). Unlike UNCCROS 1986, UNCLOS does not stipulate any direct responsibilities on maritime administrations and leaves all relevant regulatory functions to be performed by the state (UNCLOS, Article 94). When compared, one can observe some similarities between Article 5(3) of UNCCROS and Article 94(4) of UNCLOS with regard to the necessary arrangements that to be ensured. Article 94(4) of UNCLOS is observed to embody the key elements of Article 5(3) of UNCCROS 1986 with reference to survey, surveyor, international laws and regulations. But when the two aforementioned Articles are compared—it is observed that Article 94(4) of UNCLOS goes further than focusing on registration aspects in so far as it highlights and stipulates the much-needed qualifications of the master and officers (UNCLOS, Article 94(4)(b) and Article 94 (4)(c)). All in all, both UNCLOS and UNCCROS 1986 proceed with one clear objective and that is to ensure "safety at sea". Unlike UNCCROS 1986, in order to ensure "safety at sea"—UNCLOS provides specific measures with regard, *inter alia*, to:

(a) the construction, equipment and seaworthiness of ships;
(b) the manning of ships, labour conditions and the training of crews, taking into account the applicable international instruments;
(c) the use of signals, the maintenance of communications and the prevention of collisions. (UNCLOS, Article 94(3))

The objective of the ship-owner is to obtain maximum profit from the maritime business venture and with the ship being the subject matter of the NMA (or maritime administration) regulatory regime; it is a pragmatic responsibility of the ship-owner to comply with the given measures. Even if it is a public company or a private company, a small company or a large company—the ship-owners have clear delineated responsibilities under international law (*See* Fig. 2). Whether ship-owners take a proactive approach or a reactive approach, they must be cognizant of the "generally acceptable international rules and standards" and in this case, the rules and standards developed by IMO. The main result is to achieve quality goals and standards in shipping and in this regard it is submitted that safety at sea is not the sole responsibility of the flag state or the maritime administration.

The concept "safety at sea" also demands that the ship-owners efficiently and effectively perform their duties, which mainly includes verifying the qualifications of the master, officer and the crew. The ship-owner must also be conscious and aware about the human element in the operation, control and management of a ship. The operation, control and management collateral to the fair treatment of seafarers has been and continues to be the subject matter of discussion in national, regional and international fora and thus, needs adequate attention.

Sub-standard shipping could also refer to the inadequate and improper manning of ships, and ship-owners should bear in mind that the safety of a ship is related to

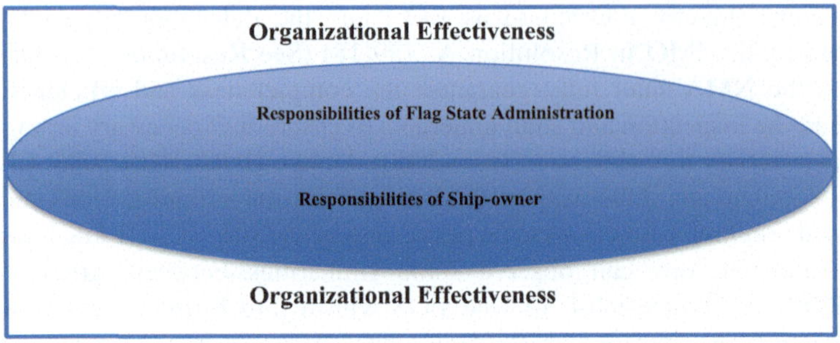

Fig. 2 Equation of Mutual Responsibilities between Flag State Administration and Ship-owner: (Square represents the all-embracing organizational effectiveness of a maritime administration; Oval represents the core of "organizational effectiveness" which is a balance between two responsibilities)

the safety of the seafarers who play a role in the operation, control and management of a ship. IMO has left no stones unturned to address the safety and security of the human element and introduced the Convention on the Standard of Training, Certification and Watchkeeping 1978, as amended 1995 (STCW95) and the International Safety Management (ISM) Code Guidelines on Implementation of the IMO Code. These Conventions and Guidelines are to be enforced through flag State implementation or port State control, yet ship-owners continue to be faced with safety and security questions, which questions all these international efforts. Ship-owners, in short, help balance the equation and when ship-owners comply with national regulations in accordance with generally acceptable international rules and standards that fall within the ambit of broader international policies, strategies and guidelines, they confirm the organizational effectiveness of flag maritime administrations.

5 Port State Control

The concept of port State control is relatively new when compared to flag State control. This is also based on the fact that previously, port states did not reflect the intention to enforce its jurisdiction over foreign ships entering their ports (Özcaryir 2001). At the grassroot level, customary international law gives a port State vast discretion to exercise control and jurisdiction over its ports (International Court of Justice 1986). Scholars have opined that a states territorial sovereignty signifies exclusive competence of the state over its own territory (Shaw 2008) and a foreign ship in the port of a state is subject to the same jurisdiction as an alien on land (McDorman 2000). Although the concept is supported by customary international law, the *status quo* port state control regime derives from a Memorandum of Understanding (MoU) between eight North Sea States in the year of 1978 (Cariou et al. 2008). This was further qualified by an MoU signed in 1982 as a result of the *Amoco Cadiz* oil spill the new MoU is observed to expand not only the scope of the agreement, but the membership as well (Cariou et al. 2008). Regional MoUs include the: (a) Paris MoU (1982); (b) Viña del Mar MoU (1992); (c) Tokyo MoU (1993); (d) Caribbean MoU (1996); (e) Mediterranean MoU (1997); (f) Indian MoU (1998); (g) Abuja MoU (1999); (h) Black Sea MoU (2000) and (i) Black Sea MoU (2004). Thus, a port State control MoU is seen as an administrative agreement among maritime authorities of different countries and as an integral part of the maritime world safety chain whereby port State control is considered as the last safety net (Özcaryir 2001). The rationale behind this consideration has been further substantiated by Cariou et al.:

> Seven of the most important conventions in the international regulatory framework for maritime safety serve as the bases upon which the regime of PSC has been institutionalized. These are the International Convention for the Safety of Life at Sea (SOLAS), International Convention for the Prevention of Pollution from Ships (MARPOL), International Convention on Load Lines (LOADLINES), International Convention on Standards of Training, Certification and Watchkeeping for Seafarers (STCW), Convention on the International Regulations for Preventing Collisions at Sea (COLREG), International Convention on Tonnage Measurement of Ships (TONNAGE), Merchant Shipping (Minimum Standards) Convention (ILO 147). This was in reaction to the generally-held belief that many *flag States are unable to adequately perform their mandated duties* of ensuring that ships flying their flag comply fully with international safety standards formulated under the auspices of the International Maritime Organization (IMO) and the International Labour Organization (ILO). As such, PSC is merely a complement, not a substitute, to effective maritime safety administration by the flag state. While it was originally intended as an interim measure, trends and developments in international enforcement indicate that PSC is here to stay. (emphasis added) (Cariou et al., 2006, p. 2).

At the international level, port State jurisdiction has been defined in relevant Articles of UNCLOS. Port state jurisdiction falls under Part XII with regard to protection and preservation of the marine environment. In an effort to analyze port State jurisdiction in terms of UNCLOS, it is observed that there are two distinct elements embedded, i.e. an element of control and an element of enforcement jurisdiction. While the control element differs from the enforcement element, it is suggested that both these elements have a common objective, i.e. protection of the marine environment. While paragraph 3 of Article 211 provides the basis of port State jurisdiction under which states may "establish particular requirements for the prevention, reduction and control of pollution of the marine environment as a condition for the entry of foreign vessels into their ports or internal waters or for a call at their off-shore terminals", states have been advised to act through competent organization and establish international rules and standards (UNCLOS, Article 211).

A competent organization, in this context, is commonly referred to as IMO. As UNCLOS establishes the universal legal principles of port State control, IMO seeks to provide an international framework, which is considered as a concrete foundation for the regional MOUs. The first effort by IMO to establish a unified framework for port State control began in 1981 with the adoption of IMO Resolution A.466(13) and since then, there have been several amendments leading to the latest adaptation i.e. IMO Resolution A.1052(27) in the year 2011 (Table 1).

Table 1 IMO Resolution on port State control and year of adoption

IMO Resolution	Adopted in the year
IMO Resolution A.542(13) Procedures for the control of ships and discharges under Annex I of the International Convention for the Prevention of Pollution from Ships, 1973, as modified by the Protocol of 1978 relating thereto.	1983
IMO Resolution A.597(15) Amendments to the Procedures for the Control of Ships.	1987
IMO Resolution A.742(18) Procedures for the Control of Operational Requirements Related to the Safety of Ships and Pollution Prevention.	1993
IMO Resolution A.787(19) Procedures for Port State Control.	1995
IMO Resolution A.882(21) Amendments to the Procedures for Port State Control.	1999

It is noteworthy that section 1.7 of IMO Resolution A.1052(27) incorporates definitions of significant terms and from a broad perspective the term inspection (section 1.7.5) is the only way to ensure effective compliance and this is done by a "visit on board a ship to check both the validity of the relevant certificates and other documents, and the overall condition of the ship, its equipment and its crew" (IMO Resolution A.1052(27)). Inspection has been termed as a powerful operational tool for the port State authority that can be exercised to prevent or interrupt unsafe operations and if deficiency is observed, the authority can then proceed towards detainment of vessels (Iarosi 1996). From a public administration perspective, inspection is defined as the process whereby the state supervises and monitors service professions (Greenwood et al. 2002; Pyper 1996) notes the increasing use of regulation and inspection during the twentieth century as crisis of self-regulation surfaced when the scope of public administrations began to widen.

Although inspection has been a central focus of Resolution A.1052(27), IMO has also incorporated Resolution A.1070(28) IMO Instrument Implementation Code (hereby referred to as the III (Triple I) Code) (adopted in 2013), which provides that states "develop an overall strategy to ensure that its international obligations as a. . .port state. . .are met" and in order to reach this objective, states are requested to "continuously review the strategy to achieve, maintain and improve the overall *organizational performance* and capability as a. . .port state" (emphasis added) (International Maritime Organization Instrument Implementation Code, Report 150). It is suggested that in order to achieve "organizational performance", maritime administrations could develop a strategic human resource development system. A good quality system, to that extent, could ensure achievement and maintenance of organizational performance.

5.1 ISO Quality Management System

The International Organization for Standardization (ISO) sets out a criteria for quality management system and the standard criteria "can be used by any organization, large or small, regardless of its field of activity" (Official homepage of ISO). A technical committee develops the ISO 9000 series and the series sets out the requirements of a "quality management" system within the framework of contractual relations between a company and its client;

ISO 9001:2015—sets out the requirements of a quality management system
ISO 9000:2015—covers the basic concepts and language
ISO 9004:2009—focuses on how to make a quality management system more *efficient and effective* (emphasis added)
ISO 19011:2011—sets out guidance on internal and external audits of quality management systems. (Official homepage of ISO)

Although ISO 9000 series are an effective way to develop quality management for all types of organizations, it is to be noted that implementation and certification within ISO are generally done on a voluntary basis (Jedral 2000). It can be asserted that a maritime administration does not have any influence in the implementation of ISO standards and the only role they play in ISO standard implementation is to participate in the preparation of the norms and rules of certification, which is based on inspection (Jedral 2000). A state needs to become a member of ISO, which is the best way forward for a state administration to effectively set out requirements of a quality management system (Jedral 2000). The paradigm shift has already begun whereby maritime administrations are recognizing a quality management system as an important tool to ensure quality and organizational effectiveness (Jedral 2000) (*See* Diagram 2).

6 Maritime Administrations of Developed and Developing Countries

In order to understand the level of a maritime administration's organizational effectiveness, one must first observe the performance aspects, which indicate: (a) whether administrations have developed and maintained best practices of ocean governance; and (b) to what extent do those best practices reflect social responsibility towards stakeholders at large. In short, the national laws and regulations by which the maritime administrations are governed, need to provide specific reference to either maritime governance or ocean governance. It is a rather daunting and challenging task to explore each and every maritime legislation of each and every maritime nation and confirm whether ocean governance is concretely defined. However, the common perception is that, national maritime legislation of developed and developing countries do not precisely and clearly express or readily observe the term "ocean governance" with only a handful of exceptions, namely Korea, New Zealand, Australia and Canada. To understand ocean governance in the context of national legislation, reliance has to be made on: (a) the general idea gathered from the texts of the maritime legislation; (b) the interpretation of the texts and their incorporation in the maritime administration's work; and (c) results of incorporation reflected through reports of survey, inspection and relevant tasks. In this context, it is noteworthy that that there is no specific reference to maritime or ocean governance in key international instruments. Reference to international instruments is highly relevant due to the fact that member states are under an obligation to consider the implementation of "generally acceptable international rules and standards". These are the rules and standards that have been implemented and enforced at the international level. While the concept of ocean governance resides somewhat in a legal vacuum, the process of connecting this term to maritime administrations is frustrated because of the often wide differences in the organizational structure.

Although there has been an effort to provide a blueprint of a model organization structure (Vanchiswar 1996), the existing differences in the organizational framework of various maritime administrations make it clear that the governments have adopted their own strategies. The differences can be further confirmed by a comparative study through which a lack of symmetry is observed among the various maritime administrations across the globe (EMSA 2004). This is especially the case in the European Union whereby the European Maritime Safety Agency (EMSA) prepared a report in 2004 showing the different organizational structures of maritime administrations of 29 European Union member states (EMSA 2004). In order to understand how major maritime states (developed countries) have structured their maritime administrations and implemented respective strategies, it is important to observe the differences in their organizational division framework. To highlight the differences, the authors have carefully selected the organizational structure of 11 developed countries, which are enlisted in the following chart (Table 2):

Similar to the developed countries of the European Union, there exists variation in the organizational structure of maritime administrations of developing countries. In this context, the maritime administration organizational structure of two maritime nations, i.e. India and Vietnam can be taken into consideration. The reason behind this consideration is largely due to the fact that these two developing countries have opened their own economies to take full advantage of the opportunities for economic development through trade (Official homepage of the International Monetary Fund; Srinivasan and Bhagwati 1999). In India, the Director General of Shipping is the statutory maritime authority and is appointed by the government of India under the Merchant Shipping Act of 1958 and deals with all matters concerning the maritime administration, maritime education and training, development of shipping industry and other related subjects (DG Shipping, Official homepage of the Directorate General of Shipping). The Indian structure can be contrasted with the Vietnamese maritime administration structure, which is based on a divergent framework and involves a number of Ministries including the Ministry of Transport, the Ministry of Planning and Investment, the Ministry of Finance and the Ministry of Defence (Quang 2000). At the commercial level, the Vietnamese government has involved

Table 2 Organizational structure of maritime administrations of selected European Union member states (and Canada)

European Union member state	Head of maritime administration/Name of agency	Division
Austria	The Minister for Transport, Innovation and Technology	1. Air/water belongs to the "Infrastructure" section. 2. Air/water infrastructure has three departments i.e. law, water policy and Federal waterways.
Denmark	The Danish Maritime Authority.	The Danish Maritime Authority of Denmark is a government agency that governs maritime affairs. The authority is comprised of: (1) board of Directors; (2) Secretariat for Maritime Policy; (3) Strategic Planning Division; (4) Centre for Internal Staff, Services and Finances; (5) Centre for Maritime Regulation; (6) Centre for Ships; (7) Centre for Seafarers and Fishermen; (8) Centre of Maritime Health Service; and (9) Division for Investigation of Maritime Accidents.
Finland	"The Finnish Maritime Administration, reporting to the Ministry of Transport and Communications, is the competent authority for maritime issues in Finland".	The Administrative sector of the Ministry of Transport and Communications is divided into: 1. Government offices and agencies and; 2. State-owned Enterprises and 3. State-owned companies.
France	"The Ministry of Transport, Infrastructure, Tourism and the Sea; and the Ministry for Ecology, Sustainable Development and Special Planning is responsible for preparing and fine tuning France's Maritime Policy".	The Directorate for Sea and Transport has two divisions: 1. Directorate for sea, road and river transport and 2. Directorate for Maritime Affairs.
Germany	"The Sub-Department titled "Shipping" is the competent authority for maritime issues within the Federal Ministry of Transport, Building and Urban Affairs".	

(continued)

Table 2 (continued)

European Union member state	Head of maritime administration/Name of agency	Division
		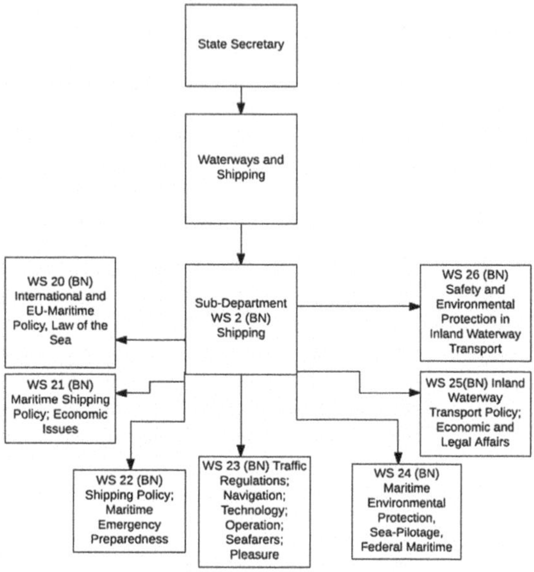
Greece	"The Ministry of Mercantile Marine is the competent Greek Maritime Authority and performs its duties mainly through the Hellenic Coast Guard".	"The operations which are institutionally conducted by the Ministry of Mercantile Marine, the Aegean and the Island Policy, are to a large extent complicated, inquiring implication and collaboration of a great amount of Public Services, Regional Services, International Organizations as well as cooperation of the Social Partners. It should be emphasized that, according to the current European and International regulations in force, rarely can we find any other corresponding government agencies having such a wide range of responsibilities falling within the Ministry's operational activities".
Italy	"The Navigation, Maritime Transport and Aviation Department is the competent authority for maritime issues within the Ministry of Transports in the Italian Republic. The following picture shows its position within the Ministry".	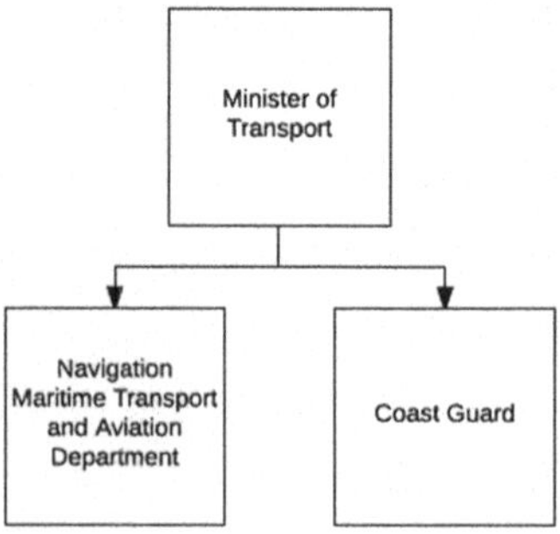

(continued)

Table 2 (continued)

European Union member state	Head of maritime administration/Name of agency	Division
Spain	"The Dirección General de la Marina Mercante (DGMM) (Directorat-e General for merchant navy) is a Department of the Ministerio de Fomento (Ministry of Public Works)".	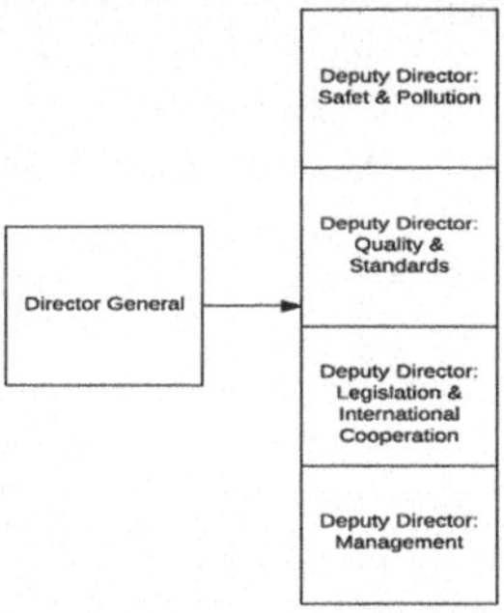
Sweden	"The Swedish Maritime Administration is a public enterprise within the transport sector, governed by the Ministry of Enterprise, Energy and Communication. The Swedish Maritime Administration is a self-financing public enterprise, i.e. its activities are, with some exceptions, financed through fees and charges on shipping, outside the government budget".	
UK	"The Maritime and Coast Guard Agency is an executive agency of the Department for Transport".	The Maritime and Coastguard Agency "is responsible throughout the UK for implementing the government's maritime safety policy. That includes co-ordinating search and rescue at sea through Her Majesty's Coastguard, and checking that ships meet UK and international safety rules. The Directorate of Operations consists of six separate parts: Enforcement, Survey, Inspection including Port State Control, Her Majesty's Coastguard (HMCG) Search & Rescue and Incident Prevention and Counter Pollution. These branches provide statutory survey and inspection services to the UK fleet and carries out Port State Control of non UK ships, investigates and prosecutes breaches of Merchant Shipping legislation, coordinates search and rescue and maintains a marine counter pollution response capability. MCA is an organization certified according to ISO 9001: 2000 standards by an external auditing body".

(continued)

Table 2 (continued)

European Union member state	Head of maritime administration/Name of agency	Division
Canada	Ministry of Transport and the Canadian Coast Guard	The Ministry of Transport is responsible for implementation of national law and policy and overseeing the federal government's transportation regulatory departments. The Canadian Coast Guard is largely responsible for the operational delivery of all at sea programs and obstacles.

Source: European Maritime Safety Agency (EMSA) (2004), "An Overview of the 29 European Maritime Administration"

two major state-owned corporations, namely the Vietnam National Shipping lines and the Vietnam Shipbuilding Industry Corporation (Quang 2000). In short, considering the maritime administration organizational of India and Vietnam, it is safe to assert that developing countries do not follow any ideal blueprint when structuring respective maritime administrations and their departments. Even though the organizational structure of maritime administrations in the developed nations vary from one state to another, it is relatively easy for developed countries to implement the new global measures largely due to the fact that they have an effective maritime or coast guard administration or both (Herbet-Burns et al. 2008).

In retrospect, the effectiveness of a maritime administration relies heavily on how well it is synchronised with the national maritime legislation, which is formulated taking into account the generally acceptable international rules and standards and their acceptance by a particular State. Developed countries of the European Union have an improved system due to the fact that the EU is based on the "rule of law". A further examination reveals that, every action taken by the European Union is founded on treaties approved voluntarily and democratically by all European Union member States (Official homepage of the European Union). In addition, European Union Directives are used as a legislative tool to bring different national laws into line with each other (Official homepage of the European Commission) and this makes the transposition phase more easier for the European Union member States. It should be noted that failure to transpose the Directives into national law renders the European Commission a right to instigate an infringement case against member States for non communication and thus, a mandatory regime begins to unravel. This mandatory regime is marked by a positive aspect and one that includes a form of confirmation that a developed country within the European Union has fined tuned it's national legislation with laws of other member States. Completeness in the individual measures of all the member States confirms and is indicative of the fact that there is absolute completeness in the European Union altogether. Although the word completeness can often be seen as a vague term, for European Union member States it translates into two consecutive steps: (a) to what extent the national laws are congruous with the European Union Directives; and (b) whether the national laws are complete and sufficient enough to govern the maritime administrations. Here, the common element or media is national law, a channel through which the proper functioning of the principle law i.e. European Union Directive is ensured. For the developed European Union member States, that principle law is Directive 2009/16/EC of the European Parliament and of the Council of 23 April 2009 on port State control (Directive 2009/16/EC). Directive 2013/38/EU of the European Parliament and of the Council of 12 August 2013 (hereby referred to as Directive 2013/38/EU has been introduced as an amendment to Directive 2009/16/EC on a significant number of Articles (Directive 2013/38/EU). It is noteworthy that, even though Directive 2013/38/EU is an amendment of Directive 2009/16/EC, the main objective tends to be generic and takes into consideration the international standards for safety, pollution prevention and on-board living and working conditions;

Preamble, Paragraph 7 of Directive 2009/16/EC

> Responsibility for monitoring the compliance of ships with the international standards for safety, pollution prevention and on- board living and working conditions lies primarily with the flag State. Relying, as appropriate, on recognised organisations, the flag State fully guarantees the completeness and efficiency of the inspections and surveys undertaken to issue the relevant certificates. Responsibility for maintenance of the condition of the ship and its equipment after survey to comply with the requirements of Conventions applicable to the ship lies with the ship company. However, there has been a serious failure on the part of a number of flag States to implement and enforce international standards. Henceforth, as a second line of defence against substandard shipping, the monitoring of compliance with the international standards for safety, pollution prevention and on-board living and working conditions should also be ensured by the port State, while recognising that port State control inspection is not a survey and the relevant inspection forms are not seaworthiness certificates. (2009/16/EC)

Preamble, Paragraph 4 of Directive 2013/38/EC

> In order to ensure a harmonised approach to the effective enforcement of international standards by Member States when performing both flag and port State control inspections and to avoid friction between international and Union law, Member States should aim at ratifying the Conventions by the date on which they enter into force, at least those parts thereof falling under Union competence. (Directive 2013/38/EC)

One of the unique features of Directive 2009/16/EC is the submission of a report or information by any person or organization with a legitimate interest in safety at sea, which takes into account: (a) the safety of the ship including the human element; and (b) the prevention of pollution aspect. This mindset remains unaltered in Directive 2013/38/EC whereby the submission of a report by an inspector remains an obligatory task. In general, the report submitted by an inspector following a detailed inspection highlights the deficiencies with regard to "the living and working conditions on the ship" and identifies the parts that do not conform to the Maritime Labour Convention of 2006 (Directive 2013/38/EC, Article 1(7)). Article 1(7) of Directive 2013/38/EC further states that this report comprised of deficiencies is brought to the attention of the shipowners' organizations or to the member State in which the inspection is carried out. The report prepared by the inspector is forwarded to the shipowners' organization for consideration and enforcement of immediate measures to resolve the deficiencies. From an organizational aspect, corporations (companies) have a similar reporting responsibility and the report so prepared is mainly shared with the stakeholders. The only difference is that the reporting system for public and private corporations (company) is seen as a voluntary task and it is further argued that CSR actually functions as an informal law (Buhmann 2006) because the entire facet of CSR is influenced by the notion of self-governance.

Relevantly, business and or/civil society organizations have come to terms with the fact that responsible stewardship in terms of both resources and public opinion is necessary to ensure their longevity and thus, the growing number of company reports that mirror the effort to be more corporate and socially responsible (Hohnen 2007). Some of the better known non-profit CSR institutions and resources established by these business and or/civil organizations include Accountability, African Institute of Corporate Citizenship, Business and Human Rights Resource Centre, Business Social Compliance Initiative, Business for Social Responsibility, Business in the Community, Coalition for Environmentally Responsible Economies, the Conference Board, Ethos Institute, Ethical Trading Initiative, European Academy of Business in Society, Extractive Industries Transparency Initiative, Fair Labor Association, Fundacion Entorno, Social Accountability International, World Business council for Sustainable Development, Vincular, World Council for Corporate Governance (Hohnen 2007). In the maritime sector, a detailed report on CSR has the potential to show the influence that a particular maritime administration has on finances, people (employees and societal) and the environment. Unlike business corporations (companies), a different term is used in lieu of CSR Report whereby current practice in the maritime field revolves around the publication of a sustainability report by maritime administrations. The so-called sustainability report is marked by similar objectives. Maritime administrations of developed countries within the European Union have focussed their attention on delivering a sustainability report, which is evident from the current efforts of Swedish Maritime Administration (via annual publication of sustainability reports) and the Danish Maritime Authority (via Blue Denmark), to name a few.

7 Conclusion

The notion of CSR recognizes that companies have obligations that extend beyond short-run profit maximization. This extended obligation also incorporates social and environmental concern by taking into account the stakeholders who are directly or indirectly affected in the operation of business. Although the interest in CSR at both the professional and academic level has increased considerably in recent decades, for business corporations, defining CSR remains as a challenging task (Masaka 2008). While some authors believe that organizations should have a one solution fits it all approach (van Marrewijk 2003), other authors draw a concrete conclusion stating that the moral underpinnings of CSR are neither clear nor agreed upon (Frederick 2006). A few authors are observed to rest on an all-embracing definition:

> The term [social responsibility] is a brilliant one; it means something, but not always the same thing, to everybody. To some it conveys the idea of legal responsibility or liability; to others, it means socially responsible behavior in an ethical sense; to still others, the meaning transmitted is that of "responsible for," in a causal mode; many simply equate it with a charitable contribution; some take it to mean socially conscious; many of those who embrace it most fervently see it as a mere synonym for "legitimacy," in the context of "belonging" or being proper or valid; a few see it as a sort of fiduciary duty imposing higher standards of behavior on businessmen than on citizens at large (Carroll 1999, pg. 280).

Whereas authors of business administration tend to debate on the existence of a particular definition of CSR, it gradually becomes complicated when the term is incorporated in the maritime field. In the maritime sector, the trend is to focus on government organizations, more specifically, maritime administrations and their (maritime) governance capacity to control sub-standard shipping via flag State control and port State control. It is, therefore, submitted that CSR is connected to a maritime administration through the concepts of effectiveness and efficiency, which is an intricate part of the good (maritime) governance strategy. Even if this hypothesis is rejected, one cannot deny the fact that maritime administrations can be linked to CSR through the model provided by ISO 26000. ISO 26000 delineates the seven core subjects of social responsibility as: (a) organizational governance (at the core); (b) community involvement and development; (c) human rights; (d) labor practices; (e) the environment; (f) fair operating practices; and (g) consumer issues (Discovering ISO 26000). The amalgamation of these core subjects of social responsibility reflects a holistic approach whereby organizational governance acts as the nucleus (Discovering ISO 26000, p. 9, see Figure). Even though the subject matters of social responsibility have been successfully identified, now-a-days it is commonly understood that whether it is a small or a big business corporation, every corporate entity is entitled to tailor their corporate policies for self-regulation, which they unanimously agree to be governed by in the process of conducting business.

Again, for business corporations, CSR emanates from the will to be dedicated, both for the cause and the reputation. CSR, thus, takes the shape of informal law, which is embedded into the business model for the corporate managers to follow. Although maritime administrations function with the same cause and reputation ideology and the same subject matters including human rights, labor practices and the environment, the laws governing the functionality of a maritime administration are far from informal. Under international maritime law, there exists both formal prescriptive and enforcement jurisdictions and these are further formalized through implementation in national law. From a formal law perspective, a maritime administration needs to work effectively and efficiently to reach organizational effectiveness or administration effectiveness and simultaneously provide a check and balance in the operations of shipping companies via surveys, inventories and reports. A striking difference is that reports issued by a maritime administration (inspector) differs from the CSR reports published a company. The former is seen as a compliance report that embodies the deficiencies to address urgent matters to deter sub-standard shipping, and the latter is mainly a performance indicator whereby the CSR report is a voluntary publication that evaluates the company's overall environmental and safety performance. But whether it is a complaint or a performance indicator, the common objective is to be socially responsible to the stakeholders, both minor and major. These stakeholders are the one's who are directly or indirectly impacted by sub-standard shipping or in the company's business process. Then again, the three aforementioned elements i.e. human rights, labor practices and the environment (as a part of ISO 26000's seven core subjects) are the key elements of UNCLOS, UNCCROS 1986 and the Maritime Labour Convention of 2006 and marked by the term safety at sea. This safety aspect is mainly ensured and verified by the maritime administration (by the dual role they play in flag State control and port State control) and the laws governing safety at sea are already implemented at the international level and acceptable by, more or less, all governments in general.

These generally acceptable international rules and standards with regard to safety at sea ought to be implemented and enforced at the national level as a part of state responsibility i.e. *pacta sunt servanda* (observation of treaties) pursuant to the Vienna Convention on the Law of Treaties of 1969. For the developed countries of the European Union, the rigidity is observed once the rules and standards are enacted in the form of a Directive. It is only then the European Union member States need to conscientiously transpose them into national legislation, and the national legislation in turn adds to the functional-strength of maritime administrations, which can work to ensure quality management and intra-organizational effectiveness and provide the government with the necessary tools to complete the national and international maritime functions. For the maritime administrations of developing countries, the quest to achieve organizational effectiveness still continues. On the bright side, India, a developing country that tends to take the lead position in maritime affairs among South-East Asian countries, has come forward in establishing a CSR mandate by implementing the Companies Act in 2013 (The Companies Act, 2013, s. 135), considered to be the first update of the country's corporate law in more than 50 years. Schedule VII of the 2013 Act defines CSR as activities relating to: (1) eradicating extreme hunger and poverty; (2) promotion of education; (3) promoting gender equality and empowering women; (4) reducing child mortality and improving maternal health; (5) combating human immunodeficiency virus, acquired immune deficiency syndrome, malaria and other diseases; (6) ensuring environmental sustainability; (7) employment enhancing vocational skills; (8) social business projects; (9) contribution to the Prime Minister's National Relief Fund or any other fund set up by the Central government or the State governments for socio-economic development and relief and funds for the welfare of the Scheduled Castes, the Scheduled Tribes, other backward classes, minorities and women; and (10) such other matters as may be prescribed (The Companies Act, 2013, schedule VII). The CSR requirements of the 2013 Act apply to any company incorporated in India, whether it is domestic or a subsidiary of a foreign company (The Companies Act 2013). Although CSR has become mandatory for companies incorporated in India, the state legislation which governs the structure and operation of maritime administrations are still out-of-date. If this is the *status quo*, then developing countries including India and Bangladesh are well overdue for a major reform. Major reform, in this sense, refers to compliance with the international safety at sea regulations in order for the maritime administrations to be effective and efficient and the departments to be well synchronized. After this is achieved, the administrations can proceed to ensure that shipping companies align their business with society's expectations and continue to maintain a good CSR status by putting social responsibility equally alongside their business goals.

References

Abe, M. (2000). Classification societies: Their roles, duties and responsibilities. *BIMCO Review*, 116.

Arat, L. (2011). *Corporate Social Responsibility in Shipping Conpanies in the Baltic Sea*. University of Turku, Centre for Maritime Studies, CAFE project. Work Package (Task A): Theory of corporate social responsibility (CSR) and implications to the maritime sector. http://www.merikotka.fi/julkaisut/CafeCSRraportti_LauraArat.pdf. Accessed 1 August 2016.

Bigg, T., & Ward, H. (2007). *Linking CSR, good governance and corporate accountability through dialogue* (p. 5). International Institute for Environmental Development.

Borcherding, T. E., Pommerehne, W. W., & Schneider, F. (1982). Comparing the efficiency of private and public production: The evidence from five countries. *Zeitschrift für Nationalökonomie, 89*, 127–156.

Buhmann, K. (2006). Corporate social responsibility: What role for law? Some aspects of law and CSR. *Corporate Governance, 6*(2), 188–202.

Carroll, A. B. (1999). Corporate social responsibility – evolution of a definitional construction. *Business and Society, 38*(3), 268–295.

Cariou, P., Mejia, M. Q., Jr., & Wolff, F.-C. (2008). On the effectiveness of port state control inspections. *Transportation Research Part E, 44*, 491–503.

Chartered Institute of Public Finance and Accountancy (CIPFA) and International Federation of Accountants (IFAC). (2013). *Good Governance in the Public Sector – Consultation Draft for an International Framework*. Consultation Draft.

Curristine, T., Lonti, Z., & Joumard, I. (2007). Improving public sector efficiency: Challenges and opportunities. *OECD Journal on Budgeting, 7*(1).

Chrzanowski, I. (1985). Types of operations. In S. J. Wiater (Ed.), *An introduction to shipping economics*. London: Fairplay Publication.

Committee of Inquiry into Shipping. (1970). *Report (Rochdale Report)*. Cmnd. 4337. London: HMSO.

D'Amato, A., Henderson, S., & Florence, S. (2009). *Corporate social responsibility and sustainable business: A guide to leadership tasks and functions*. Centre for Creative Leadership, CCL Press. http://insights.ccl.org/wp-content/uploads/2015/04/CorporateSocialResponsibility.pdf. Accessed 2 August 2016.

DG Shipping, Official homepage of the Directorate General of Shipping, http://www.dgshipping.gov.in/Content/OrganisationChartAbout.aspx. Accessed 12 December 2015.

Directive 2009/16/EC of the European Parliament and of the Council of 23 April, 2009 on port State control. http://eur-lex.europa.eu/legal-content/EN/TXT/PDF/?uri=CELEX:02009L0016-20130820&rid=1. Accessed 18 December 2015.

Directive 2013/38/EU of the European Parliament and of the Council of 12 August, 2013. http://eur-lex.europa.eu/legal-content/EN/TXT/PDF/?uri=CELEX:32013L0038&from=EN. Accessed 18 December 2015.

Discovering ISO 26000, ISO 26000 Guidance on Social Responsibility. http://www.iso.org/iso/discovering_iso_26000.pdf. Accessed 20 December 2015.

Etzioni, A. (1960). Two approaches to organizational analysis: A critique and suggestion. *Administrative Science Quarterly, 5*, 257–258.

European Maritime Safety Agency (EMSA). (2004). *An Overview of the 29 European Maritime Administration.* http://www.emsa.europa.eu/overview-maritime-administrations/download/1031/621/23.html. Accessed 12 December 2015.

COM (20001) 366 Final, European Union Commission. http://eur-lex.europa.eu/LexUriServ/LexUriServ.do?uri=COM:2001:0366:FIN:en:PDF. Accessed 21 December 2015.

Fare, R., & Lovell, C. A. K. (1978). Measuring the technical efficiency of production. *Journal of Economic Theory, 19*, 150–162.

Farthing, B., & Brownrigg, M. (1997). *Farthing on international shipping* (3rd ed.). London, Hong Kong: LLP Limited.

Frederick, W. C. (2006). *Corporation, be good! The story of corporate social responsibility.* Indianapolis: Dog Ear Publishing.

Good Governance. (2005). *Official Homepage of UNESCO.* http://portal.unesco.org/ci/en/ev.php-URL_ID=5205&URL_DO=DO_TOPIC&URL_SECTION=201.html. Accessed 7 December 2015.

Greenwood, J. R., Pyper, R., & Wilson, D. J. (2002). *New public Administration in Britain* (p. 14). Psychology Press.

Hawker, G. (1983). Review of third report from the treasury and Civil Service Committee: Efficiency and effectiveness in the Civil Service London. *Journal of Public Policy, 3*, 233–234.

Henri, J.-F. (2004). Performance measurement and organizational effectiveness: Brdiging the Gap. *Managerial Finance, 30*(6), 93–123.

Herbet-Burns, R., Bateman, S., & Lehr, P. (Eds.). (2008). *Lloyd's MIU handbook of maritime security* (p. xxi). CRC Press.

Hohnen, P. (2007). In J. Potts (Ed.), *Corporate social responsibility: An Implementation Guide for Business*. International Institute for Sustainable Development. http://www.iisd.org/pdf/2007/csr_guide.pdf. Accessed 13 August 2016.

Hubbard Michael J. (IMO Consultant) and Hoppe Heike (IMO Technical Officer) (Possible Framework for a Model Maritime Administration). (2001). *Possible Framework for a Model Maritime Administration.* http://www.imo.org/blast/blastDataHelper.asp?data_id=3935&filename=modeladministration.pdf. Accessed 7 December 2015.

Iarosi, F. (1996). The future relationship of classification societies to port states. *BIMCO Review*, 130–132.

IMO. (2013). *World Maritime Day: A Concept of a Sustainable Maritime Transportation System, World Maritime Day.* http://www.imo.org/en/About/Events/WorldMaritimeDay/WMD2013/Documents/CONCEPT%20OF%20%20SUSTAINABLE%20MARITIME%20TRANSPORT%20SYSTEM.pdf. Accessed 15 August 2013.

IMO Member State Audit Scheme, Original homepage of the International Maritime Organization. http://www.imo.org/en/OurWork/MSAS/Pages/AuditScheme.aspx. Accessed 15 August 2016.

IMO Resolution A.1052(27). Procedures for Port State Control, 2011. http://www.imo.org/en/KnowledgeCentre/IndexofIMOResolutions/Documents/A%20-%20Assembly/1052(27).pdf. Accessed 11 December 2015.

IMO Resolution A.946 (23). *Voluntary IMO Member State Audit Scheme*. London: IMO.

International Maritime Organization Instrument Implementation Code, Report 150. file://Users/tafsir/Downloads/Chapter3%20(1).pdf. Accessed 11 December 2015, p. 15

International Court of Justice. (1986). The republic of Nicaragua v. The United States of America (1986 WL 522 (I.C.J.), 1986 I.C.J. 14) https://www.ilsa.org/jessup/jessup08/basicmats/icjnicaragua.pdf. Accessed 11 December, 2015, p. 6.

ISO 9000 – Quality Management, Official homepage of ISO. http://www.iso.org/iso/home/standards/management-standards/iso_9000.htm. Accessed 11 December 2015.

Jan-Erik, L. (2000). *The public sector: Concepts, models and approaches* (3rd ed.). SAGE Publications.
Jedral, K. M. (2000). *Maritime safety and environmental protection: Enhancement through quality and safe management systems: IMO and EU approaches and their adoption in Poland* (p. 13). Unpublished masters dissertation, World Maritime University.
Kalb, A. (2010). *Public sector efficiency: Applications to local governments in Germany*. Springer Science and Business Media.
Kopp, R. J. (1981). The measurement of productive efficiency: A reconsideration. *Quarterly Journal of Economics, 96*, 477–503.
Li, S. (2000). *Effeciency and effectiveness in Maritime Safety Administration* (p. 92). Unpublished masters dissertation, World Maritime University.
March, J. G., & Sutton, R. I. (1997). Organizational performance as a dependent variable. *Organization Science, 8*(6), 688–706.
Masaka, D. (2008). Why enforcing corporate social responsibility (CSR) is morally questionable. *Electronic Journal of Business Ethics and Organizational Studies, 13*(1), 13–21.
McDorman, T. L. (2000). Regional port state control agreements: Some issues of international law. *Ocean & Coastal Law Journal, 5*, 207–227.
Mihaiu, D. M., Opreana, A., & Cristescu, M. P. (2010). Efficiency, effectiveness and performance of the public sector. *Romanian Journal of Economic Forecasting, 13*(4), 133.
Mueller, D. C. (1989). *Public Choice II*. Cambridge: Cambridge University Press.
Mukherjee, P. K. (1993). Flagging options: Legal and other considerations. *Mariner*, January/March, pp. 31–37.
Mykoo, W. A. (2003). *The role and responsibility of minor Stakeholders in the elimination of substandard shipping: A critical analysis* (p. 27). Unpublished masters dissertation, World Maritime University.
Official homepage of DNV GL, ISO 26000 & Social Responsibility. http://www.dnvba.com/US/sustainability/corporate-responsibility/Pages/ISO26000.aspx. Accessed 21 December 2015.
Official homepage of the European Union. http://europa.eu/eu-law/index_en.htm. Accessed 17 December 2015.
Official homepage of the European Commission. http://ec.europa.eu/atwork/applying-eu-law/implementation-monitoring/index_en.htm. Accessed 17 December 2015.
Official homepage of the International monetary Fund. https://www.imf.org/external/np/exr/ib/2001/110801.htm. Accessed 11 August 2016.
Özcaryir, Z. O. (2001). The role of port state control. *Journal of International Maritime Law, 8*(5).
Pamborides, G. P. (1999). *International shipping law: Legislation and enforcement*. Brill/Nijhoff Publishers.
Pyper, R. (Ed.). (1996). *Aspects of accountability in the British System of Government*. London: Tudor Business Publishing.
Quang, V. T. (2000). *Proposals for the improvement of Maritime Administration and Policy in Vietnam* (p. 36). Unpublished masters dissertation, World Maritime University.
Resolution A.739(18) – Guidelines for the Authorization of Organizations Acting on Behalf of the Administration, Adopted on 4 November 1993. http://www.sjofartsverket.se/upload/5121/739.pdf. Accessed 9 December 2015.
Roe, M. (2015). *Maritime governance: Speed, flow, form, process* (pp. 3–5). Springer.
Shaw, M. N. (2008). *International law* (6th ed.). Cambridge: Cambridge University Press.
Shenhav, Y., Shrum, W., & Alon, S. (1994). Goodness' concepts in the study of organizations: A longitudinal survey of four leading journals. *Organization Studies, 15*(5), 753–776.
Srinivasan, T. N., & Bhagwati, J. (1999). *Outward orientation and development: Are the revisionists right?* Yale University Economic Growth Center Discussion Paper No. 806.
Stopford, M. (2009). *Maritime economics* (3rd ed.). Routeledge.
The Companies Act, 2013, No. 18 of 2013, Ministry of Law and Justice, India. http://www.mca.gov.in/Ministry/pdf/CompaniesAct2013.pdf. Accessed August 2016.

United Nations Conference on Trade and Development. (2013). Recent developments and trends in international maritime transport affecting trade of developing countries. Note by the UNCTAD secretariat, TD/B/C.1/30. http://unctad.org/meetings/en/SessionalDocuments/cid30_en.pdf. Accessed 1 August 2016.

United Nations Convention on the Conditions for Registration of Ships, 1986, United Nations Conference on Trade and Development. http://unctad.org/en/PublicationsLibrary/tdrsconf23_en.pdf. Accessed 9 December 2015.

United Nations Convention on the Law of the Sea, 1981. http://www.un.org/depts/los/convention_agreements/texts/unclos/unclos_e.pdf. Accessed 9 December 2015.

van Marrewijk, M. (2003). Concepts and definitions of corporate social responsibility: Between agency and communion. *Journal of Business Ethics, 44*, 95–105.

Vanchiswar, P. S. (1996). *The establishment and administration of maritime matters with particular reference to developing countries* (pp. 1–25). Unpubslihed course material, World Maritime University, Malmö, Sweden.

Vienna Convention on the Law of Treaties, 1969, No. 18232. https://treaties.un.org/doc/Publication/UNTS/Volume%201155/volume-1155-I-18232-English.pdf. Accessed 9 December 2015.

Worthington, A., & Dollery, B. (2000). An empirical survey of frontier efficiency measurement techniques in local government. *Journal of Local Government Studies, 26*(2), 23–52.

Energy Management in the Maritime Industry

Aykut I. Ölçer and Fabio Ballini

1 Background

Corporate Social Responsibility (CSR) and energy management are highly interrelated with each other. Energy management serves and contributes to the targets set by a CSR policy of a shipping company or a port authority. Managers of some of these organizations have responsibilities for the effective implementation of energy efficient measures both in ship operations and in port activities under the fulfilment of their CSR (Kitada and Ölçer 2015).

Two thirds of all Green House Gases (GHGs), which result from human activities, come from energy production and its consumption in the world (IEA 2015), noting that GHGs are the main drivers for the climate change causing the increase of global temperatures and sea level. The GHGs emitted from international shipping are within the remaining one-third (IMO 3rd GHG Study 2014). International shipping has a role to play to contribute to the reduction of GHGs, which was resulted in an IMO regulation on energy efficiency, MARPOL Annex VI Chapter 4, that entered into force on the 1st of January 2013. According to this regulation, there are Energy Efficiency Design Index (EEDI) limits for new ship designs to comply with. In addition, a Ship Energy Efficiency Management Plan (SEEMP) needs to be developed for existing ships and kept onboard.

World seaborne trade including oil and gas, dry bulk and container has started to increase again after the marginal fall in 2009 (Clarkson 2016), and will most likely follow the same pace in the near future. In line with this, energy demand to carry more cargo and passengers onboard ships and to handle them at ports is being increased.

Fuel prices are unstable. Minimising energy consumption will lead to lower air emissions and lower fuel oil cost regardless of the price of fuel oil. The times when

A. I. Ölçer (✉) • F. Ballini
World Maritime University, Malmö, Sweden
e-mail: aio@wmu.se; fb@wmu.se

L. L. Froholdt (ed.), *Corporate Social Responsibility in the Maritime Industry*, WMU Studies in Maritime Affairs 5, https://doi.org/10.1007/978-3-319-69143-5_8

fuel oil price is high, environmental and economical gains were naturally high due to decreased energy consumption or increased energy efficiency. Here economical gain is the benefit for shipowner whereas environmental gain is a positive thing for the society and the world.

It is a known fact that fossil fuel reserves (oil, gas and coal) will run out in the near future if we continue to consume them at the rate we consume today (Global Marine Trends 2030 Report). New and advanced technologies should therefore be developed to be able to meet the future energy demand for the world's sustainable economic growth. In this respect, renewable energy is one of the promising alternatives to fossil fuel trio in addition to energy efficiency. Due to the scarcity of resources, increased rate of resource efficiency should be the way forward in the near future.

Sustainable and constant supply of energy sources at an affordable cost is called energy security, and this is vital to an effective energy management in the industry (Thorpe 2014).

The maritime industry responded to the above-mentioned drivers (shown in Fig. 1) in almost every platform, from relevant regulations to technical and operational measures for ships, to energy management in ports to becoming more energy efficient and environmentally friendly. To name a few;

- Ships are becoming more energy efficient than ever due to the recent advancements in computers and simulation programs,
- The training needs for crew awareness for energy efficient ship operations is not seen as voluntary any more,
- Energy efficiency related barriers at organizational and individual levels is now started to be discussed in detail (Johnson et al. 2014),
- Energy management through energy audit and implementing energy saving potentials has become became a good practice in some ports, not only in Europe,

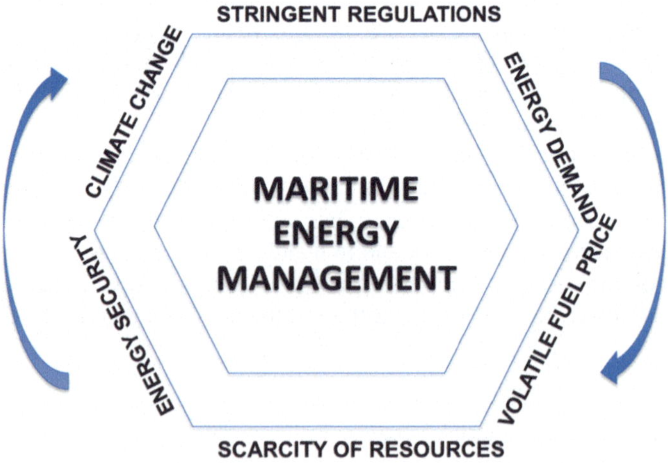

Fig. 1 The motivational drivers of maritime energy management

- There are ships operated with hybrid propulsion, which includes classical, renewable energy, and other means of power production,
- Wind assisted ship propulsion has regained its popularity however their application is limited to small ships

The literature is full of these types of examples and therefore not limited to the above.

There is no widely accepted definition of maritime energy management in the formal literature. The authors propose the following definition: Energy management in the maritime industry, called maritime energy management (MEM):

- Understanding the transformation of energy sources into different energy forms, and
- Managing its consumption in an optimised way in order to be able to minimise negative environmental and economical consequences resulting from this consumption

The above definition is mainly for ships, however, to a certain extent, the same also applies to ports. The only difference is that in the first point above ships differ from ports since energy is not produced at ports in most cases whereas energy is produced and consumed onboard ships.

Whenever energy consumption is decreased or energy efficiency is increased, clear benefits would be obtained. The benefits of an appropriate energy management would be as follows (Doty and Turner 2013):

- Compliance with the relevant environmental regulations
- Reduced GHGs
- Decreased energy consumption
- Decreased energy costs, increased profits and competitiveness
- Improved energy productivity

In this chapter, maritime energy management is discussed through sub-chapters, starting with energy efficient ship design and operation and continuing with energy management in ports. Considering the size of the topic, this chapter introduces the concept at a descriptive level.

2 Energy Efficient Ship Design and Operation

The first important stage when discussing energy management is ship design. All the decisions required for production and operation of ships are taken during this stage and therefore all these decisions will have either a negative or a positive impact on the energy efficiency performance of ships. Some examples could be:

- If the ship designer selects a good hull form or manages to optimise the hull for a ship, then water resistance (opposite force produced by water due to ship's

movement in the sea) will be minimised for the rest of her life as long as the condition of the hull is properly maintained,
- Similarly, main engine selection specifies the fuel consumption for power generation which has financial implications on ship operation cost.

The ship designer has more flexibility during the early phases of design than later. Therefore, it is important to make the right decisions at an early stage in order to ensure an energy efficient ship. Otherwise, it can be very costly to fix. It should also be borne in mind that early decisions have an impact not only on later design phases but also on ship operations (Vassalos 2009).

When it comes to being more energy efficient during the phase of ship design, there are mainly two areas to be looked into: ship resistance and ship propulsion.

2.1 *Ship Resistance and Propulsion*

Here, without going into the details of ship resistance, we will focus on the means for reduction of resistance or resistance related energy saving potentials (ESPs) and their impact on fuel consumption. First, the relationship between speed and water resistance and power requirement (thereby fuel consumption) needs to be addressed. The faster the ship travels, the more resistance is produced and thus more power is needed to maintain the desired speed (Fig. 2). If ship speed is kept constant during operation, one of the main ways to decrease fuel consumption is to decrease resistance during the design phase.

Firstly, it is important to understand how much of the total energy produced onboard a ship is lost prior to talking about resistance related ESPs. Ships need energy to be able to perform their main functions such as advancing in the water,

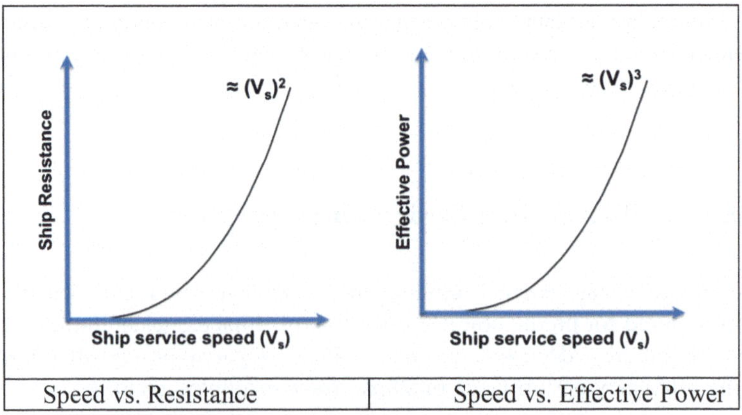

Fig. 2 The typical relation between speed and resistance/effective power

providing hotel facilities to the crew and passengers, loading/unloading the cargo and so on. According to IMO 2nd GHG study, 2009, if total energy produced by fuel on board a small cargo ship is 100, 57% of this energy is lost in the form of heat and exhaust. Only 43% of the total energy is transformed into shaft power and used to propel a ship. 28% of the total energy within 43% goes to overcoming hull friction (16%) and others (air resistance, weather resistance, residual hull losses, wave generation). The percentages given here are generic, not ship specific. Losses would be obviously different for various types of ship as well as for different environmental conditions such as sea state.

When it comes to hull friction, air resistance, wave generation, weather resistance and residual hull losses, ship total resistance is the main naval architectural concept to be dealt with in order to decrease fuel consumption and to become energy efficient. Ship total resistance has four main components (Molland et al. 2011), which are:

- Wave-making resistance: When a ship travels at a constant speed, it produces two types of waves, transverse and divergent. These waves possess energy that comes from the ship; the ship therefore loses a certain fraction of her total energy. This type of resistance is called wave-making resistance.
- Viscous resistance: When a ship travels at a constant speed, there exists a frictional force against her movement between her hull and the water. The viscous resistance is the summation of this force (frictional resistance) and form resistance.
- Air resistance: Air drag results from wind resistance affecting the ship surface above the water line.
- Appendages resistance: This type of resistance is due to the appendages such as bilge keels, shaft, or rudders attached to the ship to perform her functions.
- Engine and hull/propeller maintenance

In terms of their relative share within total resistance, viscous and wave-making resistances are two major contributors. Therefore during ship design, these two components have the greatest ESP.

For each resistance component, there is a different way of decreasing resistance. In order to reduce wave-making resistance, the most widely employed technique is hull form optimisation. The aim of hull form optimisation is to find the best hull form that gives the least resistance. The focus areas of this approach are bulbous bow and stern hull.

Integration of a bulbous bow into a ship's hull has a positive effect on bow wave and its resistance. The important gain can only be obtained at higher speeds since lower speeds do not have too much advantage for bulbous bow inclusion. Another factor is loading condition. Naval architects take into consideration design condition to find optimal bulbous bow. Therefore, bulbous bow might present different performance for different loading conditions. Similarly, stern waves are also affected by the form of stern. The gain or fuel/CO_2 saving potential from an optimised hull shape in still water would be within the range of 5–20% (IMO 2nd GHG Study 2009).

Frictional resistance, the main component of the viscous resistance, is mainly the function of fluid properties (density and viscosity), under water surface area, ship speed, and Reynolds Number (function of ship speed and length, and kinematic viscosity). So, logically speaking, minimising frictional resistance of a ship necessitates decreasing her under water surface area, which is not easy to achieve. Due to the viscosity of the fluid, the second potential area to reduce frictional resistance is hull surface characteristics or the flow around the hull.

How can you change the surface properties of a ship or flow around a hull? The answer is good quality paints, surface patterns and air lubrication. There are advanced new paints that mimic sharkskin which helps to reduce viscous resistance.

The main principle of air lubrication is to produce air on board ship and inject it into underwater surface of the hull in the form of bubbles, partial cavity and layer, which are schematically represented in Figs. 3, 4, and 5 respectively. Despite the fact that there are clear benefits for reducing frictional resistance, producing air injection consumes some of ship overall energy.

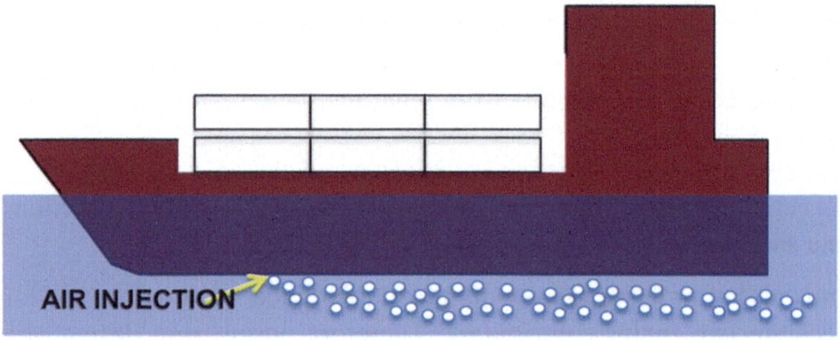

Fig. 3 Air lubrication—bubbles

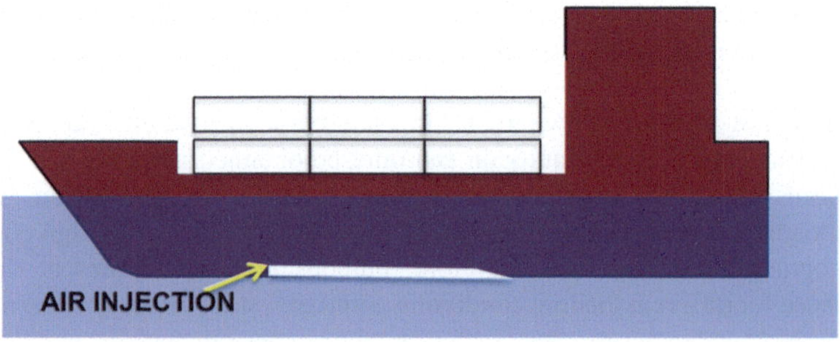

Fig. 4 Air lubrication—partial cavity

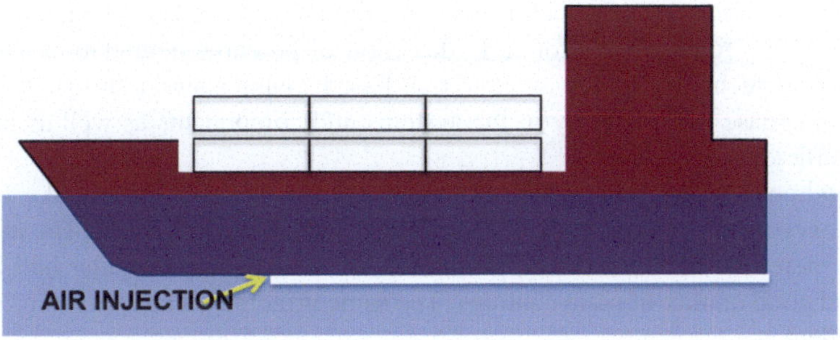

Fig. 5 Air lubrication—air layer

2.2 The Potential During Ship Operation

After the investigation of ESPs during ship design, there is still energy saving potential for improving energy efficiency of a ship through her operational life-cycle. This potential is not as big as that in the design phase, nevertheless it cannot be omitted from consideration.

ESPs during ship operation are classified under ship level, fleet level and ship-port interface. Fleet level is here referred as the situation in which the whole fleet is operated at reduced speed. Ship-port interface can be explained through effective traffic management and communication between port and ship to reduce time in ports.

This chapter focuses on ship level and thereby ESPs during ship operation at ship level can be classified into three main areas:

- Voyage specific optimization: the optimal characteristics of a voyage
- Ship operation specific optimization: Performing ship operations in an optimised way (optimised ship handling).

Ship Routeing

The first area during ship operation to be looked into is to find the most optimal characteristics for ship's voyage for efficient fuel consumption. It might be either optimising voyage route by determining the least distance, determining optimised speed or selecting the best route by taking into consideration environmental conditions (weather routing). It might even be the different combinations of those. There is software developed for the implementation of weather routing or route optimisation.

Ship Handling

The second area is optimised ship handling that mainly covers optimum trim and ballast. Trim, by definition, is the difference between aft draft and forward draft of a ship. Finding the right trim is crucial for optimal fuel consumption during a ship's operation. Trim optimisation might present fuel savings of up to 3–4%.

Maintenance

Maintenance not only for ships but also for all engineering systems have a positive impact on energy efficiency. For a poorly maintained hull of a ship, increase in C_T (coefficient of total resistance) can be 10–30%/year (Molland et al. 2011). Hull and propeller maintenance is crucial for fuel consumption and needs to be monitored and controlled on a regular basis for early detection of potential degradation. Different maintenance techniques such as condition-based maintenance play a key role in order to increase the reliability of the systems and components as well as improve energy efficiency.

Smoothness of the hull, which is mainly affected by the factors like fouling, quality of coating and corrosion, is one of the drivers for hull friction. The means to prevent increased hull friction are proper maintenance through regular hull inspections and good quality of paint coatings. The same principles also apply to propellers and rudders.

Engine maintenance, both main and auxiliaries, is different from hull/propeller maintenance in the sense that engine manufacturers employ more systematic and condition monitored procedures with regularly conducted planned inspections.

Improving energy efficiency of a ship is a continuous effort throughout her life cycle. Ships are retrofitted for that purpose on top of design and operation. It might be fitting an energy saving device into a propeller or replacing old engine with a dual fuel engine. Whoever decides for retrofitting option, s/he faces a trade-off between pros (gain) and cons (cost). The main cost elements here are investment and operating costs. The challenge would be to make rational and right decisions under these trade-off situations (Ölçer and Ballini 2015). With the right preferences of decision maker(s) and the selection of the most appropriate decision making technique, correct decisions can be made which will lead to beneficial solutions.

Ballast water operations during varying modes of operation of a ship have impacts on safety, environment and fuel economy. There are already IMO regulations such as Load Line, MARPOL and Ballast Water Management Conventions, and rules at national level regulating those operations with regards to safety, environment and energy efficiency. Nevertheless, it is all about the way we deal with these operations and sometimes compliance has been a single dimensional approach, in the sense that one discipline (energy efficiency or fuel consumption) is given attention and others are compromised. For example, safety of a vessel in terms of ship stability and structural integrity is the main concern during de/ballasting, which can be employed for trim optimisation.

Therefore, it should be always kept in mind that safety should never be compromised whenever an ESP is found and applied. This would be another challenge that decision makers will face in the future.

3 Energy Management in Ports

3.1 The Linear Economy: Reaching the Limit of Resource Consumption

The linear model of consumer consumption is based on the premise of take, make and dispose—a model that has prevailed from the very early days of the industrial revolution. Raw materials are harvested and extracted and used in the manufacture of products before being discarded by consumers after they have served their purpose. And throughout each step of the industrial production process, waste is generated that must be disposed of. However, this linear model has been increasingly challenged since the 1970s and 1980s by a growing awareness across all industries of the necessity to recycle and move towards a low-carbon economy. This development is due to a greater appreciation of the fact that the world is reaching the boundaries of sustainable consumption with a detrimental effect on the climate and wider environment (Rockström et al. 2009). Indeed, four out of nine quantifiable planetary boundaries ([1])have already been crossed as a result of human activity (Steffen et al. 2015): climate change, loss of biosphere integrity, land system change and altered biogeochemical cycles (phosphorus and nitrogen). As human activity pushes the Earth system beyond planetary boundaries, the implications are, for instance, that marine ecosystems may change dramatically (as a result of ocean acidification and eutrophication). Temperature increases may also be so significant that they pose threats to agricultural production, infrastructure and human health (Steffen et al. 2015).

Throughout most of the twentieth century, commodity prices fell as production became more efficient. But as a result of a narrower scope for efficiency improvements within industry and with a rising global population, a higher demand on resources will eventually lead to resource scarcity and subsequent markedly higher prices. Already we are seeing a considerable rise in demand. In terms of volume, around 65 billion tons of raw materials entered the economic system in 2010, a figure that is set to increase to approx. 82 billion tons by 2020 (Ellen MacArthur Foundation 2013).

Commodity prices are currently volatile relative to the past few decades, which is consistent with cyclical supply and demand fundamentals (Dwyer et al. 2011). Volatility has also previously occurred during supply and demand spikes globally throughout the past century. However, when raw material prices eventually start to rise due to a growing global population the subsequent price spikes will pose great risks for many businesses, yet also offer new opportunities for those industry sectors that are helping the economy to transit to a more sustainable circular economy (Commodity Special Feature 2016).

---

[1]Planetary Boundaries is the central concept in an Earth system framework proposed in 2009 by a group of environmental scientists led by Johan Rockström from the Stockholm Resilience Centre and Will Steffan from the Australian National University. The concept seeks to define a so-called safe operating space for humanity in relation to the consumption of Earth's resources as a precondition for sustainable stewardship.

3.2 The Circular Economy: Moving from Waste Disposal to Resource Management

As we reach the limits of what our planet can sustain, we are experiencing an increasing trend among industries, innovators and decision-makers to refocus attention on the opportunities offered by a more sustainable circular (or non-linear) model of consumption, in which the concept of 'waste disposal' is replaced by that of 'resource flows'. As much as possible is recycled. Around the world, the concept of circular economy (CE) has become central to addressing environmental sustainability (Murray et al. 2015). Moving to a circular economy requires resource efficiency, which is promoted through effective management that retains the value of raw materials and promotes energy efficiency throughout all stages of the value chain (Yuan et al. 2006). Ways to achieve resource efficiency include light-weighting, durability, efficiency, substitution, eco-design, industrial symbiosis, and leasing/renting. The transformations needed to achieve such resource efficiency are based on technical, social, and organisational innovations throughout the value chain (European Commission 2014).

As commodity prices will eventually rise due to scarcity, circular business models will gain a competitive edge since they create more value from each consumed resource unit than the traditional linear model (Ellen Macarthur Foundation 2014). Within a circular economy, companies will be encouraged by market forces to make, improve and renew so that raw materials are kept in the value chain for as long as possible, thereby eliminating waste (Bilitewski 2012). Companies will therefore constantly seek to re-engineer their production processes to increase productivity and resource efficiency by substituting high-priced materials with lower-priced alternatives, while also enhancing their efforts to upcycle or down-cycle their waste as valuable bi-products rather than having to pay the costs of traditional waste disposal.

Four principles that define the circular economy:

1. Minimise the use of resources and eliminate waste and pollution.
2. Maximise the value at each stage of production.
3. Manage flows of bio-based and non-renewable resources in closed loops.
4. Establish mutually beneficial relationships between industries within each supply chain.

3.3 The Pathway to Circular Economy: The Transition Process

Moving from a linear economy to a circular economy requires a concerted effort both at a political and a business level. Industries need to see a competitive advantage in becoming part of the circular economy, which will initially be driven by new regulatory targets. These initiatives will subsequently give rise to new business models and new technological approaches. A good practice example of the potential for transition from linear to circular economy models is the Pathways to a Circular Economy (Rabobank Industry 2012), a strategic project conduced for the Rotterdam/Delta Region in the Netherlands and Belgium, an area that include the major ports of Rotterdam and Antwerp. The report sets out models for four sectors (gas and carbon in the energy sector, copper in the metals sector, plastic in the chemicals sector and aquaculture in the agriculture sector).

The project also defined four stages in the transition:

1. Business as usual where initiatives are introduced on the fringes.
2. Recycling and alternative production methods take hold. Regulatory targets are based on benchmarking and best practice. The emergence of new business models for the collecting, processing and recycling of waste.
3. The new circular economy emerges and starts to demand new kinds of infrastructure and markets. Higher value application of by-products and recycled materials across supply chains.
4. The circular economy takes hold. New concepts, technologies and markets have replaced the linear economy. Businesses identify ways to eliminate or minimise waste disposal and reuse waste as by-products across several supply chain.

4 Circular Economy in Port Management: Regulatory Measures and CSR

Regulatory measures and government-sponsored initiatives, including subsidies, are among the important drivers when transitioning from a linear to circular economy. With the EU Energy Efficiency Directive, EU Air Quality Framework Directive; Directive 2000/59/EC on port reception facilities for ship-generated waste and cargo residues, the EU has set a 20% energy savings target by 2020 in relation to the projected use of energy in 2020. Based on an analysis of Member State actions and additional forecasts, the Commission estimates that the EU will achieve energy savings of around 18–19% in 2020. This means falling short of the 20% savings target by 20–40 Mtoe (COM(2014) 520 final).

The main goals behind the EU's energy policy are the security of energy supply and combating climate change. Furthermore, the United Nations General Assembly has adopted the 2030 Agenda for Sustainable Development that includes a bold set of Global Goals called Sustainable Development Goals (SDGs). Goal number 7 is to ensure access to affordable, reliable, sustainable and modern energy for all and Goal number 13 takes urgent action to combat climate change and its impacts. These goals have an important target: by 2030, the share of renewable energy in the global energy mix is to be substantially increased and the global rate of improvement in energy efficiency is to be doubled. So before industries necessarily experience a competitive economic incentive to embrace circular economy models, governments, regions and international bodies will pave the way for a more eco-sustainable economy through a wide range of regulatory measures.

The first steps in introducing a circular economy strategy in port management involve embracing wider environmental concerns in Corporate Sustainability

Policies (CSP). Ports are increasingly engaging in developing such policies, not only to respond to legislation and regulation but also to enhance their competitive edge since sustainable ports are increasingly likely to be selected as preferred supply chain partners (Acciaro 2015). Ports increasingly adopt internationally recognised standards as ISO (ISO 9001 Quality Management, ISO 14001 Environmental Management, etc.). For instance, the environmental review of 2016 prepared by the European Sea Port Association (ESPO) shows that 70% of European ports are certified under either ISO 14001 or EMAS (European Management and Audit Scheme) or under the EcoPorts Port Environmental Review System (PERS). Furthermore, since 1996 European ports have been reporting on the sector's performance through dedicated surveys by ESPO and EcoPorts. The review of 2016 shows that two out of three European ports produce a publicly available environmental report on a regular basis. This figure has more than doubled from 30% in 2004 and the positive trend demonstrates a development towards increased transparency (Trends in EU ports governance 2016).

Corporate environmental policies at ports generally evolve over time, addressing a whole host of priorities that change as a result of the success or failure of such policies. They also reflect a shifting focus on specific issues over time. The European Sea Ports Organization has monitored the top-10 environmental priorities of the European port sector over time. The issue of air quality has replaced water quality as the top concern at European ports over the period between 1996 and 2016 (European Sea Ports Organisation 2016).

This shift in priorities reflects general changes in industrial policies that have introduced better wastewater management in cities and a reduction in industrial water consumption. When it comes to dealing with air pollution from ports, on the other hand, the culprit is fuel consumption on vessels both during navigation and hoteling. This environmental challenge is therefore directly related to port energy management.

4.1 Circular Economy in Port Management: Industrial Ecology and Best Practice

Transport is one of the cornerstones of globalisation. Of the world's 20 economically leading and most competitive cities, 14 are port cities. Additionally, 65% of cities in the world with populations above 1.3 million are coastal cities (Vallega 2001). Urban areas in general are also responsible for 80% of greenhouse gas emissions generated by human activity (Feng et al. 2013).

Although major European ports have often migrated toward peripheral urban areas or 'greenfield sites' (Hoyle 1989), ports throughout the world are nevertheless predominantly integrated with urban industrial complexes, supply chains, urban transport infrastructure and utility services. Ports also play an important role in enhancing efficiency and reducing the costs of international seaborne trade

(Sanchez et al. 2003; Nordas and Piermartini 2004). Ports are therefore set to become increasingly important players as cities address pollution issues and adopt smart city solutions to energy conservation and resource management and adopt a more sustainable economy. In recent years, cities worldwide have embarked on initiatives to promote industrial ecology (IE). The aim of industrial ecology is to optimise resource management by densifying interactions between stakeholders within a defined geographical area (Cerceau et al. 2014).

As an example of IE good practice, Japan introduced circular models in port management in 1996 in no less than 26 cities. This project sought to promote industrial symbiosis among industry players to minimise waste and maximise energy efficiency in the region. Among the aims of the program was to maximise the economic and environmental benefits from the close geographic proximity of industrial and urban areas of ports by ensuring that previously discarded industrial waste material was recycled alongside household waste. Approx. US$ 1.65 billion was invested in a total of 61 innovative recycling projects backed by an average state subsidy of 36%. In addition, 107 non-subsidised recycling plants were also constructed. The success of the program was ensured by setting ambitious product-specific targets for the recycling programs and by ensuring general access to private sector technological resources as well as encouraging a widespread awareness of environmental issues among private and public players (Girard 2013).

A European example of IE best practice is The Symbiotic Bioenergy Port Integration with Cities by 2020 project (EPIC 2020) coordinated by the city of Malmö and covering four harbour cities: Malmö in Sweden, Mantova in Italy, Navipe-Akarport in Greece, and Wismar (including Rostock) in Germany. The project targets the untapped bioenergy resource potential of ports and port regions and the challenge of generating urban economic growth based on bioenergy resources. The bio-based economy aims to reduce dependence on fossil fuels and introduce production processes based on organic material, which ports have significant access to in the surrounding urban areas in the form of bio waste and other bioenergy resources. Another European example of an IE project is the Port of Marseilles-Fos, France, which has since 2000 focused on the local generation and distribution of energy, including solar and wind power, geothermal energy and biomass. Initial studies were carried out in 2004 and 2005 (Junqua et al. 2005, 2006; Junqua and Moine 2007) to identify and model potential industrial synergies and new initiatives, which have subsequently been implemented as part of a drive towards sustainable port management.

5 Circular Economy in Port Management: Energy Management

Energy consumption is a major overhead in port operations (Boile et al. 2015). Any environmental policy for a port must therefore address energy management. The overall aim of Port Energy Management (EnMP) is to promote the development towards an economically, environmentally and socially sustainable port aligned with local, regional, national, international and European policies.

An energy management system (such as ISO 50001) helps an organisation to internalise the necessary policies, procedures and tools to systematically track, analyse and improve energy efficiency. A number of established standards already exist that ports can adopt as part of their environmental management systems, such as EcoPorts, ISO 14001 and Eco-Management and Audit Scheme (EMAS). The benefits of better energy efficiency are manifold. Substantial energy savings can be achieved through the streamlining of operations, adoption of new technologies and by utilising renewable energy sources (Wiegmans and Louw 2011; Acciaro et al. 2013; Denktas-Sakar and Karatas-Cetin 2012; Yap and Lam 2013; ESPO 2016). Energy efficiency cuts overall costs and enhances competitiveness. It is also instrumental in moving ports away from fossil fuel to embrace renewables. Utilising sustainable energy sources furthermore helps ports comply with stricter air pollution limits and embrace the wider trend towards a circular economy.

The objectives of energy management (Hippinen and Federley 2014; Boile et al. 2015) can be summarised as follows:

- Reduce energy consumption
- Increase energy supply from renewable sources
- Provide better planning and management
- Introduce production systems with low environmental impact
- Deliver on relevant CSR targets
- Promote recycling
- Support the transition from a linear to circular economy

When defining the objectives and goals of an energy management plan the following five energy pillars should be addressed (Burns and McDonnell 2014):

1. Resiliency: the ability to sustain operations continuity during a power blackout and to resume operations after a catastrophic event. The factors include: physical threats to transmission and distribution lines, cyber security threats and electrification of cargo handling equipment.
2. Availability: access to energy generation, transmission and distribution sources required in order to meet present and future power demands
3. Reliability: availability of consistent energy supply during peak demand
4. Efficiency: reduced energy requirement through management practices and technologies that maximise operational productivity and cost-effectiveness
5. Sustainability: adopting energy management practices and utilising renewable power sources to ensure environmental sustainability

The tasks involved in setting up an energy management system include:

- Monitoring and analysing the port energy using a benchmarking process with Key Performance Indicators (KPIs)
- Assessing the existing energy profile and energy usage to identify target areas

- Identifying opportunities to save energy, e.g. by carrying out an energy audit using the Self Diagnosis Methodology (SDM)
- Identification and implementation of economically feasible energy-saving measures
- Creating and implementing a beneficial energy procurement strategy

6 Energy Audit

The aim of an energy audit is to analyse the energy use of a facility and to identify solutions that can help conserve energy (Motiva 2011). Energy audits are a beneficial analytical tool with which to identify economically feasible energy-saving solutions. They can help develop an understanding of specific energy-using patterns. They involve gathering system information, measuring energy use, developing conservation strategies, choosing the most cost-effective plan, implementing changes, and verifying results. Also, a proactive facility will seek to continue to improve energy efficiency by regular audits, which aligned with the company's general operational procedures are to ensure a high level of energy efficiency.

Energy audits can be carried out either independently or in combination with the energy management system based on the ISO 50001 standard. This international standard specifies requirements for the audit process to achieve an Energy Audit certificate. The Directive of the European Parliament and of the Council 2012/27/EU on energy efficiency sets out measures to promote the use of energy audits among small and medium-sized enterprises, encouraging them to implement the recommendations resulting from these audits.

The energy audit process consists of several steps, as follow:

- Energy audit planning: Define the goal of the energy audit and collect the preliminary information.
- Opening meeting and data collection: The energy auditor collects all the relevant documents and records useful for conducting the energy audit and assessing the energy efficiency potential.
- Site visits (walkthrough survey): The auditor visits the facilities to interview staff, collect data and visually inspect the buildings
- Analysis: The energy auditor will evaluate utility and site data to subsequently identify energy and cost saving. A list of recommended measures is compiled.
- Energy auditing reporting: Summarising the findings and presenting the recommendations.

An example of an energy audit program is one embraced by the Antwerp Port Authority. Launched in 2010, the program offers expert guidance to all port user stakeholders on the implementation of energy-saving initiatives. The program's audits include proposals for concrete measures and estimations as well as their economic feasibility. The Antwerp Port Authority also shares its knowledge with the stakeholders of available subsidies for efficient energy use and even provides assistance with regard to subsidy applications. By developing this initiative, the port authority intends to encourage private companies to invest in energy efficiency measures.

7 Conclusion

Energy management in the maritime industry is a concept, which is part of the CSR agenda for shipping companies, under the environmental leg of CSR, and it is evident that strides are being taken to address the challenges and opportunities that energy management involves. This chapter has addressed the importance of maritime energy management in relation to CSR, beginning with energy management on ships, and then continuing in relation to ports. The authors of this chapter have also put forward a definition of the concept of maritime energy management.

The linear model of consumer consumption has resulted in four out of nine planetary boundaries being crossed: climate change, loss of biosphere integrity, land system change and altered biogeochemical cycles. There is an increasing awareness among industries, innovators and decision-makers to move towards a more sustainable circular model of consumption in which raw materials are retained in the value chain and where growth is sustained in a world with rising populations. Moving from a linear economy to a circular economy requires a concerted effort both politically and on a business level.

Across the world, urban areas in general are responsible for 80% of greenhouse gas emissions generated by human activity. And of the world's 20 economically leading and most competitive cities, 14 are port cities. Ports are, therefore, central to the wider development of industrial ecology. Regulatory measures, including the EU Energy Efficiency Directive, Port Reception Facilities Directive, Air Quality Framework Directive, and UN 2030 Agenda for Sustainable Development in addition to government-sponsored initiatives are among the important drivers when transitioning to a circular economy. For ports, the first steps in introducing a circular economy strategy therefore involve embracing wider environmental concerns. Such CSR not only seek to respond to environmental regulatory requirements but also seek to enhance the competitive edge of ports since sustainable and cost-effective ports are increasingly likely to be selected as preferred supply chain partners.

Energy consumption is a major operative cost for ports. An energy management system (such as ISO 50001) helps an organisation to internalise policies, procedures and tools to systematically track, analyse and improve energy efficiency. Energy audits are part of such an energy management system. They allow both ships and ports measure energy use and develop solutions to conserve energy. Substantial energy savings can be achieved through the streamlining of operations, adoption of new technologies and by utilising renewable energy sources.

References

Acciaro, M. (2015). Corporate responsibility and value creation in the port sector. *International Journal of Logistics: Research and Applications, 18*(3), 291–311.

Acciaro, M., Hoffmann, P. N., & Eide, M. S. (2013). The energy efficiency gap in maritime transport. *Journal of Shipping and Ocean Engineering, 3*(10), 1–10.

Bilitewski, B. (2012). The circular economy and its risks. *Waste Management, 32*, 1–2.

Boile, M., Theofanis, S., Sdoukopoulo, E., & Plytas, N. (2015). *Developing a port energy management plan: Issues, challenges and prospects*. Transportation Research on Board of the National Academic. (GREENBERTH project).

Burns & McDonnell Engineering Company. (2014). Port of Los Angeles: Energy 44 Management Action Plan. Draft Report.

Cerceau, J., Mat, N., Junqua, G., Lin, L., Laforest, V., & Gonzalez, C. (2014). Implementing industrial ecology in port cities: International overview of case studies and cross-case analysis. *Journal of Cleaner Production, 74*, 1–16.

CLARKSON. (2016). https://www.clarksons.net, Seaborne Trade Monitor, *3*(1), January 2016, ISSN: 2058-7570.

Commodity Special Feature from World Economic Outlook, International Monetary Fund. (April 2016). https://www.imf.org/external/pubs/ft/weo/2016/01/pdf/SF_Commod.pdf.

COMMUNICATION FROM THE COMMISSION TO THE EUROPEAN PARLIAMENT AND THE COUNCIL, Energy Efficiency and its contribution to energy security and the 2030 Framework for climate and energy policy, COM(2014) 520 final, Brussels, 23.7.2014.

Denktas-Sakar, G., & Karatas-Cetin, C. (2012). Port sustainability and stakeholder management in supply chains: A framework on resource dependence theory. *The Asian Journal of Shipping and Logistics, 28*(3), 301–319.

Doty, S., & Turner, W. C. (2013). *Energy management handbook* (8th ed.). Liburn, GA: The Fairmont Press.

Dwyer, A., Gardner, G., & Williams, T. (2011). *Global commodity markets – price volatility and financialisation*. Bulletin June Quarter 2011.

Ellen MacArthur Foundation. (2013). *Towards the circular economy, Economic and business rationale for an accelerated transition*. Ellen MacArthur Foundation.

Ellen MacArthur Foundation. (2014). *Towards the circular economy, Accelerating the scale-up across global supply chains*. Ellen MacArthur Foundation.

ESPO/EcoPorts Port Environmental Review. (2016). Insight on port environmental performance and its evolution over time April 2016.

European Commission. (2014). *Towards a circular economy: A zero waste programme for Europe*. Brussels: European Commission.

Feng, Y. Y., Chen, L. X., & Zhang, S. Q. (2013). System dynamics modeling for urban energy consumption and CO2 emissions: A case study of Beijing, China. *Ecological Modelling, 252*, 44–52.

Girard, L. G. (2013). Toward a Smart Sustainable Development of Port Cities/Areas: The Role of the "Historic Urban Landscape" Approach, sustainability, ISSN 2071-1050.

Global Marine Trends 2030 Report, Commercial Sector, pp. 52–53. http://www.lr.org/en/marine/projects/global-marine-trends-2030.aspx.

Hippinen, I., & Federley, J. (2014). *Fact-finding study on opportunities to enhance the energy efficiency and environmental impacts of ports in the Baltic Sea Region*. Motiva Services Ltd.

Hoyle, B. S. (1989). The port-city interface: Trends, problems and examples. *Geoforum, 20*, 429–435.

International Energy Agency (IEA). (2015). Energy and climate change, World Energy Outlook Special Report.

International Maritime Organization (IMO). (2009). *Second IMO Greenhouse Gas Study*. London: IMO.

International Maritime Organization (IMO). (2014). *Third IMO Greenhouse Gas Study*. London: IMO.

Johnson, H., Johansson, M., & Andersson, K. (2014). Barriers to improving energy efficiency in short sea shipping: an action research case study. *Journal of Cleaner Production, 66*(1), 317–327.

Junqua, G., & Moine, H. (2007). Utilisation de l'écologie industrielle et de l'intelligence économique territoriale pour le développement durable d'une Zone Industrialo-Portuaire. *Déchets Sciences et Techniques*, (46), 19–23.

Junqua, G., Moine, H., & Bouzidi, Y. (2006). *Développement durable d'une zone industrialo-portuaire: utilisation de l'écologie industrielle et de l'intelligence économique et territoriale.* Paris: Colloque Européen EMUE, May 18–19, 2006.

Junqua, G., Moine, H., Bouzidi, Y., Abriak, N. E., & Damidot, D. (2005). L'écologie industrielle, outil de l'intelligence économique et territoriale. In: *Conférence Internationale d'Ingénierie Urbaine e technologies innovantes pour les infrastructures et l'habitat* (pp. 385–393). Lille, October, 12–13, 2005.

Kitada, M., & Ölçer, A. (2015). Managing people and technology: The challenges in CSR and energy efficient shipping. *Research in Transportation Business & Management, 17*, 36–40.

Molland, A. F., Turnock, S. R., & Hudson, D. A. (2011). *Ship resistance and propulsion: Practical estimation of propulsive power.*, Cambridge University Press, 8 Aug 2011, ISBN: 9781107641259.

Motiva, 2011. Motiva Oy, Energiakatselmustoiminta, 2011. http://www.motiva.fi/toimialueet/energiakatselmustoiminta.

Murray, A., Skene, K., & Haynes, K. (2015). The circular economy: an interdisciplinary exploration of the concept and application in a global context. *Journal of Business Ethics.*

Nordas, H., & Piermartini, R. (2004). Infrastructure and Trade, World Trade Organisation Staff Working Paper ERSD-2004-04.

Ölçer, A., & Ballini, F. (2015). The development of a decision making framework for evaluating the trade-off solutions of cleaner seaborne transportation. *Transportation Research Part D: Transport and Environment, 37*, 150–170.

Pathways to a Circular Economy, Rabobank Industry Note #343 - October 2012.

Rockström, J., Steffen, W., Noone, K., Persson, Å., Stuart Chapin, F., Lambin, E. F., et al. (2009). Planetary boundaries: Exploring the safe operating space for humanity. *Ecology and Society, 14*(2), 32.

Sanchez, R., Hoffmann, J., Micco, A., Pizzolitto, G., Sgut, M., & Wilmsmeier, G. (2003). Port efficiency and international trade: Port efficiency as a determinant of maritime transport costs. *Maritime Economics & Logistics, 5*, 199–218.

Steffen, W., Richardson, K., Rockström, J., Cornell, S. E., Fetzer, I., Bennett, E. M., Biggs, R., Carpenter, S. R., de Vries, W., de Wit, C. A., Folke, C., Gerten, D., Heinke, J., Mace, J. M., Persson, L. M., Ramanathan, V., Reyers, B., & Sörlin, S. (2015). Planetary boundaries: Guiding human development on a changing planet. *Science, 347*(6223), 1259855.

Symbiotic bio-Energy Port Integration with Cities by 2020 (EPIC 2020) https://ec.europa.eu/energy/intelligent/projects/en/projects/epic-2020

The Economist Intelligence Unit Hot Spots. Benchmarking Global City Competitiveness. A Report from the Economist Intelligence Unit. http://www.citigroup.com/citi/citiforcities/pdfs/eiu_hotspots_2012.pdf

Thorpe, D. (2014). *Energy management in industry.* New York: Routledge. ISBN: 978-0-415-70647-6.

Trends in EU ports governance 2016, European Sea Ports Organisation (ESPO) http://www.espo.be/media/espopublications/Trends_in_EU_ports_gouvernance_2016_FINAL_VERSION.pdf.

Vallega, A. (2001). *Urban waterfront facing integrated coastal management.* Ocean Coastal. Management.

Vassalos, D. (2009). Chapter 2-Risk based ship design. In: A. Papanikolaou (Ed.), *Risk-based ship design; methods, tools and applications* (p. 25). ISBN 978-3-540-89041-6.

Wiegmans, B. W., & Louw, E. (2011). Changing port–city relations at Amsterdam: A new phase at the interface. *Journal of Transport Geography, 19*(4), 575–583.

Yap, W. Y., & Lam, J. S. L. (2013). 80 Million-TEU container port? Sustainability issues in port and coastal development. *Ocean & Coastal Management, 71*, 13–25.

Yuan, Z., Bi, J., & Moriguichi, Y. (2006). The circular economy: a new development strategy in China. *Journal of Industrial Ecology, 10*, 4–8.

Sulphur Directive, Short Sea Shipping and Corporate Social Responsibility in a EU Context

Patrick Donner and Tafsir Johansson

1 Introduction

When considering the beneficial aspects and dynamics of shipping, it is stated as being, statistically, the least environmentally damaging mode of transport (IMO Marine Environment Policy 2008; Mitropoulos 2007). Whilst this acknowledgment is derived from quantitative research analysis (Whitelegg 1993; Hecht 1997; IMO Marine Environment Policy 2008, p. 1), maritime transport is not completely free from negative externalities and may pose a threat to fragile marine ecosystems and to those who value and depend on the sea (Lindén et al. 2007). Although regulation of maritime transport continues to progress with a proactive approach from IMO and sometimes driven by initiatives from the European Union, it is observed that since the early 1960s the focus has shifted to air pollution, more specifically to air emissions. At the request of the Council of Europe's Parliamentary Assembly, the Council of Ministers held a conference in 1965 and set up a Committee of Experts to examine the possibilities to "convene a European Convention on Air pollution" (Gillespie 2005, p. 191). This led to the 1968 Declaration of Principles of Air Pollution (Gillespie 2005) adopted by the Ministers' Deputies on the 8th of March 1968 (Resolution (68) 4). Subsequently, the Council of Europe adopted resolution 70 (11) in 1970 and declared that a restriction is desirable to limit altogether the concentration of sources of emissions of air pollutants, irrespective of their source (Gillespie 2005). Parallel to regional efforts, the international effort to control air pollution commenced in 1968 when the World Meteorological Organization provided the framework for a global network to monitor atmospheric chemical components related to climate change and environmental issues (Kiss and Shelton 2007). Although air pollution is not considered a major environmental consequence of

P. Donner (✉) • T. Johansson
World Maritime University, Malmo, Sweden
e-mail: pd@wmu.se; tj@wmu.se

L. L. Froholdt (ed.), *Corporate Social Responsibility in the Maritime Industry*, WMU Studies in Maritime Affairs 5, https://doi.org/10.1007/978-3-319-69143-5_9

shipping, emissions from ocean-going vessels while in port can nevertheless, be of great concern due to the fact that they are more likely to affect the population of adjacent coastal areas (Hecht 1997). These ocean-going vessels are said to contribute significantly to global emissions of inter alia SO_2, and it is projected that by 2020, the contributions of ship emissions to the European Union NOx and SOx inventories will exceed all other emission sources in the European Union nations (Friedrich et al. 2007, p. 31, Commission of the European Communities 2005). It is, therefore, important to analyse pertinent European Union legislation on SO_2 emission against the backdrop of Corporate Social Responsibility (CSR) and examine how the voluntary aspect of CSR functions under emission reduction strategies that are "strict compliance" in nature.

1.1 Evolution of International Regulation of Air Pollution

In retrospect, air pollution control via regional initiatives within Europe can be marked as a dramatic, continuous and long-standing progress since the late 1960s. This momentum reached a high plateau in 1975, the year when the Final Act of the Helsinki Conference on Security and Cooperation in Europe gave the United Nations Economic Commission for Europe (UNECE) the responsibility to develop and structure an international treaty concerning air pollution (Kiss and Shelton 2007). This in turn became the Geneva Convention on Long-Range Transboundary Air Pollution (LRTAP), which was adopted in 1979 (Geneva Convention on Long-Range Transboundary Air Pollution 1979) and in the same year all EU member states adopted the "air pollution" framework convention. It is noteworthy that the LRTAP is built on progressive co-operation and does not stipulate any precise rules (Kiss and Shelton 2007). The LRTAP does not consider individual polluter-responsibility due to the fact that the person or entity cannot be identified and it proceeds to lay down a form of general obligation on the state parties, i.e. "to protect man and his environment" from the detrimental effects of air pollution and "to limit, and, as far as possible, gradually reduce and prevent" it (Article 2 of the Geneva Convention on Long-Range Transboundary Air Pollution 1979). Although the term "air pollution" has been used throughout the convention, the term "emission" has been cited in a number of articles when referring to sulphur compounds and other major air pollutants. The term "emission", as such, is introduced in the definition of "Long-range transboundary air pollution" in Article 1(b) of the Convention:

> Long-range transboundary air pollution means air pollution whose physical origin is situated wholly or in part within the area under the national jurisdiction of one State and which has adverse effects in the area under the jurisdiction of another State at such a distance that it is not generally possible to distinguish the contribution of individual *emission* sources or groups of sources. (Emphasis added) (Article 1(b) of the Geneval Convention on Long-Range Transboundary Air Pollution, 1979).

Successive Protocols were adopted following the LRTAP and the first LRTAP instrument that adopted direct restrictions on air pollutants was the 1985 Protocol to the 1979 Convention on Long-Range Transboundary Air Pollution on the reduction of Sulphur Emissions or their Transboundary Fluxes by at Least 30 Per Cent (Helsinki Protocol) (The Helsinki Protocol 1985). With regard to the control of other significant air pollutants, a number of Protocols were introduced following the introduction of the Helsinki Protocol. These include the 1988 Protocol Concerning the Control of Emissions of Nitrogen Oxides or Their Transboundary Fluxes, the 1991 Protocol Concerning the Control of Emissions of Volatile Organic Compounds or their Transboundary Fluxes and the 1994 Protocol on Further Reductions of Sulphur Emissions (Oslo Protocol) (Gillespie 2005). The Oslo Protocol, in the context of air pollution control, is referred to as a target-based protocol whereby differentiated targets for Sulphur Dioxide (SO_2) were used (Gillespie 2005. This was based on the idea that restriction of SO_2 emissions should be founded on the ecosystem's tolerance of SO_2 emissions, given the fact that different ecosystems have various levels of tolerance (Gillespie 2005). With this idea in mind, the Oslo Protocol developed the concept of Sulphur Oxide Management Areas (SOMA), which require extra stringent management due to their ecosystem sensitivity (Article 2 of the Oslo Protocol).

Mandated SO_2 reductions in accordance with the Oslo Protocol vary in terms of type and location and the emission reductions range from 80% for the United Kingdom of Great Britain and Northern Ireland (highest), through to 4% for Greece (lowest) (the Oslo Protocol as amended in December 2004). It is to be noted that the control of "sulphur emission" has been addressed in two separate LRTAP Protocols and the latter protocol, i.e. the Oslo Protocol mirrors the concern of the international community with regard to sulphur emissions and the need to take immediate measures to further reduce the emission levels in order to strengthen the objectives of protection of human health and protection of the environment as marked out by the LRTAP. It is submitted that the regulations incorporated in the Oslo Protocol have a form of cohesion with relevant rules of the United Nations Convention on the Law of the Sea of 1982 (UNCLOS) concerning control of atmospheric pollution. In this context, Article 212 of the UNCLOS prescribes that member states should adopt laws and policies to "prevent, reduce and control pollution of the marine environment from or through the atmosphere..." and in doing so, member states should comply with the international rules and standards (Article 212 of UNCLOS). Although the Oslo Protocol maintains the same status as UNCLOS, the protocol can nevertheless, be characterized by its all-embracing feature in so far as it takes into consideration the human health factor (Article 2(1) of the Oslo Protocol). It is submitted that a rationale for consideration of the human health factor within the ambit of the Oslo Protocol is based on the number of premature deaths per year in Europe caused by air pollution from international shipping (Transport and Environment). The exact number is difficult to prove and claimed numbers have been disputed. In Europe alone, air pollution from ships has been claimed to cause as many as 50,000 premature deaths and it is further claimed that the sulphur limits introduced by IMO in 2008 (see below) could reduce the number of premature deaths by about half. The emission of SO_2 is considered to be one of the main elements that poses a threat to human health (Transport and Environment; Brandt et al. 2013) and can, therefore, be seen as a negative externality of international shipping. Thus the need to reduce and control sulphur emissions from ships.

2 Ship-Sourced Sulphur Emissions

Ship-emission is considered as an important source of anthropogenic particles (result of human activity) and it has been observed that the chemical composition of particles from ship-emissions is most likely to be dominated by sulphur and other organic matters, with a slightly lower content of black-carbon (Mauritzson 2015). Bill Hemmings, Policy Team Programme Manager for Aviation and Shipping at the NGO Transport & Environment, has claimed that "shipping is now the biggest emitter of SOx pollution in Europe" (European Policy Centre 2012) and Helfre and Couto Boot (2013), citing the European Policy Centre and IMO, stated the following findings:

> The shipping industry is among the top emitters of SOx A total of 2.3 million tonnes of SO_2 (the most common sulphur oxide) was emitted by ships in the seas surrounding Europe in the year 2000. Globally, 15 million tonnes of SOx were emitted by shipping in 2007, representing a 50% increase from 1997 levels. SOx emissions from shipping represent between 5% and 8% of the world's total SOx emissions. (Helfre and Couto Boot, 2013, p. 4).

Various stakeholders and interest groups have presented differing estimates on ship-sourced emissions, but although exact measures and numbers are hardly available, the total emissions will not reduce without changes in technology and regulations to enforce their use.

Ships vary in size and type and different types of ships run on different types of engines, such as large slow-speed diesel engines or medium speed-diesel engines (Lack and Corbett 2012). In the absence of international regulations governing the usage of a particular type of engine and an appropriate environment-friendly quality fuel (Mauritzson 2015), it was still considered that in terms of emissions neither the engines nor the quality of fuel had improved over the past few decades (Fridell et al. 2008, pp. 1160–1168). It could be argued that advancement of technology in recent years with development of ships with LNG-powered and dual-fuel engines and scrubbers will bring a gradual change with respect to emissions. So far relatively few such ships have been commissioned, but currently an increasing interest in LNG as marine fuel is evident. However, considering that the lifecycle of an average ship is at least 20–25 years, it will take a long time for such technology to have full effect. Retrofitting of scrubbers is easier, but still represents a significant investment, and shipowners appear to have decided on such investments only when they have faced mandatory emission limits. Engines and heavy fuel oils are a part of a shipping company's financial investment and unless regulated in mandatory rules, this aspect cannot be dictated by policies established by international organisations as shipping companies tend to invest in cheap but more polluting fuel (The Guardian 2014). Although the International Convention on the Prevention of Pollution from Ships of

1973 as modified by the Protocol of 1978 (MARPOL 73/78) adopted by the International Maritime Organization has its roots in the Torrey Canyon incident, the Convention was amended by the 1997 Protocol and the amended version includes Annex VI. Annex VI entitled "Prevention of Air Pollution from Ships" regulates the emission of substances including sulphur oxides (SOx), nitrogen oxides (NOx) and particulate matters (MARPOL 73/78, Annex VI). The most stringent changes in the amendment relate to SOx emission and reduction of SOx emissions, which can be achieved by limiting the maximum sulphur content of the fuel oil used onboard. Annex VI, to that extent, entitles a contracting state to submit or jointly submit with other contracting states a proposal of designating specific areas of coastal waters as a SOx Emission Control Area (SECA). A SECA has been defined as "an area where the adoption of special mandatory measures for SOx emissions from ships is required to prevent, reduce and control air pollution from SOx and its attendant adverse impacts on land and sea areas..." (Annex VI, Regulation 2 (11), MARPOL 73/78). A proposal for the designation of an area as a SECA needs to be submitted to the IMO and must comply with six SECA pre-requisites as incorporated in Appendix III (2.2):

1. a clear delineation of the proposed area of application of controls on SOx emissions from ships, along with a reference chart on which the area is marked;
2. a description of the land and sea areas at risk from the impacts of ship SOx emissions;
3. an assessment that SOx emissions from ships operating in the proposed area of application of the SOx emission controls are contributing to air pollution from SOx, including SOx deposition, and their attendant adverse impacts on the land and sea areas under consideration. Such assessment shall include a description of the impacts of SOx emissions on terrestrial and aquatic ecosystems, areas of natural productivity, critical habitats, water quality, human health, and areas of cultural and scientific significance, if applicable. The sources of relevant data, including methodologies used, shall be identified;
4. relevant information pertaining to the meteorological conditions in the proposed area of application of the SOx emission controls and the land and sea areas at risk, in particular prevailing wind patterns, or to topographical, geological, oceanographic, morphological, or other conditions that may lead to an increased probability of higher localized air pollution or levels of acidification;
5. the nature of the ship traffic in the proposed SOx emission control area, including the patterns and density of such traffic; and
6. a description of the control measures taken by the proposing Contracting State or Contracting States addressing land-based sources of SOx emissions affecting the area at risk that are in place and operating concurrent with the consideration of measures to be adopted in relation to provisions of regulation 14 of Annex VI of the present Convention. (Appendix III of Annex VI, MARPOL 73/78).

New requirements reflecting significant improvements were introduced in Annex VI in the year 2008 which included "new fuel quality requirements" and this requirement entered into force from the beginning of July 2010. In terms of new fuel quality requirements and fuel-emissions, two sets of requirements were defined in Annex VI. The former is a requirement, which is global in nature, while the latter requirement specifically applies to Emission Control Areas (referred to as ECA), which includes emission control areas for SOx or SECAs. Currently, there are four regions in the world that are defined as SECAs, namely: (1) Baltic Sea area; (2) North Sea area (3) North American area (covering designated areas off the United States and Canada); and (4) United States Caribbean Sea area (International Maritime Organization Sulphur oxides (SOx)—Regulation 14). It is noteworthy that Annex VI regulations include limits or caps on sulphur content of fuel oil as a part of the MARPOL 73/78 control mechanism. The permissible sulphur content of the fuel inside an ECA prior to July 2010 was 1.50% m/m (by mass) when this rate was reduced to 1.0% (by mass) and further reduced to 0.10% m/m (by mass) on and after 1 January 2015 (International Maritime Organization, Sulphur Oxides (SOx)—Regulation 14). The Baltic Sea was designated as the first SECA in Annex VI of the 1997 Protocol of MARPOL 73/78, which prohibited the usage of fuel-oil with a sulphur content exceeding 1.50% and came into effect from May 2006. The same standard was established for the North Sea at the 44th session of IMO's Marine Environment Protection Committee (44/11/4), and came into effect on 22 November 2007 (Marine Environment Protection Committee, 44th session, 2000). At the EU level, the MARPOL 73/78 prescribed rate of 1.50% was given effect as of 11 August 2006 for the Baltic Sea and 11 August 2007 for the North Sea. Within the Member States of the European Union new maximum permitted rates of sulphur content in marine fuels were mandated through Directive 2005/33/EC of the European Parliament and of the Council of 6 July 2005 (Directive 2005/33/EC), which amended Directive 1999/32/EC. When the EU regional legislative efforts on sulphur emission are compared to the legislative efforts of the IMO, it is observed that the EU Directive 2005/33/EC is not precisely aligned with the earlier MARPOL 73/78 Annex provisions. Although the two instruments are parallel initiatives at the international and regional level, and seem to voice a strong sense of determination to control sulphur emission, subtle differences remain between Annex VI of MARPOL 73/78 and Directive 2005/33/EC in terms of sulphur limits, sulphur content of marine fuels and the commencement date of effect.

Seven years into the application of Directive 2005/33/EC, the EU felt the need to align its efforts with international law and practice and hence, a new set of amendments was introduced in 2012. The new Directive took into account a higher level of protection pursuant to international commitments and re-confirmed the EC's intention to adhere to the sulphur limits set out by international law. Directive 2012/22/EU of the European Parliament and of the Council of 21 November 2012 (Directive 2012/33/EU) can be termed as an attempt to end all incoherence between the former Directives (including Directive 1999/32/EC) and the revised Annex VI to MARPOL 73/78 (Directive 2012/33/EU). A "statutory alert" was published by Lloyd's Register in December 2012 detailing specifics of the changes implemented through Directive 2012/33/EU (Lloyd's Register Classification News, No. 32/2012). The "statutory alert" acknowledged the alignment of EC regulations with the revised Annex of MARPOL 73/78 and highlighted the key elements of change brought by

Directive 2012/33/EU with regard to sulphur limits for marine fuel in and outside of EU SECAs. In terms of sulphur limits for marine fuel inside SECA, the new Directive implemented a strict reduction from 1.00% m/m (by mass) to 0.10% m/m (by mass), which was a dramatic decrease by 0.9% m/m (by mass). The reduced rate of sulphur content, i.e. 0.10% has now been in effect since 1 January 2015. For areas outside EU SECAs, the set limit for maximum sulphur content of fuel is 3.50% m/m (by mass), which has been in effect from 18 June 2014. This rate needs to be reduced to 0.50% m/m (by mass), which is a sharp drop by 3.0% and is expected to become effective from 1 January 2020 regardless of the outcome of the IMO fuel availability review, which is due by 2018. It should be noted that these rates apply to all ships excluding passenger ships on regular services to/from EC ports and ships at berth in EC ports. For ships at berth and passenger ships, Directive 2012/33/EU places the following requirements (Table):

From the original initiatives, the introduction of the LRTAP in 1979 and the Oslo Protocol in 1994, European regional efforts via Directives 1999/32/EC, 2005/33/EC and 2012/33/EU, the EU have set a landmark for other regions of the globe in the field of ship-sourced air pollution control and, more specifically, the control of sulphur emissions. In general, the European Commission has made advancements over the years to regulate air pollution through other mechanisms, e.g. product standards, environmental quality standards, flag state control, port state control, market mechanisms and global action. But in a maritime context, Directive 2012/33/EU reflects the EU's bonafide intention to govern maritime transportation with the sole intention to reduce the detrimental effects of sulphur emissions from ships. In all of this, the objective of the EU is transparent and straightforward—to align the regional standards with the international standards, which finally narrows down to the core objective—protection of the marine environment. The ideology behind labelling the Baltic Sea and the North Sea Areas as ECAs in conformity with Annex VI of MARPOL 73/78 clearly demonstrates the EU's intention to regulate maritime transportation and to ensure the member states fulfil their international obligations in accordance with Article 192 of UNCLOS, which stipulates that "states have the obligation to protect and preserve the marine environment". This international obligation is satisfied, to some extent, by ensuring strict compliance with the aligned sulphur content rates in those control areas. But the protection and preservation of the marine environment aspect is only one side of the entire maritime

Table Fuel sulphur content pursuant to Directive 2012/33/EU

	Maximum fuel sulphur content (by mass) outside EU SECAs	Maximum fuel sulphur content (by mass) inside EU SECAs
(a) All ships excluding (b) and (c) below	3.50% from 18 June 2014 0.50% from 1 Jan 2020	1.00% until 31 Dec 2014 0.10% from 1 Jan 2015
(b) Passenger ships on regular services to/from EC ports excluding ships at berth in EC ports	1.5% until 1 Jan 2020 0.50% from 1 Jan 2020	1.00% until 31 Dec 2014 0.10% from 1 Jan 2015
(c) Ships at berth in EC ports	0.10%	0.10%

Lloyd's Register Classification News, No. 32/2012

governance scenario. If the European Commission is considered the vanguard of the EU marine environment (including the SECAs), the governee would inevitably be the shipping sector. Although the aim of ISO 26000 is to contribute to sustainable development by encouraging companies to go beyond mere compliance with applicable law and act in consistence with international norms of behaviour (International Organization for Standardization 2010), strict compliance with the prescribed rates of fuel sulphur content pursuant to Directive 2012/33/EU can be seen as the mechanism that can help govern the shipping sector. Although CSR involves companies voluntarily addressing concerns related to, among others, social and environmental issues, the inevitable question is how can we define CSR in the context of air emission?

3 CSR and Ship-Sourced Air Emissions

While the conceptual definition of CSR has been explained over the years against the backdrop of societal contributions of business corporations (Bowen 1953; Carroll 1999; Moir 2001), the theory has been extended to include shipping companies and the effect maritime transportation may have on various stakeholders in the business-process (Progoulaki and Roe 2011). It is noteworthy that different authors have followed different methodological approaches since 1999 to establish a better understanding and a robust definition of CSR. These efforts were gathered and compiled by Dahlsrud (2008) and subsequently, through content analysis, coding scheme and frequency counts he observed that the definition of CSR had branched into five main dimensions: (1) the environmental dimension, (2) the social dimension, (3) the economic dimension, (4) the stakeholder dimension and (5) the voluntariness dimension (Dahlsrud 2008). Regardless of the multitude of definitions developed over time, the environmental dimension was emphasized much less frequently, partly due to the fact that "corporate environmental responsibility" was often used as a distinct concept. Nonetheless, the "environmental dimension" is directly or indirectly related to the others.

To confirm whether the environmental dimension is truly related to any of the other four dimensions by Dahlsrud (2008), the intentions behind the implementation of the LRTAP, which was developed by the UNECE, needs to be observed. The central objective of the LRTAP was "to protect man and his environment" and "the history of the LRTAP can be traced back to the 1960's, when scientists demonstrated the interrelation between sulphur emissions in continental Europe and the acidification of Scandinavian lakes" (UNECE). Following the objective, i.e. "to protect man and his environment", as observed in the regional-international interplay in the LRTAP, the environmental dimension (marine environment) appeared in parallel with the stakeholder dimension (human health) in the Council Directive 1999/32/EC of 26 April 1999 (Directive 1999/32/EC), but finally, the environmental dimension was incorporated within the scope of Directive 2012/33/EU:

(1) The environmental policy of the Union, as set out in the action programmes on the environment, and in particular in the Sixth Environmental Action

Programme adopted by Decision No 1600/2002/EC of the European Parliament and of the Council, has as one of its objectives to achieve levels of air quality that do not give rise to significant negative impacts on and risks to human health and the environment.

(2) Article 191(2) of the Treaty on the Functioning of the European Union (TFEU) provides that Union policy on the environment is to aim at a high level of protection taking into account the diversity of situations in the various regions of the Union. (Preamble (1) and (2) of Directive 2012/33/EU).

Through Directive 2012/33/EU shipping companies are required to observe the prescribed limits on sulphur content in fuel inside and outside of the European Union SECAs. Although the term CSR is not explicit in either of the aforementioned Treaty or Directive, it can be inferred that the prescriptive nature of the sulphur content in fuel imposes a form of environmental obligation on shipping companies, and still belongs to the broad category of CSR. Since this obligation to operate the vessel within the prescriped sulphur limit has an implied connection with the environmental dimension, it is safe to assert that the voluntary environmental-responsibility aspect of CSR transposes to a form of company-obligation under the relevant provisions of Directive 2012/33/EU. Regardsless of whether it is seen as a corporate social responsibility or an environmental social responsibility, shipping companies are obliged to adhere to the given limits inside and outside the European union SECAs. Furthermore, the European Commission linked the notion of responsible business with the definition of CSR, i.e. a "concept whereby companies integrate social and environmental concerns in their business operations and in their interaction with their stakeholders on a voluntary basis" (Commission of the European Communities 2006). So the integration of social and environmental concerns is a priority for the shipping companies and with the help of CSR tools, i.e. survey, inspection, publication of reports, etc., companies, whether large or small, together with their stakeholders, can work towards reconciliation of economic, social and environmental ambitions (Commission of the European Communities 2006). The intention of the European Commission was to provide a political impetus to CSR, to give recognition to the work that had already been done by companies (including shipping companies) and to boost the level of encouragement to do more in this field (Commission of the European Communities 2006). Although academics, scholars, proponents of CSR and the school of business administration have strongly opined that the concept is in itself voluntary in nature (Carroll 1983), there appears to be a shift from the voluntary nature of CSR to a more mandatory and strict compliance nature. This is broadly due to the fact that shipping companies registered within the EU must comply with the new standards and the EU member states have an obligation to confirm that the new sulphur limits are maintained, which is done through flag state control and port state control. It is submitted that the notion of protection and preservation of the marine environment in Directive 2012/33/EU relates to the environmental dimension of CSR and ensures that shipping companies are environmentally conscious when conducting business within the SECAs of the EU and conscientiously adhere to the sulphur limits in their shipping operations.

Shipping companies and enterprises can be primary actors of CSR and by maintaining the principles of better regulation, they not only exhibit ethical and legal compliance, but also actively participate in the promotion of CSR.

Although an aberration from the traditional concept, CSR can be hypothesized as being closely related to the new standards and regulations in directive 2012/33/EU. While the sulphur content in ships' fuel has been revised and reduced in the EU since 1999 through three successive Directives, the contents and amendments of these Directives leave little room for critique. The only question that remains to be answered is how do the sulphur content requirements in the EU SECAs impact on shipping companies in the EU? It has been observed that some ships, which conduct business operations exclusively in the Baltic Sea have consumed fuel with a lower shulphur content than the applicable SECA requirement (at the time), for example passenger ferries between Sweden and Finland have used Low Sulphur Fuel Oil (LSFO), estimated at 0.50% or even less (Nugraha 2009). In 2002, it was observed that some 65% of the ferries had switched to LSFO and dozens of ferries within the EU had installed Selective Catalytic Reduction Technology to comply with the sulphur reduction rate embodied in Directive 1999/32/EC (Corbett and Farrell 2002, pp. 197–211; Lock 2013). Passenger ships on regular services to/from EU ports face a practical problem since the permissible sulphur content in fuel for operating outside SECAs is currently 1.5% (until 2020) whereas the permissible rate is reduced to 0.10% for operating inside SECAs. Consequently, they can choose to operate continuously on fuel with 0.1% sulphur content, which is more expensive, but being a voluntary choice, could be seen (and promoted) as an expression of CSR. Alternatively, they will need to deal with dual-fuel systems, but a dual-fuel operation system is considered to have implications on engine condition, lubrication complexity and tank segregation etc. (Nugraha 2009; Nersesian 2016). A further potential problem for ships entering a SECA is that the prescribed limits apply to the actual emissions and not to the fuel currently being used, so the emissions may exceed the limit even if the ship believes it has changed to low-sulphur fuel in good time before entering the SECA. The problem also remains for ships at berth in EU ports and inland waterways operations where the sulphur content in fuel inside and outside of the SECA must be within the rate of 0.10% pursuant to Directive 2012/33/EU. There exist alternative forms of compliance, such as several types of LSFO, including low-sulphur distillate oil, hybrid fuel oil, Liquefied Natural Gas (LNG), Liquefied Petroleum Gas (LPG), biofuels, Dimethyl Ether (DME), ethane and methanol (Lloyd's Register Marine 2012). Furthermore, it has been estimated that Low Sulphur Distillate Oil (LSDO) will generally be used to comply with the reduced rate and falls within the category of LSFO (Lloyd's Register Marine 2012). LSDO comprises of marine diesel oil (MDO) or marine gas oil (MGO) and the Baltic Ports Organization Secretariat considered MGOs to be the first viable option for operators in the Baltic Sea SECA due to the fact that using marine distillate fuel in the main engines normally does not pose major technical challenges (TransBaltic 2012). From an International Organization for Standardization (ISO) aspect, MGOs are categorised as distillate marine grades pursuant to ISO standard 8216:2010 (Lloyd's Register Marine 2012). However, it should be noted that LSDO and MGOs are not completely trouble-free and Lloyd's Register has summarised the problems related to compliance as follows:

> The availability of LSDO is an industry concern. There has been a tightening of distillate fuel supplies as a result of EU requirements for ultra-low sulphur automotive fuels and an increasing demand in emerging markets. In 2009, Conservation of Clean Air and Water in Europé (CONCAWE) estimated that a USD 50 billion investment in refineries was needed to meet European automotive and industrial demand for distillates, with a further USD 17.5 billion investment needed to meet potential additional demand from shipping. Little of this investment has been in Europe and in fact Europe has been losing refining capacity. There is significant investment in upgrading refineries outside of Europe, for example in Russia. This may offset expected shortfalls. The IMO will review LSDO availability in 2018 to see whether the 2020 global sulphur limit reduction is achievable. At the time of writing, LSDO is typically 300 US dollars per tonne more expensive than 380 centistokes (cSt) Residual Fuel Oil (RFO), and while long-term fuel cost forecasting is notoriously unreliable it is generally accepted that it will remain significantly more expensive than RFO (Lloyd's Register Marine, 2012).

Regarding the second option, the Baltic Ports Organization Secretariat considers LNG as an alternative fuel. Although challenges are posed with the use of LNG, it has proven to be a popular option for ship operators operating in the Baltic Sea and the North Sea Areas (Rozmarynowska and Oldakowski 2012). There are certain advantages with the usage of LNG since no additional abatement measures are required in order to comply with international (IMO) standards (Rozmarynowska and Oldakowski 2012). Given the fact that LNG contains virtually no sulphur, operators do not need to worry about the sulphur content in LNG since sulphur emissions are reduced by virtually 100% (Rozmarynowska and Oldakowski 2012). LNG has been used as a marine fuel in the EU since the beginning of the century and in order to meet the LNG demand, the Danish Maritime Authority (DMA) published a summary report in 2012 with business models for the establishment of an LNG Bunkering Infrastructure in the EU (Danish Maritime Authority 2012). While Norway has been a forerunner in this respect, establishing LNG terminals in the EU is an ongoing process. For example, the LNG terminal in Nynäshamn in Sweden, which became operational in 2011, was the first one in the Basltic Sea and there were plans to upgrade the terminal so that it can load LNG on vessels that could in turn supply other vessels with the required amount of LNG fuel (Rozmarynowska and Oldakowski 2012). The interest in LNG as a marine fuel has increased exponentially and in early 2017 the estimated number of LNG-powered ships exceeded 100 vessels with an equal number under construction (Yep 2017), but in relation to the total fleet, this number still represents a drop in the ocean.

While alternative fuels may provide a sense of comfort to ship operators, the negative implications of alternatives will be widespread. There is a possibility that the operational costs will increase for shipping companies who wish to convert to LNG and a possible rapid uptake of scrubber technology raises the question as to whether manufacturing supply will meet demand (Lloyd's Register Marine 2012). The disadvantages were highlighted by the International Chamber of Shipping (ICS) in 2013 when they presented an estimate of the cost for the global shipping industry of complying with the already adopted regulations related to SOx, NOx, CO_2,

United Nations Framework Convention on Climate Change (UNFCCC) and Ballast Water Management, which, according to ICS' estimate totals about USD 750 billion over the next decade. Of these estimated total investments and increases in operational costs, as much as USD 200 billion is estimated to stem from the 0.1% sulphur limit in the SECAs (International Chamber of Shipping 2013). In this context, the financial challenges are considered to be enormous, particularly at a time when few (if any) shipowners have readily available cash reserves. Stringent regulations have impacts on the budgets and investments of shipping companies, because they affect fuel costs, which represent significant costs borne by shipping companies (Helfre and Couto Boot 2013). At the same time, banks are generally less willing to provide loans for investments to upgrade ships (Hadhi 2017) compared to financing ship acquisitions or newbuildings, particularly when many clients are already technically in default on loan covenants.

4 Sulphur Directive: Possible Impact on Short Sea Shipping

There have been fears that the cost of the new requirements to control and reduce SOx emissions in the SECAs could result in a modal shift from sea to land-based transport, which is presumed to have negative effects on the competitiveness of short sea shipping, but also the competitiveness of export industries in comparison with companies in countries outside the SECAs. In order to avoid the challenges associated with operational costs emanating from strict compliance with Directive 2012/33/EU when using MGO instead of heavy fuel oil, shippers in the EU member states could consider the "truck only" option, which was studied extensively and explained by the European Community Shipowners' Associations (ECSA) in 2010 (European Community Shipowners' Associations 2010). The study showed that the Baltic States can be reached from Western Europe by following the highways and main roads connecting Germany, Poland and the eastern Baltic and the study provided a comparative cost-analysis between the Short Sea Shipping (referred to as SSS) combined with truck transport (short sea/truck) and "truck only" options (European Community Shipowners' Associations 2010). In some cases the "truck only" option proved to be more competitive. For example, on the trade lane between Germany/Denmark and Sweden, where the sea leg is quite short, a projection showed a price gap which, although small, could trigger a modal shift from sea to road in a scenario where fuel prices were projected to be high (European Community Shipowners' Associations 2010). The comparative disadvantage of the short sea/truck alternative increased with the length of the sea leg. However, the comparative cost-analysis reflected other disadvantages when considering the "truck only" option, which was observed by the European Commission in so far as an "increasing share of goods being transported by road would in many cases run counter to the Union's climate change objectives and increase congestion" (Directive 2012/33/EU):

> ...The Rotterdam-Harwich short sea link shows the most competitive profile on all routes considered except for traffic flows to and from Manchester (price dominance of Rotterdam-Hull), but also here the use of MGO is expected to make its competitive position weaker. The narrowing of the price gap implies that the Rotterdam-Harwich short sea route moves towards a situation of increased competition with the truck/rail option. Such a development should raise great concern given longer truck distances on the already highly congested motorways in the southeast of the UK (European Community Shipowners' Associations, 2010).

If the truck option is disregarded in this scenario, shippers are left with the SSS alternative, which has numerous positive attributes and is said to: (1) facilitate regional trade, (2) facilitate distribution of goods, (3) stimulate development of remote areas, (4) save investment in infrastructure, (5) reduce congestion on roads and railways, and (6) contribute to development of support industries. The main container lines (trunk lines) utilise larger ships, which, as a consequence, only call at a few hub ports. These goods need to be further distributed to other parts of the EU region, which is often done by road or rail, but it can also be done by feeder services or by inland waterways, which is traditionally seen as a separate mode of transport rather than as a part of SSS. It is furthermore, acknowledged that SSS can reach remote and peripheral areas of a region or country, which may be disadvantaged by the lack of adequate land connections. The use of SSS and coastal services save investments in road and rail infrastructure and, most importantly, SSS preserves the investments already made by reducing wear and tear on road networks. However, in 1999 the European Commission highlighted a significant drawback of SSS observing that the amount of documentation needed in the process created an inherent burden to SSS (Communication from the Commission 1999). The study published by the European Commission concluded that "...the documentation required in road transport was in all cases less than short sea shipping" (Communication from the Commission 1999). It is noteworthy that SSS has all along been subject to the competition rules of the Treaty of the EU, Articles 81 and 82 (previously Treaty of Rome, Articles 85 and 86), which raises complicated questions relating to market share and dominant position in the market, which are real concerns when operating to smaller ports. Moreover, in 2001, the European Conference of Ministers of Transport reviewed the obstacles to the development of SSS and reflected on the major barriers of SSS, which included *inter alia*: (1) costs and standards of port services as disincentive, (2) intermodal competition, and (3) pre- and post-shipment carriage (European Conference of Ministers of Transport 2001). Although the European Commission has recommended that the procedures including documentation be simplified, the implementation of it all lies with respective member states and despite efforts to reduce the documentation formalities, this issue has not yet been satisfactorily resolved (European Community Shipowners' Association 2016).

5 Conclusion

Proponents of SSS argue that in comparison with road transport, SSS is a better alternative from the point of view social and environmental sustainability. In this respect a modal shift from SSS to road transport could be said to be a negative reflection of CSR. Towards the end of 2014, there were grave concerns that the entry into force of the reduction of the permissible shulphur content in marine fuel in the SECAs and the attendant rises in operating costs would sound the death knell for many SSS services. Two years after the entry into force of the 0.1% sulphur cap it could be noted that these doomsday prophecies had not materialised, primarily due to the global drop in the price of oil. However, although the operating costs for shipping had not increased, at least not due to fuel prices, the competitive disadvantages are a reality, since the price differences between heavy fuel oil and LSFOs remain. In an effort to understand whether there exists a balance between (a) the new requirements, which underpin environmental protection through control of sulphur content in fuel, and (b) cost effectiveness, which is significant to shipping companies whether at the EU level or the global level, it can clearly be concluded that the perfect balance is yet to be achieved. From a thorough examination of quantitative and comparative analyses conducted at the governmental and non-governmental level, it is easy to deduce that alternatives in which shipping companies will be able to benefit from business while complying with SECA sulphur rates will be difficult (European Community Shipowners' Associations 2010; Rozmarynowska and Oldakowski 2012; Boer et al. 2015). When operating within the SECAs of the Baltic Sea and the North Sea Areas, both shippers and shipping companies will need to be more tactical and apply strategic thinking. Whether the decisions relate to the choice of fuel or the use of short sea shipping, short sea/truck combinations or truck only alternatives, the primary actors need to calculate beforehand so that there is a sufficient amount of profit in whatever choices are made. It is now safe to assert that corporate responsibility in the area of emissions is regulated by mandatory legislation whereby the EU maritime administrations are asked to deter sub-standard shipping and control maritime transportation via survey, inspection and, in the worst-case scenario, detention. The paradigm shift from a soft-law approach to an obligatory approach for EU member states began with the implementation of the "Treaty on the Functioning of the European Union". Since then, implementation of rules at the national level has become mandatory for each and every EU member state, but the level of enforcement may vary. For example, in 2015 Norway (which is not a member of the EU) conducted 204 inspections of the sulphur content and in 11 of the samples the sulphur content exceeded 0.1% and in three cases ships had been fined for failing to switch to low-sulphur fuel while verdicts had not been returned in the remaining cases (Bergman 2016). In other instances, the European Commission has been in favour of a zero tolerance policy when it comes to protection and presevation of the marine environment. This is mainly due to the fact that the buzzword in all of today's shipping related policy development is sustainability, but the question has arisen whether the regulations, which have already been adopted, make for a sustainable shipping industry. While the notion of zero tolerance policy could ensure perfect sustainability by reducing all emissions and pollution by 100 %, the inevitable question is whether this will falter the traditional concept of CSR, which supports business endeavours to the extent that shipping companies are corporately and socially responsible and contribute to the welfare of the five dimensions, including the economic dimension. But whether or not the shipping companies operating in the EU SECAs will be able to cope with the current changes, and the upcoming changes that will come with the next step of sulphur-reduction, is still a burning question. Now that this environmental dimension of CSR has become an issue of compliance, rather than choice for shipping operators, the baton has been passed to shippers to exercise CSR by voluntarily opting for SSS as the most sustainable mode of transport.

References

Bergman, A. (2016). Eleven SECA–transgressions in Norway (in Swedish: Elva SECA-överträdelser i Norge). *Sjöfartstidningen* 2016, 15 January, http://www.sjofartstidningen.se, Retrieved January 15, 2016.

Boer, E. D., Ahdour, S., & Meerwaldt, H. (2015). SECA assessment: Impacts of 2015 SECA marine fuel sulphur limits: First drawings from European experience. *CE Delft*, Retrieved from the World Wide Web, https://www.nabu.de/imperia/md/content/nabude/verkehr/nabu-seca-studie2016.pdf, Retrieved July 22, 2016.

Bowen, H. R. (1953). *Social responsibilities of the businessman*. New York, NY: Harper and Row.

Brandt, J., Silver, J. D., Christensen, J. H., Andersen, M. S., Bønløkke, J., Sigsgaard, T., et al. (2013). Assessment of past, present and future health-cost externalities of air pollution in Europe and the contribution from international ship traffic using the EVA model system. *Atmospheric Chemistry and Physics, 13*(5), 7747–7764.

Carroll, A. B. (1983). Corporate social responsibility: Will industry respond to cut-backs in social program funding? *Vital Speeches of the Day, 49*(19).

Carroll, A. B. (1999). Corporate social responsibility: Evolution of a definitional construct. *Business & Society, 38*(3), 268–295.

Commission of the European Communities. (2005). *Communication from the Commission to the Council and the European Parliament, Thematic strategy on air pollution, COM (2005) 446 Final,* Retrieved from the World Wide Web, http://eur-lex.europa.eu/legal-content/EN/TXT/PDF/?uri=CELEX:52005DC0446&from=en, Retrieved July 22, 2016.

Commission of the European Communities. (2006). *Communication from the Commission to the European Parliament, the Council and the European Economic and Social Committee: Implementing the Partnership for Growth and Jobs: Making Europe a pole of excellence on Corporate Social Responsibility", COM(2006) 136 Final,* Retrieved from the World Wide Web, http://eur-lex.europa.eu/LexUriServ/LexUriServ.do?uri=COM:2006:0136:FIN:en:PDF, Retrieved December 31, 2015.

Communication from the Commission (to the Council, the European Parliament, the Economic and Social Committee and the Committee of the Regions). (1999). *The development of short sea shipping in Europe: A dynamic alternative in a sustainable transport chain.* Retrieved from the World Wide Web, Retrieved January 1, 2016, http://aei.pitt.edu/3565/1/000714_1.pdf.

Corbett, J. J., & Farrell, A. (2002). Mitigating air pollution impacts of passenger ferries. *Transportation Research Part D: Transport and Environment, 7*(3), 197–211.

Council Directive 1999/32/EC of 26 April 1999. Official Journal of the European Communities. Retrieved from the World Wide Web, http://eur-lex.europa.eu/legal-content/EN/TXT/PDF/?uri=CELEX:31999L0032&from=EN, Retrieved December 31, 2015.

Dahlsrud, A. (2008). How corporate social responsibility is defined. An analysis of 37 definitions. *Corporate Social Responsibility and Environmental Management, 15*, 1–13.

Danish Maritime Authority. (2012). North European LNG infrastructure project: A feasibility study for an LNG filling station infrastructure and test of recommendations. *Summary Report*. Retrieved from the World Wide Web, http://www.dma.dk/themes/LNGinfrastructureproject/Documents/Final%20Report/LNG_Summary_Report_20120522_optimerad.pdf, Retrieved January 1, 2016.

Directive 2005/33/EC of the European Parliament and of the Council of 6 July 2005. Official Journal of the European Union. Retrieved from the World Wide Web, http://eur-lex.europa.eu/LexUriServ/LexUriServ.do?uri=OJ:L:2005:191:0059:0069:EN:PDF, Retrieved December 30, 2015.

Directive 2012/33/EU of the European Parliament and of the Council of 21 November 2012. Official Journal of the European Union. Retrieved from the World Wide Web; http://eur-lex.europa.eu/LexUriServ/LexUriServ.do?uri=OJ:L:2012:327:0001:0013:en:PDF, Retrieved December 31, 2015.

European Community Shipowners' Associations. (2010). *Analysis of the consequences of low sulphur fuel requirements*. Retrieved from the World Wide Web; http://www.schonescheepvaart.nl/downloads/rapporten/doc_1361790123.pdf, Retrieved January 1, 2016.

European Community Shipowners' Associations. (2016). *European shipowners showcase short sea shipping*. Retrieved from the World Wide Web; http://www.ecsa.eu/9-latest-news/237-european-shipowners-showcase-short-sea-shipping, Retrieved February 16, 2016.

European Conference of Ministers of Transport. (2001). *Short sea shipping in Europe*. Retrieved from the World Wide Web; http://www.internationaltransportforum.org/IntOrg/ecmt/pubpdf/01ShortSea.pdf, Retrieved January 1, 2016.

European Policy Center. (2012). *Reducing CO emissions from shipping - rethinking European policies*, 18 September 2012. Retrieved from the World Wide Web; http://www.epc.eu/themes_details.php?cat_id=6&pub_id=2932&theme_id=32, Retrieved December 29, 2015.

Fridell, E., Steen, E., & Peterson, K. (2008). Primary particles in ship emissions. *Atmospheric Environment, 42*(6), 1160–1168.

Friedrich, A., Heinen, F., Kamakate, F., & Kodjak, D. (2007). Air pollution and greenhouse gas emissions from ocean-going ships: Impacts, mitigation options and opportunities for managing growth. *The International Council on Clean Transportation*.

Geneva Convention on Long-Range Transboundary Air Pollution. (1979). Retrieved from the World Wide Web; http://www.unece.org/fileadmin/DAM/env/lrtap/full%20text/1979.CLRTAP.e.pdf, Retrieved December 29, 2015.

Gillespie, A. (2005). *Climate change, ozone depletion and air pollution: Legal commentaries with policy and science considerations*. Leiden: Martinus Nijhoff Publishers.

Hadhi, A. (2017). ABN AMRO offers financing for ballast water treatment systems as deadline nears. *Lloyd's List 2017*, 3 May.

Hecht, J. (1997). *The environmental effects of freight*. Paris: Organisation for Economic Co-operation and Development.

Helfre, J.-F., & Couto Boot, P. A. (2013). Emission reduction in the shipping industry: Regulations, exposure and solutions. *Sustainalytics*. Retrieved from the World Wide Web; http://www.sustainalytics.com/sites/default/files/shippingemissions_july2013.pdf, Retrieved December 29, 2015.

International Chamber of Shipping. (2013). Annual Review 2013.

International Convention on the Prevention of Pollution from Ships of 1973 as modified by the Protocol of 1978, Annex VI. Retrieved from the World Wide Web; https://www.ufpe.br/engnaval/images/pdf/Normas/Marpol/marpol_7378_parta.pdf, Retrieved December 30, 2015.

International Maritime Organization. (2008). *IMO Marine environment policy*. Background paper at sixteenth OSCE Economic and Environmental Forum - Part 1: Maritime and inland waterways co-operation in the OSCE area: Increasing security and protecting the environment, Vienna, 28–29 January 2008.

International Maritime Organization. (n.d.) *Marine Environment*. Retrieved from the World wide Web; http://www.imo.org/en/OurWork/Environment/Pages/Default.aspx, Retrieved December 27, 2015.

International Maritime Organissation. (n.d.) *Sulphur oxides (SO_x) –Regulation 14*. Retrieved from the World Wide Web; http://www.imo.org/en/OurWork/environment/pollutionprevention/airpollution/pages/sulphur-oxides-(sox)-%E2%80%93-regulation-14.aspx, Retrieved April 30, 2017.

International Organization for Standardization. (2010). *ISO 26000:2010 Guidance on social responsibility*. Retrieved from the World Wide Web; https://www.iso.org/standard/42546.html, Retrieved May 8, 2017.

Kiss, A., & Shelton, D. (2007). *Guide to international environmental law*. Leiden: Martinus Nijhoff Publishers.

Lack, D. A., & Corbett, J. J. (2012). Black carbon from ships: A review of the effects of ship speed, fuel quality and exhaust gas scrubbing. *Atmospheric Chemistry and Physics, 12*(9), 3985–4000.

Lindén, O., Chircop, A., Pourzanjani, M., Schröder, J.-U., & Raaymakers, S. (2007). *PSSA in the Baltic Sea: Present situation and future possibilities*. Malmö: World Maritime University.

Lloyd's Register. (2012). Statutory alert: Amendments to EC sulphur regulations to align them with MARPOL Annex VI. Lloyd's Register Classification News, No. 32/2012. Retrieved from the World Wide Web; https://www.cdlive.lr.org/information/Documents/classnews/2012/CN3212.pdf, Retrieved December 31, 2015.

Lloyd's Register Marine. (2012). *Your options for emissions compliance: Guidance for shipowners and operators on the Annex VI SOx and NOx regulations (first launched in 2012 as "Understanding exhaust gas treatment systems")*. Retrieved from the World Wide Web; http://www.lr.org/en/_images/213-35826_Your_options_for_emissions_compliance.pdf, Retrieved January 1, 2016.

Lock, L. M. (2013). *Future fuel for worldwide tanker shipping in spot market*. Master's Degree Project in Naval Architecture, KTH Engineering Sciences, Stockholm, Sweden.

Marine Environment Protection Committee, 44th session, 12 April 2000. Report of the Marine Environment Protection Committee on its Forty-Fourth Session. Retrieved from the World Wide Web; http://www.crs.hr/Portals/0/docs/eng/imo_iacs_eu/imo/mepc_reports/MEPC44.pdf (Retrieved 30 December 2015).

Mauritzson, N. (2015). *Soot particles from shipping: Analysing emission factors*. Unpublished Master's Dissertation, University of Lund, Sweden.

Mitropoulos, E. E. (2007). Ship shape. *Our Planet, The Magazine of the United Nations Environment Programme*, December 2007, 8–9. Retrieved from the World Wide Web; http://www.unep.org/pdf/Ourplanet/2007/dec/en/OP-2007-12-en-FULLVERSION.pdf, Retrieved June 1, 2016.

Moir, L. (2001). What do we mean by corporate social responsibility? *Corporate Governance. The International Journal of Business in Society, 1*(2), 16–22. https://doi.org/10.1108/EUM0000000005486.

Nersesian, R. L. (2016). *Energy economics: Markets, history and policy*. Oxon: Routledge.

Nugraha, F. (2009). *Effective implementation of emission control area towards Cleaner shipping operations: Focusing on sulphur oxides (SOx) emission reduction*. Unpublished Master's Dissertation, World Maritime University, Sweden.

Progoulaki, M., & Roe, M. (2011). Dealing with multicultural human resources in a socially responsible manner: A focus on the maritime industry. *Journal of Maritime Affairs, 10*(7), 7–23.

Resolution (68) 4, Approving the "Declaration of principles" on Air Pollution Control, Retrieved from the World Wide Web; https://wcd.coe.int/com.instranet.InstraServlet?command=com.instranet.CmdBlobGet&InstranetImage=584176&SecMode=1&DocId=632300&Usage=2, Retrieved December 29, 2015.

Rozmarynowska, M., & Oldakowski, B. (2012). *Implications of new regulation regarding sulphur content in ship's fuel on maritime transport sector within Baltic Sea Region on the basis of the TransBaltic and Baltic Ports Organization's port debate: Implications of the IMO regulations on the future pattern of the cargo flow in the Baltic held on 15th June 2012 in Helsinki, Finland.* Retrieved from the World Wide Web; http://www.transbaltic.eu/wp-content/uploads/2013/05/ImplicationsofnewRegulationFINAL.pdf, Retrieved July 22, 2016.

The Guardian (2014). Retrieved from the world wide web; http://www.theguardian.com/sustainable-business/2014/aug/01/sustainable-shipping-is-making-waves, Retrieved December 30, 2015.

The Helsinki Protocol, 1985. Protocol to the 1979 Convention on Long-Range Transboundary Air Pollution on the reduction of sulphur emissions or their transboundary fluxes by at least 30 per cent. Retrieved from the World Wide Web; http://www.unece.org/fileadmin/DAM/env/lrtap/full%20text/1985.Sulphur.e.pdf, Retrieved December 29, 2015.

The Oslo Protocol, 1994. Protocol to the 1979 Convention on Long-Range Transboundary Air Pollution on further reduction of sulphur emissions. Retrieved from the World Wide Web; http://www.unece.org/fileadmin/DAM/env/lrtap/full%20text/1994.Sulphur.e.pdf, Retrieved December 29, 2015.

Transport and Environment. (n.d.). Air pollution from ships. Retrieved from the World Wide Web; http://www.transportenvironment.org/what-we-do/shipping/air-pollution-ships, Retrieved December 29, 2015.

United Nations Economic Commission for Europe. (1979). *The 1979 Geneva Convention on Long-range Transboundary Air Pollution*. Retrieved from the World Wide Web https://www.unece.org/fileadmin/DAM/env/lrtap/full%20text/1979.CLRTAP.e.pdf, Retrieved December 31, 2015.

Whitelegg, J. (1993). *Transport for a sustainable future: The case for Europe*. London and New York: Belhaven Press.

Yep, E. (2017). Is this the tipping point for LNG fuel? *Lloyd's List 2017*, 2 May

Green Ports and Economic Opportunities

D. S. H. Moon, J. K. Woo, and T. G. Kim

1 Introduction

Port development in recent decades has been remarkable, having been driven mainly by international trade and containerisation. Many ports, particularly in Western Europe and East Asia including China, have developed at a faster rate and experienced sustained growth. Here the outcome on the one hand has been incentivised by economic growth, while on the other new challenges have emerged in the form of environmental awareness for the port developers.

It is clear that the environmental impact of ports is closely related to shipping and operations on the port site, including cargo handling and other port related activities. The international and national legislations for new ports or extensions of existing ports incorporate these issues and are increasingly based on strict regulations aiming at creating designs that minimise environmental impact and sustainable operations in the long-term. The regulations are enforced through a system of permits in which certain construction and operation methods are pre-defined, including mitigation and compensation measures. There are several drivers (or policies) that make ports

D. S. H. Moon (✉)
World Maritime University, Malmö, Sweden
e-mail: dm@wmu.se

J. K. Woo
Department of International Logistics, Division of Port Logistics System, Tong Myong University, Busan, Republic of Korea
e-mail: jkwoo@tu.ac.kr

T. G. Kim
Division of Maritime Transportation Science, Korea Maritime and Ocean University (KMOU), Busan, Republic of Korea
e-mail: teddykim48@kmou.ac.kr

L. L. Froholdt (ed.), *Corporate Social Responsibility in the Maritime Industry*, WMU Studies in Maritime Affairs 5, https://doi.org/10.1007/978-3-319-69143-5_10

greener including regulations, information, incentives, and technology upgrades. Many different instruments are connected to these, with various levels of intervention, ranging from global to local (Merk 2013).

However, it is known that any policy instrument that reduces environmental impact, e.g. air emissions in ports, results in a cost for the relevant parties, particularly ports and terminals. This is the main reason why some ports are reluctant to implement environmental programmes in their own region. Much of the challenge of choosing and implementing an appropriate policy solution comes in how to weave more flexible economic instruments into the existing policy and institutional conditions in the country. Taking both economic and environmental aspects into consideration in ports guarantees corporate credibility; not only by considering the protection of environment but also addressing the interests of stakeholders, ports can fulfill the requirement of Corporate Social Responsibility (CSR).

Essentially, these environmental policy instruments could be of great help to the regional economy if they are implemented in conjunction with proper economic policy options. In other words, the environment could also be an economic opportunity in a more fundamental way, using the several main drivers that could be identified to create economic value from ports. For example, the domain of port industrial development and maritime clusters could be the area in which the environment presents new economic opportunities.

The purpose of this chapter is to discuss the usefulness of implementing these policy instruments with the conceptual model that is based upon the system dynamics (SD) technique. With this model, a good business case resulting in greening ports will be examined.

2 International Seaborne Trade, the World Fleet and Port Developments

2.1 International Seaborne Trade and the World Fleet

For the last couple of decades, world economic development has been phenomenal and this has resulted in the rapid growth of seaborne trade. As shown in Fig. 1, growth in GDP, merchandise trade and seaborne shipments are interlinked and continue to move in tandem. Trade can generally grow faster or slower than GDP, although since the 1990s it has tended to grow about twice as fast (WTO 2014).

Further, prospects are overall positive for global economic and industrial outputs, with world GDP forecasted to expand continuously. World merchandise trade prospects are also improving and are expected to increase thanks to an increased demand from Europe, a strengthening recovery in the United States and rising intra-Asian trade (UNCTAD 2015).

In January 2014, the world fleet reached a total of 1.69 billion dwt. As shown in Fig. 2, bulk carriers account for 42.9% of the total tonnage, followed by oil tankers (28.5%) and container ships (12.8%). Since 1980, the global share of dry-bulk

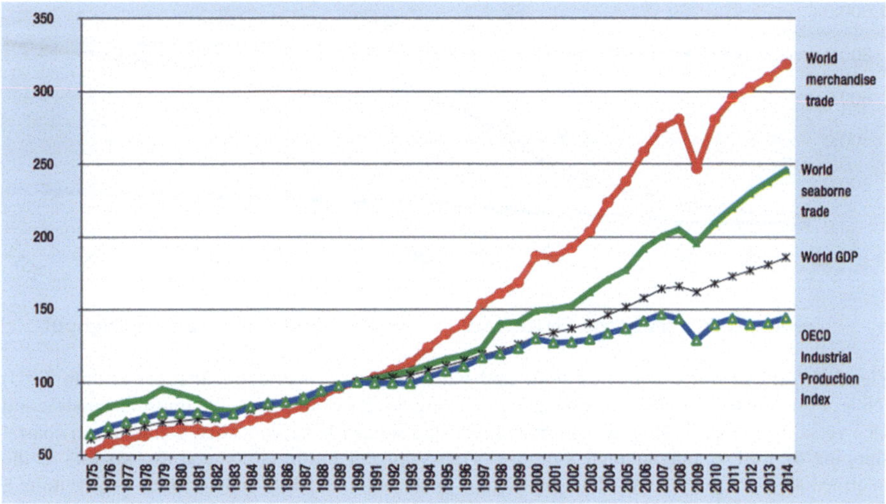

Fig. 1 World economic growth and world seaborne trade (1990 = 100). Source: (UNCTAD 2015)

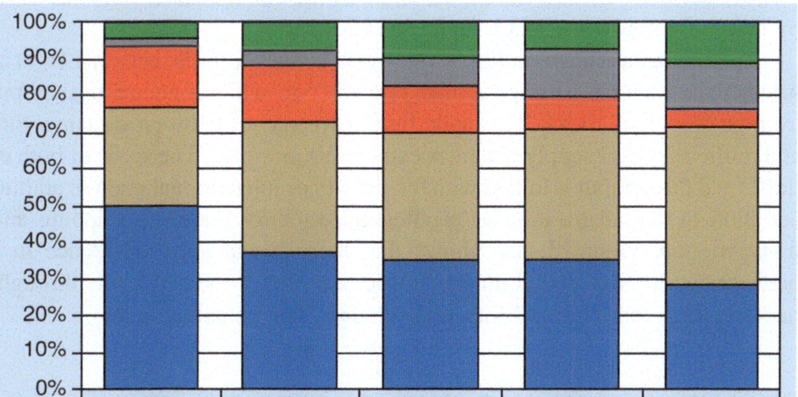

	1980	1990	2000	2010	2014
Other	4.5	7.5	9.4	7.2	11.2
Container	1.6	3.9	8.0	13.3	12.8
General cargo	17.0	15.6	12.7	8.5	4.6
Dry bulk	27.2	35.6	34.6	35.8	42.9
Oil tanker	49.7	37.4	35.4	35.3	28.5

Fig. 2 World fleet by principal vessel types, 1980–2014 (Beginning-of-the-year figures, % share of dwt) Source: (UNCTAD 2015)

carriers has gone up by 58%, while that of oil tankers has declined by 43%. In particular, it is noticeable that non-bulk cargo has dramatically been containerised. According to UNCTAD report, with the reduction of the general cargo (non-bulk

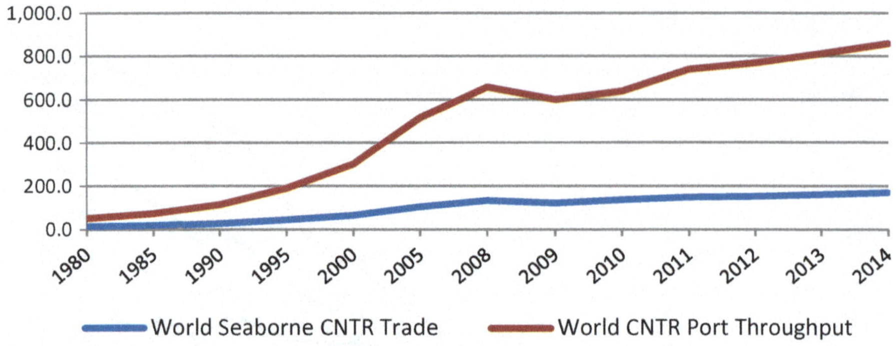

Fig. 3 World seaborne container trade and world container port throughput (in million TEU) (Note: Port container traffic measures the flow of containers from land to sea transport modes, and vice versa, in twenty-foot equivalent units (TEUs), a standard-size container. Data refer to coastal shipping as well as international journeys. Transshipment traffic is counted as two lifts at the intermediate port (once to off-load and again as an outbound lift) and includes empty units.). Source: Reproduced from the source of (Drewry Maritime Research 2012) (data.worldbank.org; www.clarksons.net)

cargo) fleet share by two-thirds, the share of the containership fleet has skyrocketed by nearly 7 times since 1980 (UNCTAD 2015).

In particular, as shown in Fig. 3, the world container traffic between 1980 and 2014 has increased with an average growth rate of 9.5%, while container throughput had an average growth of 10.5%. This underlines a divergence between container throughput and traffic as global supply chains became more complex. The surge of both container traffic and throughput is linked with the growth of international trade in addition to the adoption of containerisation as privileged vector for maritime shipping and inland transportation. Figure 3 also shows that there is the large difference in quantity between world seaborne container traffic and world container port throughput that has been between three and four times greater than container trade.

2.2 *Port Developments*

Ports are important nodal points of a global transport system and have played a key role in the economic development of any country in the world. UNCTAD report has clearly explained the importance and the role of ports as follows:

> Ports are channels for international trade and the gateway to accessing global trading partners and shipping is one of the most cost-effective means of transport over long distances. Historically, ports have been regarded as critical public assets as, in addition to being the gateway to a country, they are also placed where taxes on imports and excise duties are collected. However, the port's role is continuing to evolve although there is a difference in the rate between developing and developed countries. (UNCTAD 2015)

A timely port development, therefore, is a very important process for a country wishing to successfully engage in international trade. Understanding the medium and long- term development affecting ports is vital for making strategic business decisions.

Port development over the last three decades has been phenomenal; mainly being driven by population growth, economies, external trade and containerisation. Almost all worldwide ports have experienced a sustained period of growth, and many new ports have developed at astonishing pace in terms of throughput, especially in markets such as China and Southeast Asia (Fig. 4). These port developments have not only fuelled economic growth, but also brought environmental challenges. The environmental impact of ports is related to shipping, hinterland traffic and operations on the port site, including cargo handling and industrial activities. (Merk 2013)

Ports are important nodes in view of transport networks but at the same time environmental hotspots. Port functions near highly populated areas have been constrained because of public resistance to their negative impact, e.g. poor air quality, noise, dust and congestion. Increased knowledge of the consequences of cumulative exposure to harmful pollutants implies a necessity for ports to actively promote environmental sustainability and green management practices.

3 Sustainable Development, Green Growth, Green Guide and Green Ports

With the publication of the report 'Limits of Growth' (Meadows et al. 1972) by the Club of Rome in 1972, the United Nations and its agencies have made great efforts to promote an environmental conscience in leaders and people in general. These efforts led to the establishment of the United Nations Environment Programme (UNEP) in 1972 and the creation of a World Commission on Environment and Development (WCED), chaired by Gro Harlem Brundtland, in 1983. The WCED, also known as the Brundtland Commission, released the report called 'Our Common Future: A Global Agenda for Change' in October 1987. This document, also known as the Bruntland Report, was the first to coin the meaning of the term 'sustainable development', defined as "development that meets the needs of the present without compromising the ability of future generations to meet their own needs". Since this publication, the definition of 'sustainable development' has been widely used by many institutions and organisations (WCED 1987).

The PIANC Report No.150 in 2014 has further extended the coverage of 'sustainable development' by adopting the framework of the Triple Bottom Line (TBL) as follows:

> Today, the idea of sustainability is generally accepted to cover much more than strictly environmental issues. The Triple Bottom Line (TBL) encompassing people, profit, planet is a concept that extends the frame of sustainability to include social, economic and environmental aspects. The TBL refocuses the measurement of corporate performance from the perspective of a shareholder (predominantly financially driven) to that of a stakeholder (anyone affected by the actions of a firm) and coordinates three interests: 'people, profit

	1985	1990	1995	2000	2005	2010	2012	2013	2014
1	Rotterdam (2,665)	Singapore (5,224)	Hong Kong (12,550)	Hong Kong (18,090)	Singapore (23,192)	Shanghai (29,069)	Shanghai (32,529)	Shanghai (33,620)	Shanghai (35,290)
2	NY/NJ (2,367)	Hong Kong (5,101)	Singapore (11,830)	Singapore (17,090)	Hong Kong (22,427)	Singapore (28,431)	Singapore (31,649)	Singapore (32,580)	Singapore (33,870)
3	Hong Kong (1,519)	Rotterdam (3,667)	Kaohsiung (5,232)	Busan (7,540)	Shanghai (18,084)	Hong Kong (23,532)	Hong Kong (23,097)	Shenzhen (23,280)	Shenzhen (24,040)
4	Kobe (1,519)	Kaohsiung (3,495)	Rotterdam (4,787)	Kaohsiung (7,426)	Shenzhen (16,197)	Shenzhen (22,509)	Shenzhen (22,941)	Hong Kong (22,290)	Hong Kong (22,230)
5	Antwerp (1,350)	Kobe (2,596)	Busan (4,503)	Rotterdam (6,274)	Busan (11,843)	Busan (14,194)	Busan (17,041)	Busan (17,680)	Ningbo (19,450)
6	Yokohama (1,327)	LA (2,587)	Hamburg (2,890)	Shanghai (5,613)	Kaohsiung (9,471)	Ningbo (13,144)	Ningbo (16,830)	Ningbo (17,350)	Busan (18,680)
7	Hamburg (1,159)	Busan (2,348)	Long Beach (2,844)	LA (4,879)	Rotterdam (9,287)	Guangzhou (12,550)	Guangzhou (14,743)	Qingdao (15,660)	Qingdao (16,820)
8	Keelung (1,158)	Hamburg (1,969)	Yokohama (2,757)	Long Beach (4,601)	Hamburg (8,088)	Qingdao (12,012)	Qingdao (14,500)	Guangzhou (15,320)	Guangzhou (16,630)
9	Busan (1,148)	NY/NJ (1,872)	LA (2,555)	Hamburg (4,248)	Dubai (7,619)	Dubai (11,600)	Dubai (13,265)	Dubai (13,640)	Dubai (15,520)
10	Long Beach (1,141)	Keelung (1,826)	Antwerp (2,329)	Antwerp (4,082)	LA (7,485)	Rotterdam (11,146)	Tianjin (12,295)	Tianjin (13,010)	LA/LB (15,610)

Fig. 4 World Top 10 container ports (1985–2014) (Unit: 000 TEU). Source: Reproduced from many sources by authors

and planet'. When there is a balance between these three 'P's, there is sustainability. (PIANC 2014)

The concept of 'sustainable development' provided important context for green growth.[1] The world needed a new growth paradigm to maintain the sustainable economic development while ensuring climatic and environmental sustainability. This was the key message in the OECD Report on Green Growth Strategy—'Towards Green Growth' (OECD 2011).

With this new paradigm, the PIANC Report (No.150) suggested the possibility of using the environmental challenges (or issues) as economic opportunities for new growth from macroeconomics point of view:

> While economic activities and environmental protection are conventionally perceived as two separate domains adversely affecting each other, green growth calls for a conceptual shift to recognise that both can be achieved complementarily. Under this new paradigm, challenges such as climate change and energy crises are no longer considered as problems that need to be addressed, but as opportunities for new growth from the viewpoint of macroeconomics. Unlike the past labour and capital-intensive methods of production, the driving factors of green growth are comparatively new ideas, transformational innovations and the state-of-the-art technology. (PIANC 2014)

In particular, by applying this new paradigm to a port sector, green growth can be taken as an economic driver. In a green growth or green port strategy,

> sustainability is an economic choice based on a proactive long-term vision. As ports are typically located along coasts, estuaries, river deltas and/or canals and ports are connected to cities and nature, the interactions of transport systems, natural systems and social systems are eminent. Sustainable port strategies consider the integration of these different systems to be fundamental. In sustainable port strategies, the planning and managing of port activities is done by looking at the activity's effect on all systems and in cooperation with the stakeholders belonging to these systems. Port authorities and their (private) tenants must plan and manage their operations and future expansions together in order to cope with the limited or decreased environmental space and (in some cases) increased interactions between port and cities/nature. By accommodating this planning in harmony with the surrounding cities and nature, green growth can clearly be seen as an economic driver. (PIANC 2014)

In its Green Guide in 2012, the European Sea Ports Organisation (ESPO)[2] was trying to influence public policy in the EU in order to achieve a safe, efficient and environmentally sustainable European port sector, operating as a key element of a transport industry where free and undistorted market conditions prevail, as far as practicable (ESPO 2012). The ESPO Environmental Code of Practice in 1994 was the first official policy document that was ever published by ESPO. The Code

[1]Green growth is not a replacement for sustainable development, but rather should be considered a subset of it. It is narrower in scope, entailing an operational policy agenda that can help achieve concrete, measurable progress at the interface between the economy and the environment. It focuses on fostering the necessary conditions for innovation, investment and competition that can give rise to new sources of economic growth—consistent with resilient ecosystems.

[2]Founded in 1993, it represents the port authorities, port associations and port administrations of the seaports of the Member States of the European Union and Norway. As of 2015, ESPO, headquartered in Brussel, consists of 24 member countries and 1 observer country.

regulating environmental practices among its member port authorities was then updated in 2003 (ESPO 2003) and in 2012 this ESPO-developed Environmental Code of Practice was again revised and replaced by the ESPO Green Guide that consists of three main parts; to trigger port authorities to be proactive and to commit to sustainable development and the continuous improvement of their environmental performance.

In 2014, PIANC[3] published the report on providing information and recommendations on good practice, particularly by focusing on the sustainable development and green growth of ports and the related logistic chain and added value activities. This report aimed to contribute thus in the shift of thinking away from a reactive 'ports or nature/environment' approach towards a proactive 'ports and nature/environment approach' that add value through stakeholder participation. The Green Port concept not only changes the role of the port authority, but also the way in which operations are carried out. Under this concept, the port operates proactively and beyond legislation in a way based on a long-term vision. This report has also emphasised the green port strategy that is to accommodate the future development of the port in harmony with the region and natural system. Important aspects of Green Port strategy are: efficiency and sustainability as complementary drivers; pro-active approaches like working with nature, CSR, stakeholder participation and responsible innovation; and attract frontrunners, which attract other frontrunners and better prepares the port for any future. The report has finally ended up with recommendations that 'sustainable ports' use their roles to a maximum to accommodate the transition to green growth for their own benefit and the prosperity of the region they serve from the viewpoint of area manager, estate owner, manager in the logistics chain, administrators, regulators and enforcing agents, developers and managers of infrastructure, port operators, central points for knowledge, facilitators of innovation, partner in community and port authority as economic developer (PIANC 2014).

In its practical guide for a sustainable seaport for the PIANC WG 150 in 2010, the working group has clearly defined Green Ports as follows:

> Green Ports are widely regarded as the answer to those challenges mentioned previously. However, there is no clear and comprehensive description of what a Green Port actually is. Environmental issues regarding ports have been studied in great detail before, but there is a need for a step forward towards an integrated approach in which all separate measures,

[3]PIANC is the forum where professionals around the world join forces to provide expert advice on cost-effective, reliable and sustainable infrastructures to facilitate the growth of waterborne transport. Established in 1885, PIANC continues to be the leading partner for government and private sector in the design, development and maintenance of ports, waterways and coastal areas. As a non-political and non-profit organisation, PIANC brings together the international experts on technical, economic and environmental issues pertaining to waterborne transport infrastructures. Members include national governments and public authorities, corporations and interested individuals. PIANC has Technical Commissions concerned with inland waterways and ports (InCom), coastal and ocean waterways (including ports and harbours) (MarCom), environmental aspects (EnviCom) and sport and pleasure navigation (RecCom). For more information, please see www.pianc.org.

> including climate change adaptation and mitigation measures, are merged into the concept of a single package: the Green Port. (PIANC 2010)

This was the first comprehensive definition of what a Green Port actually is: a Green Port is a port that sees green growth as a prime economic driver and as key to its commercial and operational activities.

The PIANC report in 2014 has given guidance on the needs for, and how, to adopt the green ports philosophy, and refers to the best practices of 'climate change mitigation and adaptation' and 'environmentally friendly and sustainability issues' from existing ports and their effectiveness and economic potential to be used as examples for other ports (PIANC 2014).

A green port is a port that implements a green business strategy and that understands the ecological and commercial mechanisms of environmental incentive schemes. Further, its sustainability work is a component in the long-term strategy for the development of the port. The overall idea is a continuous reduction of negative environmental impacts without jeopardising economic growth (Pavlic et al. 2014).

According to Professor Vellinga, who has established several of the conceptual ideas of Green Ports, ports are in a unique and privileged position in the global logistic chain to capture and evolve their roles to initiate and consolidate the needed change, for their own benefit and the prosperity of the region that it serves (Vellinga 2011). He has defined a sustainable port (or a green port) as:

> one in which the port authority together with port users, proactively and responsibly develops and operates, based on an economic green growth strategy, the working with nature philosophy and on stakeholder participation starting from a long-term vision on the area in which it is located and from its privileged position within the logistic chain, thus assuring development that anticipates the needs of future generations, for their own benefit and the prosperity of the region that it serves. (PIANC 2014)

The following sections will discuss how green port strategy can be adopted and utilised as an economic driver to reinvigorate the national (or regional) economy.

4 Environmental Policy (EP) Instruments for Green Ports: Focusing on Air Quality in Port

According to ESPO and EcoPorts, there are more than 30 environmental issues in the European port sector. They have been monitoring the environmental priorities of the European port sector since 1996 through regular respective surveys. Figure 5 shows the changes in port environmental priorities from 1996 to 2016. Priority issues change their ranking with time but certain components retain their significance for the sector, e.g. garbage/port waste, noise and air quality.

These negative environmental impacts in ports are closely related to shipping activities in a port, port operations and hinterland transport to and from ports. Mitigating negative port impacts is essential for the long-term survival of ports

	1996	2004	2009	2013	2016
1	Port Development (water)	Garbage / Port waste	Noise	Air quality	Air quality
2	Water quality	Dredging: operations	Air quality	Garbage / Port waste	Energy consumption
3	Dredging disposal	Dredging disposal	Garbage / Port waste	Energy consumption	Noise
4	Dredging: operations	Dust	Dredging: operations	Noise	Relationship with local community
5	Dust	Noise	Dredging disposal	Ship waste	Garbage / Port waste
6	Port Development (land)	Air quality	Relationship with local community	Relationship with local community	Ship waste
7	Contaminated land	Hazardous cargo	Energy consumption	Dredging: operations	Port Development (land related)
8	Habitat loss / degradation	Bunkering	Dust	Dust	Water quality
9	Traffic volume	Port Development (land)	Port Development (water)	Port Development (land)	Dust
10	Industrial effluent	Ship discharge (bilge)	Port Development (land)	Water quality	Dredging: operations

Fig. 5 Top 10 environmental priorities of European port sector over time. Source: ESPO and EcoPorts (2013), EcoPorts (2016)

and port-cities. If ports want to have sustainable future perspectives, ports must get rid of negative impacts related to their developments.

Many ports recognise the need to develop 'green policies' supported by incentives to encourage ports to implement green practices. This section assesses the main policies to mitigate these impacts, particularly focusing on the issue of 'air quality'.

As seen in Fig. 5, the issue of air quality has not been keen to port sector in Europe until the 2004 survey. Ports, however, have been challenged by the air pollution issue in particular. Ranked in the 6th in 2004 and the 2nd in 2009, air quality was the top environmental issue by the European port sector in the 2013 and 2016 surveys. This reflects the priority given to issues related to the health of people working or living around ports, and is in line with the European political agenda, through the ongoing review of the EU Air Quality policy but also the several ongoing initiatives that aim to control the exhaust emissions of air pollutants by ships (ESPO and EcoPorts 2013, EcoPorts 2016)

Increasing rules & regulations (R/R), and the growing importance of port authorities' corporate social responsibility (CSR), result in the need and necessity to actively develop air pollution reduction strategies and measures. According to the Ocean Shipping Consultants (OSC) report (Stenvert and Penfold 2010), there are 50 ways to ease air pollution for shipping lines, port (or terminal) operators, inland transport companies and others (Fig. 6).

As shown in Fig. 7, these diverse ways to ease air pollution in ports can be grouped into four drivers (or policies) to make ports (or terminals) greener: regulation, information, incentives and technology upgrades. Various policy instruments are used to tackle the main environmental impacts associated with ports, with various levels of intervention ranging from global to local. A broad range of solutions has been identified to reduce air emissions in ports from 5 groups of polluters[4]. However, it is not always clear which of these have worked quite well, as there is a relative lack of evaluation of each policy instrument. Even though there is some convincing evidence of the effectiveness of various policy instruments with examples (or cases) around the world, many complexities would need to be resolved to increase the effectiveness of port impact mitigation, particularly in terms of the air quality in ports.

Further, it has been known that any policy instrument to mitigate air emissions in ports, as shown in Fig. 7, results in a cost for the relevant parties, and particularly the ports themselves. However, these environmental policy instruments could be of great help to the regional economy if they are implemented in conjunction with proper economic policy options. The following sections discuss the usefulness of implementing these policy instruments.

[4]Ocean-going ships, harbour craft, cargo handling equipment, heavy duty vehicles and rail locomotives.

Shipping lines	1. Carriers using clean ships 2. Maintain reduced vessel speed in coastal waters 3. Vessels using low-sulphur diesel when approaching port and while at dock 4. Minimise smoking 5. Clean up air emissions by capturing emissions 6. Deepsea vessels using shore-side power while berthed 7. Barges, short-sea vessels and tugboats using shore-sided power while berthed 8. Repower / refitting with cleaner diesel engines 9. Maintain high schedule integrity	Terminal operators	10. Secure multi-user capacity 11. Implement robotised operational system instead of on-wheels 12. Use low sulphur diesel and diesel emulsions for diesel powered equipment 13. Equip diesel engines with diesel oxidation catalysts(DOCs) 14. Equip diesel engines with diesel particulate filters (DPFs) 15. Install idling controls on diesel powered equipment for automatic shut-off 16. Secure replacements that run on alternative fuels 17. Facilitate cold ironing 18. Realise spread of vessel arrivals 19. Minimise stack movements by improved pre-information 20. Realise on or near dock rail facilities 21. Secure sufficient gate capacity 22. Install automatic gates 23. Implement a truck appointment system on the terminal 24. Implement a port-wide appointment system 25. Extend the gate hours into the evening and night 26. Realise a true 24/7 operation 27. Incentivise off-peak hour deliveries 28. Install guaranteed window systems for barges and feeders 29. Improve terminal performance to reduce terminal times
Inland transport companies	30. Promote a modal shift towards rail and barge transport 31. Increase the frequency of current rail and barge connection 32. Set up new rail and barge conncections 33. Install dedicated railway corridors 34. Maximise the full use of existing corridors 35. Use bigger barges to increase capacity 36. Realise dedicated truck lanes on highways 37. Incentivise off-peak hour road traffic 38. Maintain reduced/constant speed limits for trucks 39. Use 6 TEU trucks 40. Perform modal scan with shippers/receivers 41. Realise fleet modernisation for trucks, barges or locomotives 42. Equip existing diesel engines with diesel particulate filters (DPFs) 43. Equip existing diesel engines with Nox catalysts (LNCs) 44. Use alternative fuels	Others	45. Avoid empty legs by better forecasting and planning 46. Implement virtual markets to better align supply to demand 47. Coordinate transfers of empty containers/improve repositioning 48. Improve container management/share containers between shipping lines 49. Intensify the use of inland empty depots 50. Use environmental friendly fumigation techniques

Fig. 6 Fifty ways to ease air pollution in port. Source: Reproduced from the source of (Stenvert and Penfold 2010)

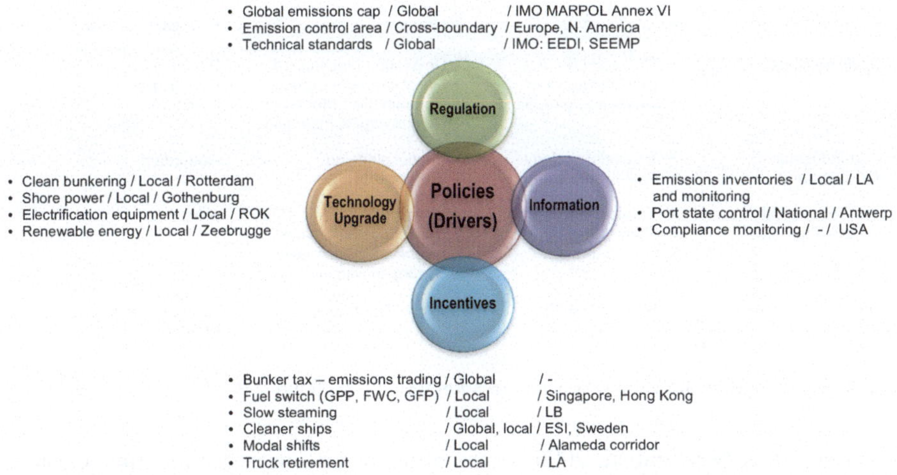

Fig. 7 Policy instruments to mitigate air emissions in ports. Source: Reproduced from the source of (OECD 2014)

5 Policy Options (PO) for Economic Value Creation in Ports

By traditional definition, ports are places where there is the interchange of cargo and passenger traffic among vessels, between vessels and overland carriers or sites alongshore. However, ports become more meaningful nodes in terms of the international transport chain (or international logistics chain). Their effectiveness depends ultimately on how they link up with these chains both by sea and by land, and also how port operations are aligned with shipping and hinterland transport.

Ports are also places where cargoes are handled and act as facilitators of trade. These cargo handling activities in port have an economic impact on the port region and country from the viewpoint of macro-economics; creation of value-added activities through economic interactions in port regions and the translation of economic interactions into port-related employment (Moon 1995). Further, ports offer spatial clusters for innovation, research and development.

As shown in Fig. 8, there are several policy options for economic value creation from ports. The formation of maritime clusters[5] (Langen 2002, Wijnolst 2006, Brett

[5]Clusters are especially important to the maritime domain, because the shipping and ports industries are highly dependent on subcontracting and various kinds of services, and because they require a very specialised local workforce.

For firms, participation in maritime clusters is said to generate increasing productivity through the creation of cost-reducing linkages between suppliers and customers, the formation of larger and more qualified labour pools, and through spillovers of knowledge that work through inter-firm interaction. Particularly for shipping, ports and maritime manufacturing, clusters can facilitate better

Policy option	Related sectors	Instruments	Examples
Maritime clusters	• Port and Logistics • Maritime services • Shipbuilding/repair	• Developmental support • Fiscal incentives/grants • Co-ordination/information • Human capital matching	Singapore Hong Kong London
Port-industrial developments	• Industrial ecology • Renewable energy	• Spatial planning • Investments	Rotterdam
Port-related waterfront (re)developments	• Tourism/recreation • Food • Events industry	• Master planning • Project implementation • Incentives/investments • Synergies with port	Barcelona
Urban diversification	• Non-port sectors	• Similar instruments	London, Liverpool, Boston

Fig. 8 Policy options for economic value creation from ports. Source: (OECD 2010)

and Roe 2010, Weissenberg 2006) is one of them and successful maritime clusters enhance the port's contribution to its surrounding city and region (TheCityUK 2011). For this reason, the formation of maritime clusters has been considered as a policy objective in many parts of the world, and governments in many countries have at their disposal a diverse range of instruments that may help embryonic maritime clusters to emerge, consolidate, and enhance mature clusters.

The port is the most important component of the maritime cluster in conjunction with such others as shipping/maritime services and shipbuilding/repairs[6] (Lam and Zhang 2011). In order for these sectors to be successful in promoting maritime clusters, certain instruments must evolve Fig. 8 indicates that there are four types: development support, fiscal and financial incentives, co-ordination and information-sharing, and human capital matching. Singapore and London are exemplary cases of showing what a maritime cluster is all about.

A port-industrial development policy could also provide new economic opportunities in port through environment-oriented options such as industrial ecology[7] and renewable energy.

Port sites have great potential for ecological industrial projects, inspired by various motives ranging from pollution prevention, process optimisation, and waste management to internalisation of environmental costs, local economic development and competitiveness (OECD 2014). Examples of these are the transformation of several

interactions with a range of ancillary services (finance, brokerage, insurance), and can enable access to information and expertise that might open new markets and provide opportunities for expansion.

[6]Maritime cluster consists of port, marine insurance, financial service, ship registry, shipowners/operators/managers, ship classification society, ship agency & forwarding, ship brokers, legal services, ship building & repair, marine personnel, research education & training, information & communication technology (ICT) services, regulators such as maritime organisations, associations, exchange market and etc.), governmental support and maritime culture & heritage.

[7]Also referred to as circular economy. Its aim is to provide systematic management of material and energy flows, using waste from one process as input for another process.

Japanese ports into recycling hubs (OECD 2013), and the promotion of the use of waste heat capacity in the Port of Rotterdam (Baas and Huisingh 2008).

Ports are also places for renewable energy production, including solar, tidal and wind energy, both onshore and offshore. This renewable energy sector could attract employment and provide an added value to the ports through constructing future power-supply systems and clustering related industries in the port areas, thus revitalising the economy of port-cities (Ragwitz et al. 2007, McNeil et al. 2013).

Further, ports should be considered laboratories for green innovation. Being vulnerable to the impact of climate change, port-cities could use their advanced knowledge of climate change adaptation technologies, such as the floodwalls, and commercialise their findings or by sharing their knowledge with other ports. The CleanTech Programme developed by the Port of Los Angeles aims to develop the port as a site for innovative green technologies (Merk 2013).

6 Environmental Policies (EP) Versus Policy Options (PO)

Policies in ports fall into two general categories: environmental policies (EPs) and policy options (POs). They interact with each other, both positively and negatively, by influencing the level of environmental standards and the cost of logistical activities in ports.

EPs encompass a range of policy tools from incentives (e.g. pollution taxes and slow steaming) to regulation (e.g. ECA, EEDI and SEEMP) by international bodies. The common element of all EPs is that they operate on a case-by-case basis globally, except for regulation. Much of the challenge of choosing and implementing an appropriate policy solution comes from how to weave more flexible environmental instruments into the existing policy in the country. POs are policies that a port authority can devise to create economic values from ports.

As indicated in Fig. 9, the conceptual system dynamic (SD) model that shows the relationship between EPs and POs is assumed. EPs have both the incentive and the power to act in a more environmentally responsible manner to make ports greener. However, EPs drive up the cost of implementing various environmental tools (or instruments). In most cases, EPs shift the costs and responsibilities associated with pollution back to the polluter. The implementation of EPs entails considerable investment that will be a burden for either the port or the port user. This is the main reason why some ports are reluctant to introduce environmental instruments into them.

POs can accomplish a number of important changes in making ports places where economic values are created. They can be considered as the positive aspect of implementing certain policies in the port region from the viewpoint of macroeconomics. This encourages ports to adopt policy options such as maritime clusters, port-industrial developments and port-related waterfront (re)developments.

Better air quality in port derived from the implementation of EPs will definitely improve the quality of life in port regions affect, once again, the introduction of POs in a positive way. As shown in Fig. 9, EPs in conjunction with POs by a port

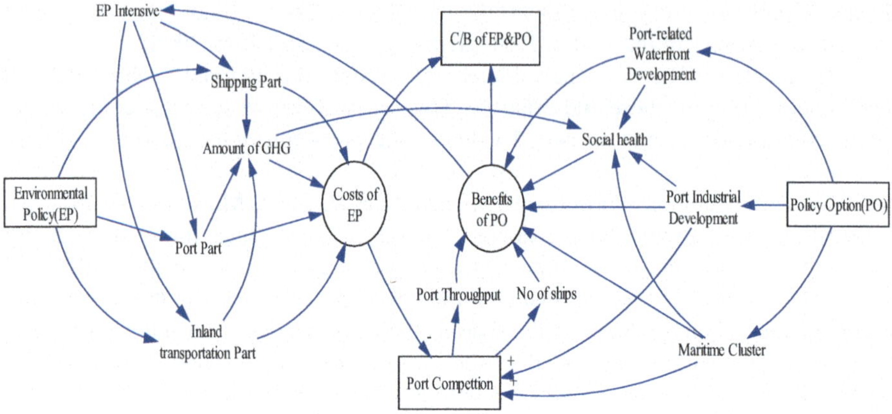

Fig. 9 Concept of model (SD)

authority will have a direct impact on the competitiveness of ports (or port region) in terms of throughput handled, the value added and the ships visited.

EPs have been proposed and implemented around the world to address a host of environmental concerns, including the issue of air quality in port. They have had varying degrees of success. EPs involve various policy instruments (or tools) that will cost ports and users. POs have the benefit that they generate employment, incomes, taxes, and the value-added for the regional economy.

A combination of components in Fig. 9 seems to explain the usefulness of the model in a more positive way by comparing the cost of implementing EPs with the benefit of introducing POs. Taken together, if the benefit is smaller than the cost, EPs will remain as a burden to ports and port users. However, in the opposite case where the benefit is larger than the cost, the implementation of EPs together with POs will be a much-needed encouragement for the port.

7 Conclusion

As ports have developed, people in port regions have become aware of their environmental impact, thereby creating new challenges for the development of ports, i.e. green ports.

These environmental issues have been reflected by international and national legislation for new ports or extensions of existing ports that are based upon strict regulations aiming at creating designs with minimal environmental impact and sustainable operations in the long-term. There are several drivers (or policies) to make ports greener including regulations, information, incentives, and technology upgrades. Many different instruments are connected to these, with various levels of intervention, ranging from global to local.

It is axiomatic that any policy instrument to mitigate the environmental impact, e.g. air emissions in ports, results in a cost for the relevant parties, i.e. ports per se as well as their customers. This is why not all ports prefer to implement an environmental programme in their own region. However, these impacts can be turned around and used to a port's advantage as an economic opportunity. There are complementary aspects of port environmental policies and economic policy options.

The objective of this chapter was to discuss the usefulness of implementing these policy instruments with the conceptual SD model. It has been known that there is a good business case for making a port greener. Greening ports could therefore be used as a development tool to generate new business in a port region.

In summary, these environmental policy instruments could be of great help to the regional economy if they are implemented in conjunction with proper economic policy options. In other words, the environment could also be an economic opportunity in a more fundamental way, using the several main drivers that could be identified to create economic value from ports. For example, the domain of port industrial development, maritime clusters and port-related waterfront (re)developments have positive effects on regional economy with the implementation of environmental instruments.

However, if the environmental policy generates just additional costs or expenses without creating additional valuation, the port authorities, although they recognise the necessity of it, will reduce the level of policy intensity or delay the policy's enforcement as much as they can. Otherwise, the port authority is likely to support and promote the environmental policy actively. Therefore, further study should be done to investigate the environmental policy issues in port concerning how and how much the environmental policy affects the cost-benefit structure in port from the economic and environmental perspectives. In other words, the impact of a green policy, i.e. environmental policies (EPs) and policy options (POs), in the balance of cost-benefit and amount of port emissions from the medium and long term perspectives could be simulated by using a system dynamics simulation modelling technique.

References

Baas, L., & Huisingh, D. (2008). The synergistic role of embeddedness and capabilities in industrial symbiosis: illustration based upon 12 years of experiences in the Rotterdam Harbour and Industry Complex. *Progress in Industrial Ecology-An International Journal, 5*(5/6), 399–421.

Brett, V., & Roe, M. (2010). The potential for the clustering of the maritime transport sector in the Greater Dublin Region. *Maritime Policy and Management, 37*(1), 1–16.

Drewry Maritime Research. (2012). *Container Market Review and Forecast: Annual Report-2012/13*. London: Drewry.

ESPO. (2003). *ESPO Environmental Code of Practice*. Brussels: ESPO.

ESPO. (2012). *ESPO Green Guide: Towards excellence in port environmental management and sustainability*. Brussels: ESPO.

ESPO, EcoPorts. (2013). *Top environmental priorities of European Ports for 2013*. http://www.espo.be/media/espopublications/Analysis_of_top_environmental_priorities_2013.pdf. Accessed 29 November 2016.
EcoPorts. (2016). *Top 10 environmental priorities 2016*. https://www.ecoports.com/publications/top-10-environmental-priorities-2016
Lam, J. S., & Zhang, W. (2011). *Analysis on development interplay between port and maritime cluster*. Singapore: National University of Singapore.
Langen, P. D. (2002). Clustering and performance: The case of maritime clustering in the Netherlands. *Maritime Policy and Management, 29*(3), 209–221.
McNeil, C., Straw, W., & Rowney, M. (2013). *Pump up the volume: Bringing down costs and increasing jobs in the offshore wind sector*. London: Institute for Public Policy Research.
Meadows, D. H., Meadows, G., Randers, J., & Behrens, W. W., III. (1972). *The limits to growth*. New York, NY: Universe Books.
Merk, O. (2013). Green ports: Impacts, policies and economic opportunities. *Ports and Harbors, 58*(6), 35.
Moon, S. (1995). Port eocnomic impact model (PIM) and its planning applications. *Maritime Policy and Management, 22*(4), 363–387.
OECD. (2011). *Towards green growth*. Paris: OECD Publishing.
OECD. (2013). *Green growth in Kitakyushu, Japan*. Paris: OECD Publishing.
OECD. (2014). *The competitiveness of global port-cities*. Paris: OECD.
Pavlic, B., et al. (2014). Sustainable port infrastructure, practical implementation of the green port concept. *Thermal Science, 18*(3), 935–948.
PIANC. (2010). *A practical guide for a sustainable seaport*. Brussels: PIANC WG 150 ENVICOM.
PIANC. (2014). *Sustainable Ports: A guide for port authorities*, s.l.: Brussels: The World Association for Waterborne Transport Infrastructure.
PIANC, 2015. www.pianc.org. [Online].
Ragwitz, M., Held, A., Resch, G., Faber, T., Haas, R., Huber, C., et al. (2007). *Assessment and optimisation of renewable energy support schemes in the European electricity market*. Germany: Fraunhofer IRB Verlag.
Stenvert, R., & Penfold, A. (2010). *Container port strategy - Emerging issues*. London: Ocean Shipping Consultants Ltd.
TheCityUK. (2011). *Maritime services*. London.
UNCTAD. (2015). *Review of maritime transport 2014*. New York and Geneva: United Nations.
Vellinga, T. (2011). *Green Ports - Fiction, condition or foregone conclusion?*. Delft.
WCED. (1987). *Our common future*. New York, NY: Oxford University Press.
Weissenberg, P. (2006). European economic clusters: The European commission perspective. In N. Wijnolst (Ed.), *Dynamic European maritime clusters* (pp. 11–22). Amsterdam: IOS Press BV.
WTO. (2014). *World Trade 2013, prospects for 2014*. Geneva: WTO.

Energy-Efficient Ship Operation: The Concept of Green Manoeuvring

Michael Baldauf, Knud Benedict, Matthias Kirchhoff, Michèle Schaub, Michael Gluch, and Sandro Fischer

1 Introduction: Problem Description and Scope

Corporate Social Responsibility (CSR) has raised to the top of today's agendas of many companies to apply concepts in their companies and enterprises to ensure for more social balance and justice. Academics and research has developed various theories and models to explain and teach CSR. However, there is no common harmonized approach to CSR yet. Despite the many definitions, it is agreed that CSR is nowadays a core business issue (Pava and Krausz 1996). As a result of comprehensive reviews Dahlsrud (2008) has indicated five main categories of CSR: mentioning stakeholders, social, economic, voluntariness and environment. Moreover, the European Commission has made these categories integrated parts of its own CSR definition (EC 2001) stating that CSR is "A concept whereby companies integrate social and environmental concerns in their business operations and in their interaction with their stakeholder on a voluntary basis". This original definition has been further developed and according to latest developments CSR is indicated as "the responsibility of enterprises for their impacts on society" (EC 2011). In this respect, shipping companies are expected to integrate social, environmental, ethical, human rights and consumer concerns into their operation and spend efforts to

M. Baldauf (✉)
World Maritime University, Malmö, Sweden

Department of Maritime Studies, Institute of Innovative Ship Simulation and Maritime Systems (ISSIMS), Hochschule Wismar, University of Applied Sciences: Technology, Business and Design, Rostock, Germany
e-mail: mbf@wmu.se

K. Benedict • M. Kirchhoff • M. Schaub • M. Gluch • S. Fischer
Department of Maritime Studies, Institute of Innovative Ship Simulation and Maritime Systems (ISSIMS), Hochschule Wismar, University of Applied Sciences: Technology, Business and Design, Rostock, Germany

L. L. Froholdt (ed.), *Corporate Social Responsibility in the Maritime Industry*, WMU Studies in Maritime Affairs 5, https://doi.org/10.1007/978-3-319-69143-5_11

minimize potential negative effects of operating their fleets. Air pollution is one of the identified negative effects of shipping and among many others there is a clear link to manoeuvre ships in an environmentally friendly manner. The concept of green manoeuvring is an approach to integrate the aspects of minimizing GHG and particle emissions and energy efficiency into the conventional process of manoeuvre a ship.

Manoeuvring of ships is a human centred process. Most important elements of this process are the human itself and technical equipment to support his task (see Fig. 1).

However, most of the work is to be done manually because even today nearly no automation support is available for complex manoeuvres. Normally ship officers have to steer the ships based on their mental model of the ships motion characteristics only. This mental model has been developed during the education, specifically training in ship handling simulators (SHS) and most important during their sea time practice.

Ship Handling Simulation for simulator training has a proven high effect for the qualification, however, it is based on real time simulation, i.e. 1 s calculation time by the computers represents 1 s manoeuvring time as in real world. This means despite all other advantages of full mission ship handling simulation that collecting/gathering of manoeuvring experiences remains a utmost time consuming process. Up to now there is no electronic tool to design a manoeuvring plan effectively, even in briefing procedures for ship handling training the potential manoeuvres will be explained and drafted on paper or described by sketches and short explanations.

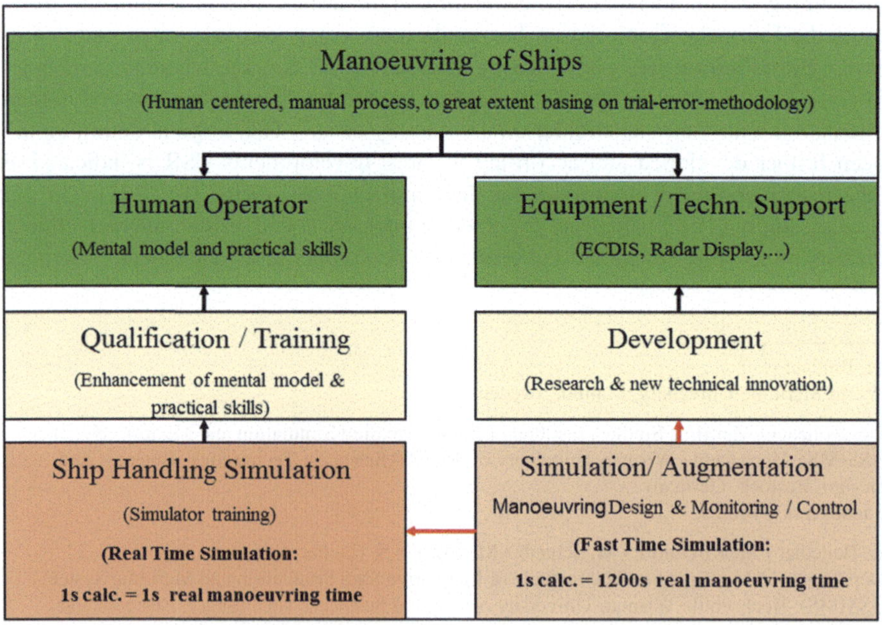

Fig. 1 Elements of the manoeuvring process and potential for enhancement by new Simulation/ Augmentation methods (adapted from Benedict et al. 2009a, b)

For increasing the effectiveness of training and also the safety and efficiency for manoeuvring real ships the method of Fast Time Simulation will be used in future. This innovative method enables simulation of ship manouves lasting up to 20 min in only one second calculation time of even standard computers. This allows for substantial support both the training process and the real manoeuvring process on board ships.

In Fig. 2 a comparison is given for the some essential elements of the real manoeuvring process on ships and in training in with/on the ship handling simulators as well.

Additionally in the right column some of the Fast Time Simulation (FTS) tools are mentioned and their roles to support each element of the manoeuvring process are indicated. These tools origin from research activities at the Maritime Simulation Centre Rostock-Warnemuende (MSCW) at the Department of Maritime Studies of Hochschule Wismar, University of Applied Sciences: Technology, Business and Design (HSW). Continuous scientific and technical development of the tools are realized through the Institute of Innovative Ship Simulation and Maritime Systems (ISSIMS).

A brief overview is given on the modules for the FTS tools and its potential application:

Elements of Manoeuvring Process on Ships & in Training and support by Fast Time Simulation Tools		
Real World / Ship	**Ship Handling Simulator Training**	**Fast Time Simulation Tools**
Real ship	Math model of the ship for simulation	SIMOPT/ SIMDAT tool for developing & tuning of parameters of math models
Mission / Planning	Scenario / Briefing	MANOEUVRING DESIGN & PLANNING tool to generate and edit a manoeuvring plan
Manoeuvring Operation	Execution of exercise	MULTIPLE DYNAMIC PREDICTION tool to monitor and control the vessel
Recording (VDR, ECDIS)	Recording by simulator	SIMDAT tool to display and assess recordings
Evaluation of success	Debriefing	MANOEUVRING TRIAL tool for verification Rof esults by simulation & prediction

Fig. 2 Elements of Manoeuvring Process on Ships (real world left column) & in Training (centre column) and process support by Fast Time Simulation Tools for Simulation/Augmentation (left column; adapted from Benedict et al. 2009a, b)

- SAMMON stands for "Simulation Augmented Manoeuvring – Design, Monitoring & Control". It is an innovative system providing four software modules for Manoeuvring Design and Planning, Monitoring, Multiple Dynamic Prediction. It furthermore allows for Manoeuvring Control as well as for free Simulation and Trial of manoeuvres. It is made both
  - for application in maritime education and training to support lecturing for ship handling to simply demonstrate and explain manoeuvring technology details and more specifically to prepare manoeuvring training in SHS environment i.e. for developing manoeuvring plans in briefing sessions, to support manoeuvring during the exercise run and to help in debriefing sessions for analysis in replays and discussions of quick demonstration of alternative manoeuvres and
  - for the application on-board to assist manoeuvring of real ships e.g. to prepare manoeuvring plans for challenging harbour approaches with complex manoeuvres up to the final berthing/unberthing of ships, to assist the steering by multiple prediction during the manoeuvring process and even to give support for analysing the result and for on board training with the Simulation and Trial module.
- SIMOPT is a Simulation Optimiser software module based on FTS for optimising Standard Manoeuvres and modifying ship math model parameters both for simulator ships and FTS Simulation Training Systems and for on board application of the SAMMON System. The quality of the math model for the simulation and the parameters in the equations are of high importance for the effectiveness of the simulation. There is a great need for fast and effective modelling/tuning processes both for the general operation of SHS where clients from several shipping companies need to be trained on their specific ship types and for the SAMMON dynamic predictor and manoeuvre planning modules. The advantage of module is to be seen in: it is remarkably faster than real time and the steering of vessels is organized by prepared files from a library for Manoeuvre-Control Settings/Commands for standard procedures and individual manoeuvres.
- SIMDAT is a software module for analysing simulation results both from simulations in SHS or SIMOPT and from real ship trials: the data for manoeuvring characteristics can be automatically retrieved and comfortable graphic tools are available for displaying comparing and assessing the results.

The SIMOPT and SIMDAT modules were described earlier (see Benedict et al. 2003, 2006) and also the modules for MULTIPLE DYNAMIC PREDICTION AND CONTROL have been introduced already (refer to Benedict et al. 2009a, b).

In this chapter the focus will be laid on the planning process as part of the route planning, addressing IMO's e-Navigation initiative and its specific requirement to cover safety of navigation from berth to berth by specifically supporting the most complex manoeuvring planning in ports or for the harbour approaches.

2 A Fast-Time Simulation Tool Using Full Dynamic Model for Manoeuvre and Route Planning

2.1 Ship Dynamic Model for Manoeuvring Simulation

The following equation of motion was used as math model for the ships dynamic:

$$\begin{aligned} X &= m(\dot{u} - rv - x_G r^2) \\ Y &= m(\dot{v} + ru + x_G \dot{r}) \\ N &= I_z \dot{r} + m x_G(\dot{v} + ru) \\ Q &= I_{ME} \dot{n}_{ME} \end{aligned} \tag{1}$$

On the right side are the effects of inertia where u and v represent the speed components in longitudinal and transverse direction x and y, r is the rate of turn of the ship. The ships mass is m and x_G is the distance of centre of gravity from the origin of the co-ordinate system, I_z is the moment of inertia around the z-axis.

The ship's hull forces X and Y as well as the yawing moment N around the z-axis are on the left side. Their dimensionless coefficients are normally represented by polynomials based on dimensionless parameters, for instance in the equation for transverse force Y and yaw moment N given as the sum of terms with linear components N_r, N_v, Y_r and Y_v and additional non-linear terms depending on speed components u, v and rate of turn r, revolution n. Other forces as for instance rudder forces and wind forces are expressed as look up tables. There are other models, e.g. for the engine or thruster operation: for the sample in the fourth equation in (1) Q represents the sum of the torque components of engine, propellers and others; on the right side there is the inertia moment of the rotation parts around the propeller axis.

Additional differential equations represent the calculation of heading and position. The solution of this set of differential equations is calculated at least every second; some internal calculations are even done with higher frequency.

This equation of motion (1) can be written in the form:

$$x'(t) = f(x, u_c, t) \tag{2}$$

where:

- State spaces with track co-ordinates ζ-η, heading ψ:

$$x = [u, v, r, \xi, \eta, \psi, \delta, n_{ME}, n_{TH}, \ldots]$$

- Controls with commanded values Cmd for main engine ME and thrusters TH:

$$u_c = [\delta_{Cmd}, n_{ME\_Cmd}, n_{TH\_Cmd}, \ldots]$$

- with initial conditions at: $t = t_0 : x(t_0) = x_0, \quad u(t_0) = u_{c0}$:

$$\mathrm{x}_0 = [u_0, v_0, r_0, \xi_0, \eta_0, \psi_0, \delta_0, n_{ME0}, n_{TH0} \ldots]$$
$$\mathrm{u}_{c0} = [\delta_{Cmd0}, n_{ME\_Cmd0}, n_{TH\_Cmd0}, \ldots]$$

This equation of motion (2) can be solved by numerical integration for the prediction time period t0 to t1 in the form of the general solution:

$$x(t) = x(t_0) + \int_{t_0}^{t_1} x'(t)\,dt$$

i.e. for the full set of states and controls:

$$x(t) = x_0 + \int_{t_0}^{t_1} f(x, u_c, t)\,dt \tag{3}$$

For a very simplified simulation for the so called "curved headline" for static prediction a solution is used by integration of track and heading assuming only constant speed u0, v0 and rate of turn r0, which results always in a circular motion with constant speed and will be used for simplified prediction with reduced accuracy or to indicate the current motion status valid only for a small time span:

$$x(t) = x_0 + \int_{t_0}^{t_1} f(u_0, v_0, r_0)\,dt \tag{4}$$

2.2 *Technological Setup for Manoeuvring Simulation Within the Route Planning*

The technological setup and the elements to use this math model for manoeuvring design within the route planning process is shown in Fig. 3. The planning data are collected by the interfaces of the Planning Data Collector. By means of the ship simulation parameters from the Ship Data Base Module the Fast Time Simulation Module executes the simulation of the manoeuvring segment and presents the results in the Presentation and Displaying Module. If the results are acceptable the segment will be stored in the Manoeuvre Data base. All the organization for this process will be done by the Data base manager Module.

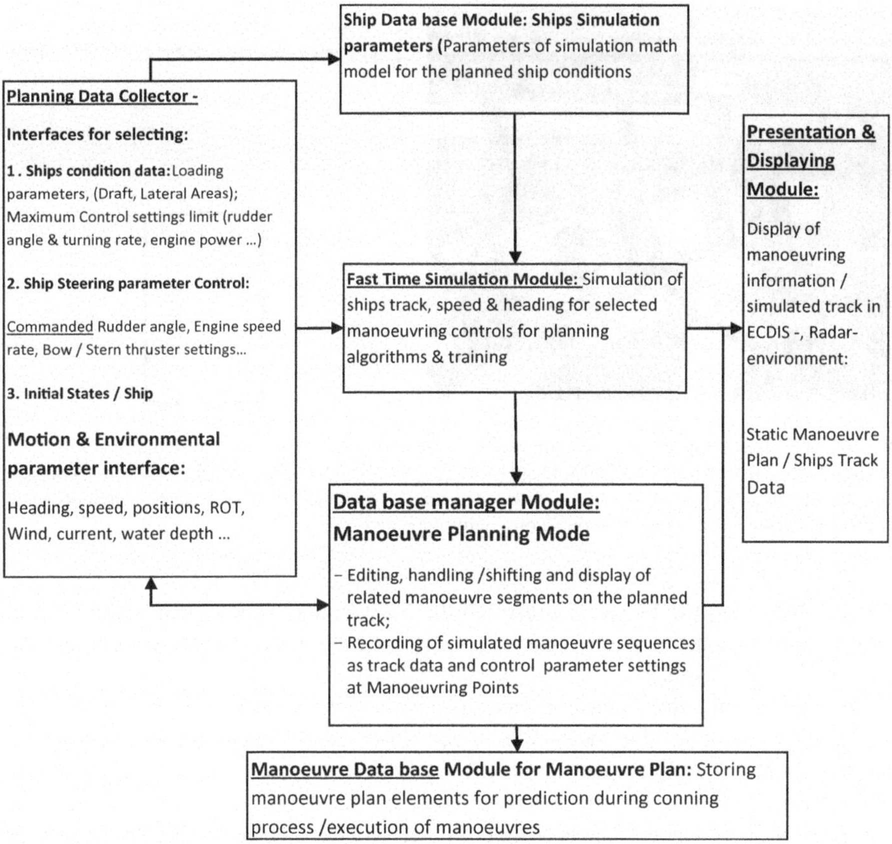

Fig. 3 Elements of Manoeuvre Planning Process using FTS Tools for designing manoeuvre plans (adapted from Benedict et al. 2012)

3 Fast Time Simulation for Designing Manoeuvres for Detailed Route Planning

3.1 Principle of Fast Time Simulation of Manoeuvres in ECDIS and Sample Data

The fast time simulation method is used to find out efficient manoeuvres for the design of manoeuvring plans within the route planning process. The use of this tool will be explained by some sample scenarios:

The sample ship is the RO-PAX Ferry "Mecklenburg-Vorpommern" with Loa = 200 m, Boa = 28.95 m, Draft = 6.2 m, Displacement = 22,720 t and Speed = 22 kn. She has two variable pitch propellers and two rudders located behind the propellers and additionally one bow thruster (Navigation Bridge as in Fig. 4 left). The test area is the Rostock Sea Port. The RO-PAX ferry is entering the

Fig. 4 Left: Test setup for new Conning/ECDIS Display on Bridge 1 in Ship-handling Simulator during Test trials for new Prediction Display. Right: ECDIS chart showing the test-bed (approach and basins of sea port of Rostock) with one sample scenario track of a ferry's manoeuvres: approach, turning and astern motion to one berthing position

fairway from north to be steered through the fairway and to be turned at the turning area followed by astern motion into ferry basin or alternatively to the berth at west pier (as in Fig. 4 right).

Some basic functions and interface displays are shown in the next figures.

Figure 5 explains the method in a sea chart environment represented by an interface which combines the electronic navigational chart ENC window (centre), the interface window for the steering panel of the ship (right) for adjusting the controls for the selected manoeuvring point MP and the interface to display the status of the current actual ship manoeuvring controls (left) at the position of the next manoeuvring point which is indicated as ship shape in red colour in the ENC.

For purposes of demonstration for a complex manoeuvre procedure the ship is initially positioned in the fairway (black contour) and is going to enter the turning area as objective for the first manoeuvring segment. For the planning procedure the ships motion can be controlled by the settings in the control panel window on the right side. Any manoeuvre can be generated and will be immediately displayed in the ENC in less than one second with full length. In this case the rudders are set 10° to STB to achieve a small turning rate ROT = 4.5°/min to port. The length of the simulated track corresponds to the settings in the prediction window (left top corner): the range value represents the duration of the simulated manoeuvre and that means the track length of that manoeuvring segment; the interval value controls the number of displayed ship contours on that predicted manoeuvre track. The selected end position of the manoeuvring segment is indicated by the red ships contour; its position can be shifted and adjusted using the slider at the bottom line which is adjusted to 165 seconds after the beginning of the manoeuvre at MP 1. If this position is accepted it will assigned the next manoeuvring point MP 2.

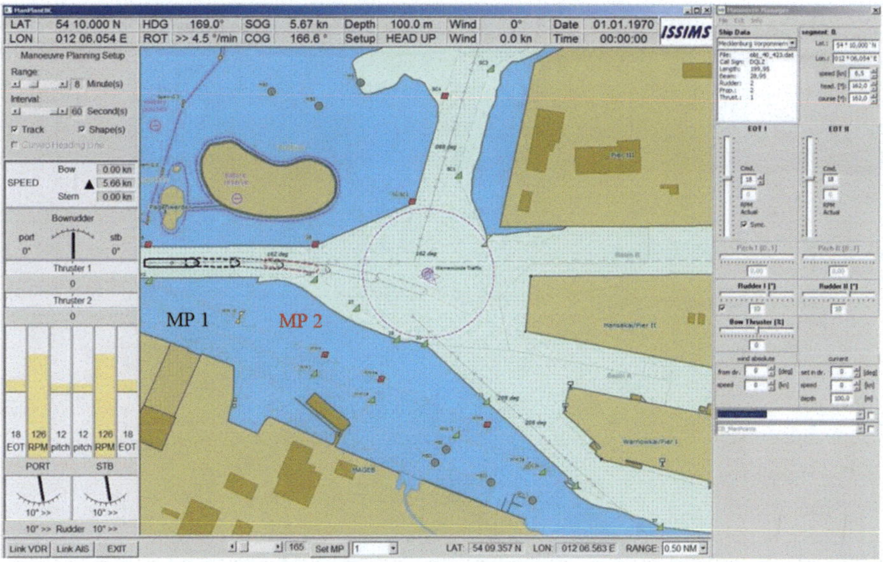

Fig. 5 Display for Manoeuvring Design by Fast Time Simulation for immediate presentation of manoeuvring results: Sample for entering the turning area with slight turning to STB from initial conditions in a fairway at manoeuvring point MP 1 (originally presented in Benedict et al. 2009a, b)

This planning process guarantees the full involvement of the navigating officer: The best version of the manoeuvres can be found to be trial and error but it is possible to bring in his full knowledge and to take advantage of his skills—it is possible to see and to verify immediately the results of the own ideas and to make sure that the intentions will work. This is important for safety and efficiency, but also for gaining experience for future manoeuvres.

3.2 *Sample of Designing a Full Manoeuvring Sequence as Part of Route Planning*

The planning procedure for a complete complex manoeuvring plan follows the principles as described for a single segment and is shown in Fig. 5 as follows:

- Figure 6 presents the situation after accepting the manoeuvre previously planned—now the next segment is to be planned from MP 2 to MP 3: the ship is going to enter the turning area and to slow down both engines are set to STOP (EOT 0).
- In Fig. 7 the initial complex turning manoeuvre is to be seen: the ship is using both engines, rudders and the bow thruster to turn as fast as possible while Fig. 8 shows the planning of the smooth change from turning the vessel into going astern (Fig. 8).

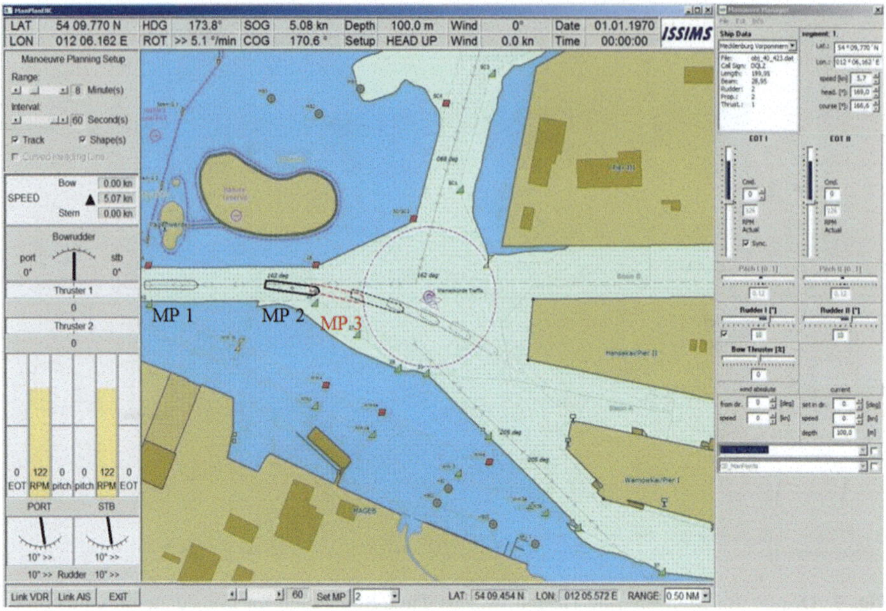

Fig. 6 Planning of the next segment from MP 2 to MP3: adding a speed reduction manoeuvre (originally presented in Benedict et al. 2009a, b)

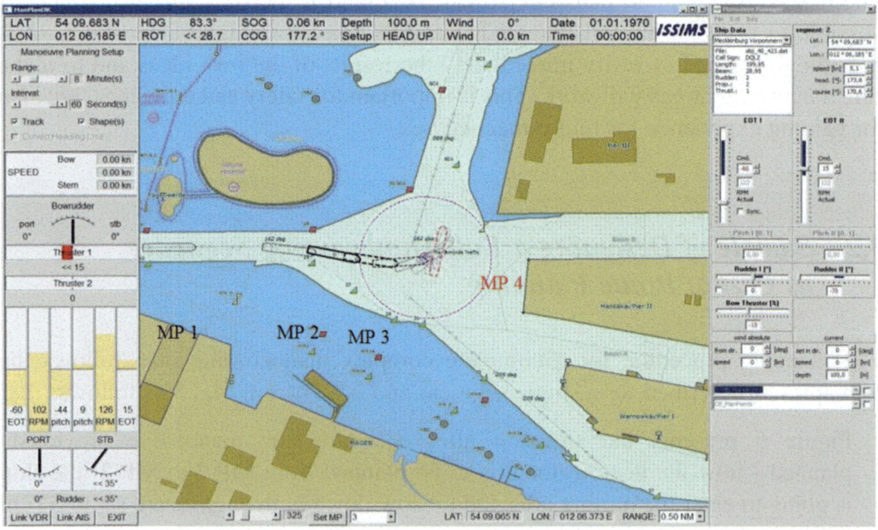

Fig. 7 Planning of the next segment from MP 3 to MP4: complex turning and stopping with engines, rudders and thruster (presented in Benedict et al. 2009a, b)

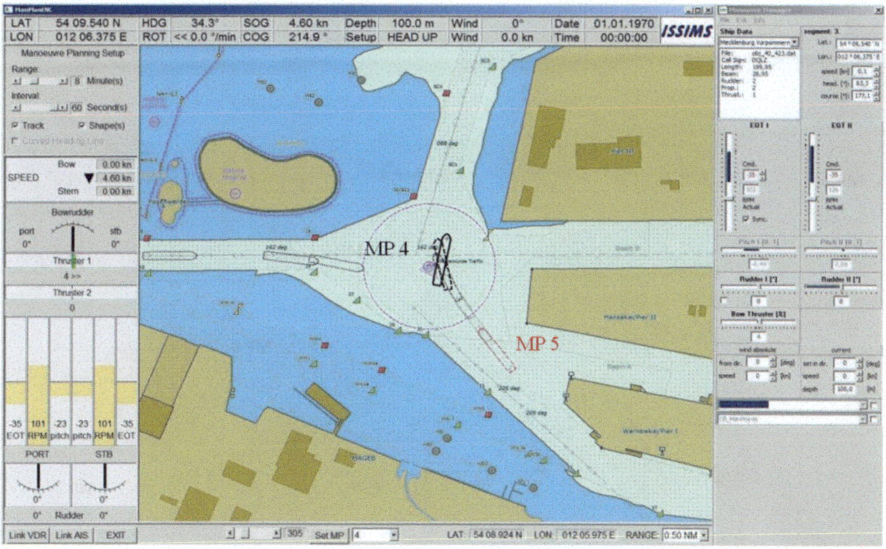

Fig. 8 Planning of the next segment from MP 4 to MP5: completion of turning and going astern (presented in Benedict et al. 2009a, b)

- In Fig. 9 the result for the full manoeuvring plan is to be seen with the list of Manoeuvring Points (MP) for the complete approach and the berthing manoeuvre.

The different settings of the controls and the track of the planned manoeuvre sequences are stored in a manoeuvre planning file to be displayed in the ENC. For the execution of the manoeuvre this plan can be activated later to be superimposed in ECDIS together with the actual position of the ship and most important with the prediction of manoeuvring capabilities (see Sect. 4) for effective steering under the actual manoeuvring and environmental conditions.

4 Overlaid Prediction for On-line Manoeuvring Decision Support Using Manoeuvring Plans and the Multiple Manoeuvring Prediction Module

4.1 Presentation of Dynamic Predictions in ECDIS Environment

For a compact presentation of information to the captain, pilot and responsible navigating officer respectively a new layout of a conning display was designed and implemented into the equipment installed on an integrated navigation system. For the purpose of testing the technical feasibility and user acceptance the new

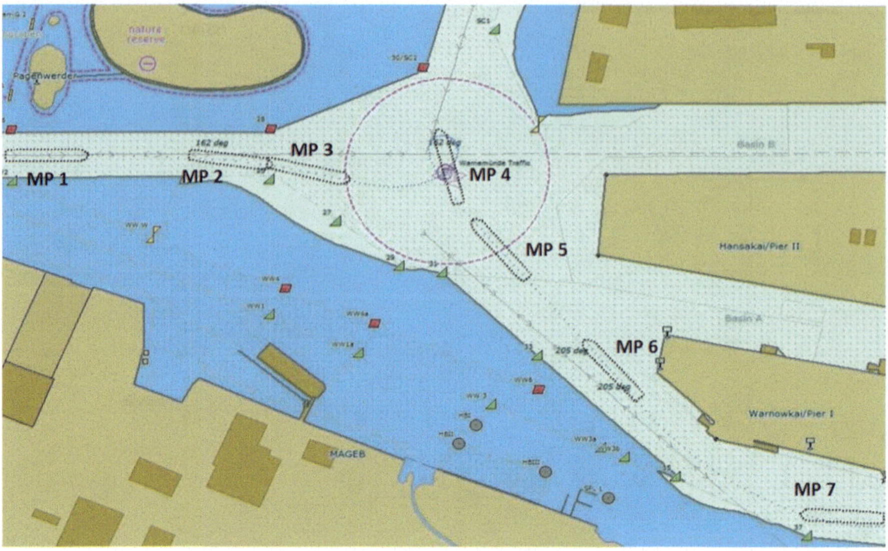

Fig. 9 Complete manoeuvring plan for the route segment for passing the turning area and approaching the berth in astern motion (presented in Benedict et al. 2009a, b)

conning display with the integrated MULTIPLE MANOEUVRING PREDICTION MODULE was implemented in the INS equipment of the large full mission simulator bridge of the ship handling simulator of MSCW. The sample ship is again the RO-PAX Ferry "Mecklenburg-Vorpommern", the test area is the Rostock Sea Port; the RO-PAX ferry is leaving the berth to be steered through the fairway and to leave the port.

The layout of a dedicated prediction display integrated into an ECDIS is shown in Fig. 10. It contains CONNING information together with the prediction and the planned manoeuvring track. The centre window shows the ENC in Head up Mode together with motion parameter for longitudinal speed and transverse speed as well as a circle segment with the rate of turn is shown. The ships position is displayed in the centre of the ENC as ships contour where also the track prediction can be indicated as curved track or as chain of contours for the selected prediction time. The prediction parameters as range or interval of presentation can be set in the control window at the right side.

The Dynamic Path Prediction with the sophisticated simulation model is shown as chain of ships contours based on full math model (ship contours every 60 s for 5 min with turning to STB). This dynamic prediction reflects already the effect of the setting of rudder and propeller control parameters shown in the left bottom window: In this sample the two rudders of the ferry used are set to 12° Starboard and the Engine Order Telegraph for the two controllable pitch propellers are set to 50% representing 130 rpm of the propeller. The actual pitch status is 19. This interface allows for a presentation of dynamic predictions of steering and stopping characteristics as an immediate response according to the current steering handle or engine

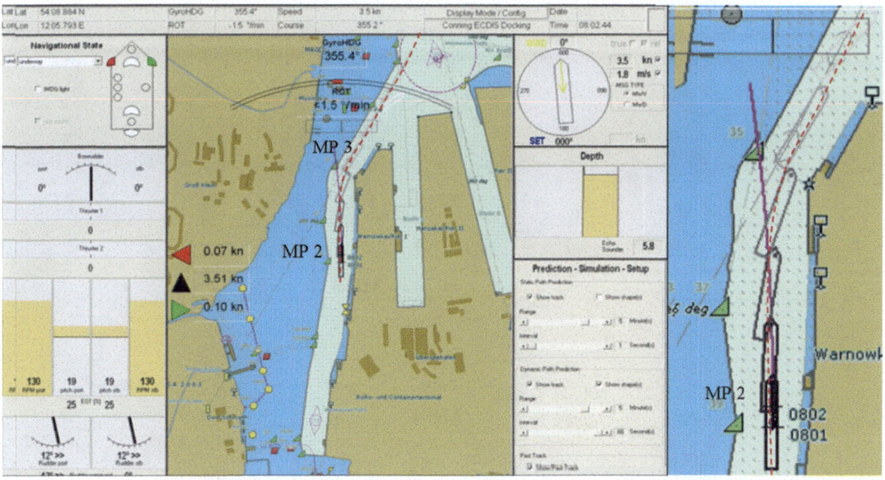

Fig. 10 Layout concept for Manoeuvring Prediction integrated into ECDIS (left) and comparison of static and dynamic predictions (right) together planned manoeuvring track (red broken line) (presented in Benedict et al. 2009a, b)

order telegraph position. It can be perfectly compared with the planned manoeuvring track as a reference line or curve, shown as red broken line in the ENC window.

The predicted track for the simplified static path prediction based on of current constant motion parameters (implemented as add-on in some ECDIS solutions) are shown as magenta curve: According to the actual/present small rate of turn to port the predicted track is presented as a circle segment to the left side.

4.2 *Test Set Up and Sample Scenario for Using the Manoeuvring Plan Together with On-line Prediction*

The following series of figures will indicate the effect of the dynamic predictor and the advantage of displaying the planned manoeuvring track as a reference for the future manoeuvring decisions. In Fig. 11 the manoeuvring plan is to be seen for a concept to leave the berth and the port, prepared by the method from the previous section.

The figure shows the start of the scenario from the berth: at MP 1 a suitable rudder angle is adjusted to steer the ship along the planned track through the fairway (red broken line) using dynamic predicted contours. The magenta line of the static motion prediction follows slowly according to the change of the current rate of turn. Figure 12 show the course change onto the turning area and then into the next fairway segment reversing the turning by counter rudder to steer the ship into the next straight fairway segment.

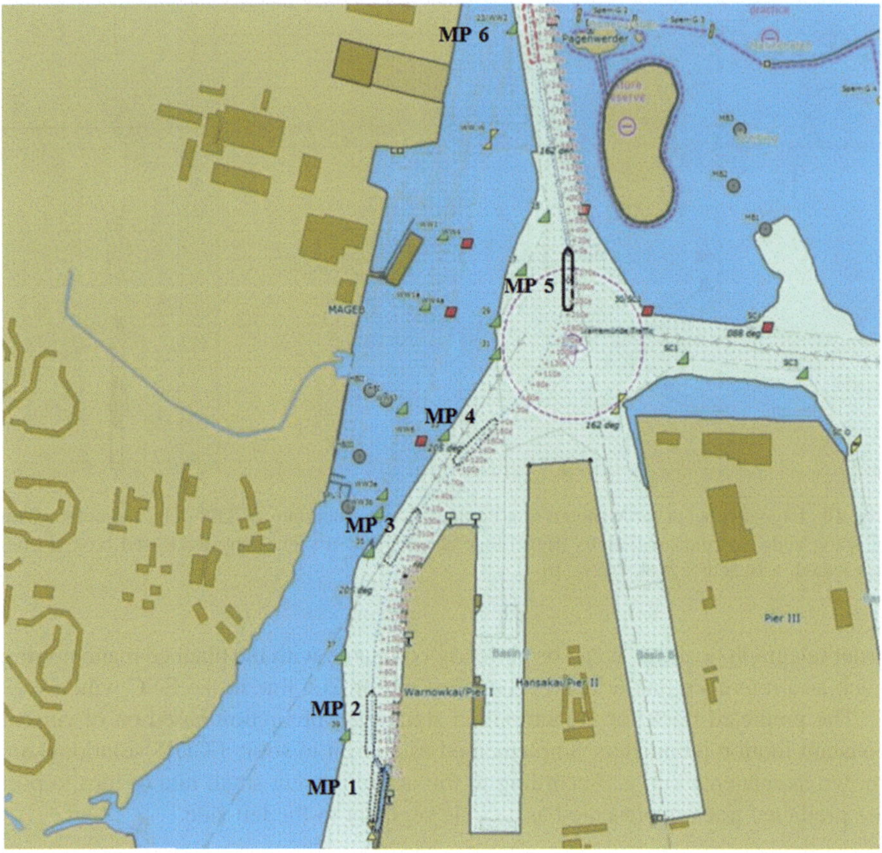

Fig. 11 Complete manoeuvring plan for the route segment for leaving the berth/port (presented in Benedict et al. 2009a, b)

Investigations for improving manoeuvres in ferry operation in the port of Rostock were made to analyse the performance specifically in the turning area. Analysing the VDR recordings from ferry approaches it was found that there is some space for improvements. Applying the predictor new strategies were found to save some minutes in this area which is very important in tight time schedules (Fischer and Benedict 2010). Alternative manoeuvring strategies were developed in the ship handling simulator by combining stopping and turning on turning area for non-interrupted turning and backing to berth. As a result it was found a potential of saving up to 25% of the total manoeuvring time for the respective route segment.

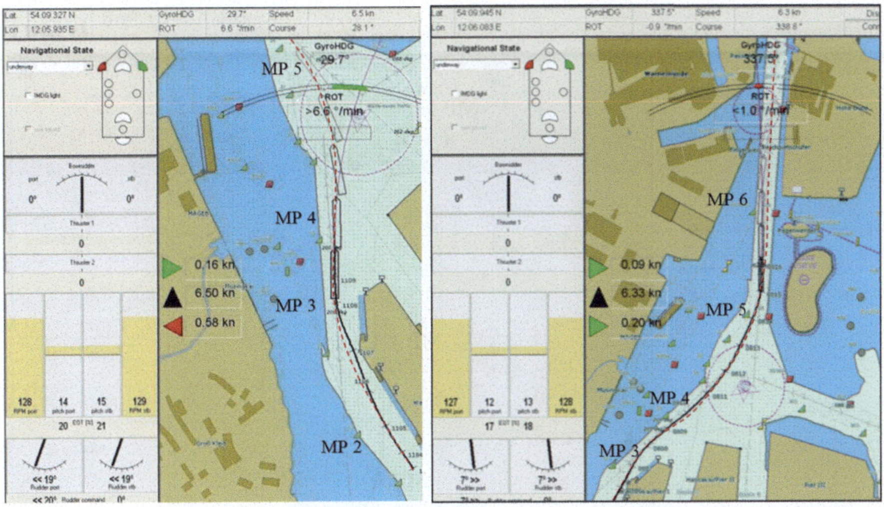

Fig. 12 Manoeuvring Sequences in ECDIS using Prediction methods and planned manoeuvring track for steering the ship onto turning area (left) and reverse turning to steer into the straight fairway segment (right) (presented in Benedict et al. 2009a, b)

4.3 Manoeuvring Simulation and Trial Module

This module combines a full simulation module for the ship manoeuvring process with all the modules above in order to test and try out manoeuvring plans and strategies, to be used both

- as training tool in maritime education
  - both in briefing/debriefing sessions for ship handling simulator training,
  - and in lectures on ships manoeuvring in classes and
- as training tool on board ships.

Figure 13 shows the interface of this module: In order to control the virtual ship during the simulation process the manoeuvring panel on the right side allow steering the ship in real time along the planned route supported by the Multiple Predictor.

4.4 Potentials of Enhanced FTS-Based Manoeuvre Planning and Monitoring

Voyage planning usually including route planning nowadays, in the era of e-Navigation, also needs to cover appropriate planning processes of manoeuvres in shallow waters when approaching ports and even berthing operation in harbour

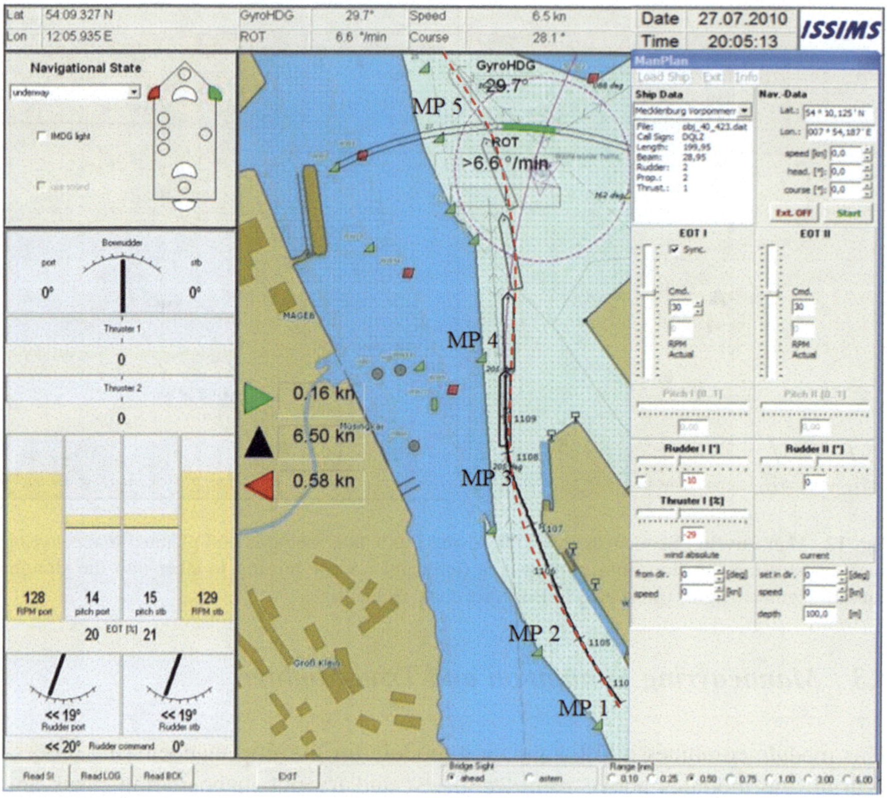

Fig. 13 Simulation interface for the Manoeuvring Simulation & Trial Module providing real time simulation and Predictions together with planned manoeuvring track for steering by means of the panel interface on the right side (presented in Benedict et al. 2009a, b)

basins. Correct conduction of ship manoeuvres are essential for the safety and efficiency of maritime transport and provide facilities to also reduce emissions. New innovative technologies and enhanced algorithms and procedures have great potential for advanced support of the bridge team when manoeuvring a ship. Moreover, such tools may contribute to improve ship handling training as well.

Selected aspects of past and on-going investigations regarding on-board manoeuvring assistance and into the integration of new maritime technologies on-board ships have been presented in the chapters. As a main outcome the concept of a comprehensive SAMMON tool box for simulation augmented design, monitoring and control of manoeuvres has been introduced and exemplarily discussed for use on-board and in ship-handling training with full mission simulators. Core element of the universal tool box is the implementation of innovative “Fast-Time-Simulation” technology which allows for dynamic predictions of ship motions taking into account the actual steering commands for immediate display of the expected path. The system was tested using the excellent resources for research and development of the Maritime Simulation Centre Warnemuende. During test trials several manoeuvring situations were managed with an increased performance when using the FTS tool.

The presented new applications have demonstrated great potential to contribute to safe ship handling and emission reduction in challenging sea areas and harbour basins and critical environmental conditions. Ship-handling training using full-mission simulators can also be improved by enhanced support for briefing, monitoring and analysis of performance data for de-briefing purposes.

5 Green Manoeuvring Integrated into Routine Ship Operation and IMO's e-Navigation Strategy

5.1 Tools to Support Energy Efficient Ship Operations

Several technical systems and tools are available on the market dedicated to the support of energy efficient and environmentally friendly ship operations during several phases of a voyage.

5.1.1 Weather Routing

Compared to manoeuvre planning weather routing can be seen as a kind of the mother or father for planning on a more detailed level. Weather routing is dealing with estimating the optimal route for a ship's voyage aiming at minimizing consumption of time and fuel and consequently saving costs. Weather routing addresses crossing of the oceans. One may say the macro level of a voyage plan, while manoeuvre planning addresses purposes of micro level voyage planning.

The use of weather information supports the ship operation to avoid unforeseen circumstances that may influence the ship itinerary and voyage plan. Also weather routing service providers can develop proper estimation tools to assess the fuel saving levels for reconciliation according to agreements between the parties. The fuel consumption for a ship not only depends on speed, but also on water depth and weather conditions. The optimal speed distribution along the route can be calculated in advance, if a weather forecast is available.

Table 1 exemplarily shows the fuel consumption increase (%) for different water depths W_D and speeds v (Hellstrom 2003).

Table 2 describes a typical and approximate relation between increased wind strength, direction, and increased fuel consumption for each unit of Beaufort (adapted from Hellstrom 2003).

Example: This specific example is to calculate fuel consumption increase based on the figures given in the above tables. The ship's speed is 18 knots. The current is 1 knot along the direction of the ship. The wind blows 4 Beaufort points straight

Table 1 Increase in relative fuel consumption (%) caused by shallow water depth at different speeds

v [kn]	W_D [m]	Increase of fuel consumption [%]
10	8	5
10	10	3
10	100	0
17	8	20
17	15	10
17	100	0
20	8	30
20	15	20
20	100	0

Table 2 Increase in fuel consumption (%) caused by wind forces from different directions (adapted from Hellstrom 2003)

w_{dir} [°]	Class of wind	Relative increase in fuel consumption [%]
315–360, 0–45	Head wind	4
45–135, 225–315	Side wind	2
135–225	Tail wind	1

against the starboard side of the ship ($w_d = 90°$). The water depth W_D is 15 m below the keel. The speed through water is then $18 - 1 = 17$ knots. The fuel consumption at 17 knots before the wind and limited depth effects is 1300.00 l/h. According to Table 1, fuel consumption increases by 10% caused by the water depth. According to Table 2, fuel consumption increases by 8% (4*2) due to the side wind.

The total estimated fuel consumption is therefore $1300.00 * 1.10 * 1.08 = 1544.00$ l/h.

Weather routing develops an optimum track for ocean voyages based on weather forecasts, sea conditions, and a ship's individual features for a particular transit. Within specified weather limits and sea conditions, the term means minimum fuel consumption while maximising safety and crew comfort and minimising time underway.

5.1.2 Tools to Support Energy Efficient Ship Operations at Sea

- Voyage performance analyser: There are systems that can routinely measure ship speed, shaft propulsion power and environmental conditions. These systems could be used for monitoring voyage performance. They could also help to identify reasons for poor performance, deviations in speed and so on.
- ECDIS (Electronic Chart Display and Information System): The electronic chart and information system could be used by means of integrated information for voyage management purposes and especially may support energy efficient ship operations in several ways.

- Autopilot: The new generation of Autopilots are under development or already available on the market and are provided by several manufacturers. Sophisticated autopilot systems provide technical facilities to also adapt the steering actions to prevailing weather conditions and especially the sea states, even automatically. Those systems are providing dedicated functions such as ‘precision’ and ‘economy’ modes. An Autopilot operating in Economy mode reduces rudder movements and consequently contributes to fuel savings. On the other hand, using Autopilot in the Precision mode allows for the best accuracy and ensures safe navigation.

5.1.3 Tools to Support Energy Efficient Ship Operations in Coastal Areas and Harbours

Generally, ship manoeuvres can be divided into routine manoeuvring and manoeuvring in safety-critical and emergency situations. This division can be developed further by considering different sea areas where manoeuvres have to be performed: e.g. in open seas, in coastal waters and fairways as well as in harbour approaches and basins. Routine manoeuvring in open seas covers ship-handling under normal conditions, e.g. in order to follow a planned route from the port of departure to the port of destination; this includes simple course change manoeuvres, speed adaptations etc. according to the voyage plan. Manoeuvring in coastal areas, at entrances to ports and in harbour basins include manoeuvres, e.g. to embark and disembark a pilot, to pass fairways and channels and even berthing manoeuvres with or without tug assistance. However, manoeuvring is always connected to fuel saving and emission reductions and therefore is crucial for energy-efficient and environmentally friendly ship operations.

Ships, during their normal operation, generate different kinds of pollutants emitted into the atmosphere. For example, the refrigeration plants of ships can contain ozone depleting substances; these are hydro- and chlorofluorocarbons. On the other hand, greenhouse gases (CO_2) are emitted during the normal combustion processes with fossil fuels. These are mainly generated in the main and auxiliary engines, the boilers and the incinerators. It is assumed that during combustion all of the carbon in the fuel is converted into CO_2 and that therefore the emission factor is dependent on the carbon content of the fuel (e.g. Endresen et al. 2003; Corbett 2004).

It is known that shipping is a contributor to air pollution, especially in coastal zones and harbour areas where many people are concerned. An inventory of air pollution caused by ship emissions have been provided for instance by Whall et al. (2007) for the Mediterranean Sea. Measurements in the south Sweden region (Winnes and Fridell 2010) have shown that almost 70% of SO_2, approximately half of NO_x and 20% of particles in the air are caused by shipping activities. The manoeuvring activities in coastal zones, port approaches and harbour areas are usually higher than when sailing in open seas (see Fig. 14).

Optimized manoeuvring regimes have great potential to decrease the negative effects and also may reduce fuel consumption. This can be realized by using manoeuvring assistance tools.

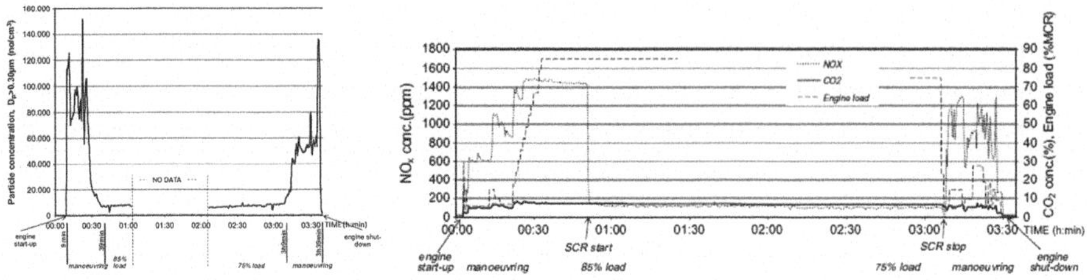

Fig. 14 Particle concentration (left), NO_x and CO_x emissions during different manoeuvring phases of a ferry (source: adapted from Winnes and Fridell 2010)

- Manoeuvring assistance tools: With the introduction of modern information and communication technologies, more and more assistance tools have been introduced additionally to standard mandatory navigational bridge equipment. Among those integrated systems there are tools for planning and monitoring purposes on the macro and micro level. Macro planning deals with waypoint planning for the sea trail of any voyage from point A to B (see Sect. 5.1.1). Micro planning is dedicated to the planning of detailed steering sequences for complex manoeuvres in harbour areas, even including berthing operations.
- Sophisticated manoeuvring assistance tools take into account not only the prevailing environmental conditions (especially wind, current and water depth), but also the actual ship status conditions and the impact of their parameters (beside course, speed and heading also i.a. draught and trim among others). The purpose of using such systems is to foresightedly adapt the manoeuvring strategies and regimes into an energy-efficient range with the efficient use of energy and resources and consequently minimize the emissions of GHG. One of the main aims of pre-planning manoeuvres regarding energy-efficient ship operations is the adaptation of the number of elementary manoeuvres. Elementary manoeuvres are defined as each single manoeuvre or command of rudder, engine and thrusters and any further steering equipment.

Once the planning process is completed and approved the bridge team can follow the steering sequence using any dedicated display to check the plan is being kept.

The use of sophisticated planning and monitoring tools optimizes the number of elementary manoeuvres in order to meet the requirements for the safety of navigation while also meeting the requirements for the minimum use of the steering equipment and saving fuel and time and simultaneously reduce GHG emissions when operating in coastal and harbour areas.

5.2 *Outlook: Potential Impact of e-Navigation Developments*

According to the definitions given by IMO and IALA, "e-Navigation" is defined as the harmonised collection, integration, exchange, presentation and analysis of maritime information onboard and ashore by electronic means to enhance berth-to-berth navigation and related services, for safety and security at sea and for the protection of the marine environment. Within this concept new approaches to provide advanced support for energy-efficient and environmentally-friendly GHG reduced ship operations are under development.

According to the plans of IMO and IALA the aim of the e-Navigation concept is that "... Onboard navigation systems will be developed that benefit from integration of own ship sensors, supporting information, a standard user interface and a comprehensive system for managing guard zones and alerts." It is quite obvious that such systems will also have strong effects on energy-efficient ship operations and contribute to the reduction of greenhouse gas emissions.

A principle overview of the e-Navigation concept is given in the descriptive model sketched in Fig. 15.

Those developments related to e-Navigation have to be taken into consideration for application onboard and ashore as well to guarantee the highest standard in environmental protection under all circumstances (environmental and ship's status) and in all areas at sea.

Some expected future new or enhanced applications are e.g.:

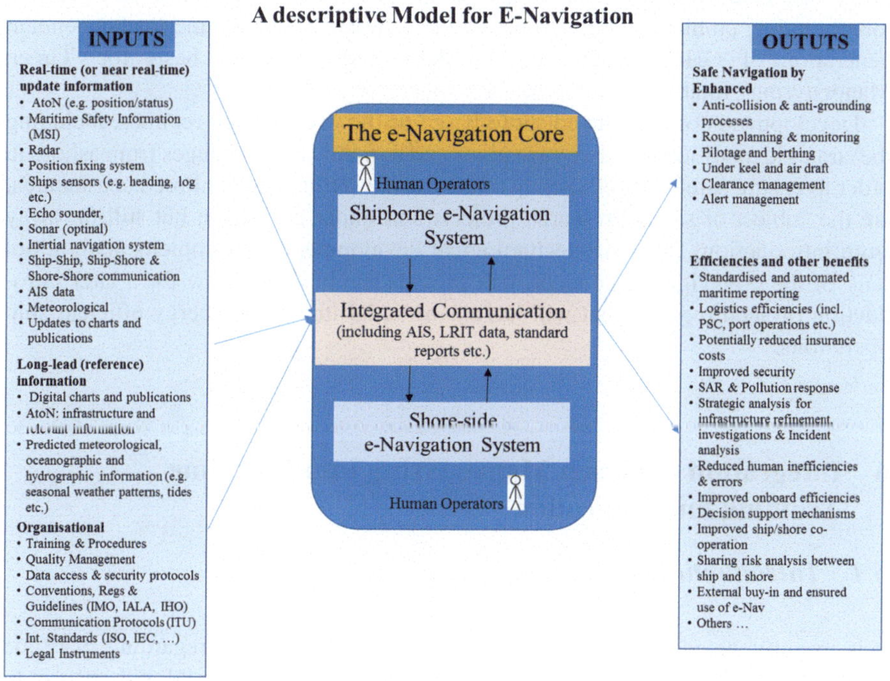

Fig. 15 Principle outline and basic elements of the e-Navigation concept (taken and adapted from IMO/IALA documents)

- passage planning with applied dynamic under keel clearance criteria
- on-line monitoring of ships' routes related to GHG emissions and further parameters of energy-efficient ship operation
- Integrated Navigation systems with specialized applications for specific users in particular regions
- Any further integrated solution.

It is stated and intended that e-Navigation will not only improve navigation safety. It is also stated that e-Navigation, due to the fact that there will be a reduction in the risks, will also contribute to the improved protection of the marine environment, especially by the enhanced avoidance of shipborne pollution caused by collisions and groundings. There are ongoing activities supported by IMO and IALA to determine if e-Navigation may have uses to help reduce carbon, sulphur and nitrogen emissions from ships through more efficient vessel routeing and handling. It is intended to potentially use e-Navigation as one tool for auditing the measurement of emissions offset claims and credits trading.

The main and fundamental change of the introduction of e-Navigation related applications will be the closer relation between the OOW on the bridge and the potential assistance provided from shore-based stations in order to meet also environmental rules and regulations. However, the stepwise implementation of the e-Navigation concept are providing a infrastructure that will allow for the application of FTS on-board ships. The simultaneous enhancement of modelling ships behaviour including emulating engine processes to estimate power-engine-load dependent generation of GHG (Schaub et al., 2015) will form the basis for "Green Manoeuvring" finally.

Developments of centralized shore-based traffic organisation regimes, including the strategic modification of voyage plans and dynamic route changes from ashore in order to ensure safety and efficiency of the overall traffic in a monitored coastal area, are the subject of several research projects and under discussion but still far away from introduction. However, technological developments and implementation, not only of the e-Navigation concept, will provide the basis to allow for a later introduction of such regimes that will have substantial impact on energy-efficient ship operations.

6 Integration of Green Manoeuvring into Maritime Training and Education

6.1 Introduction

It is recently stated and very well recognised, that best results regarding maritime safety and efficiency is basing on well-trained crews. Same is valid with respect to environmentally-friendly operation of ships. Only mariners and crews who have background knowledge and who know how they can contribute in the best way to energy efficient and emission reduced ship operation will be able to contribute to the ambitious aims.

Despite of a good overall energy balance of maritime transportation compared to other transport modes, it is known, that shipping is a main contributor to air pollution especially in coastal zones and harbour areas where a lot of people are concentrated and affected. It is assumed that e.g. optimized manoeuvring regimes have potential to reduce GHG emissions. Such procedures and supporting technologies have can decrease the negative effects on the environment and also may reduce fuel consumption. However, related training tools and methods have to be developed and to be integrated into existing course schemes accordingly.

The International Maritime Organization (IMO), through its Maritime Environmental Protection Committee (MEPC), has been carrying out substantive work on the reduction or limitation of greenhouse gas emissions from international shipping since 1997, following the adoption of the Kyoto Protocol and the 1997 MARPOL Conference. While to date no mandatory GHG instrument for international shipping has been adopted, IMO has given significant consideration of the matter and has been working in accordance with an ambitious work plan with a view to adopting a package of technical provisions.

In continuation of those efforts IMO developed a Model Course aiming at promoting the energy-efficient operation of ships. This Course contributes to the IMO's environmental protection goals as set out in resolutions A.947(23) and A.998 (25) by promulgating industry "best practices", which reduce greenhouse gas emissions and the negative impact of global shipping on climate change. These developments went along with new challenges and requirments for maritime education and training as discussed e.g. in (Bai et al. (2012)). To meet those new challenges IMO also provided supporting Train-the-Trainer courses (e.g. Baumler et al. (2014)) for use on a global level.

In this chapter the overall structure and the development of detailed content of the Model course will be exemplarily explained. Also, developed draft modules for the model course and samples of the suggested integrated practical exercises will be introduced and discussed. One example for an integrated simulation-based training module of the course is presented.

6.2 *Draft IMO Model Course on "Energy-Efficient Operation of Ships"*

The International Maritime Organization (IMO), through its Maritime Environmental Protection Committee (MEPC), has been carrying out substantive work on the reduction or limitation of greenhouse gas emissions from international shipping since 1997, following the adoption of the Kyoto Protocol and the 1997 MARPOL Conference. While to date no mandatory GHG instrument for international shipping has been adopted, IMO has given significant consideration of the matter and has been working in accordance with an ambitious work plan with a view to adopting a package of technical provisions to include:

- an energy efficiency design index (EEDI) for new ships;
- an energy efficiency operational indicator (EEOI), which will enable operators to measure the fuel efficiency of an existing ship and, therefore, gauge the effectiveness of any measure adopted to reduce energy consumption; and
- a Ship Energy Management Plan (SEMP) that incorporates guidance on best practices, which include improved voyage planning, speed and power optimization, optimized ship handling, improved fleet management and cargo handling, as well as energy management for individual ships.

It is in continuation of such efforts that a Model Course aiming at promoting the energy-efficient operation of ships was delivered and adopted. The Course will contributes to the IMO's environmental protection goals as set out in resolutions A.947 (23) and A.998(25) by promulgating industry "best practices", which reduce greenhouse gas emissions and the negative impact of global shipping on climate change.

Based on literature and database reviews, questionnaires, interviews with stakeholders and further data collection a draft model course has been developed and submitted to IMO MEPC and was finally adopted. The model course provides some kind unique a set of examples for practical activities by which both theoretical knowledge and practical skills can be easily obtained by participants to the course.

The initial course development was mainly be based on the introduced management tool of a Ship Energy Efficiency Management Plan (SEEMP) as agreed and circulated by MEPC 59/24 (Annex 19) as well as on the Guidance for the development of a SEEMP as agreed and distributed in MEPC.1/Circ.683.

Performed survey studies have shown that there have already been many courses or materials in terms of the energy-efficient operation of ships mainly developed by classification societies and shipping companies in the world. Though each of them is well developed and recognised as a good reference for the model course.

The final draft of the model course contains the core part for the energy efficient operation of ships. The developed and suggested outline of the draft model course is given in Fig. 16.

The finally adopted draft clearly stated that its main purpose is to assist training providers and their teaching staff in organising and introducing new training courses, or in enhancing, updating or supplementing existing training material, so that the quality and effectiveness of the training courses may thereby be improved.

6.3 Investigation into Green Ship Operation

As also already reflected in the structure of the draft IMO model course, green ship operation comprises a wide variety of legal-administrative, technical but also operational aspects. The focus in the context of this study is on the aspect of reducing emissions of particles and greenhouse gases (GHG) and the potentials for its reduction by measures onboard related to the process of ship's navigation.

	Module & Task	Lecture	Practice (Demo/Sim)	Total course hours
1	**Background**	**4 hours**	**0 hours**	**4 hours**
1.1	Climate Change	4	0	4
1.2	IMO related work			
2	**Guidance on Best Practices**	**14 hours**	**4 hours**	**18 hours**
2.1	Fuel efficient operations	3	1	4
2.2	Improved voyage planning			
2.3	Weather routeing			
2.4	Just in time			
2.5	Speed optimization			
2.6	Optimized shaft power			
2.7	Optimized ship handling	3	1	4
2.8	Optimum trim			
2.9	Optimum ballast			
2.10	Optimum propeller and propeller inflow considerations			
2.11	Optimum use of rudder and heading control systems			
2.12	Hull maintenance	3	1	4
2.13	Propulsion system			
2.14	Propulsion system maintenance			
2.15	Waste heat recovery			
2.16	Improved fleet management	3	1	4
2.17	Improved cargo handling			
2.18	Energy management			
2.19	Fuel type			
2.20	Other measures			
2.21	Compatibility of measures	2	0	2
2.22	Age and operational service life of a ship			
2.23	Trade and sailing area			
3	**Application**	**3 hours**	**3 hours**	**6 hours**
3.1	Planning	3	3	6
3.2	Ship-specific measures			
3.3	Company-specific measures			
3.4	Human resource development			
3.5	Self-evaluation and improvement			
3.6	Voluntary reporting/review			
4	**Implementation and Monitoring**	**2 hours**	**0 hours**	**2 hours**
4.1	Implementation	2	0	2
4.2	Monitoring			
	Total Course hours	**23 hours**	**7 hours**	**30 hours**

Fig. 16 Outline of the draft IMO model course for "Energy Efficient Operation of Ships" (originally shown and adapted from Baldauf et al. 2013)

As explained in Sect. 5.1.3 ship operation are critical in respect to emissions when in manoeuvring mode rather than when sailing in open sea. That is why, it is assumed that optimized manoeuvring regimes contribute to decrease Greenhouse gas emissions, reduce fuel consumption and helps to save energy. However, this aspect of energy-efficient manoeuvre strategies has not been addressed sufficiently yet, especially by navigators when operating their ships in harbour areas.

The inter-disciplinary research project "Simulation-based training module to promote green energy-efficient ship operation" (Baldauf et al. (2012), (2013) & (2014)) brought together four recognized IAMU institutions by merging and combining their research competencies related to environmentally friendly shipping. The partners World Maritime University (Sweden—Coordinator), Hochschule Wismar, University of Applied Sciences: Technology, Business and Design (Germany), University of Catalonia Barcelona (Spain) and Australian Maritime College of University of Tasmania commonly investigated potentials for the enhancement of maritime education and training schemes (MET) by taking especially into account the challenges connected to IMO's aims in reducing greenhouse gas emissions when operating a ship. The first phase dealt with basic investigations to identify potentials for energy-efficient ship operation focusing on manoeuvring in harbour areas and into the fundamentals for the development of a simulation based training module. In a later stage the concept for simulation-based exercises should be applied by exemplarily integrating and demonstrating the module in a simulation environment of a ship-handling simulator.

The main objective was the development of a simulation based training module that supports optimized ship operation by means of enhanced integrated manoeuvring planning to assist captains, pilots and navigating officers when entering (or leaving) port entrances and when manoeuvring in harbour areas. Manoeuvres shall be performed so that time saving will allow for reducing greenhouse gas emissions by the reduction of fuel consumption while keeping the economic constraints of the voyage time schedule. For this purpose an onboard prototyped manoeuvring assistance system was integrated into a full-mission simulation environment in order to provide situation dependent recommendation for optimal manoeuvring strategies and steering sequences (Fig. 17).

For the mentioned purposes a combined field and simulation study has been performed. The field study was carried out to research the actual real situation regarding the applied manoeuvring strategies of ferries in a harbour area. Real manoeuvres have been recorded onboard the ship in order to identify potentials for improvement and to derive and test alternative concepts for energy efficient manoeuvring strategies with supporting computer-based assistance in a simulation environment secondly. Figure 18 depicts one section of the harbour area considered in the field study and additionally shows exemplarily the tracks recorded onboard and ashore (synchronized VDR and AIS data).

The simulation studies have been conducted at the MSCW of HSW. For the purpose of analysis real manoeuvre tracks and strategies were compared with simulated alternative ones. One main outcome of the analysis is that the support of dynamic path predictions taking into account ordered manoeuvre handle settings has

Fig. 17 Recorded real track of harbour manoeuvres of a ferry (presented in Benedict et al. 2009a, b)

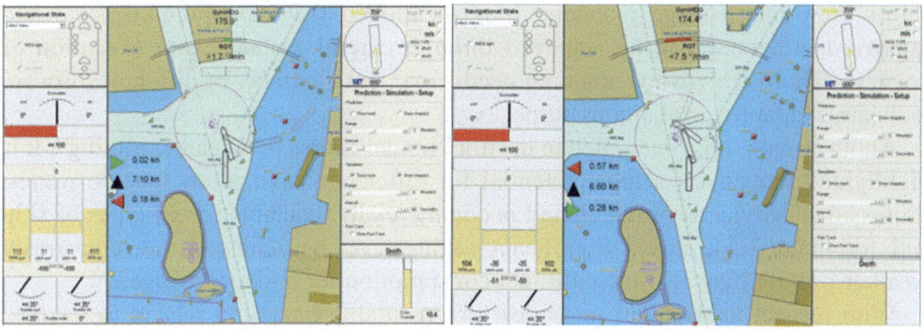

Fig. 18 Adjustment of manoeuvre setting when approaching the turning basin (Left: prediction shows, that vessel is in risk of grounding, right: adapted setting predict smaller turning diameter) (presented in Benedict et al. 2009a, b)

huge potential to contribute to time and energy savings. With the support of such predictions the navigators have been able to better estimate the effects of e.g. ordered engine or rudder commands well in advance and consequently as the steering equipment was used much more target oriented than without the supporting tools.

6.4 Approach for an Integrated Simulation-Based Training Module

From research studies into the application of tools for enhanced manoeuvre planning in coastal areas, approaches to ports and even in harbour basins especially using enhanced Fast-Time-Simulation technologies it can clearly be concluded and stated that the approach of introducing sophisticated assistance tools for enhanced manoeuvring planning can significantly contribute to more energy-efficient ship operation in the harbour areas. On the other hand, as demonstrated in the simulations studies, there is clear potential for time and fuel savings and consequently the reduction of GHG emissions.

The gained results are in accordance with IMO's intention to contribute to green shipping as also supported by the development of a model course for "Energy-efficient Operation of Ships". The first draft of the model course contained a suggestion for a 1 week (5 days) training course for ships technical and nautical crew and shore-based personnel as well. As a core element the drafted course framework provided a wide range of and room for practical exercise in order to learn about best practices related to energy efficient operations of a ship and shall be discussed here a bit more detailed.

Five main subject areas for training have been defined. Especially section I and II are relevant for an integrated simulation based training module. Section I is entitled "Fuel efficient operations" and addresses e.g. the fields of voyage planning, weather routing as well as "Just-in-time" operations and others.

The subject "Improved voyage planning" is foremost dedicated to the appropriate implementation of procedures according to IMO resolution A.893(21) (25 November 1999) on voyage planning as this resolution provides essential guidance for the ship's crew and voyage planners. It is mentioned that the optimum route and improved efficiency can be achieved through careful planning and execution of voyages. Thorough voyage planning needs time, but a number of different software tools are available for planning purposes.

Another main topic integrated in the draft model course is "Weather routing". It is highlighted that it has a high potential for efficiency savings on specific routes. Professional service is provided and is commercially available for all types of ship and for many trade areas. Significant savings can be achieved, but conversely weather routing may also increase fuel consumption for a given voyage.

With respect to potential measures for green ship operation related to nautical departments, voyage planning and weather routing are seen as the "macro (planning) level" for rather strategic decisions whereas manoeuvring planning is seen as the micro (planning) level belonging to tactical decisions of the ship navigation process.

Further in the first section of IMO's draft model course also "Just-in-time" practices are described. Emphasize is given to good early communication with the next port. This should be an aim in order to give maximum notice of berth availability and facilitate the use of optimum speed where port operational procedures support this approach. Optimized port operation could involve a change in procedures involving different handling arrangements in ports. Port authorities should be encouraged to maximize efficiency and minimize delay.

Moreover "Speed optimization" and "Optimized Shaft power" are topics of section I. The training modules consider that speed optimization and optimized shaft power can produce significant savings. However, optimum speed means the speed at which the fuel used per ton mile is at a minimum level for that voyage. It does not mean minimum speed; in fact sailing at less than optimum speed will consume more fuel rather than less. Reference needs to be made to the engine manufacturer's power/consumption curve and the ship's propeller curve. Possible adverse consequences of slow speed operation may include increased vibration and sooting, and these is to be taken into account as well.

As part of the speed optimization process, due account may need to be taken of the need to coordinate arrival times with the availability of loading/discharge berths etc. The number of ships engaged in a particular trade route may need to be taken into account when considering speed optimization.

The second section of the draft model course is entitled "Optimized ship handling" and should address optimum trim and ballasting but also optimum propeller and propeller inflow considerations and optimal use of rudder and heading control systems. These items have impact on manoeuvring performance on both the planning levels too and therefore are also relevant for the development of simulation-based training modules of such a training course.

6.5 *Integration of STCW Competence-Based Training Objectives into Scenarios*

As identified above, careful and thorough planning on *macro* (route optimisation including weather routeing) and *micro* level (optimisation of manoeuvring regimes in port approaches and harbour basins) are key elements for energy-efficient ship operation. Good planning needs experience and associated training.

Modern comprehensive improved voyage planning nowadays can be performed by using dedicated software system providing processed information regarding e.g. currents, tidal streams, and impact of shallow water as well as weather and related and sea state. However systems depend on reasonable and intelligent use of the provided functions taking into account the actual and forecasted prevailing circumstances.

On the other hand experienced navigators are also using manuals containing graphs indicating the performance parameter information as e.g. about pitch handling, power, speed and fuel consumption under different loading conditions and for the two main types of fairways (deep and shallow water).

A practical exercise on fuel efficient operation integrated into a course framework should make use of simulators or otherwise suitable equipped laboratories providing specific assistance systems as standalone version or integrated into a complex ship-handling simulator even connected to ship engine simulator.

In addition, there are also game-based simulators available enabling demonstrating relationships between power, speed, fuel consumption and CO_2 emissions and furthermore allows savings that can be made when the power is adjusted to ETA, instead of sailing 100% to the destination and anchoring to avoid arriving too early.

By applying the described methodology the principle framework of a practical simulation-based exercise on fuel efficient ship operation is structured as exemplarily shown in Fig. 19. The framework allows for flexible integration of the suggested exercises into an applied IMO model course.

For a simulation-based exercise dedicated to the micro level planning it is suggested to integrate practical activities to support optimized ship handling and to demonstrate effects of such actions regarding fuel saving, reduction of GHG emissions etc. and on the other hand to perform actions/tasks in simulation environment.

Practical activities on this subject can range from performing manual or desktop calculation exercises of specific case studies up to full-mission simulation exercises.

As a sample exercise the ship operation when approaching a berth in a harbour is suggested. A potential frame for the sequence of events and tasks of such an exercise is given in Fig. 20.

The emphasis of the simulation exercise is laid on planning of energy efficient manoeuvring taking into account optimized use of engine, propeller, thrusters etc. and by using available sources of information and taking into account different trim and ballast conditions.

Such an exercise can be implemented to full-mission ship handling simulators and, preferably, directly connected to a ship engine room simulator to cover the onboard regime of ship operation more completely. The sample exercises introduced here are suggested for integration into the final draft of the IMO model course and were forwarded accordingly.

6.6 Summary and Conclusion

Within this section basic investigations into potential contributions of ships to reduce greenhouse gas emissions have been performed. In the frame of the CSR concept, reduction of GHG emissions is seen as a part of ship crews environmental responsibility.

The main objective of the studies presented here, was to perform investigations into the development of the basics for a simulation based training module that supports optimized ship operation by means of enhanced integrated manoeuvring planning and monitoring to assist captains, pilots and navigating officers when entering port entrances and manoeuvring in harbour areas. Training is seen as the key element in the CSR concept. There is an obvious need to rise seafarers awareness, that they can contribute significantly to the protection of the marine environment and especially to reduce air pollution from ship manoeuvring. Dedicated

Draft sample exercise scenario "energy-efficient ship operation in open seas"	
Identifier	**Fuel efficient ship operation I** Improved voyage planning
Training objective(s)	i.a. / e.g. • Perform comprehensive voyage planning according to IMO Res. A.893 (21) and Weather routing acc. to IMO Res. A.528 (13) • Speed optimization • Use different methods for determination of optimal route (incl. weather routing) taking into account efficiency indexes and optimal fuel consumption • Draft a berth to berth voyage plan
Simulator tool	Master office / shore-based company office
Standard of competence	Master, chief mate (management level) and navigating officers, Environmental officer, chief engineers and shore based operators
Ship model	e.g. Container feeder vessel (L_{oa} = 188m; draught = 8,24m; service speed = 22kn)
Traffic situation	Varying
Time of day	Daylight
Current	n/a
Environment	Wind: moderate, < 2 Bf, Sea state: low, average high of wave ~ 0,5 m
Area	n/a
Visibility	More than 8 nm
Duration	Long, > 45 min
Event-description	• Charter party requirements delivered to ship management, crew to gather all relevant information for planning and • Heavy weather conditions forecasted with corresponding wind / wave conditions • Team determines optimal route from two/three alternative suggestions • Detailed berth-to-berth voyage planning including also the pilotage areas • Definition of monitoring parameter and criteria • Shore office to be contacted in order to coordinate decisions

Fig. 19 Draft framework for simulation exercise "Fuel efficient ship operation" (adapted from Baldauf et al. 2013)

training, as exemplarily developed here, is able to contribute to the necessary change of mariners' mind-set. Maritime education and sophisticated manoeuvring training help to understand the Whys? and provides guidance how environmental protection can be realized by the crew members.

For this purpose a prototyped manoeuvring assistance system was exemplarily integrated into a full-mission simulation environment and tested with respect to its potentials for time and energy savings. Recordings of real manoeuvre sequences at harbour entrance manoeuvres and berthing actions have been analyzed followed by a comparing simulation study. It is clearly demonstrated that by means of enhanced simulation-based technologies time savings are possible and allow for substantial

Draft sample exercise scenario "energy-efficient ship operation in harbour areas"	
Identifier	**Optimized ship handling I** Manoeuvre planning for harbour basin and berthing operation
Training objective	i.a. / e.g. • Manoeuvring in shallow water areas of harbour basin • Optimum use of steering and control systems • Use of tools for planning and monitoring ship operation considering different trim / ballast conditions
Simulator tool	Desktop up to Full mission ship handling simulator
Standard of competence	Master, chief mate (management level) and navigating officers
Ship model	e.g. RoRo Ferry (L_{oa} = 200 m; draught = 6,0 m; service speed = 24 kn)
Traffic situation	Moderate (about 3 ships per 10 min)
Time of day	Daylight
Current	Realistic (regarding area)
Environment	Wind: moderate, < 4 BF Sea state: low to moderate, average high of wave ~ 2,5 m
Area	Harbour area including approach and basins
Visibility	good, more than 8 nm
Duration	Long, > 45 min
Event-description	• Ferry/Passenger vessel (i.a. equipped with two propellers, bow thrusters) is approaching a harbour area for berthing operation, • Communication with shore-based VTS station • Passage to berth includes several rudder/engine manoeuvre, also use of thrusters is necessary • Passage planning to berth including pre-planning of manoeuvring up to berthing • Combined rudder/engine manoeuvres possible to save time while simultaneously keeping safety limits • Effects of "squat" on under keel clearance power, speed and fuel consumption in shallow water • Situation assessment (including trim operation and speed adaptation)

Fig. 20 Draft framework for simulation exercise "Optimized ship handling" (adapted from Baldauf et al. 2013)

reduction of fuel consumption at sea while simultaneously keeping the economic constraints of the voyage's time schedule and consequently reduce greenhouse gas emissions.

From the human element studies it is concluded that much more enhanced integration of technical and navigational performance data is needed on the ships navigational bridge in principle. Training scenarios for simulation exercises have been drafted and will support the effective use of enhanced manoeuvring assistance systems and substantially contribute to green ship operation with reduced GHG emissions in cleaner oceans. In this way corporate social responsibility become a living concept adapted and implemented in the working environment of maritime business.

Acknowledgements Some of the materials presented in this chapter were partly achieved in the frame of funded research projects. Firstly to mention the project "Simulation-based training module to promote green energy-efficient ship operation" (ProGreenShip). ProGreenShip was a capacity building research project of IAMU kindly supported by the International Association of Maritime Universities (IAMU) and The Nippon Foundation in Japan.

Further research work is undertaken and partly resulted from "MEmBran – Modelling of Emissions and Fuel Consumption during Manoeuvring Operation of Ships" and "MTCAS – electronic maritime collision avoidance", which are funded by the Federal Ministry for Economic Affairs and Energy (Germany), "Multi Media for Improvement of MET" (MultiSimManGREEN), funded by the Federal Ministry of Education and Research, surveyed by Research Centre Juelich PTJ and German Aerospace Agency. Finally, on-going work that contributes to the presented studies belongs partly to WMU's project on further development and implementation of the e-Navigation concept funded by Korea Research Institute Ships & Ocean Engineering (KRISO) as well as the European project for research and technological development "OpenRisk", co-financed by the EU – Civil Protection Financial Instrument as project 2016/PREV/26.

References

Bai, J., Zhang, B., & Yu, J. (2012). Response of maritime education and training to new requirements of STCW'78 Manila amendments. In R. Mercer, J. Cross, & C. McCulloch (Eds.), *Expanding frontiers – Challenges and opportunities in maritime education and training* (pp. 83–90). The Fisheries and Marine Institute of Memorial University of Newfoundland, Local Executive Committee of IAMU AGA 13.

Baldauf, M., Pourzanjani, M., Brooks, B., de Melo, G., & Benedict, K. (2012). *Simulation-based training module to promote green energy-efficient ship operation, Part I: Basics*. Tokyo: International Association of Maritime Universities Tokyo.

Baldauf, M., Pourzanjani, M., Brooks, B., de Melo, G., & Benedict, K. (2013). *Simulation-based training module to promote green energy-efficient ship operation, Part II: Application*. Tokyo: International Association of Maritime Universities Tokyo.

Baldauf, M., Baumler, R., Ölçer, A., Nakazawa, T., Benedict, K., Fischer, S., & Schaub, M. (2014). Energy-efficient ship operation – training requirements and challenges. *TransNav, the International Journal on Marine Navigation and Safety of Sea Transportation, 7*(2), 283–290.

Baumler, R., Ölçer, A. I., Pazaver, A., Nakazawa, T., Baldauf, M., Moon, D., & Cole, C. (2014). Train-the-trainer course on energy efficient operation of ships. *American Journal of Climate Change, 3*, 404–412. https://doi.org/10.4236/ajcc.2014.34035.

Benedict, K., Baldauf, M., Felsenstein, C., & Kirchhoff, M. (2003). Computer-based support for the evaluation of ship handling simulator exercise results. In *MARSIM - International Conference on Marine Simulation and Ship Manoeuvrability*, Kanazawa, Japan, August 25th–28th.

Benedict, K., Baldauf, M., Fischer, S., Gluch, M., KIirchhoff, M., Schaub, M., & Klaes, S. (2012). Fast time manoeuvring simulation as decision support for planning and monitoring of ship handling processes for ship operation on-board and training in simulators. In *MARSIM - International Conference on Marine Simulation and Ship Manoeuvrability*, 23–27 April 2012, Singapore.

Benedict, K., Baldauf, M., Fischer, S., Gluch, M., & Kirchhoff, M. (2009a). Manoeuvring prediction display for effective ship operation on-board ships and for training in ship handling simulators. In *IAMU 10th Assembly & Conference 2009* St. Petersburg/Russia at AMSMA, 19–21 September.

Benedict, K., Baldauf, M., Fischer, S., Gluch, M., & Kirchhoff, M. (2009b). Manoeuvring simulation for dynamic prediction display to be used on-board and in ship handling simulator training. In *MARSIM - International Conference on Marine Simulation and Ship Manoeuvrability*, 36th AGA of IMSF and International Conference, Panama City, Panama; August 17–20. Conference Proceedings, pp. S-60–S-70.

Benedict, K., Baldauf, M., Kirchhoff, M., Koepnick, W., & Eyrich, R. (2006). Combining fast-time simulation and automatic assessment for tuning of simulator ship models. In *MARSIM - International Conference on Marine Simulation and Ship Manoeuvrability*, Terschelling, Netherlands, June 25th–30th Proceedings, M-Paper 19, pp. 1–9.

Corbett, J. J. (2004). *Verification of ship emission estimates with monitoring measures to improve inventory and modeling*. California 2004. Report for the California Air Resources Board and the California Environmental Protection Agency.

Dahlsrud, A. (2008). How corporate social responsibility is defined: An analysis of 37 definitions. *Corporate Social Responsibility and Environmental Management*, 15, 1–13.

EC. (2001). Commission Green Paper 2001 "Promoting a European Framework for Corporate Social Responsibility", (COM(2001)366 Final)

EC. (2011). EC MEMO/11/730 "Corporate Social Responsibility: A new definition, a new agenda for action", Brussels, 25 October 2011

Endresen, O., Sörgard, E., Sundet, J. K., et al. (2003). Emission from international sea transportation and environmental impact. *Journal of Geophysical Research, 108*(D17), 4560.

Fischer, S., & Benedict, K. (2010). *Analyses of manoeuvring procedures on ferry "Mecklenburg-Vorpommern" in Rostock Sea Port and potential improvements using alternative manoeuvring concepts with Dynamic Predictor*. Hochschule Wismar, Dept. of Maritime Studies, Warnemuende 2010.

Hellstrom, T. (2003). Three levels of fuel optimisation at sea. In *The Proceedings of 2nd International EuroConference on Computer and IT Applications in the Maritime Industries (COMPIT)*, 2003.

IMO MEPC 62/INF.39: Draft Model Course "Energy-efficient operation of Ships" London, November 2011.

Pava, M. L., & Krausz, J. (1996). The association between corporate social responsibility and financial performance:the paradox of social cost. *Journal of Business Ethics*, 15, 321–357.

Schaub, M., Benedict, K., Kleas, S., & Baldauf, M. (2015). Fast-time simulation for prediction of fuel consumption and emissions during ship manoeuvres. In O. Turan (Ed.), *International Conference on Shipping in Changing Climates. SCC 2015 Proceedings* (Vol. 1, pp. 171–183). Glasgow, UK: University of Strathclyde.

Whall, C., et al. (2007). *Ship emissions inventory - Mediterranean Sea*. Brussels. Report for Lourens Post, CONCAWE.

Winnes, H., & Fridell, E. (2010). Emissions of NO_X and particles from manoeuvring ships. *Transportation Research Part D: Transport and Environment, 15*(4), 204–211.

A Financial Business Case for Corporate Social Responsibility

Ioannis Oikonomou, Aspasia Pastra, and Ilias Visvikis

1 Introduction: Environmental and Social Challenges in Shipping

The shipping industry facilitates substantially the operation of a global supply network and plays a pivotal role in the global transport of products. Shipping positively affects the lives of billions of people, with 90% of the world's international trade travelling by sea. The challenges of the sector are multiple due to the cyclical nature of the industry, the global political and economic instability, the bulk volume of environmental laws and the volatility of bunker fuel and freight rates. The international nature of the industry possesses significant challenges because regulations are usually taken in a global level and enforced on the local level in which there are various environmental and national peculiarities.

Usually, shipowners are taking environmental and pollution incidents very seriously, following the increasing volume of regulations that are promoted by the International Maritime Organisation (IMO). In order to better understand the financial business case of shipping and Corporate Social Responsibility (CSR) someone has to start from the basic environmental challenges and risks that the sector encounters (and the relevant IMO instruments). The following summary provides an overview of regulatory regimes, challenges and actions being taken, providing

I. Oikonomou
ICMA Centre, Henley Business School, University of Reading, Reading, UK

A. Pastra
World Maritime University, Malmö, Sweden

I. Visvikis (✉)
School of Business Administration, American University of Sharjah, Sharjah, United Arab Emirates
e-mail: ivisvikis@aus.edu

L. L. Froholdt (ed.), *Corporate Social Responsibility in the Maritime Industry*, WMU Studies in Maritime Affairs 5, https://doi.org/10.1007/978-3-319-69143-5_12

clarity on what is compliance in the industry and how companies go beyond compliance in order to address the CSR agenda:

- **Marine pollution**: Pollution from ships by oil; noxious liquid substances; sewage and garbage; ballast water; and ship paints comprise a thorny issue for the maritime industry. The adoption of the International Convention for the Prevention of Pollution from Ships (MARPOL) led to a dramatic decrease in pollution from international shipping. Furthermore, the increasing amount of invasive alien species has necessitated measures to reduce the risk of non-indigenous species being introduced through the discharge of ship's ballast water. The proposed IMO Ballast Water Management (BWM) Convention, along with relating Guidelines relating to the uniform implementation of the Convention, aims at providing guidance on Port States, Flag States and ship operators to reduce the transfer of harmful aquatic organisms in ships' ballast water.
- **Greenhouse gas emissions**: CO_2, CH4, N2O, HFCs, PFCs, SF6 and relevant substances (NOx, NM VOC, CO, PM, SOx) are causing climate change. Despite that shipping is the cleanest mode of transport per capita, there is growing scrutiny on the limits of greenhouse gas emissions. The IMO GHG Study (2014) reports that in 2012 international shipping emitted no more than about 2.2% of the total CO_2 emission volume for that year. However, various mandatory technical and operational measures have been introduced since it is expected that by 2050 there will be a substantial increase, between 50% and 250%, in the CO_2 emissions from international shipping (Third IMO Greenhouse Gas Study, 2014).

  The IMO, especially through the International Convention for the Prevention of Pollution from Ships, plays the most important role in addressing the issue of greenhouse gas emissions and has created an international regulatory regime for monitoring of CO_2 emissions and Sulphur limits for ships fuel. Within the industry, there are also some shipping firms that are exploring the possibility of taking further action and shift to lower-carbon fuels. Speed reduction, new fuels and new technologies could prove important solutions to the emission problem.
- **Ship recycling**: Ship recycling raises serious concerns about a number of health, safety, and environmental problems and vessels should be recycled only in facilities that are environmental friendly. To this direction various guidelines and tools have been formed to help states and ship-owners to take control over recycling methods, the conditions under which their ships are demolished and the handling of waste materials.

  The Hong Kong International Convention for the Safe and Environmentally Sound Recycling of Ships, upon enforcement, will addresses all the relevant issues for scrapping ships and the conditions at recycling locations. Besides, the EU Ship Recycling regulation aims to the reduction of the adverse impacts associated with the recycling of EU flagged ships and is considered as an early implementation of the prerequisites of the Hong Kong International Convention. Furthermore, the Basel Convention, which has been ratified by several member countries, aims to control the transport, recycling, and disposal of hazardous wastes (i.e. toxic, poisonous and explosive).

To further appreciate the business environment that shipping companies operate, then the social challenges of the sector need to be highlighted. More specifically, some of the most important social issues of the sector that are usually high on the agenda of IMO's Maritime Safety Committee, Marine Environment Protection Committee, as well as in a number of Sub-Committees, are presented hereto:

- **People retention and motivation**: Human capital is the most important asset of the organization. Shipping firms should find ways to motivate their employees both at the offices and onboard the ships. A safe working environment, responsible human resource management policies and wellbeing benefits usually lead to an organizational competitive advantage in recruiting of the most talented employees. Especially, when it comes to the manning of ships, shipowners should be vigilant in the selection of flags (despite being an economic decision) and emphasize on the recruitment and proper training of their seafarers.
- **Safety at sea and prevention of accidents**: Working at sea exposes individuals to various occupational accidents and injuries. General shipboard safety and accident prevention on-board is a major concern for governments, organizations and shipowners. The regulatory regime for safety is the IMO's International Convention for the Safety of Life at Sea (SOLAS) along with its International Safety Management (ISM) Code. SOLAS is of paramount importance when addressing maritime safety because it specifies the safety standards for the construction, equipment and operation of ships. Besides, a number of guidelines and regulations have been implemented at the international and national level about seafarers' rights and working conditions, search and rescue, maritime traffic, and the carriage of dangerous goods and tonnage measurement.
- **Security, piracy and armed robbery**: The deteriorating security situation in various regions and seas calls for a well-organized coordinated effort between countries and naval forces. There are still a number of steps that need to be taken to support international effort to suppress maritime crime. Shipowners should take measures to protect their crews and educate seafarers on the steps that have to be taken in cases of attack alert due to cases of pirate attacks and armed robbery.
- **Community outrage**: The shipping industry is very sensitive when it comes to pollution and oil incidents at sea. The negative societal and environmental effects that an oil pollution incident brings are so severe that the public image of the firm and the sector is completely destroyed. Incidents like those of Exxon Valdez (24th March 1989) and MV Prestige (19th November 2002) oil spill affected people's lives, both economically and culturally. Shipowners should manage the reputation risk and demonstrate to their stakeholders that their ships and operations are environmentally friendly. Proactive measures through communicated CSR initiatives could enhance public awareness about the environmental friendly practices both of the company and the industry. Communicated CSR initiatives, local community involvement and use of local suppliers are means to assume a corporate citizenship-role and contribute in the case of an environmental crisis.

From the above summary it is clear that there are many CSR issues that are crucially relevant to the shipping industry and there is ample room for shipping owners to incorporate social considerations in their priorities. However, in order to give a more holistic approach on the topic we will take a step back from our maritime perspective and look at the issue of the financial relevance of CSR more broadly, drawing on theoretical and empirical work that has been conducted in the field.

2 Skepticism Towards the Business Case for CSR

Traditionally, the view that CSR could be a seen as a sound set of business policies, which could preserve and even enhance corporate value has been met with strong opposition and has been subject to a variety of different criticisms. The most notable of these is based on the strict neoclassical view which posits that CSR is something extraneous and irrelevant to the core business of a firm, lacks the ability to lead to any tangible, demonstrative economic benefits (Aupperle et al. 1985) while at the same time, its application comes with significant costs. As such, it may constitute a misappropriation and misallocation of scarce and valuable corporate resources (Margolis and Walsh 2003; Waddock and Graves 1997) and a simple cost-benefit analysis would convince corporate managers to steer clear from it.

Perhaps the most famous critique of this kind came from seminal economist Milton Friedman (1970). In an article tellingly entitled "*The social responsibility of business is to increase its profits*", Friedman chastised the increasing interest towards the concept of CSR by academics and practitioners. He emphatically proclaimed that CSR constitutes an implicit "*tax imposition*" to firm shareholders for the sole purpose of allowing the top firm executives to promote their own social, environmental and ethical agendas. As such, he claimed, it is both a bad business practice and fundamentally undemocratic; that is, it is the government's job to create laws, rules and regulations to promote social cohesion and environmental stability, not the firm's.

This line of reasoning, in different variants, has been echoed in many theoretical papers and opinion articles since the 1970s (see Doane and Abasta-Vilaplana 2005, as an example). However, it is solely based on the key assumption that CSR is taking away focus from maximising shareholder value to other external issues and cannot possibly lead to a net economic/financial benefit. Hence, it should not be considered by any conscientious and capable manager who upholds his role as an agent and tries to maximise shareholders' value. But need this theoretically be the case, i.e. does performing well financially and promoting social or environmental good need to be mutually exclusive in the corporate world? And purely based on the data, is it empirically the case? These questions have been the object of a significant body of academic research for the past 40 years. The answers provided to each question are next examined in turn.

3 Arguments in Favour of the Value Relevance of Corporate Social Responsibility

So is it possible for pro-social, pro-environment, strong corporate governance practices to also be value-enhancing? A framework created principally by Organizational Management scholars and referred to as Stakeholder Theory says that it is not just possible but highly probable. Originally developed by Freeman (1984), stakeholder theory broadly posits that in order to sustain and create value, a firm need to take into consideration the needs, requirements and demands of all individuals and institutions that affect and are affected by the firm's activities. This view drastically shifts (or at least broadens) the scope of corporate operation.

Many would argue that the above definition of a stakeholder is so generic and inclusive that it does not provide a meaningful and tractable goal for managers. How can a firm try to balance the swarm of demands, often conflicting, placed upon it by different groups—some of which crucial and others tangentially related to and affected by the firm's activities? Jensen (2002) recognises the practical difficulties in managing such trade-offs and makes a proposition about the path firms should follow: *Enlightened Stakeholder Theory*. The central idea is very simple. Firms should maintain long-term shareholder value maximization as the goal they are striving to achieve but they should certainly consider all-important constituencies.[1] In Jensen's own words: "*It is obvious that we cannot maximise the long-term market value of an organization if we ignore or mistreat any important constituency. We cannot create value without good relations with customers, employees, financial backers, suppliers, regulators, communities and so on*" (Jensen 2002, p. 246). According to this view, issues related to CSR could be crucially important to firm valuation so long as they influence the firm's relationships with key stakeholders.

Going a step further, Clarkson (1995) argues that firms should prioritise according to the importance of constituents to the firm by separating them in primary and secondary. Strong relationships with primary stakeholders are of strategic important to the firm as they can lead to the creation of sustainable comparative advantages. Employee attraction, retention, loyalty and effort can improve. Local communities can provide support and a hospitable business environment. The firm will find it easier to lobby for tax-breaks and less stringent regulation from the part of local (or even central) governing bodies and regulatory agencies. Environmental and other activist groups can provide their seal of approval to the products and services of a firm, which can go a long way with consumers who share the respective sensitivities. All these will eventually create a differential advantage for the firm vis-à-vis its competitors, which will translate into tangible benefits, increased cash-flows and improved market valuation. On the other hand, resources spent to ingratiate (or appease) secondary stakeholder will not have a material effect on the firm's bottom line and thus fall under the Friedman critique. Hillman and Keim (2001)

[1]In mathematical terms, the firm's problem remains maximising long-term value in its objective function but additional constraints (stakeholder restrictions) should be considered in solving it.

provide empirical support to this rationale by showing that, at least for large US firms, strategic stakeholder management (i.e. CSR practices related to primary stakeholders) leads to improved shareholder value while social issues participation (CSR practices related to broader issues) has the exact opposite effect.

But how does a firm recognise key stakeholders and distinguishes them from more peripheral constituents? Mitchell et al. (1997) provide a framework for measuring stakeholder salience. The principal criteria for this identification are power (the degree to which the stakeholders can impose their will in their relationship with the firm), legitimacy (the extent to which stakeholder claims are in line with socially accepted and expected behaviour) and urgency (the extent to which the stakeholders' claims tend to be characterised by criticality and time-sensitivity). The degree to which all three of these criteria are met determines the importance of a stakeholder group to the firm and makes them more value relevant. For example, employees going on strike making allegations of a very unsafe working environment have power, legitimacy and urgency on their side, and hence their CSR related claims should be seriously considered by the firm's management.

A different prospective about the likely economic/financial effects of CSR is offered by Godfrey (2005) who suggests that CSR's role is even more crucially important in protecting rather than enhancing the firm's bottom line. Godfrey proclaims that when a firm has been shown to conduct some sort of transgression, the impact on its valuation will partly depend on the stakeholders' judgment of its underlying character. In such situations, CSR can act as "*mitigating evidence*" in favour of the firm, having a positive influence on its moral coloration and blurring the line on whether its recent controversy was intentional and indicative of the usual way it does business or incidental and uncharacteristic. In this way, CSR acts as a form of "*reputational insurance*" and can preserve firm value by making it less likely for employees to go on strike, consumers to boycott, regulators to impose fines, activists to protest and so on. So CSR may be more useful as a means of value protection rather than value creation.

Lastly, it has also been theorized that apart from the inherent value-relevance of CSR, it may additionally function as a signal to the market for identifying good managers, i.e. the good management hypothesis (Waddock and Graves 1997). The rationale behind this proposition is that because CSR is something that would *prima facie* be viewed as a peripheral business issue and its efficient application is hard due to the trade-offs between conflicting demands by different stakeholder groups, only the most competent managers would consider and practice it. Hence, part of the positive financial effects of CSR will be a product of the correlation between CSR practices and managerial ability.

In summary, theory suggests that be it through building stronger long-term relationships with key stakeholders or due to the comparatively high managerial competence of individuals using it, CSR can lead to the enhancement of the firm's value or at least to its preservation during systemic and idiosyncratic turmoil. But is this empirically validated or is it does just ivory tower wishful thinking? The next section will investigate what is the empirical evidence in the literature on the financial management impact of CSR.

4 The Evidence on the Financial Impact of CSR

Researchers in scholarly fields as varied as Environmental Economics, Marketing, Business Ethics, Strategic Management and Finance have attacked the issue regarding the existence, size, sign and relevance of the relationship between CSR and firm valuation for decades. There are literally hundreds of published studies on the subject from the late 1970s until nowadays and many more working papers produced at a very high frequency. Accordingly, a variety of different data sets (ranging from firm disclosures of CSR practices to third-party CSR ratings and inclusion to CSR stock indices) and methodologies have been applied in this effort. Add to that the different sample characteristics in terms of size, geographic coverage, time window, sectoral diversity and type of CSR dimension examined and you get a sense of the breadth of the CSR-firm value literature which makes general conclusions hard to reach (Griffin and Mahon 1997).

In order to address this issue, researchers have produced extensive qualitative literature reviews, succinctly summarising broad common conclusions that can be drawn and stylised characteristics of the CSR-financial performance link. Margolis and Walsh (2003) examine more than 120 studies that had been published by that moment in time and point out that 71% of them find a positive relationship between corporate social and financial performance at the firm level, some of them fail to detect any statistically significant link, while very few reveal a negative association between the CSR and firm value. More recently, Schröder (2014) notes that the literature fails to detect significant differences in the performance of Socially Responsible Investment (SRI) funds or equity indexes and their otherwise comparable conventional counterparts. However, when long-short SRI portfolios are created (i.e. portfolios where firms with the best CSR ratings are overweighed and firms with the worst CSR ratings are sold-short), they manage to capture the most extreme CSR performers and consistently beat their conventional peers.

Many would argue though that such qualitative summaries (Margolis and Walsh 2003; Schröder 2014) are merely "*vote counting*" exercises and not necessarily reflective of the true burden of evidence towards any direction. With that in mind, statistical meta-analyses have been produced. These studies aggregate the statistical evidence of empirical papers in bulk and provide an overarching quantitative estimation regarding the average strength of the relationship between a variable X (metrics of CSR in this case) and a variable Y (measures of firm value in this case). Similar conclusions are drawn from this strand of research. Orlitzky and Benjamin (2001) conduct a meta-analysis on the link between CSR and various financial risk metrics and find a strong inverse relationship between the two, running from the former to the latter and being more powerful when reputational measures of CSR are used. More broadly, Orlitzky et al. (2003) accumulate data from 52 studies (total sample of nearly 34,000 observations) and reveal that the true (bias-adjusted) correlation between CSR and financial performance is positive and stands at approximately 36%. A more recent meta-analysis of 251 empirical studies by Margolis et al. (2009) verifies that there is a statistically robust association between CSR and firm performance but estimates the economic significance of this association to be lower at approximately 13% on average.

So although the question concerning the value effects of CSR has not been definitively answered, the empirical evidence is quite lopsided. The vast majority of the literature supports that there is at least a modest positive link between CSR and firm financial performance and at the very least, CSR does not appear to be value decreasing. There are also indications that it acts as a reputational buffer for firms caught up in various controversies and thus assists in preserving firm value.

If anyone is still skeptical about these results and is considering whether they are driven by the socio-political biases of academics, it is perhaps worth noting that the increased demand for CSR-related investments has led professional fund managers to create a host of different financial products, which fall under the umbrella of SRI.[2] According to the Global Sustainable Investment Review 2012, approximately US $13.6 trillion of assets under professional management incorporate environmental, social or governance considerations into the asset allocation or security selection process. In addition, the 2014 report on the US Sustainable, Responsible and Impact Investing Trends reveals that "*The total US-domiciled assets under management using SRI strategies expanded from $3.74 trillion at the start of 2012 to $6.57 trillion at the start of 2014, an increase of 76 percent. These assets now account for more than one out of every six dollars under professional management in the United States*".[3] So given the very significant size and tremendous growth this industry has exhibited, would investors place so many funds for so many years in a strategy that would diminish their returns? It would be very hard to reconcile such behaviour if CSR was value-destroying. The next step is to investigate how CSR impacts on the financial risk management position of companies.

5 Financial Risk Management and CSR

In today's global economy, firms and institutions face new challenges as they have to cope with the rapidly changing business environment, including market developments, economic shocks, technological progression, regulatory changes, and increased environmental concerns. Firms are exposed to a number of market risks, which if they are not handled or managed properly can lead to business disruptions, or even failures. Firms today are pressed by investors, shareholders, clients, regulators, among others, for growth and sustainability, in a challenging market landscape with tight capital opportunities, blurred future market expectations, and increased volatility in rates and prices.

---

[2]Also referred to as Sustainable and Responsible Investing, Environmental, Social and Governance Investing or Impact Investing.

[3]http://www.ussif.org/Files/Publications/SIF_Trends_14.F.ES.pdf.

Efficient risk management has been viewed by institutions as of paramount importance, especially following the global financial meltdown in late 2008. Corporate risk management has attracted a lot of attention, as it is incorporated in business strategies for growth, sustainability, competitiveness, and shareholder value creation. CSR, under its social, environmental and economic aspects, can enhance corporate sustainability and contribute towards the efficient management of risk. In efficient markets, positive (or negative) CSR announcements must positively (or negatively) affect corporate performance. Altschuller and Smith (2001) argue that a CSR program should be integrated into management standards and be part of the firm's business strategy. Such an efficient CSR program can decrease the legal disputes and divestment activities.

An early association of CSR to strategic risk management discusses adjusting returns to risk in order to make returns comparable between firms (see Alexander and Buchholz 1978; Aupperle et al. 1985). Financial risk management and CSR involve maintaining profits, shielding investments and shareholder value, and sustaining commercial growth (see Anderson 2006; Anderson and Anderson 2009, amongst others). Non-financial risk management relates to "*social and environmental concerns that relate to CSR*" (see Wong 2014). According to the United Nations Environmental Programme's (UNEP) Financial Initiatives (2003), non-financial risk management relates to managing risks concerning issues of sustainability.

According to Baron (2001), firms undertake CSR activities because they expect a net benefit from them. CSR processes that maximise profits can lead to diversification strategies and a competitive advantage (Siegel and Vitaliano 2007). It is argued in the literature that CSR contributes to enhance capital that protects firms from the adverse effects of future economic sock events in the market (see Godfrey 2005, among others). Boutin-Dufresne and Savaria (2004) suggest that "*socially responsible companies tend to show less diversifiable risk in their stock behavior than non-socially responsible companies*". Thus, implementation of CSR can assist in decreasing the overall business risk of a firm, and improve its long-run performance.

Husted (2005) develops a model for CSR as a real option in strategic risk management and argues that CSR should be negatively related to the firm's business risk; that is, business risk is decreasing with CSR activities. Coleman (2009) argues that by including CSR risk management issues into strategic planning, CSR becomes an important part of the company's business strategy. Boatright (2011) suggests that the source of risk for each stakeholder in an organisation should be considered in order for a holistic approach of CSR risk management to be established at a management level. Sharfman and Fernando (2008) establish that institutional-level environmental performance is negatively related to systematic risk (also known as "*undiversifiable risk*" or "*market risk*," affects the overall market, not just a particular company), resulting in lower cost of equity capital, and thus better financial performance. Oikonomou et al. (2012) confirm that CSR is negatively associated to systematic risk, arguing that social irresponsibility is related with higher systematic risk. Albuquerque et al. (2013) approaches CSR processes as an investment in client devotion, and show that CSR decreases systematic risk and increases institutional value. Finally, Wong (2014) argues that incorporating CSR issues into the business operations can assist an organization to detect risks but also opportunities and returns.

So far, it seems that from the arguments, evidence and trends described earlier in this chapter, CSR tends to enhance and protect firm value and does not seem to detract from it. Let us now return to the *maritime perspective* and examine the business impact of CSR more closely within the framework of this sector.

6 Corporate Performance and CSR in Shipping

Following from the above, performance is a multidimensional construct, which can be broadly classified into financial performance (i.e. profits, Return on Investments) and non-financial performance that includes operational measures, such as market share and value (see Venkatraman and Ramanujam 1986). Barnett and Salomon (2012) underline the long-standing conflict that exists between those who support that the implementation of a CSR increases firm's administrative costs and those who support the argument that an improved social performance attracts more investments and businesses. The results of their study show that the truth stands somewhere in the middle since different social responsible initiatives affect differently the financial performance. Within the same approach, Lu et al. (2009) find that in container shipping "*community involvement and environment*" and "*disclosure*" dimensions have positive effects on financial performance, whereas the employee and consumer interests' dimension positively influences non-financial performance.

The direct benefits that a firm could achieve for its corporate performance by implementing CSR initiatives are specified clearly in the work made in shipping from previous scholars (for example, see Hopkins 2004; Grewal and Darlow 2007; Poulovassilis and Meidanis 2013; Sprinkle and Maines 2010; Kunnaala et al. 2013, amongst others) the important corporate benefits of socially responsible initiatives could be summarised as follows:

- Competitive advantage and differentiation from the competitors
- Reputation, enhanced firm's and industry's image by investors, owners, donors and local communities
- Development of trust with investors and different stakeholders
- Important cost savings in the value chain through pro-active decision-making leading to the avoidance of negative societal effects
- Maintenance and boosting of employees' morale, commitment and productivity

Sprinkle and Maines (2010) support that a significant benefit of CSR is "*free*" advertising, since the initiatives of the organisation are published on newspapers, magazines, radio and television without imposing communication costs. Furthermore, the authors underline that through CSR firms are attracting, motivating, and retaining the best talent in the industry. Frynas (2012) investigates the progress of 20 oil and gas firms from around the world towards oil spill prevention, and based on the results of previous studies (Sharma and Vredenburg 1998; Frynas 2009), concludes that environmental initiatives (besides good corporate management and CSR) lead to: (a) increased profits, (b) innovations such as technology patents in the areas of sulfur dioxide recovery, waste reduction and disposal, (c) reduction of carbon dioxide emissions, and (d) implementation of a zero spill policy for the firm. CSR has been linked with many corporate benefits and specific CSR behaviors are linked with different specific strategic outcomes. For example, Burke and Logsdon (1996) support that:

- Philanthropic contributions, such as community support donations, lead to customer loyalty and future purchases.
- Employee benefits (i.e. financial and non-financial motives, flexible working hours) are linked to productivity gains.
- Environmental initiatives bring marketing strategic advantages.

Shipping firms should focus on the long-term benefits that a CSR strategy can bring rather than quick short-term profits. The benefits that a shipping organization can achieve from the integration of financial, environmental and social factors could enhance substantially the overall quality of shipping sector. Quality management practices can be incorporated under the umbrella of CSR. Cheng and Choy (2007) identified four success factors of quality management in shipping industry: (a) top management commitment, (b) quality information and performance measurement, (c) employee training and empowerment, and (d) customer focus. In a subsequent study, Cheng and Choy (2013) showed that all these four quality management practices are positively associated with superior financial performance, marketing performance and shore-based staff/seafarer performance. Consequently, the adoption of CSR initiatives such as investment in employee training and crew welfare boost the quality of management practices in the industry. In the next section we provide suggestions of how to achieve this integration through the implementation of CSR initiatives.

7 Implementation of CSR Initiatives for Shipping Companies

Many of the basic environmental and social challenges presented above are mainly tackled at the global level through the rules adopted under the auspices of IMO. Governments have a crucial role to play in implementing regulations and creating the proper climate for assisting the industry in investing energy-efficient technologies, alternative fuels and safety advances.

The maritime industry has a very important role in addressing the environmental and social challenges of the sector. Shipping firms should take steps to improve their public image and raise the sustainability of their operation both at the offices and on board on their ship. One point that should be taken into serious consideration is that the CSR strategy cannot be separated from the overall strategy of the organization.

The integration of CSR into business strategy encompasses various concerns. According to Galbreath (2009), the way that CSR fits into corporate strategy is dependent upon the organizational goals, the identification of internal and external issues and the development of internal resources (assets, skills, competencies, financial resources). The model presented by Husted and Allen (2011) encompasses the basic seven steps that a firm should follow to develop its CSR strategy and, among others, these include external and internal environmental analysis as well as resource-based analysis:

1. Analyse social issues and the external competitive environment
2. Analyse the internal resources and capabilities of the organisation
3. Evaluate firm identity in terms of social needs and opportunities
4. Determine the cost of acquiring necessary resources and capabilities
5. Create an integrated plan including different stakeholders and outcomes
6. Implement the plan
7. Evaluate objectives and performance

Despite the pressures that the various stakeholders impose on firms to implement sustainable strategies, only a few have managed to successfully embed them into the organizational vision. Unfortunately, many leaders still have not identified the roadmap to integrate environmental, social, and financial goals, but several shipowners already have. Lubin and Esty (2010) underline that the basic problem with business leaders is that they have not perceived the CSR as a megatrend, and as a result they have failed to involve every function, process, business line, and employee in CSR initiatives. Especially in the maritime sector, which there is an indirect interaction with final consumers, the implementation of CSR strategies has been delayed and when shipping firms explore the possibility of implementing them, then they focus their attention on environmental concerns (see Kunnaala et al. 2013).

The study of Fafaliou et al. (2006) in Greek Shipping firms shows that small firms are not involved in CSR. The few medium or large shipping firms that are involved in such activities are either subsidiaries of international conglomerates or managed by owners who are fully aware of the benefits that derive from setting up a CSR strategy.

Apart from the Husted and Allen's (2011) seven-step CSR model, this chapter includes a few practical guidelines that firms could follow to encounter the social and environmental challenges of shipping. For example, shipping firms are advised to implement the guidelines of ISO 26000 (2010), which facilitate the implementation of socially responsible practices throughout the organization. ISO 26000 addresses seven core subjects of social responsibility and these are: human rights, labour practices, the environment, fair operating practices, consumer issues, community involvement and organizational governance.

Shipping firms should complement governmental and international regulation on responsible environmental and social practices. They should also minimize the environmental impact of their activities through improved efficiency in their operations, management and resources. Shipowners could invest on innovative practices on reduced consumption, alternative energy sources such as LNG, biodiesel, reduction of Sulphur emissions, exhaust gas cleaning systems, advances in ships design and technology, research and development projects. The implementation of a "*green ship plan*" includes low pollution objectives throughout the entire life of ship from design, construction and operation to recycling.

Shipping firms are strongly advised to implement sustainable initiatives for environment, safety, employees, customers, investors, suppliers and the community. This commitment to CSR implies that the firms depart from the traditional reporting framework and encompasses environmental, economic and social performance disclosure. Unfortunately, only a limited number of firms are releasing information about CSR initiatives, demonstrating a gap between what stakeholders want and the information being provided.

In the maritime domain, the literature between CSR activities and shipping firm performance is still limited. Drobetz et al. (2014) investigates the relationship between corporate performance and CSR disclosure in the shipping industry, by employing a sample of 111 listed firms, over 2002–2010. They argue that there is a strong positive relationship between the two investigated variables. Andreou et al. (2014) examine the relationship between corporate performance and corporate governance, by employing 26–32 shipping firms (according to available data), over 1999–2010. They also find a strong positive relationship between the variables. Kavussanos and Tsouknidis (2015) argue that CSR performance leads to higher performance in the shipping industry. More specifically, by employing a sample of 33 shipping firms, between 2002 and 2013, their study finds a positive relationship between firm performance and CSR performance with 1-year lag.

Any CSR strategy in shipping should fulfill various objectives both for the employees working offshore and on-board vessels in the areas of environmental protection, safety, wellbeing, the relation with customers, suppliers, investors and communities. Table 1 provides a combination of regulations and guidelines of IMO along with exemplary CSR practices that depict what social responsible initiatives could mean for a shipping company. These suggestions can be adopted by shipping companies.

Over the last years a few shipping firms have started to implement sustainable initiatives mainly because stakeholder groups are demanding that firms operate in a socially responsible manner. However, there are substantial steps that have to be taken by the majority of shipping firms. If firms want to reap the benefits of a CSR they must integrate it into their overall strategy and set sustainable objectives into the day-to-day operation of the organisation. Green shipping initiatives combined with social initiatives should be embedded in the main philosophy of the organization so as each employee earns the respect and trust of society.

Table 1 Social responsible initiatives for shipping firms

Employees working on land
• Enhancement of the **Health and Safety Management System** that safeguards staff's occupational health and safety.
• Implementation of an **Environment Management System** committed to sound environmental practices. Application of the ISO 14000 series of standards for an environmental management system for responsible practices in the areas of prevention of pollution and sustainable resource use.
• Ensure that safety and environmental awareness are an integral part of the firm's daily life through **training workshops** and continuous improvement of the competencies of employees, both at sea and ashore.
• Respect **human rights** providing equal opportunities to all employees and create a workplace without discrimination or harassment. Gender diversity in Top Management Team and Board of Directors. Empower female employees to contribute even more to the vision and goals of the organization.
• **Social benefits** for employees: Good benefit packages for employees and retirement programs.
• Creation of an **Ethics Code** that ensures that each employee behaves with honesty, responsibility, respect and fairness and applies these values in the daily activities.
• Set up an **Expert Team** that works on initiatives for technical and operational optimization, renovation plans in the fleet, energy-efficient operations, optimization of auxiliary machine.
Employees working on board
• Ensure that **Health and Safety** of the seafarers are priorities for the organization. Continuous education and update on regulations and guidelines such as the Safety of Life at Sea (SOLAS), International Safety Management Code (ISM Code) and the Maritime Labour Convention (MLC).
• **Security** measures for terrorism and piracy are implemented and revised when needed. Contingency plans are tested continuously in order to optimize the ability of the crew to respond to a pirate attack. Firm's and industry security experts monitor the organization's vessels in high-risk areas on a daily basis and obtain the intelligence reports from the relevant authorities.
• Implement **environmentally responsible practices** in the daily activities of the crew, monitor the objectives and disclose the environmental performance of the vessels.
• Efficient **green recycling** of the vessels. Vessels are demolished in a way that ensures safe working environment at the yard, together with safe removal and disposal of hazardous materials on board.
• Development of **Training Programmes** for Seafarers and provision of improved onboard training facilities. Support systems for **female seafarers**, to assist re-entering employment after maternity leave
Suppliers and subcontractors
• Creation of a **Supplier Code of Conduct** to ensure that all the suppliers and contactors are willing to work with the demands set forth in the Code. In the Code cover issues in the supply chain like legal compliance, fair trade, trustworthiness, safety and security, environment, human rights, tackling corruption in the supply chain.
• Choosing suppliers and sub-contractors based on pre-determined set **criteria** and engage in dialogue (or online discussions) with them about their labour conditions, heath, safety and social performance.
Customers
• Strive to create **value to your customers through** creative and innovative solutions.
Investors
• Provision of extensive **annual reporting** and communication of economic, environmental, social and governance performance. Utilize the Global Reporting Initiative (GRI) G4 guidelines and the sector-specific Oil and Gas Industry Guidance on voluntary sustainability reporting of IPIECA.

(continued)

Table 1 (continued)

• Setting up of an **Internal Audit Department** that implements and monitors the anti-fraud controls of the organisation in combatting financial fraud. The Department will be responsible for promoting good corporate practice and monitoring the ethical climate in the organisation. • Setting up of **a whistleblower policy** and ethics hotlines for anonymous reporting of fraud, corruption and other corporate wrongdoing.
Communities
• **Assess** the potential environmental, health and community impact of the firm's operation. • Collaborate with **educational institutions** and provide scholarships to young maritime talents. • Motivate your employees to get involved in the environmental activities of the community and give financial aid to nonprofit organisations.

Source: Authors

8 Conclusion

In this chapter we made a holistic presentation of the special environmental, economic and social challenges of the shipping sector and we concluded that there are many CSR issues that are crucially relevant to the shipping industry. In our attempt to give a holistic approach on the topic we examined also the financial relevance of CSR more broadly, drawing on scholar and empirical work that has been conducted in the field. We gave special emphasis to explaining the concept of CSR, describing the skepticism towards a business case, as well as the arguments in favour of its financial relevance.

Based on the strength of these arguments, as well as the enormity of evidence from the empirical literature, we support the thesis that CSR can lead to the generation of sustainable comparative advantages and via this avenue to improved operating/financial performance and reduced exposures to various risks. Within the specific framework of the shipping industry, we suggest that shipowners should examine the business impact of CSR initiatives and to initiate their integration in the operation of their firms. We advocate that shipping companies should raise the CSR levels of their activities both at the offices and on board the ships of their fleet. To that end, this chapter provides some practical guidelines that shipping companies could follow in order to tackle the social and environmental challenges of the sector. Member states, voluntary bodies and shipping companies should cooperate in sharing best practices on CSR and shaping the business agenda on responsibility and competitiveness.

References

Albuquerque, R., Durnev, A., & Koskinen, Y. (2013). *Corporate social responsibility and firm risk: Theory and empirical evidence*, No 9533. Centre for Economic Policy Research (CEPR) Discussion Papers, London.

Alexander, G. J., & Buchholz, R. A. (1978). Corporate social responsibility stock market responsibility. *Academy of Management Journal, 21*, 479–486.

Altschuller, S. A., & Smith, G. A. (2001). *Making corporate social responsibility systemic*. Executive Counsel, Feb/Mar.

Anderson, D. (2006). The critical importance of sustainability risk management. *Risk Management, 53*(4), 66.

Anderson, D., & Anderson, K. E. (2009). Sustainability risk management. *Risk Management and Insurance Review, 12*(1), 25–38.

Andreou, P. C., Louca, C., & Panayides, P. M. (2014). Corporate governance, financial management decisions and firm performance: Evidence from the maritime industry. *Transportation Research Part E: Logistics and Transportation Review, 63*, 59–78.

Aupperle, K. E., Carroll, A. B., & Hatfield, J. D. (1985). An empirical examination of the relationship between corporate social responsibility profitability. *Academy of Management Journal, 28*, 446–463.

Barnett, M. L., & Salomon, R. M. (2012). Does it pay to be really good? Addressing the shape of the relationship between social and financial performance. *Strategic Management Journal, 33*(11), 1304–1320.

Baron, D. P. (2001). Private politics, corporate social responsibility, and integrated strategy. *Journal of Economics and Management Strategy, 10*, 7–45.

Boatright, J. R. (2011). Risk management and the responsible corporation: How sweeping the invisible hand? *Business and Society Review, 116*(1), 145–170.

Boutin-Dufresne, F., & Savaria, P. (2004). Corporate social responsibility and financial risk. *Journal of Investing, 13*(1), 57–66.

Burke, L., & Logsdon, J. M. (1996). How corporate social responsibility pays off. *Long Range Planning, 29*, 495–502.

Cheng, T. C. E., & Choy, P. W. C. (2007). Measuring success factors of quality management in the shipping industry. *Maritime Economics and Logistics, 9*(3), 234–253.

Cheng, T. C. E., & Choy, P. W. C. (2013). A study of the relationships between quality management practices and organizational performance in the shipping industry. *Maritime Economics & Logistics, 15*(1), 1–31.

Clarkson, M. E. (1995). A stakeholder framework for analyzing and evaluating corporate social performance. *Academy of Management Review, 20*(1), 92–117.

Coleman, L. (2009). *Risk strategies: Dialing up optimum firm risk*. Gower Publishing Ltd.

Doane, D., & Abasta-Vilaplana, N. (2005). The myth of CSR. *Stanford Social Innovation Review, 3* (3), 22–29.

Drobetz, W., Merikas, A., Merika, A., & Tsionas, M. G. (2014). Corporate social responsibility disclosure: The case of international shipping. *Transportation Research Part E: Logistics and Transportation Review, 71*, 18–44.

Fafaliou, R., Lekakou, M., & Theotokas, I. (2006). Is the European shipping industry aware of corporate social responsibility? The case of Greek-owned short sea shipping companies. *Marine Policy, 30*(4), 412–419.

Freeman, R. E. (1984). *Strategic management: A stakeholder approach*. Boston: Pitman.

Friedman, M. (1970). *The social responsibility of business is to increase its profits*. New York.

Frynas, J. G. (2009). *Beyond corporate social responsibility – Oil multinationals and social challenges*. Cambridge, UK: Cambridge University Press.

Frynas, J. G. (2012). Corporate social responsibility or government regulation? Evidence on oil spill prevention. *Ecology and Society, 17*(4), 4.

Galbreath, G. (2009). Building corporate social responsibility into strategy. *European Business Review, 21*(2), 109–127.

Godfrey, P. C. (2005). The relationship between corporate philanthropy and shareholder wealth: A risk management perspective. *Academy of Management Review, 30*(4), 777–798.

Grewal, D., & Darlow, N. J. (2007). The business paradigm for corporate social reporting in the context of Australian seaports. *Maritime Economics and Logistics, 9*(2), 172–192.

Griffin, J. J., & Mahon, J. F. (1997). The corporate social performance and corporate financial performance debate twenty-five years of incomparable research. *Business and Society, 36*(1), 5–31.

Hillman, A. J., & Keim, G. D. (2001). Shareholder value, stakeholder management, and social issues: What's the bottom line? *Strategic Management Journal, 22*(2), 125–139.

Hopkins, M. (2004). *Corporate social responsibility: An issues paper*. Policy Integration Department, World Commission on the Social Dimension of Globalization, International Labour Office, Working Paper No. 27. Geneva: International Labour Organization.

Husted, B. W. (2005). Risk management, real options, and corporate social responsibility. *Journal of Business Ethics, 60*, 175–183.

Husted, B. W., & Allen, D. B. (2011). *Corporate social strategy: Stakeholder engagement and competitive advantage*. Cambridge: Cambridge University Press.

IMO. (2014). *Third IMO Greenhouse Gas Study*. www.imo.org/en/OurWork/Environment/PollutionPrevention/AirPollution/Documents/Third%20Greenhouse%20Gas%20Study/GHG3%20Executive%20Summary%20and%20Report.pdf. Accessed 1 December 2015.

ISO. (2010). *ISO 26000 Standard*. www.iso.org/iso/home/standards/iso26000.htm26000. Accessed 1 December 2015.

Jensen, M. C. (2002). Value maximization, stakeholder theory, and the corporate objective function. *Business Ethics Quarterly, 12*(02), 235–256.

Kavussanos, M., & Tsouknidis, D. (2015). Corporate social responsibility performance and firm performance in the global shipping industry. In *6th National Conference of the Financial Engineering and Banking Society (FEBS)*, 20–21 December, Piraeus, Greece.

Kunnaala, V., Rasi, M., & Stogard, J. (2013). *Corporate social responsibility and shipping: Views of Baltic Sea shipping companies of the benefits of responsibility*. Publications of the Centre for Maritime Studies University of Turku, A70.

Lu, C. S., Lin, C. C., & Tu, C. J. (2009). Corporate social responsibility and organisational performance in container shipping. *International Journal of Logistics Research and Applications, 12*(2), 119–132.

Lubin, D., & Esty, D. (2010). The sustainability imperative. *Harvard Business Review*, 43–50.

Margolis, J. D., Elfenbein, H., & Walsh, J. (2009). *Does it Pay to be Good... and Does it Matter? A meta-analysis and redirection of research on corporate social and financial performance*. Harvard University Working Paper.

Margolis, J. D., & Walsh, J. P. (2003). Misery loves companies: Rethinking social initiatives by business. *Administrative Science Quarterly, 48*(2), 268–305.

Mitchell, R. K., Agle, B. R., & Wood, D. J. (1997). Toward a theory of stakeholder identification and salience: Defining the principle of who and what really counts. *Academy of Management Review, 22*(4), 853–886.

Oikonomou, I., Brooks, C., & Pavelin, S. (2012). The impact of corporate social performance on financial risk and utility: A longitudinal analysis. *Financial Management, 41*(2), 483–515.

Orlitzky, M., & Benjamin, J. D. (2001). Corporate social responsibility firm risk: A meta-analytic review. *Business Society, 40*, 369–396.

Orlitzky, M., Schmidt, F. L., & Rynes, S. L. (2003). Corporate social and financial performance: A meta-analysis. *Organization Studies, 24*(3), 403–441.

Poulovassilis, A., & Meidanis, S. (2013). *Sustainability of shipping – Addressing corporate social responsibility through management systems*. www.commonlawgic.org/sustainability-of-shipping.html. Accessed 1 December 2015.

Schröder, M. (2014). Financial effects of corporate social responsibility: A literature review. *Journal of Sustainable Finance and Investment, 4*(4), 337–350.

Sharfman, M., & Fernando, C. (2008). Environmental risk management and the cost of capital. *Strategic Management Journal, 29*, 569–592.

Sharma, S., & Vredenburg, H. (1998). Proactive corporate environmental strategy and the development of competitively valuable organizational capabilities. *Strategic Management Journal, 19*(8), 729–753.

Siegel, D., & Vitaliano, D. (2007). An empirical analysis of the strategic use of corporate social responsibility. *Journal of Economics and Management Strategy, 16*, 773–792.
Sprinkle, B. G., & Maines, A. L. (2010). The benefits and costs of corporate social responsibility. *Business Horizons, 53*(5), 445–453.
UNEP. (2003). *Risk on trial: The changing face of non-quantitative risk*. United Nations Environmental Programme Finance Initiatives.
Venkatraman, N., & Ramanujam, V. (1986). Measurement of business performance in strategy research: A comparison of approaches. *Academy of Management Review, 11*(4), 801–814.
Waddock, S. A., & Graves, S. B. (1997). The corporate social performance - Financial performance link. *Strategic Management Journal, 18*(4), 303–319.
Wong, A. (2014). CSR: A perspective of non-financial risk management in China. In G. Eweje (Ed.), *Corporate social responsibility and sustainability: Emerging trends in developing economics, critical studies on corporate responsibility, governance and sustainability* (Vol. 8, pp. 323–345). Emerald Group Publishing Limited.

Impacts of CSR on Women in the Maritime Sector

Momoko Kitada and Pamela Tansey

1 Introduction

This chapter offers a comprehensive view of the development of women's integration in the maritime sector and examines the impact of corporate social responsibility (CSR) initiatives by shipping companies on gender equality and equity in shipping. CSR often includes gender equality within their diversity policies in line with other CSR elements. However, this paper argues that the inclusion of gender issues within a wider norm of diversities might have weakened the voice of women. The impact of CSR also seems to be limited to large shipping companies only, because medium and small firms are unlikely to be motivated due to their smaller business scales for the promotion of women. The paper recognises the need of combined efforts from both legal and social initiatives to promote women in the maritime industry. A cooperation between public and private sectors will create a synergy effect to promote maritime women from international to national levels.

After the millennium, the idea of CSR has been widely accepted among large companies as part of their marketing strategies. Some shipping companies also responded well to this strategic business trend. CSR often includes gender equality within their diversity policies in line with other CSR elements, such as safety, environmental protection, ecology, energy efficiency and so on. CSR has indeed made a positive impact on gender equality by employing more women in the shipping industry. Nonetheless, this paper argues that the inclusion of gender issues within a wider norm of diversities might have weakened the voice of women. The

M. Kitada (✉)
World Maritime University, Malmö, Sweden
e-mail: mk@wmu.se

P. Tansey
London, UK
e-mail: Tanseyconsult@yahoo.com

L. L. Froholdt (ed.), *Corporate Social Responsibility in the Maritime Industry*, WMU Studies in Maritime Affairs 5, https://doi.org/10.1007/978-3-319-69143-5_13

impact of CSR also seems to be limited to large shipping companies only, because medium and small firms are unlikely to be motivated due to their smaller business scales for the promotion of women.

The paper recognises the need of combined efforts from both legal and social initiatives to promote women in the maritime industry. While encouraging the industry's voluntary initiatives on gender equality and equity, legal instruments developed by the International Labour Organization (ILO) as well as global initiatives created by the International Maritime Organization (IMO) are both effective tools for the integration of women in the maritime sector. A cooperation between public and private sectors will create a synergy effect to promote maritime women from international to national levels.

2 Institutional Development to Support Gender Equality in the Maritime Sector

Women appeared as sailors in the maritime history in the eighteenth century and those heroines, such as Anne Bonny and Mary Read, added excitement in the male-dominated maritime story-telling. Gender has not been openly discussed in the international shipping until the International Maritime Organization (IMO) established formal institutional structures and awareness-building from 1988 onwards. At the genesis of the programme, the concept was aligned with the UN's generic approach of Women in Development (WID), changing later to the Integration of Women in the Maritime Sector. At the end of 1980s, only a limited number of maritime education and training (MET) institutions opened their doors to female students to study maritime subjects and prepare for seafaring jobs. It was a bottle neck phenomenon to produce female maritime professionals to the industry, because the industry tends to appreciate seafaring experiences even for shore-based positions (Langåker 2015). The neglect of women in shipping was a serious concern from the perspective of IMO's Integrated Technical Cooperation Programme (ITCP). The United Nations (UN) system emphasises gender equality through various instruments, including the 1995 Beijing Declaration, the Millennium Development Goals (MDGs), and the Sustainable Development Goals (SDGs), which affect the IMO governance through approval by the Technical Cooperation Committee of a series of strategies for the advancement of women in the maritime sector (Tansey 2015). With the effort of IMO, the topic of gender slowly became a common agenda in the shipping industry to address both internationally and nationally.

Attention to women in the shipping industry appeared to be more significant in conjunction with the discussion of a shortage of seafarers, with the IMO study of 1993 which highlighted the areas of shortfall in specialized maritime power, followed in 1995 when the first manpower report was published by BIMCO/ISF (1995). The shipping industry explored ideas for a solution to increase a number of seafarers to meet the future demand. One of the suggestions was to promote more women into seafaring professions which have been traditionally male-dominated.

Such an awareness for women seafarers was clearly documented in the International Convention on Standards of Training, Certification and Watchkeeping for Seafarers (STCW), 1978 as Amended (IMO 2011); The 'Manila Amendment' of STCW in 2010 includes the 'Resolution 14: Promotion of the participation of women in the maritime industry' adopted in the Final Act of the Conference of Parties to STCW (IMO 2010).

The responsibilities of shipowners in terms of women seafarers were stated in the Maritime Labour Convention (MLC), 2006 by the International Labour Organization (ILO). Flag states which ratified the MLC, 2006[1] must ensure separate sleeping rooms and separate sanitary facilities for men and women (ILO 2006). For more general terms to protect women in the maritime sector, other international instruments, including the Convention on the Elimination of All Forms of Discrimination against Women (CEDAW)[2] by UN, and the Maternity Protection Convention (C183)[3] by ILO, are also applicable for those ratified countries.

While such political efforts from the public sector support women in the maritime industry, what has the private sector done for gender issues in the past decades? In many industries, gender segregation is still commonly observed. Vertical gender segregation is broadly observed in many organisations where typically male managers and female clerks are divided in terms of their responsibilities and power within. Horizontal gender segregation is another form in which either men or women are dominated and gendered values and norms may have a strong influence.

This paper focuses on the impact of corporate social responsibility (CSR) initiatives by shipping companies and other maritime corporations in terms of gender equality and equity. It relates to the current business and management practices in the maritime sector and the paper begins with how organisations are generally ignorant about gender and in what context women workers are situated in overall.

3 Gendered organisation

The description of organisations and management tends to be biased through the lens of male managers and executives who are in the frontline of the business world (Townsley 2003). Marshall (2000, p. 171) also notes that organisations have been mostly studied by male scholars and researchers and "do not incorporate pluralist appreciations". Assumptions that organisations are gender-neutral can be a challenge to promote women in leadership and management unless they understand that organisations are gendered in multiple ways (Acker 1990). Ethics of business

---

[1]As of 01 November 2016, 80 countries have ratified the MLC, 2006.

[2]As of 20 June 2016, the CEDAW was ratified by 189 states while 2 states (the USA and Alaska) are signatory.

[3]As of 01 November 2016, 32 ratifications were made for the Maternity Protection Convention (C183).

corporations may become questionable if organisations apply a socially constructed assumption in their practice and ideology that men are the standard measurement (Larson and Freeman 1997). Feminists explain that women are assigned to be reproduction roles while men engage in production, supporting a gender role theory in a patriarchal system (Delphy 1984). Although there are reasonable evidences that women's traditional gender roles would have an impact on today's organisations, it is also important to look into how theories of organisations and feminism have been developed and what gaps still remain in the world of business.

Organisations began to be discussed in gender theories concurrently with the occurrence of 'third-wave feminism' in which they argue that second-wave feminism emphasises a hegemonic view to privilege white, middle-class, heterosexual women, ignoring heterogeneous women's identities (Harding et al. 2013) whilst the first-wave feminism fought for women's enfranchisement. This opened up the feminist approaches in those times from European/American-centric scientific knowledge to a more global and transnational knowledge system. Hence, the debates about organisations and management from those postmodern feminist perspectives are more accommodating to diversified men and women in the business strategies and practices.

Some scholars acknowledge this diversified nature of organisations. Butler (1990) believes that it is possible to construct our own gender by choosing gendered behaviour that we think appropriate. Although the ideas about 'feminine' women and 'masculine' men are produced, people can cause 'gender trouble' by going against conventional ideas about gender and change how gender operates with them. Goffman (1979) also criticises how gender displays tend to be based on social expectations about men and women: being dominants and subordinates by nature. Such a relationship between men as managers and women as clerks is still observed in organisations in both public and private sectors. Organisations where vertical gender segregation is displayed are expected to evolve into a modern organisational structure in which men and women are given equal opportunities in career development.

In contrast to vertical gender segregation, the maritime industry is often characterised as horizontal gender segregation, which in this case excludes women's participation, such as seafarers, engineers, ship inspectors, and naval architects. Acker (1990) pays attention to 'gendered institutions' underpinning the organisational logic which creates or reinforces a gendered organisational structure. Such gendered institutions can be also observed on board ships (Kitada and Langåker 2016). Gendered organisations need to be critically assessed from political, economic, environmental, institutional, and cultural perspectives in order to be sustainable.

Although various legal instruments exist at a national level, some prevent hegemonic masculinity in organisations while others technically facilitate the process of reproducing gendered components in a social system. For example, the Swedish Equality law 13 §, chapter 3 within the Swedish Discrimination Act ('Diskrimineringslagen' in Swedish) requires that "employers with more than 25 employees should establish a plan for their future equality work concerning gender, ethnicity, religion and other beliefs" every 3 years (Flykt and Holmberg 2015, p. 3). Such legal instrument is expected to reinforce a Swedish shared value of gender equality to be institutional. On the other hand, the Japanese tax system is designed based on the assumption that female workers engage in domestic work and part-time jobs are the best ideal under the protection from their male breadwinners. This illustrates how legislations can endorse a patriarchal system in a society.

The question arises how CSR can support organisations themselves to be autonomous in order to regulate their structure and practices beyond a company's legal responsibilities. What is the organisational responsibility of normalising their gender balance and recognise women's capabilities fairly according to their policies from a sustainability viewpoint?

4 Managing Diversity: A Feminist Approach to CSR

In the last century, the so-called era of neo-liberal economy, significant industrial development has been achieved, particularly in the Global North, including the West Europe, the United States, Canada, and Japan. The Global South represents the majority of Africa, South-East Asia, Pacific islands as well as some countries from Caribbean, South America, and Middle-East, which are typically below the world GDP per capita (IMF 2015). This North-South Divide, which privileged the North by colonising the South, has in fact facilitated the process of economic problems, such as poverty, health problems and income inequalities. Feminists criticise that within the scope of neoliberalism, the majority of decision-making in politics and economy was made in a masculinist way. One good example can be drawn from a disastrous accident of the space shuttle, Challenger. Maier (2012) critises a masculinist decision-making and managerial process which failed to listen to a number of warnings and recommendations. Consequently, this accelerated the process of marginalisation of women in the labour market (Eisenstein 2009). A lesson from masculinist business models alerts the importance of women's participation in management and leadership in the industries in order not to repeat the same 'mistakes' that those decision-makers had made in the past.

CSR has been paid much attention today as the responsibilities of corporations are increasingly concerned in the capitalist economy, driving a much faster process of globalisation. Business operational patterns are becoming so complex to survive in a highly competitive business environment that they sometimes go beyond the reach of the law. Indeed, a large number of shipowners register their vessels in an open registry. The responsibility of shipowners is therefore 'conveniently' limited within the bounds of law. Although their motivation for open registries ended in creating the crew to be multinational, shipowners can neglect their responsibility over the crew because the ships are not under their national flag. On the other hand, today's managers are no longer able to manage people when business structures and practices are so fragmented and outsourced to workers outside their direct management capacity (Kitada and Ölçer 2015). Reducing cost and seeking efficiency are understood as a business strategy for sustainability.

Awareness of economic, social, and environmental sustainability has been increasing and the recent adoption of the United Nation's Sustainable Development Goals (SDGs) reflects the direction of our future goals to be shared. In particular, the SDG 5: 'Achieve gender equality and empower all women and girls' emphasises the importance of gender equality as a key instrument for the world's sustainability (UN 2015). Research shows that better decision making tends to prevail with a wide range of opinions and independent thoughts, including women's perspectives, and it reduces the potential risk of making unethical decisions (Arfken et al. 2004). Ramirez (2003) states that the only ways of achieving meaningful diversity in both the workplace and society is by starting with corporate governance, in particular, boards of directors in corporations; if diversity is overlooked in corporate governance, it could increase a chance of leading to a corporate corruption.

Instead of the profit-making development that people are exploited in one way or another, more people-centered approach described in CSR can be a way forward to pursue sustainable development. Gender equality is often discussed within diversity issues in organisations under CSR. A reference to diversity as a workplace issue is common in CSR initiatives. Modern organisations need to address such diversity issues in their policies and visions in order to stand as being socially responsible. CSR also requires such policies and visions to transform to actions. Diversity management is an ongoing process that many organisations are expected to participate as part of their CSR. Creating diversity within the organisation also implies a positive organisational change and this is an unavoidable process to achieve gender equality in the organisation. In particular, the maritime industry which is led by mostly men should be targeted to promote diversity and evolve their organisational structure in order to achieve sustainable business.

5 Women at Sea: Training and Employment

Women have been regarded as minority organizational members in the maritime industry (Kitada and Langåker 2016). The percentage of women seafarers was reported as approximately 1 or 2% (Belcher et al. 2003; Drewry, ILO, and ITF 2009). This estimation includes women in non-operational sections, such as hotel and catering; therefore, female deck officers and engineers are much less on cargo ships, at 0.12% of the total seafaring population (Drewry, ILO, and ITF 2009). The recent BIMCO/ICS manpower report indicates that women represent approximately 1% of their large survey sample (BIMCO and ICS 2016). Despite a lack of periodic surveys for women seafarers, it is assumed that the actual number of women seafarers have not significantly increased over the years.

This slow development is not accidental. Whilst the second feminist wave created an awareness of gender equality in 1980s, the maritime industry lagged behind this trend for years. Until the IMO's first initiative in 1988, there were a limited number of maritime education and training (MET) institutions around the world which accepted women to enroll in nautical or engineering courses.[4] This bottle neck phenomenon caused a serious gender-imbalance in the industry, because shore-based maritime industries wanted personnel with seafaring experiences and it automatically excluded women from employment opportunities in the maritime industry. A systematic error that women are under-utilised human resources has to be corrected. Thanks to the efforts by the IMO member states which support the Technical Cooperation Committee of a series of strategies for the advancement of women in the maritime sector, more MET institutions started to open a door for female students, for example, in China (Zhang and Zhao 2015), Japan (Kitada 2015b), Bangladesh (Hussain 2014), and Egypt (Saeed 2015).

These efforts made by some MET institutions have created a positive outcome that more women are now able to access to MET. However, such positive trend in education and training would not be effective if shipping companies made limited efforts to employ female graduates from the MET institutions. In fact, the biggest challenge for female cadets is often an access to ships where they receive onboard training for 12 months in total in order to meet the condition of obtaining a license called a Certificate of Competence (CoC) based on the STCW convention. Tifuh (2014) highlights that some female cadets could not make it for receiving a CoC because they were not accepted to work on board by shipping companies. The reasons why shipping companies do not want to recruit women are typically two claims: (1) the lack of experience of recruiting women seafarers; and (2) stereo-types that women are neither physically nor emotionally suitable for working at sea. In both cases, a clear evidence is lacking to suggest that women cannot work on board. In fact, there are women seafarers who perform as good as, or even better than, men. This indicates that some shipping companies are not fulfilling their CSR by refusing women's entry without reasonable explanations.

This paper addresses two concerns in terms of gender and CSR in shipping. First, large shipping companies tend to have more resources and capitals than medium/small ones and this indeed influences their attitudes to respond to CSR, because the impact on their business is bigger. Although large shipping companies occupy a great portion of tonnage in the world, the number of seafarers assigned to each ship does not change. In other words, medium/small shipping companies which operate smaller scales of shipping business need to be equally encouraged to consider CSR and their economic, social, and environmental impacts. Second, diversity issues within CSR could mask gender issues as one of many diversity elements that organisations need to address. Especially in shipping, it is possible that shipowners, who are benefiting multinational crew as cheap labour force to deploy on board their ships, make a small effort for their multinational crew and defend that they are dealing with diversity issues under CSR, without emphasising gender aspects. Today, a multinational crew is a norm in modern shipping and the term, 'diversity'

[4]Former Soviet Union was known as having a large number of women seafarers in 1930s. Markwick and Cardona (2012) report that approximately 21,000 women worked as sailors and other related roles in Navy during the war, but the Navy was still far from female friendly.

could refer to them only partially and neglect women from the industry. Hence, gender issues should continue to be emphasised and reminded from time to time including and not only when CSR is discussed.

6 Gender and CSR from the Maritime Industry Perspectives

The relevance of CSR to gender equality can be found in various discussions, including the papers presented at the 2nd International Conference on Maritime Women: Global Leadership in Malmö, Sweden in 2014, hosted by the World Maritime University (WMU) in conjunction with IMO.[5] According to the conference-based book (Kitada et al. 2015), all these elements are, to a greater or lesser extent, relevant to CSR. Just to take an example of women seafarers, it is evident that CSR should promote gender equality policies, career development support, MET and research, leadership training, and resourcing women professionals as qualified seafarers for the sustainable shipping. The book draws a conclusion that gender equality is culturally under-developed throughout various maritime sectors. The role of CSR is hereby revisited from the articles of the book, contributed from the authors with various backgrounds around the world.

6.1 Gender Equality Policies and Women's Leadership

The global initiatives of promoting women in the maritime sector started by the IMO since 1988. Tansey (2015) describes how strategically the IMO has worked on gender issues by different phases. The first phase (1988–1996) established the formal institutional structures and awareness-building through the Integration of Women in the Maritime Sector (IWMS). The second phase (1997–2004) focused on the activities supporting capacity-building as well as fostering regional co-operation. Based on such foundation work, the third phase (from 2004 onwards) is being dedicated to the strategic development of regional associations for maritime women professionals.

Another global facilitator for the promotion of women in the maritime transport is the International Transport Workers' Federation (ITF), which primarily concerns the decent work of transport workers, including gender equality. ITF is known as a global union organisation in which member unions represent 148 countries worldwide. It includes approximately 700 unions, representing over 4.5 million workers in all transport sectors, including air, rail, road and sea. The representation of women in the unions are as low as 13–17% of the total membership. The ITF launched a

[5]The 1st Conference on Empowerment of Women in the Maritime World was held in 2008.

leadership programme for women, called 'Leading Change' and women activists in their affiliate unions within the maritime sections were invited to participate in 2011 for the first time. This attempt was received in success and the demand for a leadership programme was in fact spread out to both men and women (McGarry 2015).

The examples of IMO and ITF demonstrate the importance of women's networks to increase their visibility and voices. Meanwhile, capacity-building activities, including training for leadership, are found to be effective and successful in both cases. Pastra et al. (2015) investigated the state-owned shipping companies in Greece in terms of the Board Characteristics, such as CEO duality, board size, independent directors, cross directorships, tenure, age and gender. Their study highlight the underrepresentation of women in Boards and indicate good corporate practice would promote equal opportunities for women. Cevallos (2015) describes how the Ecuadorian Navy-owned oil transport company culturally excludes women from leadership and management. The lack of gender sensitivity in the organisation resulted in the underrepresentation of women and this can be a serious concern from an ethical viewpoint.

However, does the absence of women leaders in the maritime sector mean that women are not good leaders? Ortega et al. (2015) investigated both self-assessments and co-worker assessments of maritime officers' leadership skills, using the MLQ-5X leadership questionnaire. Their research found that female maritime officers over-estimated the level of negative leadership skill they had while under-estimated the level of their positive leadership skill instead. Interestingly, male maritime officers showed the opposite tendency and it suggests that women should understand they are better leaders than they think. Unlike technical maritime fields like seafaring and engineering that are overwhelmingly male-dominated, the field of law exhibits a slightly different landscape. Wouters (2015) describes that no overt discrimination against women is observed in laws and female enrollment percentage in the Advanced Master in Transport & Maritime Law at the University of Antwerp has been increasing from 35% in 2009–2010 to 50% in 2013–2014. Notwithstanding, her research informs that attrition rates among young women are disproportionately high in both Belgium and the Netherlands and there seems to be a relationship between withdrawing women and their lack of self-confidence.

6.2 *Career Development for Maritime Women*

One of the reasons to the low representation of women in the maritime industry is a small population of women at an entry level. This problem was highlighted by Mackenzie (2015), pointing out that women in STEM (Science, Technology, Engineering and Mathematics) fields remain much fewer than men in the UK where only 8.7% of professional engineers are women. Fewer women in STEM fields mean that potential women who choose the maritime industry for their career are equally low. With a growing potential in STEM areas in the UK maritime and offshore oil & gas industries, a number of recommendations were given to various stakeholders to increase the number of female engineers (Matchtech and IMarEST n.d.). Among those recommended actions, for instance, to encourage industry participation in local schools and to showcase the opportunities for women in engineering are good examples of CSR.

The evidence from the Caribbean (Grant and Grant 2015) confirms that gender bias still exists in the maritime sector despite the existence of organisational polices on gender equality. Their paper identifies the lack of effective enforcement mechanisms as a problem, indicating a systematic pitfall that women are left behind their career development in the maritime industry. Another example from Turkey highlights the challenges and disadvantages that Turkish women seafarers experienced during their careers, for example a work-life balance (Basak 2015). This view is also acknowledged by Kitada (2015a) and her research showcases the examples of mother seafarers who have faced extremely difficult situations by leaving their children ashore while working at sea. In fact, work-life balance problems are not only about women but also men. In this regard, shipping companies are encouraged to provide support and provisions for their employees who spend a majority of their lives at sea. To provide better conditions for a more balanced work-life relationship in the maritime industry through CSR will promote a more sustainable industry.

The importance of having a mentor to build women's self-confidence is suggested by Özdemir and Albayrak (2015). Women's professional networks, such as the IMO's regional women's associations as well as the Women's International Shipping and Trading Association (WISTA), are particularly useful for providing mentors to support women in leadership and management (Orsel 2015). While these mentorship programmes outside their own organisations would stimulate and inspire young women to meet their role models, what can their work organisations do for the employees? Employees' self-esteem directly relates to the productivity of the company. If employees quit because of the lack of motivation and career development opportunities, it would generate a big loss in human resources and investment of the company. Hence, the companies, especially in the maritime sector, foreseeing the future demand of maritime professionals, should consider how men and women in their organisations can be equally motivated and encouraged to maximise their potentials to serve the organisations. Social responsibilities of corporations thereby need to be reconsidered to include such professional support.

6.3 Transforming Maritime Education and Research for Sustainable Shipping

Maritime Education and Training (MET) is a specific STEM fields dedicated to seafaring jobs in a narrower yet commonly adopted definition. Cars and Österman (2015) examine how gender equality is addressed in the curricula of MET in three Nordic countries, namely Sweden, Norway, and Denmark. Because of the STCW convention which fundamentally determines the MET curricula, gender issues were not explicitly mentioned and a lack of clear strategy for gender-conscious pedagogy was observed throughout the sample countries. Since MET plays an important role to feed qualified personnel to the industry, it is a serious concern that the learning experience in MET does not promote gender equality, because it can be translated to the maritime sector where they will work after graduation. On the one hand, Chen (2015) reports that female students in the Massachusetts Maritime Academy (MMA), USA, mostly achieved higher performance rates in the academic years between 2010 and 2013. It implies that the shipping industry is perhaps missing out potential highly skilled workers—women—every year.

In the marine science field, Marins and da Costa (2015) explain that Brazilian women scholarship in oceanography outnumbered males since 2010, thanks to a special science network programme by the National Institutes of Science and Technology. Nonetheless, according to the "scientific productivity" indicator that shows the highest level of research scholarships in Brazil, the percentage of women never reached 30% of the total approved grants. Their paper calls for women's scientific leadership to increase the strengths of Brazilian oceanography.

Highly qualified female maritime and marine professionals are an asset to the industry. Baya (2015) suggests that the companies should consider to support educational institutions and invest in future leaders for the industry. The linkage between the education sector and the industry will mutually benefit as indicated by the triple bottom line: "People, Planet, and Profit" in the sustainable business model characterised by CSR. The importance of CSR in sustainable business is useful particularly in those economic emergence of so-called BRIC countries (Brazil, Russia, India, and China). A rapid economic growth in those countries anticipates an unpredictable large impact on the global environment. Transport sectors in China have grown in the last few decades and there is a high demand for maritime officers. Zhang and Zhao (2015) identify that the attitudes of shipping companies are problematic in terms of the recruitment of women seafarers in China. Their data showed that shipping managers were reluctant to employ women seafarers because of the complication arisen from the Chinese labour law which protects women from physical intensity on the job as well as other protection measures for women during menstruation, pregnancy, childbirth and maternity periods. Their research suggests that the maritime industry should establish its CSR which promotes gender equality in the profession. Stevenson (2015) also notes that good corporate practices will help the integration of women in the maritime sector and suggests that upgrading the employment package would actually help both male and female officers from a human resource management viewpoint.

Maritime professions are not limited to seafaring jobs which often require a long-time separation from home, which can be difficult for women to continue their careers. Calderon et al. (2015) indicate that ship inspection offers new job opportunities for women because inspection techniques are evolving in the last several years. In order to deploy the best qualified personnel in the maritime sector, the career-cycle model needs to be developed for sustainable shipping. While focusing on their own business sustainability, maritime-related companies would benefit from the idea of CSR to explore how their business could make a difference in improving the total efficiency of the industry and promoting women as contributors to the process of sustainable development.

7 Good Practices: CSR Examples Relating to Maritime Women

This paper points out a general trend of slow progress in promoting women in the maritime industries. Organisational, structural, and cultural barriers have been creating a long battle for maritime women to acquire a proper recognition as maritime professionals. However, though the number is small, there are some good practices from the maritime industry around the world to promote women as part of their CSR.

For example, as discussed in Chap. 6, The A.P. Moller–Maersk presents a good practice of launching a diversity and inclusion strategy, which aims to increase the representation of women in management, as well as implementing a new maternity policy to support women's career cycles. Their policy guarantees minimum of 18 weeks maternity leave on full pay for all employees in their company worldwide.[6] The Shipping Corporation of India established a policy to assign two women seafarers at a time on the same vessel. This approach is perceived to be helpful especially when women seafarers are at an early stage of their maritime careers.[7] Another example is the Celebrity Cruises: their mission states that they plan to have a diverse and inclusive workforce by 2020. The percentage of female deck officers in the Celebrity Cruises was 5% in 2015, but they have achieved to increase the figure to 18% in only 2 years.[8]

These examples are seen as positive responses from the maritime industry to overcome the organisational, structural, and cultural barriers to the promotion of women under CSR. Good practices may not be easily adopted in different environments as "one size does not fit all". However, by sharing good practices, CSR goes beyond a mere concept and becomes a powerful tool to promote gender equality in the maritime sector.

[6]See the press release form the A.P. Moller–Maersk, 'Maersk Group introduces improved maternity benefits worldwide' dated 14 January 2016.

[7]Capt. Anuradha Jha of the Shipping Corporation of India presented a paper titled "My journey as a seafarer" at the 2nd International Conference on Maritime Women: Global Leadership (MWGL 2014).

[8]The presentation made by the Celebrity Cruises at the CMA Shipping 2017 (Connecticut Maritime Association 32nd Annual Shipping Conference and Exhibition), Stamford, on 20–22 March 2017.

8 Conclusion

Women are generally under-utilised human resources in the maritime sector. Despite cultural and social biases that women typically experience, the effects of global initiatives driven by the IMO and ILO are evident. Many studies on women in the maritime sector, including seafaring, ship inspection, maritime education, maritime law, oceanography, and maritime management, call for strong support from the private sector to fulfill their CSR to promote women in the organisations. In this regard, CSR should be the arrow to promote women. By sharing good practices, maritime corporations would be able to increase their corporate performance and ethical awareness, which often directly affect the business outcomes. Shipping as a traditionally male-dominated industry should not hesitate to go beyond its tradition and corporate culture and to encourage women's participation in the sector. Shipping has crossed its boundaries in pursuit of effectiveness; therefore, there will be a potential in the shipping industry to lead other industries towards gender equality.

The IMO's slogan, "safe, secure and efficient shipping on clean oceans" can be achieved through shared responsibilities among all the maritime stakeholders. In this context, shipping companies and other maritime-related corporations as stakeholders have an important role to continue to push the development of the industry in a sustainable manner. Only a partial effort from either public or private sector cannot achieve the SDGs in the maritime industry. The combined efforts from both legal and social initiatives are indispensable. It is the promise that a cooperation between public and private sectors has the potential to create a synergy effect to promote the employment of women in the maritime industry.

Acknowledgement The authors would like to thank the contributors to the book on "Maritime Women: Global Leadership" to provide insights for this paper.

References

Acker, J. (1990). Hierarchies, jobs, bodies: A theory of gendered organizations. *Gender and Society, 4*, 139–158.

Arfken, D. E., Bellar, S. L., & Helms, M. M. (2004). The ultimate glass ceiling revisited: The presence of women on corporate boards. *Journal of Business Ethics, 50*(2), 177–186.

Basak, A. A. (2015). Women's role in the Turkish and global maritime industry. In M. Kitada, E. Williams, & L. L. Froholdt (Eds.), *Maritime women: Global leadership*. Heidelberg: Springer.

Baya, W. T. (2015). Education for career-building: How women in the maritime industry can use education to improve knowledge, skills, organizational learning and development, and knowledge transfer. In M. Kitada, E. Williams, & L. L. Froholdt (Eds.), *Maritime women: Global leadership*. Heidelberg: Springer.

Belcher, P., Sampson, H., Thomas, M., Veiga, J., & Zhao, M. (2003). *Women seafarers: Global employment policies and practices*. Geneva: International Labour Office.

BIMCO and ICS. (2016). *Manpower report: The global supply and demand for seafarers in 2015*. London: Maritime International Secretariat Services Limited.

BIMCO and ISF. (1995). *Manpower 1995 update: The worldwide demand of and supply for seafarers*. Coventry: University of Warwick.

Butler, J. (1990). *Gender trouble: Feminism and the subversion of identity*. London: Routledge.

Calderon, M., Illing, D., Schipperen, I., & Antão, P. (2015). Improving the current regime for ship safety inspections: Opportunities for technology research and women employment. In M. Kitada, E. Williams, & L. L. Froholdt (Eds.), *Maritime women: Global leadership*. Heidelberg: Springer.

Cars, M. B., & Österman, C. (2015). Mind the gap! Maritime education for gender-equal career advancement. In M. Kitada, E. Williams, & L. L. Froholdt (Eds.), *Maritime women: Global leadership*. Heidelberg: Springer.

Cevallos, M. D. (2015). Participation of Ecuadorian women in the maritime oil transportation sector. In M. Kitada, E. Williams, & L. L. Froholdt (Eds.), *Maritime women: Global leadership*. Heidelberg: Springer.

Chen, Q. (2015). Let numbers speak: Job opportunities and international exchange programs for female maritime cadets. In M. Kitada, E. Williams, & L. L. Froholdt (Eds.), *Maritime women: Global leadership*. Heidelberg: Springer.

Delphy, C. (1984). *Close to home: A materialist analysis of women's oppression*. Amherst: University of Massachusetts Press.

Drewry, ILO, & ITF. (2009). *Manning 2009*. London: Drewry Shipping Consultants.

Eisenstein, H. (2009). *Feminism seduced. How global elites use women's labor and ideas to exploit the world*. Boulder: Paradigm Publishers.

Flykt, S., & Holmberg, J. (2015). *Gender equality, better practiced as workforce diversity: An explorative study on how CSR focusing on gender equality policies is practiced*. Bachelor's thesis. Umeå School of Business and Economics, Umeå University.

Goffman, E. (1979). *Gender advertisements*. Basingstoke: Macmillan.

Grant, C., & Grant, V. (2015). Women in the maritime sector: Surviving and thriving in a man's world—A Caribbean perspective. In M. Kitada, E. Williams, & L. L. Froholdt (Eds.), *Maritime women: Global leadership*. Heidelberg: Springer.

Harding, N., Ford, J., & Fotaki, M. (2013). Is the 'F'-word still dirty? A past, present and future of/for feminist and gender studies in organization. *Organization, 20*(1), 51–65.

Hussain, S. (2014). *Young Bangladeshi Women embarking on blue highways!* Paper presented at the 2nd International Conference on Maritime Women: Global Leadership. 31 March–1 April, Malmö.

ILO. (2006). *The Maritime Labour Convention, 2006*. Geneva: International Labour Organization.

IMF. (2015). *World economic outlook: October 2015*. Washington, DC: International Monetary Fund.

IMO. (2010). Adoption of the final act and any instruments, resolutions and recommendations resulting from the work of the conference. I:\CONF\STCW\2\32.doc.

IMO. (2011). The International Convention on Standards of Training, Certification and Watchkeeping for Seafarers (STCW), 1978 as Amended. 2011 Edition. ISBN: 978-92-801-1528-4.

Kitada, M. (2015a). Absent mother sailors: How possible is it to do the impossible? In M. Kitada, E. Williams, & L. L. Froholdt (Eds.), *Maritime women: Global leadership*. Heidelberg: Springer.

Kitada, M. (2015b). Promoting women in the maritime industry [in Japanese]. *Maritime Transport Studies*. 64. ISSN: 0286-8679.

Kitada, M., & Langåker, L. (2016). *Women seafarers as organizational minority members*. The International Association of Maritime Universities (IAMU) Annual General Assembly, 26-–29 October. Haiphong.

Kitada, M., & Ölçer, A. I. (2015). Managing people and technology: The challenges in CSR and energy efficient shipping. *Research in Transportation Business & Management, 17*, 36–40.

Kitada, M., Williams, E., & Froholdt, L. L. (2015). *Maritime women: Global leadership*. Heidelberg: Springer.

Langåker, L. (2015). *Glass bulkheads in the Norwegian Maritime Industry*. Paper presented at the WMU Women's Association Maritime Soiree. 20 August. Malmö.

Larson, A., & Freeman, R. E. (Eds.). (1997). *Women's studies and business ethics: Towards a new conversation*. New York: Oxford University Press.
Mackenzie, B. (2015). The "Leaky Pipeline": Examining and addressing the loss of women at consecutive career stages in marine engineering, science and technology. In M. Kitada, E. Williams, & L. L. Froholdt (Eds.), *Maritime women: Global leadership*. Heidelberg: Springer.
Maier, M. (2012). "We Have to Make a MANagement Decision": Challenger and the dysfunctions of corporate masculinity. In M. E. Godwyn & J. H. Gittel (Eds.), *Sociology of organizations: Structures and relationships* (pp. 492–509). Thousand Oaks: Pine Forge Press.
Marins, R. V., & da Costa, J. B. (2015). Are women contributing equally to the oceanography science in Brazil? In M. Kitada, E. Williams, & L. L. Froholdt (Eds.), *Maritime women: Global leadership*. Heidelberg: Springer.
Markwick, R. D., & Cardona, E. C. (2012). *Soviet women on the frontline in the second world war*. London: Palgrave MacMillan.
Marshall, J. (2000). Revisiting Simone de Beauvoir: Recognizing feminist contributions to pluralism in organizational studies. *Journal of Management Inquiry, 9*(2), 166–172.
Matchtech and IMarEST. (n.d.). *Mitigating the skills gap in the maritime and offshore oil & gas market*. http://www.imarest.org/policy-news/representing-members/skills-gap/375-mitigating-the-skills-gap-in-the-maritime-and-offshore-oil-a-gas-market/file. Accessed 26 March 2016.
McGarry, A. (2015). Leading change: The ITF Women's Maritime Leadership Programme. In M. Kitada, E. Williams, & L. L. Froholdt (Eds.), *Maritime women: Global leadership*. Heidelberg: Springer.
Orsel, K. (2015). Women in shipping: Navigating to the top. In M. Kitada, E. Williams, & L. L. Froholdt (Eds.), *Maritime women: Global leadership*. Heidelberg: Springer.
Ortega, O. D., Øvergård, K. I., & Henden, V. (2015). Women are better leaders than they think: Gender differences in the self-assessment of leadership skills in the maritime industry. In M. Kitada, E. Williams, & L. L. Froholdt (Eds.), *Maritime women: Global leadership*. Heidelberg: Springer.
Özdemir, P., & Albayrak, T. (2015). How to cope with second-generation gender bias in male-dominated occupations. In M. Kitada, E. Williams, & L. L. Froholdt (Eds.), *Maritime women: Global leadership*. Heidelberg: Springer.
Pastra, A. S., Koufopoulos, D. N., & Gkliatis, I. P. (2015). Board characteristics and the presence of women on the board of directors: The case of the Greek shipping sector. In M. Kitada, E. Williams, & L. L. Froholdt (Eds.), *Maritime women: Global leadership*. Heidelberg: Springer.
Ramirez, S. A. (2003). A flaw in the Sarbanes-Oxley reform: Can diversity in the boardroom quell corporate corruption? *St. John's Law Review, 77*(4), 837–866.
Saeed, L. E. (2015). *Maritime education and training: A gender perspective*. Paper presented at the International Women's Day event, 13 March, Malmö.
Stevenson, C. J. (2015). Sustainable development issues in shipping: Women, the under-represented human resource. In M. Kitada, E. Williams, & L. L. Froholdt (Eds.), *Maritime women: Global leadership*. Heidelberg: Springer.
Tansey, P. (2015). Women at the Helm: 25 years of IMO's gender programme. In M. Kitada, E. Williams, & L. L. Froholdt (Eds.), *Maritime women: Global leadership*. Heidelberg: Springer.
Tifuh, A. N. (2014). *Women merchant mariners: Empowering West African women*. Master's dissertation. Malmö: World Maritime University.
Townsley, N. C. (2003). Review article: Looking back, looking forward. Mapping the gendered theories, voices, and politics of organization. *Organization, 10*, 617.
UN. (2015). *Sustainable development goals*. New York: United Nations.
Wouters, A. (2015). Women leadership in maritime law firms: The Antwerp case. In M. Kitada, E. Williams, & L. L. Froholdt (Eds.), *Maritime women: Global leadership*. Heidelberg: Springer.
Zhang, P., & Zhao, M. (2015). Chinese women seafarers: Past, present and prospects. In M. Kitada, E. Williams, & L. L. Froholdt (Eds.), *Maritime women: Global leadership*. Heidelberg: Springer.

Safety and Risk Management Considerations for CSR

Michael Ekow Manuel

1 Safety and Risk Management Issues in High Risk Industries

Safety has for centuries been a concept that has been relevant to human existence. Maslow's (1943) seminal work in motivation is still acknowledged to be significantly valid, although there has subsequently been significant development in motivation theories in general. His theory recognizes the primary role that safety (in a broad sense) plays in human motivation, indicating that in a hierarchical arrangement of motivation drivers, the need for safety is primary. In more contemporary times there have been wide-ranging discussions on risk, its role in society and increased discourse on its assessment and management (Beck 1992, 2009; Bernstein 1998) and the responsibilities those who assess and manage risk have to the wider society (Giddens 1999). This general increase in the awareness of risk has been in tandem with (perhaps because of) the growth of high-risk industries/organizations/corporate entities including in the maritime industry (Perrow 1999; Freudenburg 1993; Kasperson et al. 2003; Kristiansen 2005; Manuele and Main 2002; Rasmussen and Svedung 2000; Reason 1997; Renn 1992; Selmer-Olsen 2005).

Safety in not necessarily just an "antonym of risk" (Möller et al. 2006). As Manuel (2011) indicates, this can be illustrated by considering the difference between health and sickness; "to say that one is healthy would imply much more than not being sick. There are in turn different degrees of health, best conceptualised as the degree of human resilience against disease-causing influences. Similarly, safety is the degree of organizational or industrial resilience . . . to factors that could cause undesired loss". In an attempt to give a sound theoretical basis for a discussion of "safety" and its practical manifestation in policy, strategy and

M. E. Manuel (✉)
World Maritime University, Malmö, Sweden
e-mail: mem@wmu.se

L. L. Froholdt (ed.), *Corporate Social Responsibility in the Maritime Industry*, WMU Studies in Maritime Affairs 5, https://doi.org/10.1007/978-3-319-69143-5_14

operations, Möller et al. (2006) suggest that safety has to be viewed as either *relative* or *absolute*, *objective* or *subjective*, and note has to be taken of the influence on notions of safety of *uncertainty* and *control.*

Exploring the essence of safety is critical to the determination of what constitutes "corporate responsibility" in this regard. The Oxford Dictionary defines safety as "the condition of being protected from or unlikely to cause danger, risk, or injury; denoting something designed to prevent injury or damage" (Oxford English of Dictionary 2013). While such a definition may suffice for normal conversational contexts it is limited in indicating the absoluteness/relativeness of safety and consequentially the point at which a corporate entity may be deemed to be "responsible" for such safety. How safe is safe enough (Fischhoff et al. 1981)? Absolute safety would suggest that all risks are completely removed. This appears to be impossible. The alternative is a concept of "relative safety" which accommodates a threshold of "residual risk" or "incompressible risk" (Mol 2003) or risk "as low as reasonably practicable (ALARP)", i.e. tolerable, negligible or acceptable risk (International Maritime Organization [IMO] 2002; Fischhoff et al. 1981; Manuele 2013). The latter concept of "relative safety" is a more realistic one.

Underpinning all this is the subjectivity inherent in discourses about risk and safety; both concepts rely heavily on notions of uncertainty—probability and consequence. This means that safety does "lie in the eye of the beholder", so to speak. The subjective assumption of an organization that safety or risk issues have been addressed may differ significantly from the perceptions of its stakeholders, including employees and the wider social community. Furthermore, these subjective perceptions may also significantly differ from real and objective safety linked to the actual hazards that exist in that social context. To adapt and build on an example given by Möller et al. (2006), if A gives B a glass of clear liquid, believing it to be vodka (the subjective perception of A), and B takes it believing it to be water (the subjective perception of B), this does not mitigate the immediate and hazardous effect of the drink on B (and the legal implications for A) if it is indeed strong acid (the objective reality of the hazard)! Similarly, the appropriateness of safety measures from the point of view of a corporate entity may not relate cohesively to that of its stakeholders and neither point of view may relate well to safety from objective hazards.

In light of this and given the difficulty in exactly defining what constitutes "safe" in any social context in absolute and objective terms, one would suggest that a corporate entity addresses its responsibility as regards safety in the following ways:

1. By meeting all legislative and administrative requirements that set a threshold of safety both in the internal and external environments of the organization (based on macro-societal analyses of the limits of tolerable/acceptable risk). This involves:

    (a) establishing procedures for accessing knowledge of all relevant legal requirements;
    (b) generating mechanisms for effective compliance/implementation of all such requirements;

    (c) maintaining a system that monitors and evaluates the consistent implementation of requirements and meeting of all obligations.

2. By interrogating the perceptions of safety/risk of its stakeholders (both employees and external stakeholders) with a view to meet the expectations associated with these perceptions in a realistic manner.[1] This involves:
    (a) the identification of all relevant stakeholders;
    (b) establishing a discourse with stakeholders; a multi-directional communication system that allows for disclosure and transparency and the awareness and consideration of stakeholder perceptions.
3. Through the continuous development of a learning culture that proactively explores what constitutes safety and its limits. This in turn would entail:
    (a) generating key safety performance indicators (safety KPIs);
    (b) nurturing a reporting and just culture;
    (c) developing a proactive mentality; and
    (d) mastering precursor analyses.

The remainder of this chapter expands on an organization's responsibility in respect of these "requirements".

2 Intra and Extra Organizational Safety Considerations as Part of CSR

Human activity is mediated extensively in the twenty-first century by organizations (used here in the sense of corporate bodies). The reader is most likely accessing this text through the agency of many such organizations. Organizations are ubiquitous and indispensable. They manifest themselves as public and private institutions (both for profit and non-profit).

In discussing the place and value of organizational learning as a concept, Argyris and Schön (1996) asked the question, "what is an organization, that it may learn?" A similar question may be posed in the context of CSR? "What is an organization that it may be deemed to have social responsibility as a corporate body"? Aldrich (1979) has defined organizations as "goal-directed, boundary maintaining, and socially constructed systems of human activity". Scott and Davis (2007) bring together three approaches to the definition of organizations—the rational, natural and open systems perspectives. They see in these perspectives the definition of organizations:

[1] A "realistic manner" would imply an ethical consideration of the organization's own goals, resources and constraints. Safety in this context would mean reducing risk to a level which is as low as reasonably practicable, which level is defined by legislation as well as the perceptions of the corporate entity and all stakeholders.

- from a rational system perspective, as "collectivities oriented to the pursuit of relatively specific goals and exhibiting relatively highly formalized social structures";
- from a natural system perspective, as "collectivities whose participants are pursuing multiple interests, both disparate and common, but who recognize the value of perpetuating the organization as an important resource";
- from an open systems perspective, as "congeries of interdependent flows and activities linking shifting coalitions of participants embedded in wider material-resource and institutional environments".

Subsuming all the above into one definition is difficult, a difficulty which expresses the complexity of modern-day corporate entities. Different internal and external interests may exist in regard to any number of issues including "corporate social responsibility (CSR)" and "safety". Nonetheless, the complexity should not lead to denying the need for organizations as corporate bodies to understand, appreciate and take steps to fulfil their responsibilities in respect of safety.

In many jurisdictions, organizations are also deemed to have (legal) personhood, connoting an anthropomorphism that supports the notion of responsibility to communities both internal and external to itself. The legal discussion about the expression of corporate personhood and the rights and responsibilities associated with that notion is ongoing globally.[2] It is noteworthy that even Friedman in his firm rebuttal of the notion of "social responsibilities of business" appears to distinguish between "a corporation" and "business" (Friedman 1970). This chapter, while recognizing this ongoing discourse, proceeds on the basis that in almost all jurisdictions (irrespective of the totality of corporate rights and responsibilities, or whether organizations as social entities are viewed as "corporations/companies" or as "businesses") there is an increasing global expectation that such organizations be accountable to the wider society for the consequences of their actions and/or inactions particularly when there are perceptions of organizational recreancy (Ritchie et al. 2013; Freudenburg 2003, 1993). The pragmatic focus here is on corporate entities engaged in profit-generating activities (business entities) as manifested in shipping.

Alongside the growing sense of the accountability/responsibility of these corporate bodies, one finds the growing awareness of risk in general, as previously alluded to. Arguably the human race has lived with much less sensitivity to risk, even where there was palpable daily exposure to hazards. This increased sensitivity to risk is premised on the perceived lack of control, the amplified impacts of single and relatively small actions/inactions and the murky darkness of organizational behaviour, operations and in some cases deviance. The qualitative dimensions of risk (Manuel 2011) together with the increased spatial scope of consequences/impacts of decision-making as well as the novelty of many corporate operations, lead to differing perceptions of risk and significant difficulties for many societies. It is in

[2]Giddens (1999) offers an insightful treatment of the legal links between risk and responsibility.

this milieu that CSR is argued to be relevant, indeed critical, to an organizations strategic planning for sustainability and productivity.

According to Benn and Bolton (2011) the notion of CSR has evolved through a number of stages including:

1. an early period of "corporate philanthropy" which was challenged as being illegal given that such philanthropy could be deemed to "transgress business responsibilities to shareholders"[3];
2. a stage where CSR was approached from a productivity point of view—profiting commercially from "doing good"—thus generating a "'bolt on approach' focused on corporate profit maximisation";
3. a "triple bottom line" phase which looks beyond shareholders to stakeholders by focusing on environmental and social targets and reporting in much the same way as organizations had focused earlier on financial targets and reporting;
4. the contemporary phase, which is putting greater emphasis on overall accountability as well as values-based, ethical and sustainable relations with a complex number of stakeholders; a complexity relating to number, relationships and location.[4] The European Union, for example, recently recast CSR more broadly as "the responsibility of enterprises for their impacts on society" (European Commission 2011).

In contemporary society (a "risk society" as Beck (1992) has called it), the obligations, responsibility and resulting societal accountability of organizations is almost taken for granted by all stakeholders and even shareholders. Despite Friedman's (1970) rejection of businesses as moral entities, the reality is that the general public views them as such and irrespective of the merits of that perception, an organization that ignores it will be setting itself up for confrontation with the society at large and possibly even failure. Contemporary society is increasingly risk aware and risk averse and are intolerant of breaches of safety, howsoever caused, particularly when such breaches are perceived to have occurred because of the pursuit of profit maximisation. Furthermore, stakeholders have been necessarily defined in ever widening terms, given that corporate bodies are essentially open systems, which feed into and feed from their external environments. As a result, the definition, scope and value of CSR as a social construct, is determined by the context in which it is interrogated by researchers, strategists, corporate entities, their shareholders and their numerous other stakeholders. Dahlsrud (2008)—in his analysis of

[3]For a critical review of this position as expressed by Milton Friedman in his works "Capitalism and freedom" and "Social responsibility of business", see Carson (1993) and Carrol and Shabana (2010).

[4]The twenty-first century is characterised by increasing complexity. Relationships, levels of accountability and responsibility as well as the consequences of organizational actions or inactions may have far reaching consequences both in terms of time and of space. The organizational "playing field"—especially for the maritime industry—moved beyond the strictly local to a much more global stage many decades ago. However, the "couplings" between decisions and their consequences are getting tighter and with greater ramifications.

37 definitions of CSR—categorizes the construct into five dimensions: the environmental dimension, the social dimension, the economic dimension, the stakeholder dimension and the voluntariness dimension. He found that the stakeholder and social dimensions were the most significantly reflected in the definitions of CSR. However as he notes "all of the dimensions are necessary in order to understand how CSR is defined" (Dahlsrud 2008). In a similar work Rahman comes up with ten dimensions (Rahman 2011), some of which are similar to or rephrases of Dahlsrud's list. They include obligation to society, stakeholder involvement, improving quality of life, economic development, ethical business practice, law-abidingness, voluntariness, human rights, protection of the environment and transparency/accountability dimensions.

It is noteworthy that an appreciation of the dimensions may be more important than a definition per se. As Dahlsrud notes "the challenge of business is not so much to define CSR, as it is to understand how CSR is socially constructed in a specific context and how to take this into account when business strategies are developed".[5]

The following analysis of CSR and how it relates to safety/risk management is premised on dimensions derived from those of Dahlsrud and Rahman. They are:

1. Stakeholder dimension
2. Legal/obligatory dimension
3. The voluntariness dimension
4. Social (scope) dimension
5. Economic dimension
6. Environment protection dimension
7. Ethical dimension
8. Human rights dimension
9. Transparency/accountability dimension.

2.1 *The Stakeholder Dimension of CSR as it Relates to Safety*

In seeking to meet its corporate social responsibility in respect of safety, an organization will have to critically review what it views as "stakeholders". The importance of this cannot be overstated. This author agrees with Dahlsrud (2008) in suggesting Mitchell, Agle and Wood's conceptual framework (Mitchell et al. 1997) as a very good starting point to help organizations identify who their stakeholders are. Their work examines, from the literature existing then, a number of rationales for the identification of stakeholders. From such rationales, one can argue that stakeholders should at a minimum include employees of the organization and the entities (individuals and societal units) directly affected by the organization's activities of production and/or service. From the point of view of safety, stakeholders may be

[5]See also discussions by Okoye of CSR as an essentially contested concept (Okoye 2009).

those on whom the organization is dependent and who are, in turn, dependent on the organization; those who have legally-binding contractual agreements with the organization; those who have a claim (moral or otherwise) on the organization; and those who have something at risk from the operations of the organization (e.g. their financial investment, their health and safety or the pollution of their environment). The strength of the stakeholder's relationship with the organization rests on the three variables of *power*, *legitimacy* and *urgency* (Mitchell et al. 1997).

Given this, corporate responsibilities to employees as "social stakeholders" will have to include the following at a minimum:

1. The provision of a safe and secure working environment that does not expose employees to harm or compromise health in the short or long-term. It is important to stress the need to not limit the effects of the working environment to the short-term. Organizations should deem it their responsibility to investigate the long-term effects of their operational activities on employees.
2. Training and development in the area(s) in which they operate. Given the constant novelty in contemporary organizational operations, this may be deemed to be an imperative. The provision of function-specific training as well as safety training (for example in respect of identified hazardous operations, in the use of safety equipment and increasing knowledge of safety procedures/safe practices) is critical to the meeting of a corporate entity's safety responsibilities.

Other social stakeholders who are not internal to the organization may be deemed to be owed a fiduciary duty by the organization (Zakhem 2015). Such a duty is owed in respect of safety as well.

2.2 *The Legal Dimension of CSR as it Relates to Safety*

The legal challenge of "for-profit" entities being held responsible for anything other than profits and other ends deemed appropriate by shareholders has been mentioned. Despite this difficulty, stakeholder safety interests are to a large extent (depending on jurisdiction) protected under various legal instruments both at the national level and at the international level.

In the particular case of seafarers (as employees in the maritime operational context) the recent Maritime Labour Convention (MLC), 2006 (International Labour Organization 2006) encapsulates the many years of work by the ILO in this area, in one authoritative and comprehensive legal instrument with significant global reach. The MLC, among other important requirements, specifically mandates under Article IV, that "every seafarer has a right to a safe and secure workplace that complies with safety standards" and under Regulation 4.3 of Title 4 on "Health protection, medical care, welfare and social security provision" that:

1. Each Member shall ensure that all seafarers on ships that fly its flag are covered by adequate measures for the protection of their health and that they have access to prompt and adequate medical care whilst working on board.
2. The protection and care under paragraph 1 of this Regulation shall, in principle, be provided at no cost to the seafarers.
3. Each Member shall ensure that seafarers on board ships in its territory who are in need of immediate medical care are given access to the Member's medical facilities on shore.
4. The requirements for on-board health protection and medical care set out in the Code include standards for measures aimed at providing seafarers with health protection and medical care as comparable as possible to that which is generally available to workers ashore.

While these mandatory provisions are limited in how they specifically address the many issues that relate to a safe working environment on board ship, the subsequent guidelines under Title 4 of the MLC 2006, as well as the "Guidelines for implementing the occupational safety and health provisions of the Maritime Labour Convention, 2006" (International Labour Organization [ILO] 2015) give further elaboration in a much more comprehensive manner. Member states may deem it advisable to elevate these guidelines to a higher level of law, namely "hard law", in a national setting.

The International Management Code For The Safe Operation Of Ships and for Pollution Prevention (International Safety Management (ISM) Code)—mandatory under the International Convention on the Safety of Life at Sea (SOLAS)—requires that all shipping companies[6] ensure that personnel are trained, are familiar with their duties and understand all relevant safety regulations, rules, codes and guidelines (International Maritime Organization [IMO] 2015). Underpinning such training/familiarization is a requirement in the Code for companies to implement a "Safety and Environmental Protection policy" with a number of safety management measures.

Successful implementation of the requirements of the ISM is companies' corporate responsibility and to the extent that the (un)safe operation impacts both the seafarers and wider social communities (both local and global), also as shipping companies' corporate social responsibility. Obligatory maritime safety management under international law may therefore be deemed to reflect CSR with no corporate resort to voluntariness. This view is reflected in the definition of CSR as "business decision-making linked to ethical values, *compliance with legal requirements* and respect for people, communities and the environment" *(emphasis added)* (Thumwimon & Takahashi as cited by Mayes et al. 2015).

[6]"Company is defined in the Code as "the owner of the ship or any other organization or person such as the manager, or the bareboat charterer, who has assumed the responsibility for operation of the ship from the shipowner and who, on assuming such responsibility, has agreed to take over all the duties and responsibility imposed by the Code".

2.3 *The Voluntariness Dimension of CSR as it Relates to Safety*

Despite the foregoing, many definitions of CSR negate this obligatory nature of CSR. Some view CSR as *essentially* related to the notion of *voluntariness*. For example the Commission of European Communities has defined CSR as "a concept whereby companies integrate social and environmental concerns in their business operations and in their interaction with their stakeholders *on a voluntary basis*"[7] *(emphasis added)* (Commission of the European Communities 2002). With specific reference to safety, it can be argued that optimum safety has to go beyond compliance with legislation and emanate from a more proactive and voluntary organizational basis. As Hollnagel indicates,

> Both theory and practice make it clear that safety management that follows developments rather than leads them runs a significant risk of lagging behind and becoming reduced to uncoordinated and fragmentary fire-fighting... In order to prevent this from happening, safety management must look ahead not only to avoid that things go wrong but also – and more importantly – to ensure that they go right (Hollnagel 2013).

It is perhaps obvious that a compliance approach to safety will be essentially reactive in nature, particularly in a prescriptive legal paradigm (as opposed to a legal paradigm that is based on companies making a "safety case" (Kuo 2007))[8]. It is only within a voluntary paradigm that complete proactiveness can occur and where the non-routine safety issues (that are not adequately addressed by prescriptive measures) can be resolved. In other words, proactive safety can only *thrive* in a context of voluntariness, in which context there is intrinsic organizational motivation to ensure that "things go right". Given the complexity of contemporary high-risk operations, and if we view safety as organizational resilience to ever-changing variables both internal and external to the organization, it is arguably myopic to expect optimum safety levels to result from an organization's ability to comply with existing legislation. There can never be optimisation of CSR if the construct and its manifestation is limited to what can be given effect only through the agency of law (Schuck 2000; Vago 2012; Frohnen 2015). As Manuel (2011) notes:

> In the shipping industry, an emphasis has been traditionally placed on approaches to safety/quality such as training, improved design of the man–machine environment or interface and control/restraint through legislation. Although these have been largely influential in the reducing level of accidents (and although legislation is recognized to be ubiquitous and indispensable) the place of other human factors (motivational, social, psychological and organizational) is increasingly acknowledged as critical to a further advancement of a paradigm of quality. The limitation of law in achieving global goals of excellence in the maritime

---

[7]This definition is the one with the highest frequency in Dahlsrud's (2008) analysis.

[8]In a prescriptive regulatory approach, legal instruments prescribe the goals and standards of safety to be met as well as the methods/mechanisms/procedures (as statutory regulations) by which the standards should be met. Contrary to this approach, a "safety case" approach has broad goals set within a legal framework with legal instruments but then require practitioners/companies to indicate best methods for meeting these goals/standards by "making a safety case".

> industry lies mainly in the reliance of law on negative consequences of deviation. . . . However, positive reinforcement has been found to be a high-level motivator for subsequent behaviour. Organizational factors that generate intrinsic motivation for excellence, as opposed to the extrinsic motivation of legal measures, are one such category of mechanisms and should arguably be given a lot more attention at organizational, national and international levels.

The ILO Guidelines for Implementing the Occupational Safety and Health Provisions of the Maritime Labour Convention, 2006 (ILO 2015) defines "occupational safety and health" as "the science of the anticipation, recognition, evaluation and control of hazards arising in, or from, the workplace that could impair the safety, health and well-being of workers".[9] Elements of this definition, for example anticipation, are difficult to legislate in a strictly prescriptive/compliance approach. For optimum safety manifested through good CSR values, principles and behaviours, organizations must situate themselves as "excellence/safety cultures" and not as "evasive cultures" or even "compliance cultures" (Mathiesen 1994, 1996; Sudhakar 2005). In excellence/safety cultures, CSR behaviours and practices that emanate from intrinsically motivated organizational norms will take priority over a compliance mentality. An externally driven safety paradigm, which is not intrinsically owned by organizations, may actually lead to compromised safety as organizations cut corners and hide adverse practices—the classic manifestation of an evasive organizational culture.

Commenting on a major accident in the oil and gas industry, a US Presidential Commission noted that "because regulatory oversight alone will not be sufficient to ensure adequate safety, the oil and gas industry will need to take its own, unilateral steps to increase dramatically safety throughout the industry, including self-policing mechanisms that supplement governmental enforcement." (National Commission on the BP Deepwater Horizon Oil Spill and Offshore Drilling 2011). This further highlights the limitations of regulation in creating a resilient safety paradigm.

Arguably therefore, the essence of contemporary CSR lies—not in compliance with existing laws, but in "the continued commitment by business to behave ethically and contribute to economic development while improving the quality of life of the workforce and their families as well as the local community and society at large and doing so in a way that does not compromise the well-being of future generations" (adapted from World Business Council for Sustainable Development 1999). In this paradigm, such corporate behaviours do meet legislative requirements, but the commitment, ownership and values that underpin them are derived from a voluntary organizational mindset that is not just compliance-driven and in many cases, exceed legislative requirements.

[9]Citing the ILO General Survey Concerning the Occupational Safety and Health Convention, 1981 (No. 155), the Occupational Safety and Health Recommendation, 1981 (No. 164), and the Protocol of 2002 to the Occupational Safety and Health Convention, 1981, Report III (Part 1B), International Labour Conference, 98th Session, Geneva, 2009, ("General Survey on ILO standards on occupational safety and health").

2.4 The Social Scope Dimension of CSR as it Relates to Safety

In addressing a corporate entity's social responsibility in respect of safety, it will be necessary to establish the scope of the social context. To some extent this will mimic the exercise of establishing who the stakeholders are. As alluded to earlier, Mitchell et al. (1997) suggest a framework of stakeholder identification and salience that is laudable. They base their typology of stakeholders on three relationship attributes: power, legitimacy and urgency. In their review of the literature they identify a range of social stakeholders including:

> as primary and secondary stakeholders; as owners and non-owners of the firm; as owners of capital or owners of less tangible assets; as actors or those acted upon; as those existing in a voluntary or an involuntary relationship with the firm; as right-holders, contractors, or moral claimants; as resource providers to or dependents of the firm; as risk-takers or influencers; and as legal principals to whom agent-managers bear a fiduciary duty.

In the safety management context, corporate social responsibility to social stakeholders will include employees (as resource providers) and others who involuntarily are affected by the operations of the corporate entity and other "moral claimants" to whom the organization may be rightly deemed to owe a duty of care. Obviously, it is not realistic to expect that organizations can know and cater to the safety needs of all possible stakeholders. Given this limitation, it is necessary that organizations articulate a mechanism for identifying and prioritizing stakeholders and applying commensurate efforts in meeting the safety needs of these stakeholders. One would argue that of primary focus would be employees of the organization and the wider society that may be affected by the immediate consequences of a safety breach or limitation in the operational resilience of the organization. It is also worthy of note that risk signals (and associated perceptions) can be considerably amplified or attenuated by social stations with equally considerable consequences for the organization (Kasperson et al. 2003; Rosa 2003; Manuel 2011).

2.5 The Economic Dimension of CSR as it Relates to Safety

Safety is often viewed as a cost. However, it should be possible to see productive safety management as something that improves a profit-making organization's bottom line.

For decades, corporate bottom lines focused solely on the financial bottom line. Elkington's (1994, 1998) seminal work on what he introduced as the triple bottom line, significantly brought to the fore the recognition that "profit" for a business entity was best viewed in terms not limited to finances. Included in the triple bottom line are indicators for economic prosperity, environmental quality and social justice—profits, people and planet. Safety management primarily focuses on people but has substantial ramifications for profits. Despite anecdotal evidence that suggests that some consider safety as inordinately costly for organizations, it is indeed possible to have "management systems that allow production, safety and quality to be pursued concurrently" (Mol 2003) and with optimum economic outcomes. The ILO estimates that 6300 people die every day as a result of occupational accidents, and that "the economic burden of poor occupational safety and health practices" is 4% of global Gross Domestic Product (GDP) per annum (International Labour Organization [ILO] 2016). This compares unfavourably with a figure of 3.3% for global GDP real growth rate (Central Intelligence Agency of US Government 2013). Safety actually pays and the costs to organizations of ignoring safety can be substantial—to put it mildly (Behm et al. 2004). The direct costs of accidents (in terms of loss of lives and property, worker compensation payout, increase in insurance premiums, legal suits, working/productivity time etc.) as well as indirect costs such as reduced employee morale, loss of corporate reputation, cost of externalities like pollution etc. can be significant. There are indeed good grounds to suggest that the positive economic outcomes of proactive safety (particularly when juxtaposed against the costs of accidents) should give added impetus for an optimum CSR strategy in that regard. Furthermore, it is noteworthy that in an information-rich global environment characterized by an increasingly sustainability-conscious global community, shareholders' economic profits may well depend on how effectively corporate strategies address stakeholder interests regarding safety.

2.6 The Environment Protection Dimension of CSR as it Relates to Safety

This dimension of CSR has in recent times taken centre stage. This is due primarily to the global acceptance that humanity is responsible for many negative trends in the natural environment, which ironically supports human life. We appear to be our own worst enemies and this consciousness is driving a global agenda for change in behaviour, including in organizational behaviour. A prominent manifestation of this global agenda is seen in the increasing stress in the United Nations on sustainable development.

The recent United Nations Framework Convention on Climate Change[10] (United Nations 2015b) and the UN 2030 Agenda for Sustainable Development (United Nations 2015a) reflect this, with Goal 3 of the latter seeking to ensure healthy lives and to promote well-being. Health and well-being are directly related to safety. All these lofty goals and agendas require at least national and organizational behavioural optimization (in many cases extreme behavioural change). In the area of safety, one

[10]The United Nations Framework Convention on Climate Change (the Paris Agreement) was agreed to at the 21st Conference of Parties (CP.21) in Paris in December of 2015. It acknowledges "that climate change is a common concern of humankind" and agrees to "uphold and promote regional and international cooperation in order to mobilize stronger and more ambitious climate action by all Parties and non-Party stakeholders, including civil society, the private sector, financial institutions, cities and other subnational authorities, local communities and indigenous peoples".

notes that major industrial accidents have very often been associated with environmental consequences (actual or potential). Major examples of these include (among many others) the Torrey Canyon grounding, the 3-mile Island accident, the Chernobyl disaster, the Piper Alpha fire, the Exxon Valdez grounding and the Deep Water Horizon incident (see Sutton 2014 for a more comprehensive list of offshore incidents and descriptions of the events). All these go to show that when safety is compromised and/or when high-risk systems are not resilient to threatening variables, consequential harm is not limited to immediate human casualties but in many cases, is also environmental, with long-term harm to humans and nature. Safety as a corporate responsibility should have this in view. One of the ten principles (Principle 8) of the UN Global Compact (a platform for business to act on global goals), requires businesses to undertake initiatives to promote greater environmental responsibility (United Nations Global Compact n.d.). To the extent that environmental responsibility may be linked to safety management, these initiatives must include good safety management strategies as a corporate responsibility.

Apart from this macro view of the effect of safety breaches on the wider environment, there is also the issue of workplace environmental conditions as a safety issue. Specific to the maritime industry, this can be related to ergonomics in the workplace; how the work environment is adapted to the human element. This adaptation should address the effect of light, temperature, noise, vibration, anthropomorphic design (sitting, standing, walking, posture requirements) and repetitiveness of tasks among others. The guidelines for regulation 4.3 of the MLC, 2006 give a fairly comprehensive treatment of what ILO member states should address so as to ensure that this aspect of safety is properly managed. Recent research in human-centred design with specific reference to ships' crews seeks to enhance this area of study as well (Kataria et al. 2015).

2.7 *The Ethical, Human Rights and Transparency/ Accountability Dimensions of CSR as They Relate to Safety*

Is safety an ethical issue? Does failure to provide a safe and risk resilient working environment and to avoid societal harm from organizational operations constitute a breach of ethics? Many researchers seem to believe so and indeed there are grounds for this belief. Ethics has always been a difficult area in general, but more particularly in areas of risk and uncertainty (Hansson 2003). While Marcoux (2008), for example, accepts that a corporation is a person at law, he avoids the conclusion that as well as being a "legal person", a corporation is a "moral person". Nevertheless, if we define ethics simply as the moral system of beliefs underpinning perceptions of what is good or bad, one can argue that there is an ethical dimension to an organization's responsibility in respect of safety. This is especially true for corporate entities involved in high-risk operations such as are found in the maritime industry.

Where an organization does not consider treatment of its own employees or the consequences of its actions or inactions on the wider society through an ethical lens, there will be bound to be lapses in its approach to safety. In other words, the optimum provision of a safe working environment, harm-free organizational effects on society and a resilient context for high-risk operations may be deemed to be an ethical obligation over and above the requirements of the law. Accordingly, the ethics dimension of CSR in safety is strongly linked to the voluntary dimension. Unethical and corrupt practices severely limit the effectiveness of international, national and corporate strategies for optimum safety management such as through bribery of officials who should serve as verification entities for compliance with legislative and industry regimes on safety (e.g. auditors, port state control officers, inspectors etc.)

This view is supported by the increase in the number of organizations which voluntarily hold themselves to high ethical standards through self-imposed membership of associations characterised by ethical principles. An example is the Maritime Anti-corruption Network—a network of shipping companies, which among other things seeks to "provide a unique platform for businesses across industries to contribute to the elimination of corrupt practices in the maritime industry" (Maritime Anti-Corruption Network n.d.). The association is guided by an operating charter, a set of anti-corruption principles and an anti-trust policy. This approach is also supported by Principle 10 of the UN Global Compact: "Business should work against corruption in all its forms, including extortion and bribery" as well as the UN Convention Against Corruption (United Nations 2004) which is primarily addressed to States. These all require transparency. Safety thrives in transparent operations—in organizational cultures where challenging voices/perceptions of safety breaches are not stifled. Such cultures also support operations where learning is possible because accidents and near misses are transparently reported and where individuals and groups deem themselves accountable to themselves, to their teams, to the organization at large and to the society as a whole, in how they act.

Also, closely linked to the issue of ethics is that of human rights. A number of international legal instruments of different status all exhibit a spirit in which safety (broadly speaking) is deemed to be a human right:

- The UN Declaration of Human Rights (UNDHR - Article 23)—"Everyone has the right to work, to free choice of employment, to just and favourable conditions of work..."
- The Charter of Fundamental Rights of the European Union (Article 31)—"Every worker has the right to working conditions which respect his or her health, safety and dignity".
- The International Covenant on Economic, Social and Cultural Rights (ICESCR – Article 7(b))—"The States Parties to the present Covenant recognize the right of everyone to the enjoyment of just and favourable conditions of work which ensure, in particular: ... safe and healthy working conditions..."

Additionally, The UN Global Compact drawing from the UNDHR and the ILO's Declaration on Fundamental Principles and Rights at Work and the UN Convention

Against Corruption, derives 10 principles for business to commit to. The very first of these principles asks businesses to support and respect the protection of such internationally proclaimed human rights as indicated above. While these do not specifically address how businesses should be bound to the wider society in terms of safety, the spirit of all the instruments does suggest an approach of "no harm".

It can be seen from the above, that the various dimensions of CSR are related to safety management in high-risk industries, not least in the maritime industry. The CSR dimensions of stakeholder involvement, legal obligations, voluntariness, social awareness and concern, economic productivity, environmental stewardship, as well as ethical, human rights and transparency/accountability concerns are all germane to the need for strategic safety management in maritime corporate entities.

3 Risk and Safety Management in Strategic CSR

The question does remain as to what organizations should consider in an attempt to incorporate safety management into CSR strategies and policies. This section of this chapter explores different aspects of this.

3.1 Social Stakeholder Identification and Prioritization

Given the importance of "risk perception" and the possible amplification of risk signals through social stations, social stakeholder salience as a first step in strategy setting is critical. The process of stakeholder salience requires active scanning, seeking to identify, understand, prioritize and integrate the meritorious aspects of both internal and external social concerns and claims. Organizational decision makers should explicitly map out, not only shareholders but also stakeholders with reference to the three variables of power, legitimacy and urgency as suggested by Mitchell et al. (1997). The key issue, from a safety perspective, is not to restrict the determination of stakeholder power and legitimacy to legal or financial power and legitimacy, but to include morality and ethics as definitive parts of legitimacy regarding stakeholder concerns and claims. This implies that organizations may wish to explore the concerns of social groups with no easily identified advocates and who may thereby appear "voiceless". It also implies that a fourth variable (not mentioned by Mitchel et al.) becomes critical. It is that of stakeholders' awareness/knowledge. Ethical safety management, commensurate with responsible corporate social behaviour, will require that organizations do not exploit or take advantage of a labour force's or social stakeholders' lack of knowledge of safety/risk/health issues at stake, or of relevant legal requirements, to permit, maintain or instigate conditions of employment and outcomes of operations which are known to be deleterious to safety, resilience and health, especially in jurisdictions with limited accountability regimes.

3.2 Establishing a Safety Culture

Safety performance and management in an organization is influenced by or originates from one of four cultures namely, an uninformed culture, an evasion culture, a compliance culture and a safety culture (Sudhakar 2005). In an uninformed culture, there are significant gaps in safety knowledge, poor emergency preparedness and absence of exercises and drills. In an evasion culture, there is a perfunctory approach to safety, focus is on prima facie paperwork and the maintenance of a façade that is not supported by an underlying reality. A compliance culture is characterised by the organization being conversant with rules, keeping rule-related records and the extensive use of checklists, but exhibiting an unwillingness to proactively go beyond the requirements of externally-derived rules. Such organizations have an inability to deal proactively with emerging risks not addressed by existing rules. The last of the four, a safety culture, will be manifested, not only in the existence of appropriate rules and procedures, but also and more importantly, in recursive collective practices facilitated by both formal structures/systems and individual/group behaviours that lead to high levels of preparedness, proactivity and resilience. Safety awareness, appreciation and enthusiasm are visible throughout the organization.

Obviously the last of the four requires strategy and action at a fundamental organizational cultural level. It is not the kind of outcome that results from passing fads or short-lived effusions about safety after an accident. It requires consistent, long-term and strategic planning driven from the highest levels of the organization but owned across all other levels and would call for clarity of objectives and positive group dynamics. Strategic CSR for safety must be underpinned by such an entrenched safety culture, which has sub-cultures/components including but not limited to:

1. an informed culture
2. a reporting culture
3. a just culture (not primarily focused on "blame")
4. a flexible culture and
5. a learning culture.

3.3 Key Strategic Performance Indicators in the Safety Domain

One important element of strategic management is the planning, design, measuring and control of performance indicators. In process safety management, these kinds of indicators may broadly be categorized into leading and lagging indicators. Lagging indicators refer to those indicators that are measured after the fact; accident/no accident rates, number of near misses, injuries (number and severity) and resulting number of days off work, pollutant levels (noise, air, etc.). A particular problem with the lagging indicators is that the information they supply can be ambiguous. If just taken on the surface, they may actually reflect the opposite of what is really happening. For example, when using the number of accidents as an indicator for safety performance, a low number may reveal good safety performance, but may also indicate a lack of a reporting culture, a negative situation which severely limits safety performance. Furthermore, given the sometimes substantial time lag between organizational decisions and outcomes, such indicators may not reflect current safety performance but the results of previous organizational decisions and actions (Budworth 1996). Although they certainly have some value in helping measure safety performance, the philosophy that underpins their use is essentially reactive and thus is not very helpful in strategic safety management. Nevertheless, the use of lagging indicators appears to be the dominant approach in many high-risk industries mainly because of a high prevalence of the compliance culture described earlier.

Leading indicators, on the other hand, are measures that indicate safety performance a priori i.e. preceding actual safety breaches, incidents or accidents. They include such safety elements as quantity and quality of safety training,[11] design and ergonomic nature of the workplace, technical integrity of equipment, risk identification and mitigation strategies, avenues for reporting and soliciting of stakeholder perceptions of risk, credence-giving to stakeholder views and safety audits. By their very nature, leading indicators are more strategic, preventive and proactive and focus on continuously optimising safety operations with future case-based scenarios in mind. They thus require a degree of mastery over the identification of precursors (signals that indicate potential negative outcomes) and the analyses of such precursors. The use of leading safety indicators may serve to enhance the positive motivational dynamic in an organization, as they tend to recognize good initiatives as opposed to failures. They should be indispensable in safety management as part of strategic CSR and optimally be used strategically to build a safety culture while using lagging indicators to validate safety performance (through correlation with the leading indicators).

3.4 *Strategic Planning for HR Development (Education and Training)*

As alluded to earlier, one of the core elements of a safety culture is an informed workforce and a community that is "safety aware". The human element is the essence of safety management. Humans manage and operate high-risk systems, benefit from them and suffer their negative consequences. In light of this, human resource development through training (either for awareness or for competence) is essential as a component of safety management in strategic CSR.

[11]In the specific context of CSR, this kind of training could include for employees and for the society external to the formal boundaries of the organization.

In the specific context of the shipboard operation in the maritime industry, continued seafarer education and training ensures that operators of the multi-million dollar assets that facilitate world trade, do their work safely and efficiently and without having negative accidental effects on the environment. There is an undeniable "social responsibility" of shipping companies to ensure that their ships are operated in such a manner that these ships are not a risk-source for the States in whose waters they operate. Of primary importance, therefore, is the issue of competence of seafarers as an obligation. Various international instruments mandate this both for States and for shipping companies. They include the United Nations Convention on the Law of the Sea, the International Convention on Safety of Life at Sea (and also as mandated in the International Management Code for the Safe Operation of Ships and for Pollution Prevention (ISM Code) per Chapter 9 of that Convention), and the International Convention on Standards of Training, Certification and Watchkeeping for Seafarers, 1978 as amended.

3.5 Awareness of and Avoidance of Drift Into Deviance

Another basic requirement for good strategy is learning; learning from one's own experiences, those of others and extrapolating those lessons into unknown situations and in relation to combinations of contributing factors. Learning is also essential to safety and all safety strategy in the context of CSR must be learning-based. This requires that there is an active, visible process of seeking information (including stakeholder perspectives), interrogating the information in the context of a deep understanding of risk and safety theory, ethically evaluating the strategic options available to the organization, deciding on optimum performance and establishing control procedures (measuring, evaluating, noting deviations from the norm—including the tendency to normalize deviance—and correcting as a control loop). Even where an optimum safety paradigm exists, there is always the tendency to drift into deviance—a creeping entropy, "migration towards the boundary of safety margins" (Rasmussen 1997) or drift into failure (Dekker 2013). The deviance that becomes normalized[12] may be arrived at via small deviations from safe practices.

As is graphically represented in Fig. 1, operation on the safety performance line (often taken for granted in excellent safety cultures) may be negatively impacted by an occurrence (or lack of an intervention in response to changing internal or external variables) at point A which shifts the "optimum safety line" to the "normalization of deviance safety line". This shift may not be perceptible to non-vigilant

[12]The notion of "normalization of deviance" was first introduced by Dianne Vaughan in her investigation of the Challenger Disaster (Vaughan 1996), to represent the tendency in individuals and organizations to reinterpret danger signals and what is essentially deviance from optimum states and practice, and to view these states of deviance as normal over time based on different worldviews and priorities. Such normalization of deviance is reinforced when over a long period, there are no substantial negative consequences resulting from the deviance.

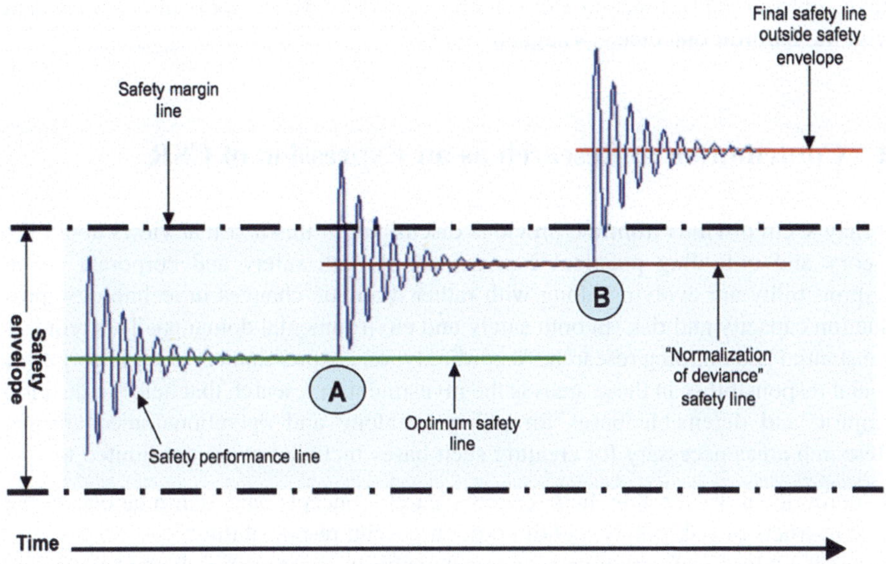

Fig. 1 Micro-steps to the normalization of deviance in a non-utopian world. Source: Manuel (2011) (used with permission from Taylor and Francis)

organizations. A similar pattern may be repeated at point B when other events impact negatively on safety choices, resulting in operating worldviews, processes and outcomes being outside the acceptable safety envelope (Manuel 2011).

Manuel (2011) further notes that decision-making about acceptable risk is generally linked to "values, beliefs and other factors" (Fischhoff et al. 1981) and that these "other factors" are mainly resource dependent. It is therefore necessary that when considering strategic CSR in safety, attention be given to the provision of adequate resources (financial, human, technological, informational, temporal, spatial etc.). Of particular note is the resource of time (temporal). In the name of "commercial pressure", time is often sacrificed in industry operations leading to what Hollnagel (2009) has called the "Efficiency-Thoroughness Trade Off" (ETTO).

Rushed operations seldom are safe operations and in the nature of most socio-technical systems, thoroughness will suffer if commercial efficiency is always prioritized without reference to available resources. In the absence of needed resources, humans (and organizations) will balance work demands and productivity expectations with available resources in a homeostatic manner often to the detriment of optimum safety outcomes.

Attention also has to be given to the influence of a culture of complacency on the safety process itself and on its outcomes, as well as the effect of the accompanying unwillingness to commit resources to avoid drift/normalization of deviance. These effects may be long-term in manifestation. As Vaughan puts it "policy decisions have deferred results, so that by the time a failure occurs, responsible administrators have left the organization or are in other positions in it, so are not publicly associated with the harmful outcome" (Vaughan 1997).

4 Contribution to Research as an Expression of CSR

It may seem obvious from the previous discussion in this text that views about the theory and unfolding practical expressions of both safety and corporate social responsibility are evolving along with rather dramatic changes in technology, production capacity and risk (in both safety and environmental domains). This requires substantial and ongoing research. Accordingly, one expression of strategic corporate social responsibility in these areas is the investment in research that helps to develop empiric and defensible bases for policy, strategy and operational mechanisms. Research areas necessary for creating such bases include but are not limited to:

- definitional issues that help create clearer concepts and delimitation of the constructs of risk, safety and of corporate social responsibility;
- the legal limits of corporate social responsibility in terms of risk and safety;
- the rationale and motivation of organization-related CSR research, strategies and practice;
- the link between CSR as practiced by an organization and fundamental cultural values and norms as they relate to ethics and morality (either in absolute terms or in relative social terms).

5 Two Cases Compared

To illustrate some of the issues raised in this chapter the following discussion about two cases is deemed relevant and helpful. It is based on an accident that did not happen in one case and another accident, which did in the second case.

In 2005, Exxon (an oil company) started drilling for oil off the US Coast via what was called the Blackbeard West well. According to Sutton (2014) this well, situated in deep water, was at the time the world's deepest oil well at 32,000 feet below the seabed. Reserves were anticipated to be in the region of 1 billion barrels (with substantial profits forecast). However, this anticipated high level of productivity was matched by an equally high level of risk. Sutton, citing a New York Times report of July 12, 2010, indicates that a decision was made by Exxon (initiated at the highest level by Rex Tillerson, then CEO of Exxon) to abandon the drill at 30,067 feet (only 2000 feet short of target) in the interest of safety. Engineers and drillers on the drill had informed corporate management of the risky levels of temperatures and pressures that made further drilling unacceptably dangerous. Their perceptions of risk were listened to, credence given to these experts and the drilling aborted despite substantial loss of investments ($US187 million and more than a year and a half of work) as well as loss of the anticipated productivity of the well (estimated at $US 150 billion) (Read 2011)). Both Sutton and Read suggest that this response was due to Exxon's learning and resulting cultural change as a direct consequence of the major oil spill from the oil tanker Exxon Valdez. That incident had cost the organization significantly in terms of finances, reputation and societal goodwill. It would appear that on the back of optimum organizational learning and an awareness of Exxon's responsibilities as a corporate entity in a high-risk industry, an organizational culture had been created which approached the excellence/safety culture described in this text. This culture facilitated the sharing of information by operational personnel, the credence-giving of management to relevant experts and the willingness to strategically and proactively abort a venture deemed to be outside the range of tolerable risk. Indeed, such cultures may actually reward employees who are proactive in safety even when such proactivity costs time and money. To quote Read in summary:

> The public is forgiving of an isolated act. However, the cost to Exxon for a repeated act would be severe indeed, and would rip off the bandages of wounds once healed. Exxon knew that it was necessary to engage in a new corporate policy that emphasized safety. Consequently, Exxon's corporate-wide safety program is now state-of- the-art in the industry.
>
> For instance, Exxon was recently willing to close up and walk away from a potentially highly profitable well, but also a highly risky well in the Gulf of Mexico (Read 2011)[13]

Juxtaposed against this, Sutton recounts the scenario five years later when BP, another oil company began drilling another well in many ways similar to Blackbeard West. Also off the coast of the US, the Macondo well in the Gulf of Mexico was also deep and just as risky. The well was being drilled by the mobile offshore drilling unit (MODU) Deepwater Horizon. A subsequent well blowout destroyed the rig and led to the loss of 11 lives. Losses include not just the productivity of the well and the investment in drilling (as in the case of Exxon), but more substantially loss of lives, long-term environmental damage, more financial losses in suits and penalties and loss of reputation and goodwill. These latter losses are certainly much more damaging to an organization, not to count the negative consequences to individuals, families, societies, nations and the global community, consequences that in many ways cannot be weighed in financial terms. The report of the Presidential Commission on the subsequent disaster, suggests an attitude by the management of BP to safety that is not ideal for such a high-risk industry. It states that:

> The most significant failure at Macondo - and the clear root cause of the blowout - was a failure of industry management. Most, if not all, of the failures at Macondo can be traced back to underlying failures of management and communication. Better management of decision-making processes within BP and other companies, better communication within

[13]Despite the fact that the abandoned Blackbeard West well was successfully drilled by a competitor after Exxon abandoned it (Read 2011), the cautious and proactive approach of Exxon, considering its own capabilities at the time, are still to be commended and recommended.

> and between BP and its contractors, and effective training of key engineering and rig personnel would have prevented the Macondo incident. BP and other operators must have effective systems in place for integrating the various corporate cultures, internal procedures, and decision-making protocols of the many different contractors involved in drilling a deepwater well. (National Commission on the BP Deepwater Horizon Oil Spill and Offshore Drilling 2011)

Interestingly and perhaps due to possible litigation exposure, BP's own investigative report (BP 2010) tends to focus more on the operational level and emphasizes engineering failures and not so much the managerial, organizational culture and decision-making failures alluded to in the quote above.

It is worrying that the National (US) Presidential Commission' Report referred to earlier, notes that:

> the immediate causes of the Macondo well blowout can be traced to a series of identifiable mistakes made by BP, Halliburton, and Transocean that reveal such systematic failures in risk management that they place in doubt the safety culture of the entire industry (National Commission on the BP Deepwater Horizon Oil Spill and Offshore Drilling 2011)

One does hope that this latter accident will cause BP, and other corporate entities particularly those involved in high-risk industries, to develop a more robust/resilient safety culture, as Exxon appears to have done after Exxon Valdez. That reactive approach (taking lessons from the Exxon Valdez accident) will have its merits but the merits of a proactive safety culture and a corporate entity's responsibility in ensuring an optimum strategic approach to it, should be recognized as being much greater!

6 Conclusion

The safety responsibility of organizations has often been addressed at the level of operational process safety. This chapter has sought to indicate that such responsibility is dependent on the strategic management level as well as corporate appreciation and valuing of some of the issues that have been raised here. In conclusion, one notes that the safety management responsibilities of business entities in the maritime industry and elsewhere, cannot be said to be based on the achievement of a paradigm of complete freedom from risk. CSR with respect to safety, will have to be interrogated in the midst of numerous other variables of productivity and resource constraints as well as the legal obligation of corporate entities to society at large. It is nevertheless the case that many of these variables are not "at war with safety". There is no basis to conclude that increased productivity or business financial sustainability can only be achieved through deliberately cutting corners with respect to safety, either by lowest threshold legal compliance, or the tolerating of or active connivance in unethical/corrupt practices. The cost of accidents, demotivation of employees and negative societal perceptions can be far more negatively impacting on the financial bottom line than prudent consideration of optimum CSR in safety matters. While organizational passion for CSR based on the financial bottom line may be deemed to be utilitarian and expressing corporate self-interest or even selfishness, it is nevertheless a target outcome in a less than ideal world. Proponents of this view believe "a business case" can be made for CSR (Carrol and Shabana 2010).

The question does remain whether it is ever possible to reach a point globally where corporate entities intrinsically value the positive impact they make on societies more than their financial bottom line. A quick review of the history of human avarice, competition and selfishness (mediated by organizations) leaves one sceptical. However, while the perfect picture of a "selfless" organization that ensures no injury or harm to all stakeholders may remain utopian, the argument that society at large and organizations in particular should strive to enhance safety cultures as a worldview, should ideally not be subject to debate.

In an ideal world, the state will be proactive about safety, give legislative effect to optimum regulations that "force" business entities in their compliance efforts to meet the best of safety standards in the interest of all stakeholders. In an ideal world, elected and appointed public officers will be the watch-keepers of the interest of the wider society (including their safety interests) and there would be no appeal to the higher ethical sense of corporate executives and their shareholders (who, based on Friedman's arguments, are arguably only responsible for profit for the shareholders in ways in which such profit is defined by those shareholders). In an ideal world, the identification of stakeholders (including voiceless ones) will be done at the macro-social level by a society that recognises its own dangers, the risks of such dangers and the vulnerability of its populace. In an ideal world, all members of society will be free partakers of a social system that puts people in public office who are able to address all the societal issues with systems that obviate the need for CSR in the first place. Unfortunately, we do not live in an ideal world and the notion of CSR (including as it pertains to safety) appears to be a new mechanism through which the wider society may encourage (even force) corporate entities to seek its best and proper interests. We do live in a world where to leave the effectuation of all that is optimum to legislative paradigms and state political forces is self-defeating. Elkington cites Pope John XXIII as follows:

> I often wake up in the middle of the night and start thinking about grave problems - and decide to talk about them with the Pope. Then I wake up completely and remember that I am the Pope. (Pope John XXIII as cited by Elkington 1994).

All of us, society at large, including governments, corporate entities, researchers etc. must "wake up completely" to the fact that in an open society we are all interconnected and when the sustainable, ethical and prudent stewardship of people and planet are made a priority (including in safety management) we all (including corporate entities) benefit. This benefiting, if not in the short term, is certainly valid for the medium to long-term. That paradigm shift requires that safety and CSR in that regards, is not an add-on management fad, reserved for the periphery, the fringes of organizational priorities, but is the core and systemic value that underpins all decision-making and organizational action.

References

Aldrich, H. E. (1979). *Organizations and environments*. Englewood Cliffs, NJ: Prentice-Hall.
Argyris, C., & Schön, D. A. (1996). *Organizational learning II: Theory, method, and practice*. Reading, MA: Addison-Wesley.
Beck, U. (1992). *Risk society: Towards a new modernity (trans: Ritter M)*. London: Sage.
Beck, U. (2009). *World at risk (trans: Cronin C)*. Cambridge: Polity Press.
Behm, M., Veltri, A., & Kleinsorge, I. K. (2004). The cost of safety: Cost analysis model helps build business case for safety. *Professional Safety, 49*(4).
Benn, S., & Bolton, D. (2011). *Key concepts in corporate social responsibility*. London: Sage Publications.
Bernstein, P. L. (1998). *Against the gods: The remarkable story of risk*. New York, NY: John Wiley and Sons.
BP. (2010). Deepwater Horizon: Accident investigation report.
Budworth, N. (1996). Indicators of performance in safety management. *The Safety & Health Practitioner, 14*(11), 23–29.
Carrol, A. B., & Shabana, K. M. (2010). The business case for corporate social responsibility: A review of concepts, research and practice. *International Journal of Management Reviews, 12*(1), 85–105.
Carson, T. (1993). Friedman's theory of corporate social responsibility. *Business and Professional Ethics Journal, 12*(1), 3–32.
Central Intelligence Agency of US Government. (2013). *The world factbook 2013–2014*. Washington, DC: Author.
Commission of the European Communities. (2002). *Communication from the Commission concerning corporate social responsibility: A business contribution to sustainable development*. http://trade.ec.europa.eu/doclib/docs/2006/february/tradoc_127374.pdf. Accessed 3 February 2016.
Dahlsrud, A. (2008). How corporate social responsibility is defined: An analysis of 37 definitions. *Corporate Social Responsibility and Environmental Management, 15*(1), 1–13.
Dekker, S. W. A. (2013). Drifting into failure: Complexity theory and the management of risk. In S. Banerjee (Ed.), *Chaos and complexity theory for management: Nonlinear dynamics* (pp. 241–253). Hershey, PA: IGI Global Business Science.
Elkington, J. (1994). Towards the sustainable corporation: Win-win-win business strategies for sustainable development. *California Management Review, 36*(2), 90–100.
Elkington, J. (1998). *Cannibals with forks: The triple bottom line of 21st century business*. Gabriola Island BC, Canada: New Society Publishers.
European Commission. (2011). *Corporate Social Responsibility: a new definition, a new agenda for action*. http://europa.eu/rapid/press-release_MEMO-11-730_en.htm. Accessed 25 January 2016.
Fischhoff, B., Lichtenstein, S., Slovic, P., Derby, S. L., & Keeney, R. L. (1981). *Acceptable risk*. New York, NY: Cambridge University Press.
Freudenburg, W. R. (1993). Risk and recreancy: Weber, the division of labor, and the rationality of risk perceptions. *Social Forces, 71*(4), 909–932.
Freudenburg, W. R. (2003). Institutional failure and the organizational amplification of risks: The need for a closer look. In N. Pidgeon, R. E. Kasperson, & P. Slovic (Eds.), *The social amplification of risk* (pp. 102–120). Cambridge: Cambridge University Press.
Friedman, M. (1970). The social responsibility of business is to increase its profits. *The New York Times*, September 13.
Frohnen, B. P. (2015). The limits of law: How formal rules undermine human relations. *Modern Age, 57*(2), 18–27.
Giddens, A. (1999). Risk and responsibility. *The Modern Law Review, 62*(1), 1–10.
Hansson, S. O. H. (2003). Ethical criteria of risk acceptance. *Erkenntnis, 59*(3), 291–309.

Hollnagel, E. (2009). *The ETTO Principle: Efficiency-thoroughness trade-off; Why things that go right sometimes go wrong*. Burlington, VT: Ashgate.

Hollnagel, E. (2013). A tale of two safeties. *Nuclear Safety and Simulation, 4*(1), 1–9.

International Labour Organization. (2006). *Maritime Labour Convention*. Geneva: Author.

International Labour Organization [ILO]. (2015). *Guidelines for implementing the occupational safety and health provisions of the Maritime Labour Convention, 2006*. Geneva: International Labour Office.

International Labour Organization [ILO]. (2016). *Safety and health at work*. http://www.ilo.org/global/topics/safety-and-health-at-work/lang--en/index.htm. Accessed 12 January 2016.

International Maritime Organization [IMO]. (2002). *Guidelines for Formal Safety Assessment (FSA) for use in the IMO rule-making process: MSC/Circ.1023 and MEPC/Circ.392*. London: Author.

International Maritime Organization [IMO]. (2015). *International safety management code*. London: Author.

Kasperson, J. X., Kasperson, R. E., Pidgeon, N., & Slovic, P. (2003). The social amplification of risk: Assessing fifteen years of research and theory. In N. Pidgeon, R. E. Kasperson, & P. Slovic (Eds.), *The social amplification of risk* (pp. 13–46). Cambridge: Cambridge University Press.

Kataria, A., Praetorius, G., Schröder-Hinrichs, J.-U., & Baldauf, M. (2015). Making the case for Crew-Centered Design (CCD) in merchant shipping. In *19th Triennial Congress of the International Ergonomics Association (IEA), Melbourne*, Australia, 9–14 August, 2015.

Kristiansen, S. (2005). *Maritime transportation: Safety management and risk analysis. Elsevier*. Oxford: Butterworth-Heinemann.

Kuo, C. (2007). *Safety management and its maritime application*. London: The Nautical Institute.

Manuel, M. E. (2011). *Maritime risk and organizational learning*. London: Ashgate.

Manuele, F. A. (2013). *On the practice of safety* (4th ed.). Hoboken, NJ: John Wiley & Sons.

Manuele, F. A., & Main, B. W. (2002). On acceptable risk: What level of risk, if any, is acceptable in the workplace? *Occupational Hazards, 64*(1), 57–60.

Marcoux, A. (2008). *Business ethics*. The Stanford Encyclopedia of Philosophy, Fall, 2008 ed. Stanford, CA: Stanford University.

Maritime Anti-Corruption Network. (n.d.). http://www.maritime-acn.org/ - home. Accessed 14 January 2016.

Maslow, A. H. (1943). A theory of human motivation. *Psychological Review, 50*(4), 370–396.

Mathiesen, T. C. (1994). Safety in shipping: An investment in competitiveness. In *BIMCO Review 1994* (pp. 56–58). London: Stroudgate Plc. for BIMCO.

Mathiesen, T. C. (1996). Safety management and loss control. In *BIMCO Review 1996* (pp. 133–134). London: Stroudgate Plc. for BIMCO.

Mayes, R. J., Bracey, P. S., Aguilar, M. G., & Allen, J. M. (2015). Identifying corporate social responsibility (CSR) curricula of leading US Executive MBA programs. In D. E. Palmer (Ed.), *Handbook of research on business ethics and corporate responsibilities*. Hershey PA: Business Science Reference (IGI Global).

Mitchell, R. K., Agle, B. R., & Wood, D. J. (1997). Toward a theory of stakeholder identification and salience: Defining the principle of who and what really counts. *The Academy of Management Review, 22*(4), 853–886.

Mol, T. (2003). *Productive safety management*. Boston, MA: Butterworth-Heinemann.

Möller, N., Hansson, S. O., & Peterson, M. (2006). Safety is more than the antonym of risk. *Journal of Applied Philosophy, 23*(4), 419–431.

National Commission on the BP Deepwater Horizon Oil Spill and Offshore Drilling. (2011). Deep water - The Gulf oil disaster (Report to the President).

Okoye, A. (2009). Theorising corporate social responsibility as an essentially contested concept: Is a definition necessary? *Journal of Business Ethics, 89*(4), 613–627.

Oxford English of Dictionary. (2013). 3rd ed. Oxford, England: Oxford University Press.

Perrow, C. (1999). *Normal accidents: Living with high-risk technologies*. Princeton, NJ: Princeton University Press.

Rahman, S. (2011). Evaluation of definitions: Ten dimensions of corporate social responsibility. *World Review of Business Research, 1*(1), 166–176.
Rasmussen, J. (1997). Risk management in a dynamic society: A modelling problem. *Safety Science, 27*(2/3), 183–213.
Rasmussen, J., & Svedung, I. (2000). *Proactive risk management in a dynamic society*. Borås: Swedish Rescue Services Agency.
Read, C. (2011). *BP and the Macondo spill: The complete story*. New York, NY: Palgrave Macmillan.
Reason, J. (1997). *Managing the risks of organizational accidents*. Aldershot: Ashgate.
Renn, O. (1992). The social arena concept of risk debates. In S. Krimsky & D. Golding (Eds.), *Social theories of risk* (pp. 179–196). Westport, CT: Praeger.
Ritchie, L. A., Gill, D. A., & Farnham, C. N. (2013). Recreancy revisited: Beliefs about institutional failure following the Exxon Valdez oil spill. *Society & Natural Resources, 26*, 655–671. https://doi.org/10.1080/08941920.2012.690066.
Rosa, E. A. (2003). The logical structure of the social amplification of risk (SARF): Metatheoretical foundations and policy implications. In N. Pidgeon, R. E. Kasperson, & P. Slovic (Eds.), *The social amplification of risk* (pp. 47–79). Cambridge: Cambridge University Press.
Schuck, P. H. (2000). *The limits of law*. Boulder, Colorado: Westview.
Scott, W. R., & Davis, G. F. (2007). *Organizations and organizing: Rational, natural and open systems*. Upper Saddle River, NJ: Pearson Prentice Hall.
Selmer-Olsen, S. (2005). The global risk perspective. In *TRENDS International Conference and Forum: Global Risk Management and Sustainable Development in the Hydrocarbon Industry* (April 6th and 7th), London.
Sudhakar, U. R. P. (2005). Promoting safety culture in shipping: Issues and strategies. In *Institute of Marine Engineers (India) - Visakhapatnam Branch*, 15th April, 2005, Visakhapatnam, India.
Sutton, I. (2014). *Offshore safety management: Implementing a SEMS program* (2nd ed.). Oxford: Elsevier/William Andrews.
United Nations. (2004). *United Nations Convention Against Corruption*. Author. https://www.unodc.org/documents/treaties/UNCAC/Publications/Convention/08-50026_E.pdf.
United Nations. (2015a). *Transforming our world: The 2030 agenda for sustainable development (A/Res/70/1)*. https://sustainabledevelopment.un.org/content/documents/21252030 Agenda for Sustainable Development web.pdf.
United Nations. (2015b). *United Nations Framework Convention on Climate Change (CP.21)*. http://www.un.org/ga/search/view_doc.asp?symbol=FCCC/CP/2015/L.9/Rev.1.
United Nations Global Compact. (n.d.). *The ten principles of the UN Global Compact*. https://www.unglobalcompact.org/what-is-gc/mission/principles. Accessed 20 January 2016.
Vago, S. (2012). *Law and society* (10 ed.). Boston: Pearson Prentice Hall.
Vaughan, D. (1996). *The challenger launch decision: Risky technology, culture, and deviance at NASA*. Chicago: University of Chicago Press.
Vaughan, D. (1997). The trickle-down effect: Policy decisions, risky work, and the challenger tragedy. *California Management Review, 39*(2), 80–102.
World Business Council for Sustainable Development. (1999). *Corporate social responsibility: Meeting changing expectations*. London: WBCSD Publications.
Zakhem, A. (2015). Can management have multi-fiduciary stakeholder obligations? In D. E. Palmer (Ed.), *Handbook of research on business ethics and corporate responsibilities*. Hershey, PA: Business Science Reference (IGI Global).

Response to Institutional Processes: A Study of Corporate Social Responsibility in Danish Shipping Companies

Jan Skovgaard

1 Introduction

Shipping is a very traditional and conservative industry. Several of the old shipping companies are originally family-owned and many still have a family foundation as a controlling shareholder. For many years, they have lived a life with very little transparency. Today, shipping carries 90% of the world trade and is therefore a significant contributor to the increasing pollution of the atmosphere and the marine environment. However, transporting cargo by ship emits less CO_2 and other harmful particles into the atmosphere than other modes of transport when comparing weight of cargo transported per mile. To mitigate the negative impact from companies on the climate, environment, and local society, the concept of Corporate Social Responsibility (CSR) has emerged.

Few studies have been conducted on CSR and shipping. CSR awareness in shipping is relatively low and only a few large companies have adopted policies and strategies to promote CSR activities (Skouloudis et al. 2011). For example, by May 2017, only two Greek companies within the Industrial Transportation sector had signed the United Nations Global Compact (UNGC). In Norway, six companies within the Industrial Transportation sector have signed the UN Global Compact. Among these is Wilh. Wilhelmsen (WW) that moved from CSR tradition to CSR leadership as described by Hargett and Williams in 2007. In Denmark, nine companies within the Industrial Transportation sector had signed the UNGC by May 2017.

Besides being a traditional and conservative industry, there are two main reasons why the shipping industry is a latecomer when it comes to CSR reporting. The first reason is that shipping mainly operates in the business-to-business (B2B) segment.

J. Skovgaard (✉)
Copenhagen School of Marine Engineering and Technology Management, Kongens Lyngby, Denmark
e-mail: js@msk.dk

L. L. Froholdt (ed.), *Corporate Social Responsibility in the Maritime Industry*, WMU Studies in Maritime Affairs 5, https://doi.org/10.1007/978-3-319-69143-5_15

Previous studies (Haddock-Fraser and Fraser 2008; Gonzalez-Benito and Gonzalez-Benito 2006) have shown that there is a relationship between closeness to market and environmental reporting. Companies proximate to the final consumer (business to consumer, B2C) have a greater inclination to report on CSR issues than B2B companies do. Even though costumers (like e.g. the big retailers and the oil majors) increasingly require CSR issues to be taken into account, most customers in the B2B segment have price as their main concern (Wolf and Seuring 2010). Furthermore, research suggests that the more companies expose their ethical and social ambitions, the more likely they are to attract critical stakeholder attention (Morsing and Schultz 2006). Likewise, contemporary research suggests that CSR communication may have a backlash effect if stakeholders become suspicious to the motives in companies' CSR initiatives (Du et al. 2010).

The second reason, for shipping to be latecomers regarding applying CSR, is the regulatory regime. Regulation is a method to control the way people, companies, or entire societies behave in order to protect public goods (e.g. clean air, clean water, wild life, or a stable climate) that cannot be regulated through the market. The market does not have any incentives to protect or reduce the use of public goods (Viscusi 1995). Consequently, authorities, in the interest of the public, have to introduce regulatory means. A lack of regulation for multi-national corporations provides a need for these companies to introduce CSR in their business operations (Campbell 2007). Therefore, the absence of an international regulatory regime triggers the need for companies to apply CSR. However, the regulation of commercial seaborne shipping has a long history and is carried out at different levels; national, supranational, and international (Selkou and Roe 2004). The International Maritime Organization (IMO) is the United Nation's specialized agency with responsibility for the safety and security of shipping and the prevention of marine pollution at sea. IMO has designed a global legal instrument to enhance the international regulatory regime, including the four pillars of the international regulatory regime consist of four conventions SOLAS (Safety of Life at Sea), STCW (Standards of Training, Certification and Watch keeping), MARPOL (Prevention of Pollution from Ships), and MLC (Maritime Labour Convention); they are internationally rooted and apply to all vessels. The issues within the four pillars are all issues that coincide with the concept of CSR, even though the four pillars do not cover the complete area of CSR.

Finally, one of the findings of Lister et al. (2015) is that shipping is lagging behind other sectors in its environmental protection due to regulatory fragmentation. Their point is that the IMO must embrace its role as orchestrating and guiding environmental progress within the shipping sector. This goes hand in hand with the thinking of Roe (2013), where it is questioned whether the framework of institutions established early in the former century can meet the challenges in a modern globalised world.

2 Theoretical Assumptions

Institutional theory states that organisations within the same field have a tendency to become increasingly similar also called isomorphism. There are three isomorphic processes. (1) The coercive process is a process, where formal and informal pressures are exerted on the organization by other organizations (or legislators), and by cultural expectations in the society. (2) The mimetic process is a process whereby companies model a leader in the field and innovate by copying the frontrunners. (3) The normative process which is a professional isomorphic process where organizations, within the same business segment, due to universities, training institutions, and trade organizations become increasingly similar (DiMaggio and Powell 1983). However, there is a lack of knowledge concerning how the institutional and isomorphic processes influence the change in socially responsible behaviour in organizations.

Oliver (1991) has identified five strategic responses to institutional processes. The five strategies, ranging from conformity to active resistance, are: (1) Acquiescence is the most submitting way of responding to different requirements. The associated tactic is to comply with new regulations or requirements. (2) Compromise is, like the strategy of acquiescence, conforming to and accepting new regulations or requirements however, the tactic is following a more self-interests path. (3) Avoid is to conceal that the company is not following the new regulations or requirements. The tactic is to decouple rhetoric from practice, to pretend to comply in words and writing while noncompliance is what really happens. (4) Defy is a more active strategy of opposition. As opposed to avoidance, the defiance strategy does not try to hide the resistance and deliberately dismiss the new rules and norms, sometimes even explaining the reasons why. (5) Manipulate is a strategy where defiance is not enough, the aim is to change or alter the new rules and norms. The tactics are to seek influence through lobbying and coalition building.

Within institutional theory, decoupling means that while organizations often official adopt formal policies and programs, the same organizations decouple the intentions of the policies and programs with the actual actions taken day-by-day (Meyer and Rowan 1977).

Based on the theoretical assumptions, the hypothesis in this chapter is that national legislation can awaken and introduce genuine social responsibility behaviour in an industry. To verify the hypothesis, the following two questions are answered:

1. Which isomorphic processes have caused the Danish shipping companies to catch up on CSR reporting?
2. What strategic responses to the before mentioned isomorphic processes have the shipping companies applied?

3 Methodology

3.1 Definitions

It is difficult to measure CSR because there is no clear definition of CSR and the concept can vary and have different meaning in different countries (Matten and Moon 2008). Some suggests that the prevailing definitions of CSR are not suitable as a basis for a comparative measure of CSR practices (Gjølberg 2009). Even though standards of CSR like SA8000, ISO26000, Global reporting initiative, and UN global compact exist, the measurement of CSR is still problematic. However, a study has identified at 37 definitions of CSR (Dahlsrud 2008). The study found that the majority of definitions consisted of five dimensions: voluntariness, stakeholder, social, environmental, and economic.

The European Commission (2001) finds that beyond compliance indicates that a company is socially responsible. The United Nations Global Compact (UNGC) is a strategic policy initiative for businesses that are committed to aligning their operations and strategies with ten universally accepted principles in the areas of human rights, labour rights, environment and anti-corruption. UNGC is one of the most influential platforms of isomorphic pressure to institutionalize the concept of CSR in the industry (Brammer et al. 2012). Therefore, the UNGC is a good indicator of how dedicated a company is to applying CSR in the organisation.

Hence, in this study, to determine whether a company has a CSR policy, a combination of the five dimensions found by Dahlsrud (2008) and the four main issues from UNGC is used. In order to have a CSR policy the company must report on the following five issues: human rights, labour rights, social supporting, environment, and anti-corruption, see Table 1.

Garriga and Mele (2004) classify the different CSR theories in four groups. The first group assumes that the corporation is an instrument for wealth creation and this is its sole social responsibility. This group is called *instrumental theory*. A second group emphasizes the social power of the corporation, specifically in its relationship with society. This second group is called *political theory*. A third group considers that business depends on society for its continuity and growth and even for the existence of business itself. This group is called *integrative theory*. Finally, a fourth

Table 1 The five CSR issues

Issue	Concerning
Human rights	Support and respect human rights
Labour rights	Right to collective bargaining, elimination of discrimination, measurement of employee satisfaction
Social supporting	Partnership with NGOs, supporting exposed and vulnerable groups, supporting education and research
Environment	Promote greater environmental responsibility, initiate precautionary approach
Anti-corruption	Work against corruption in all forms including bribery and facilitation payment

group understands that the relationship between business and society is embedded with ethical values. This group is called *ethical theory* (Garriga and Mele 2004). In practice, no company is an archetype dedication themselves to one dimension.

Among the instrumental theories is Strategic CSR, which in short states that the essential test that should guide CSR is not whether a cause is worthy but whether it presents an opportunity to create shared value (Porter and Kramer 2006). Lately, Porter and Kramer have argued that Creating Shared Value (CSV) should supersede Strategic CSR. They argue that CSR focuses too much on doing good and the reputation of the company, thereby CSR is separated from the core of doing business and does not help profit maximization (Porter and Kramer 2011).

3.2 Method

Table 2 combines the three theories of isomorphic processes, the five strategic responses, and decoupling. The figure gives examples of how a company can combine the response strategies with the existing isomorphic processes. This will be used to analyse which isomorphic processes and strategic responses the Danish shipping companies did apply in order to catch up on CSR reporting.

To determine whether a company is committed to CSR, tangible follow-up must be presented the subsequent year. To determine whether a CSR policy had been successfully integrated or not, this paper focuses on the parameters used to measure CSR achievements and actual achievements. The fact that 'what you measure is what you get' (Kaplan and Norton 1992) means that companies, who measure CSR issues are more likely to be social responsible than companies who do not measure their CSR issues.

For this study, a specific scale has been developed to determine the strategic response the Danish shipping companies adopt and presented in Table 3.

If a company responds to four or five of the five CSR issues and has tangible follow-up on these issues, this is an indication of an acquiesce strategy. If a company responds to more than two CSR issues and has tangible follow-up on two to three issues, this is an indication of a compromise strategy. If a company responds to any number of CSR issues and has no tangible follow-up, this is an indication of an avoid strategy. If a company responds to any number of CSR issues, including no issues, and has no tangible follow-up, this is an indication of a defy strategy. Finally, if a company does not respond to any CSR issues and has no tangible follow-up, this is an indication of a manipulate strategy. Largely, this tool gives an indication of the applied strategy. Combined with a text analysis of the annual reports, CSR reports, environmental reports, and transcribed interviews with key employees, it is analysed which strategy the companies apply.

Table 2 The three isomorphic processes combined with the five strategic responses and decoupling

	Coercive	Mimetic	Normative
Acquiesce	The company accepts and complies with new regulations and requirements, not only with the written words but also with the underlying intentions of the new laws, rules, and norms.	The company is inspired by peers, and is an inspiration to peers, of how to conform to or even go beyond the new rules and norms.	The company uses the expertise and knowledge from employees, consultants and trade organisation to apply, and even explore how to go beyond, the new norms and standards.
Compromise	The company accepts and complies with new regulations and requirements. However, the company only goes beyond compliance, where it is beneficial for the company to do so.	The company is inspired by peers how to conform to new rules and norms and even how to go beyond compliance, where it is beneficial for the company to do so.	The company uses the expertise and knowledge from employees, consultants and trade organisation to apply the new norms and standards and even explore how to go beyond compliance, where it is beneficial for the company to do so.
Avoid/ decoupling	The company gives loose claims to follow laws and industry norms in words and writing but not in action. The company hides their decoupling strategy.	The company copies CSR policies and strategies from leading companies within the industry without integrating these in the organisation. The company copies a decoupling strategy from peers, hiding the strategy from the public.	The company uses knowledge from employees, trade organisation, academia and peers to pretend to follow rules while actually decouple words from action.
Defy/ decoupling	The company makes use of a defiance strategy and does not try to hide the resistance and deliberately dismiss the new rules and norms. The company does nothing to hide their decoupling strategy and sometimes even explaining the reasons why.	The company copies a defiance strategy from peers within the industry. The company do not hide the decoupling strategy.	The company uses knowledge from employees, trade organisation, academia and peers to argue why it is not necessary to follow rules while actually decouple words from action.
Manipulate	The company contests new rules, requirements, and even laws.	The company challenges peers strategies and behavior.	The company disputes the educational and recruiting system.

Table 3 Scale combining number of CSR policies and tangible follow-up

Strategy	No of issues with CSR policy	No of issues with tangible follow-up
Acquiesce	4–5	4–5
Compromise	2–5	1–3
Avoid	1–5	1
Defy	0–5	0
Manipulate	0	0

Table 4 Names of the 16 shipping companies included in the study

Clipper Group	DFDS	J. Lauritzen A/S	Rohde Nielsen A/S
Color Line, Dk	D/S Torm	Maersk Line	Scandlines AG
Dannebrog Rederi A/S	D/S Norden	Mols Linien	UltraBulk A/S
Danske Færger	Erria A/S	Nordic Tankers/Herning	Unifeeder

3.3 Data

An amendment of the Danish Annual Financial Statement Act (The Danish Commerce and Companies Agency 2010) makes it mandatory for the largest Danish companies to include information on CSR in their annual financial reports. The legislation was implemented in 2010 with reference to CSR initiatives in the previous year. Reporting on CSR policy is still voluntary, but if a company has no CSR policy this information must be stated explicitly. For companies that prepare consolidated financial statements, it is sufficient that the information are provided for the conglomerate as a whole. Therefore, in this study, only one of the A.P. Moller companies is included, namely, Maersk Line, which by far is the largest company in the conglomerate. Likewise, J. Lauritzen, in this study, is considered as one company even though it actually consists of more than four different companies. Furthermore, the two companies Nordana and Danneborg refer to the same consolidated financial statement and are therefore considered as one company. Finally, Nordic Tankers and Herning Tankers merged in the time horizon of this study. Therefore, 16 companies are included in the study, see Table 4. The 16 shipping companies have all published annual statements and/or reports on CSR that cover 2009 and 2010.

Data concerning the largest Danish shipping companies were collected from two databases. The on-line website www.top1000.dk and the database 'Names & Numbers Business' have information on all VAT registered businesses, branch offices and public institutions in Denmark. Among other things the databases contain ratios and complete annual accounts at least 5 years in retrospect, ownership, corporate structure, credit rating, and industry.

To determine whether a CSR policy had been successfully integrated, this chapter focuses on the parameters used to measure CSR achievements and the actual achievements.

The statements or reports covering 2009 were analysed for policy statements within the five CSR issues and any sign of willingness to improve the company's negative influence on any of these CSR issues. Then the statements or reports covering 2010 were analysed for confirmation that the promised improvements were accomplished.

4 Findings

Three companies have policies on all five issues, two companies have policies on four issues, two companies have policies on three issues, two companies have policies on two issues, one company has policy on one issue, and six companies have no policies on CSR issues (see Fig. 1).

Figure 1 shows how many of the five CSR issues where the shipping companies have a policy in 2009. The pillars with dark black colour symbolize the number of CSR issues that a company has a policy for, in 2009. The light grey colour shows within how many issues the companies have tangible follow-up on their CSR policies in 2010. None of the companies have tangible follow-up on all five issues, four companies have tangible follow-up on three to four issue, five companies have tangible follow-up on one to two issues, and seven companies have no tangible follow-up.

Most policies are found within the environmental area, followed by labour rights and social support, while the least policies are found among human rights and anti-corruption. Most follow-ups are found with the issues environmental concern and labour rights, fewer within social supporting and anti-corruption, while no companies have a follow-up within human rights.

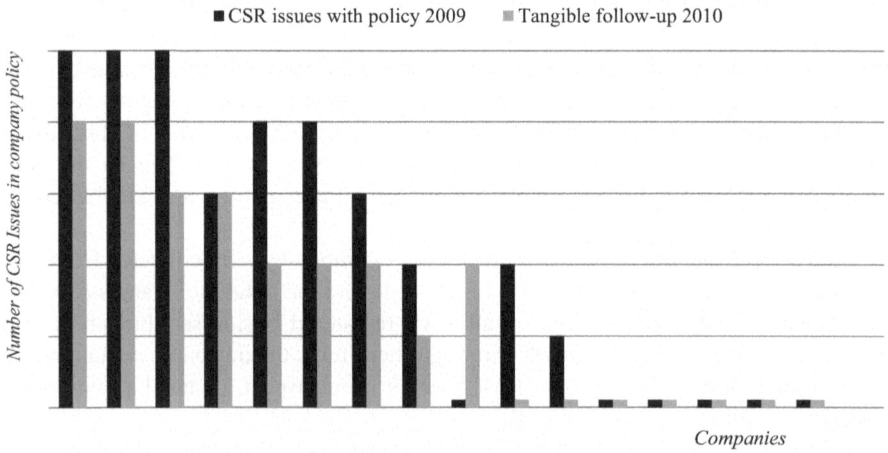

Fig. 1 Comparison of CSR policies with tangible follow-up on the policies the subsequent year

If a shipping company complies with a minimum of the Danish law concerning CSR reporting, then it means that the company is subject to a coercive isomorphic process. Examples are a company stating, "*We consider issues such as human rights, social and anti-corruption as an important part of the Group's business strategy and activities... However, at present, the company does not have comprehensive written policy on corporate social responsibility*" (Scanlines Denmark, annual report 2010). If a company does not have tangible follow-up, this indicates that the company is subject to a coercive isomorphic process. If a company states in an interview, homepage, or annual report that the CSR initiatives are triggered by legislation that respective company is subject to a coercive isomorphic process.

If a shipping company has employed specialized CSR knowledge workers from one of the major universities, this means that the company is subject to a normative isomorphic process. If a company produces tangible follow-up on issues beyond the norms and standard in the shipping industry, that company is subject to a normative isomorphic process.

If a company participates in industry network concerning CSR and CSR related issues, this may indicate that the company is subject to either a normative and/or a mimic isomorphic process. If a company states in an interview, homepage, or annual report that peers in the industry inspire the CSR initiatives, then that company is subject to a mimic isomorphic process.

Table 5 summarizes how the companies' strategic response to isomorphic processes. The main drivers are the normative and the coercive process when a shipping company engage in CSR. The mimic isomorphic process is in play and is a contributor to shipping companies engaging in CSR. However, even though present, the mimic isomorphic process is never the main driver, neither in the comply strategy nor in the decouple strategy.

To follow the coercive process alone is not recommendable as there is a great risk of a strategy of decoupling. Companies, where the coercive process is the initial trigger of engaging in CSR, can benefit from the other two processes. The mimic process where leaders in the field are followed is one way, however, the most successful path to engage in CSR activities is to follow the normative process where a company joins networks and hires employees with the knowledge and experience within the field.

Table 5 Strategic response to isomorphic processes

Strategies	Examples	N
Acquiesce	Obeying rule and accepting norms	2
Compromise	Balancing the expectations of multiple constituents	7
Avoid/decouple	Disguising nonconformity	2
Defy/decouple	Ignoring explicit norms and values	5
Manipulate	Shaping values and criteria	0
Total		16

5 Discussion

Skovgaard (2014) found that only 8% of the Danish shipping companies, compared to 59% of all Danish companies, reported on CSR prior to the implementation of the new law. This study found that the shipping companies indeed were laggards in CSR reporting. This indicates a strong coercive process, where formal pressures are exerted. However, the informal pressure is not to be neglected. Nonetheless, the new law precipitated the CSR reporting from Maersk Line where the work was initiated a few years before as a response to expectations in the society. The mimetic process, where companies model a leader in the field and innovate by copying others, might have played a role. Finally, the normative process, which is a professional isomorphic process due to universities, training institutions, and trade organizations, could also have played a role.

Most of the Danish shipping companies consider themselves to be good corporate citizens. As a top manager from one of the major Danish shipping companies explained '*We have been doing CSR for one hundred years we just called it another name*'. To follow this claim, the company states on their webpage that *'We have been monitoring our performance on quality and health, safety, security and the environment (HSSE) for many years'*.

In general, there is a weak customer pressure for introducing CSR, and the media attention on the shipping companies is limited. Furthermore, if the companies believe that they always have been doing CSR then there are no incentives for the shipping companies to change behaviour.

Skovgaard (2014) found that Danish shipping companies did not report on CSR prior to 2007. This finding confirms another study published by Det Norske Veritas (DNV 2004) which concludes that shipping is a frontrunner when it comes to globalisation but a laggard in implementing CSR in their business. This combined with the fact that, in 2009, all Danish top 10 non-shipping companies had joined the UN Global Compact, while only three of the top 10 Danish shipping companies had joined the UN Global Compact. This leaves a clear picture of the Danish shipping industry as a laggard regarding CSR prior to 2009.

Campbell (2007) argues that even though the economic condition of the company affects the likelihood of pursuing CSR activities, various institutional factors mediate the adoption of CSR practices. These factors include, amongst others, (1) the level of state regulation, (2) the level of industrial self-regulation and the degree of institutionalization of CSR issues within the industry, (3) the level of competition, and (4) the number of monitoring entities (e.g. NOGs, institutional investors and press).

There are several explanations why the shipping industry is a laggard in CSR reporting. One explanation could be that the shipping industry mainly is dominated by business to business, B2B as discussed earlier. Previous studies have shown that there is a positive relationship between closeness to the market and environmental reporting (Haddock-Fraser and Fraser 2008; Gonzalez-Benito and Gonzalez-Benito 2006). Companies closer to the final consumer, B2C, have a greater inclination to report on CSR issues compared to B2B companies. There is a lack of costumer pressure in the B2B segment. A second reason may be what some NGOs refer to as 'flying under the radar'. As earlier mentioned, Morsing and Schultz (2006) found that when companies publicly expose their ethical and social ambitions, then they are more likely to attract critical stakeholder attention. This could be an incentive to live a quiet life and not to report on your social responsibility. A third reason could be the matter of international regulation. A lack of regulation for multi-national corporations provides a need for CSR (Campbell 2007). Therefore, the fact that there exists a regulation concerning international shipping provides a less significant need for CSR in this business segment.

By 2009, 92% of the Danish shipping companies mention CSR while 96% of the top 1000 Danish companies mention CSR in their company policies. Therefore, from the year 2010, it is not fair to call the Danish shipping companies CSR laggards. This is a strong indication of the positive effect of the initiative taken by the Danish government.

Inspired by Porter and Kramer (2006), many of the shipping companies with a CSR policy, state that they apply strategic CSR. Examples are '*For A.P Moller-Maersk, sustainability is a business driven approach...*' (A.P. Moller-Maersk Group 2010) or '*In NORDEN we believe that our CSR efforts should benefit both the communities in which we operate and our business – our focus is on business-driven CSR.*' (NORDEN 2011). As earlier mentioned, in 2011 M. Porter and M. Kramer argue that the concept of Shared Value should substitute Strategic CSR. Some of the Danish shipping companies change their focus accordingly. In 2016, the CSR Direction in NORDEN is called 'Joint Efforts – Mutual Benefits' (NORDEN 2017). Likewise, A.P. Moller-Maersk operate with the concept of Shared Value (A.P Moller-Maersk 2017).

However, it is one thing is to mention CSR in annual statements and publish a CSR report, and another thing is to actually implement corporate social responsibility in the company. When legislators introduced the above-mentioned initiatives, there was a risk that some companies published a non-committal CSR policy.

Most of the Danish shipping companies have responded and mentioned CSR in their annual financial reports. However, this does not mean that all the companies have implemented CSR into their daily operation. Likewise, the findings show that while some companies have policies regarding social supporting, anti-corruption, and human rights, several of these companies have no follow-up on these issues. An explanation may be as one company states '*We mainly operate in Denmark where laws concerning human rights and anti-corruption already exist and we, off course, abide to these laws*'. Furthermore, regarding the issue of social supporting, one company states '*The owner of the company supports and sponsors a broad range of community initiatives directly or through collaboration with NGOs*'.

Of the five strategic responses to institutional processes, presented previously, four strategies are recognised among the Danish shipping companies. The four identified strategies are Acquiesce, Compromise, Avoidance, and Defiance. No strategy of Manipulate was found among the Danish shipping companies. It is arguable, though, that the strategy of manipulate is somewhat present, as the Danish

Ship-owners association (recently renamed, Danish Shipping) is actively participating in the work carried out in the European Union concerning CSR. Likewise, this can also be seen in the statement; 'We will work with regulators to raise the bar for the industry and create a level playing field, resulting in greater costs for less-sustainable competitors' (Maersk Line, Sustainability Progress Report, 2010).

The findings in this study show that of the 16 companies, seven companies responded with strategies of acquiesce and compromise and thereby accepted the new norms. These companies have CSR polices within three to five issues and tangible follow-up within two to four issues. The companies in this group have allocated resources both in terms of labour and financial to deal with the aspects of CSR. Additionally, two companies position themselves in this category. They do not fully comply, however are in the process of acquiesce and compromise.

Only two of 16 companies, used a strategy of avoidance and disguised nonconformity. These companies claim to have CSR policies within one or two issues but fail to deliver any tangible follow-up the subsequent year. Finally, five of 16 companies responded with a strategy of defy and dismissed the new norms. One shipping company stated in both 2009 and 2010 that they have no CSR policy but are working towards CSR implementation. Likewise, another company states in both 2009 and 2010 that CSR issues are important and the company wants to conform to the spirit of CSR but for the time being the company has no written policy regarding CSR.

6 Concluding Remarks

The shipping business is a reactive business (Blanco-Bazán 2004). The main reason is that the shipping business has a tradition to react to maritime accidents and learn how to avoid the same type of accident to reoccur. Therefore, it would be a sea change for the maritime sector to have a proactive approach, and commit proactively to various CSR issues.

Campbell (2006) argues that government deregulation during the 1980s and 1990s created an environment where U.S. corporations began to act in more socially irresponsible ways (Campbell 2006). Kostova et al. (2008) argue that Multi-National Corporations (MNC) experience a weaker institutional pressure, mainly because of the diversity among the many institutional systems that the MNCs are exposed to (Kostova et al. 2008). The same argument cannot be used regarding the shipping industry. Even though the Danish shipping companies operate in a multinational environment, the shipping industry is not exposed to the same diversity among the institutional systems. The regulation of commercial seaborne shipping has a long history, which is one of the factors that contribute to isomorphic processes. Furthermore, costumers (e.g. the oil majors) and Classification Societies (e.g. Lloyd's Register) ensure a certain degree of homogeneity.

Unfortunately, the concept of sustainable development and the changes in environmental laws in the 1970s did not automatically lead to changes in corporate environmental practices (Lee 2011). In relation to CSR reports, there is a risk that companies de-couple rhetoric from practice and apply a strategy of avoidance. Decoupling implies that a company consciously portrays itself as following the institutionalized rules, when in fact businesses act as usual and pursue paths believed to be more profitable. Previous studies show that the stronger influence of isomorphism, the stronger is the tendency to adopt decoupling.

A shortage of knowledge exists regarding the difference between the companies that implement CSR efficiently and the companies that adopt a decoupling approach. In recent years, several major Danish shipping companies have published an annual report on CSR according to the Danish CSR legislation. The number of companies that adopt a decoupling approach, where a company decouples rhetoric and practice, is still unknown. These are interesting questions because the companies who genuinely adopt and implement CSR policies need to differentiate themselves from the free riders in order to gain a competitive advantage.

The hypothesis in this chapter is that national legislation can awaken and introduce genuine social responsibility behaviour in an industry. In addition, to verify the hypothesis, the following two questions were addressed and answered:

(1) Which isomorphic processes have caused the Danish shipping companies to catch up on CSR reporting? (2) What strategic responses to the before mentioned isomorphic processes have the shipping companies applied?

First, this chapter demonstrates that the coercive isomorphic process is the dominating factor when the shipping companies introduce CSR policies. The coercive process created by institutional pressure has caused the Danish shipping companies to catch up.

Second, this chapter establishes that the shipping companies have applied two different strategic responses. Half of the companies chose a strategy of comply, while the other half chose a strategy of avoid/defy. It is not possible to know what would have happened if the legislation of CSR reporting had not been executed.

Finally, in conclusion, this chapter verifies the hypothesis that national legislation can awaken and introduce social responsibility to an industry.

References

A.P. Moller – Maersk Group. (2010). *Sustainability report 2009*. http://www.maersk.com/en/the-maersk-group/sustainability/~/media/82D4F989193443F183CA9FB66B28932E.ashx, Accessed May 15, 2017.

A.P. Moller – Maersk. (2017). *Sustainability report 2016*. http://www.maersk.com/~/media/the%20maersk%20group/sustainability/files/publications/2017/files/apmm_sustainability_report_2016_a3_v6.pdf, Accessed May 15, 2017.

Blanco-Bazán, A. (2004). IMO historical highlights in the life of a UN Agency. *Journal of the History of International Law, 6*(2), 259–283.

Brammer, S., Jackson, G., & Matten, D. (2012). Corporate social responsibility and institutional theory: New perspectives on private governance. *Socio-Economic Review, 10*(1), 3–28.

Campbell, J. L. (2006). Institutional analysis and the paradox of corporate social responsibility. *American Behavioral Scientist, 49*(7), 925–938.

Campbell, J. L. (2007). Why would corporations behave in socially responsible ways? An institutional theory of corporate social responsibility. *Academy of Management Review, 32*(3), 946–967.

Dahlsrud, A. (2008). How corporate social responsibility is defined: An analysis of 37 definitions. *Corporate Social Responsibility & Environmental Management, 15*(1), 1–13.

DiMaggio, P. J., & Powell, W. W. (1983). The iron cage revisited: Institutional isomorphism and collective rationality in organizational fields. *American Sociological Review, 48*(2), 147–160.

DNV. (2004). *Corporate Social Responsibility in Shipping*. [online] http://www.he-alert.org/documents/published/he00375.pdf. Accessed January 9, 2012, DET NORSKE VERITAS REPORT NO.2004-1535.

Du, S., Bhattacharya, C. B., & Sen, S. (2010). Maximizing business returns to corporate social responsibility (CSR): The role of CSR communication. *International Journal of Management Reviews, 12*(1), 8–19.

European Commission. (2001). *Promoting a European framework for Corporate Social Responsibility Brussels*, COM (2001) 366.

Garriga, E., & Mele, D. (2004). Corporate social responsibility theories: Mapping the territory. *Journal of Business Ethics, 53*, 51–71.

Gjølberg, M. (2009). Measuring the immeasurable? Constructing an index of CSR practices and CSR performance in 20 countries. *Scandinavian Journal of Management, 25*(1), 10–22.

Gonzalez-Benito, J., & Gonzalez-Benito, O. (2006). A review of determinant factors of environmental proactivity. *Business Strategy and the Environment (John Wiley & Sons, Inc), 15*(2), 87–102.

Haddock-Fraser, J., & Fraser, I. (2008). Assessing corporate environmental reporting motivations: Differences between Close-to-Market and Business-to-Business companies. *Corporate Social Responsibility & Environmental Management, 15*(3), 140–155.

Kaplan, R. S., & Norton, D. P. (1992). The balanced Scorecard--Measures that drive performance. *Harvard Business Review, 70*(1), 71–79.

Kostova, T., Roth, K., & Dacin, M. T. (2008). Institutional theory in the study of multinational corporations: A critique and new directions. *Academy of Management Review, 33*(4), 994–1006.

Lee, M. D. (2011). Configuration of external influences: The combined effects of institutions and Stakeholders on corporate social responsibility strategies. *Journal of Business Ethics, 102*(2), 281–298.

Lister, J., Poulsen, R. T., & Ponte, S. (2015). Orchestrating transnational environmental governance in maritime shipping. *Global Environmental Change, 34*(September), 185–195.

Matten, D., & Moon, J. (2008). "Implicit" and "Explicit" CSR: A conceptual framework for a comparative understanding of corporate social responsibility. *Academy of Management Review, 33*(2), 404–424.

Meyer, J. W., & Rowan, B. (1977). Institutional organizations: Formal structure as myth and ceremony. *American Journal of Sociology, 83*, 340–363.

Morsing, M., & Schultz, M. (2006). Corporate social responsibility communication: Stakeholder information, response and involvement strategies. *Business Ethics: A European Review, 15*(4), 323–338.

NORDEN. (2011). *Corportate social responsibility report, 2010*. http://www.ds-norden.com/public/dokumenter/reports/CSRReport2010WEB01042011UK.pdf, Accessed May 15, 2017.

NORDEN. (2017). *Corportate social responsibility report, 2016*. https://www.ds-norden.com/public/dokumenter/CSRrep2016/NORDEN_CSR_Report_2016.pdf, Accessed May 15, 2017.

Oliver, C. (1991). Strategic responses to institutional processes. *Academy of Management Review, 16*(1), 145–179.

Porter, M. E., & Kramer, M. R. (2006). Strategy & society: The link between competitive advantage and corporate social responsibility. *Harvard Business Review, 84*, 78–92.

Porter, M. E., & Kramer, M. R. (2011). Creating shared value. *Harvard Business Review, 89*, 62–77.

Roe, M. (2013). Maritime governance and policy-making: The need for process rather than form. *The Asian Journal of Shipping and Logistics, 29*(2), 167–186.

Selkou, E., & Roe, M. (2004). *Globalisation, policy and shipping: Fordism, Post-Fordism and the European Union Maritime Sector*. Edward Elgar Publishing.

Skouloudis, A., Evangelinos, K., & Nikolaou, I. (2011). An overview of corporate social responsibility in Greece: Perceptions, developments and barriers to overcome. *Business Ethics: A European Review, 20*(2), 205–226.

Skovgaard, J. (2014). European Union's policy on corporate social responsibility and opportunities for the maritime industry. *International Journal of Shipping and Transport Logistics (IJSTL), 6* (5), 513–530.

The Danish Commerce and Companies Agency. (2010). *Redegørelse for samfundsansvar (Statement of CSR*). [online] http://www.retsinformation.dk/Forms/R0710.aspx?id=126096. Accessed January 4, 2012.

Viscusi, W. V. J. H. J. (1995). *Economics of regulation and antitrust*. MIT Press.

Wolf, C., & Seuring, S. (2010). Environmental impacts as buying criteria for third party logistical services. *International Journal of Physical Distribution & Logistics Management, 40*(1/2), 84–102.

The manufacturer's authorised representative in the EU is Springer Nature Customer Service Centre GmbH, Europaplatz 3, 69115 Heidelberg, Germany. If you have any concerns regarding our products, please contact ProductSafety@springernature.com

Printed and bound by CPI Group (UK) Ltd, Croydon, CR0 4YY
30/09/2026
02225434-0011